THINKING OUT LOUD

_____

t

THINKING OUT LOUD

AN ESSAY ON THE RELATION
BETWEEN THOUGHT AND LANGUAGE

Christopher Gauker

PRINCETON UNIVERSITY PRESS   PRINCETON, NEW JERSEY

Library of Congress Cataloging-in-Publication Data

Gauker, Christopher.
Thinking out loud : an essay on the relation between thought and
language / Christopher Gauker.
p.   cm.
Includes bibliographical references and index.
ISBN 0-691-03400-1
1. Language and languages—Philosophy.   2. Thought and thinking.
3. Psycholinguistics.   I. Title.
P106.G35   1994
121'.68—dc20   93-50671

This book has been composed in Times Roman

Princeton University Press books are printed
on acid-free paper and meet the guidelines
for permanence and durability of the Committee
on Production Guidelines for Book Longevity
of the Council on Library Resources

Printed in the United States of America
10 9 8 7 6 5 4 3 2 1

To Alice

Contents

Preface

THIS BOOK CONTAINS MANY ARGUMENTS in support of definite conclusions. But it expresses many attitudes as well. There was a time when I had many of the attitudes but few of the arguments. I do not know why I had the attitudes before I had the arguments. No doubt part of the answer is that early on I had several teachers (Donald Davidson, Richard Rorty, Wilfrid Sellars) who shared those attitudes and whom I admired. But part of the explanation is the revulsion I felt toward certain others who apparently thought that many things were obvious and philosophy was easy.

I think of philosophy as continuous with science, but I think of science as involving a lot more philosophy than is generally recognized. Particularly in the study of language, I think that much of what passes for science is merely bad philosophy. At this point it is still far from clear how language and mind are even possible. Experimentation and data collection can hardly be expected to decide between competing theories. At most they may stimulate plausible hypotheses. The greater task at this point, though one that is usually shirked, must still be thinking such hypotheses through.

I do not know what in general it takes for a theory to make sense. But that will not prevent me from arguing, in all sorts of ways, that many contemporary theories of language and mind do not. I do not think the half-baked ideas that I will propose in their place live up to the standards I am holding others to. They are a necessary complement to my critique of the Lockean theory because they make it conceivable, I hope, that there is an alternative. Beyond that, there may be something right about them.

This is not an easy book. In our present state of ignorance the subject cannot be easy. But I have tried to write a book most of which will be accessible to careful readers with any background in the study of language. Readers acquainted with elementary formal logic will get more out of chapters 7 and 12 than others will. Readers acquainted with contemporary issues in philosophy of mind and language will better recognize the object of my criticisms in part A.

I wish to thank above all Alice Kim, on whom I depend for all things. Second, I wish to thank my colleagues in the philosophy department at the University of Cincinnati, who have helped me shape my ideas and who have always been very generous in their encouragement. I have profited from discussions with many people and will not try to list all those who have made some contribution. However, I would like to thank Bruce Aune, Lynne Rudder Baker, William Bechtel, William Lycan, and Ann Himmelberger Wald for their special help, and I would like to thank John N. Martin for helping me to discover the concept of 0-validity.

Chapters 1 and 2 contain material originally published in "The Lockean Theory of Communication," *Noûs* 26 (1992). Chapter 4 is a somewhat revised form of my paper "An Extraterrestrial Perspective on Conceptual Development," *Mind and Language* 8 (1993). Chapters 5 and 14 contain a small amount of material originally published in "Objective Interpretationism," *Pacific Philosophical Quarterly* 69 (1988). I thank Blackwell Publishers for permission to reprint this material. Chapter 3 incorporates a substantially rewritten version of my paper "Mental Content and the Division of Epistemic Labor," *Australasian Journal of Philosophy* 69 (1991). I thank the editors of that journal for permitting me to reprint this material. Bits of chapter 7 were taken from my paper "Semantics without Reference," *Notre Dame Journal of Formal Logic* 31 (1990). I thank the editors of that journal for permitting me to reprint this material. Also, a few fragments of my "Conditionals in Context," *Erkenntnis* 27 (1987), occur in chapters 7, 11, and 12. I thank Kluwer Academic Publishers for permitting me to reprint this material.

I gratefully acknowledge the support I have received for this work from the Charles Phelps Taft Memorial Fund of the University of Cincinnati.

The title "Thinking Out Loud" is a label that Wilfrid Sellars used to use for a certain kind of candid speech that he regarded as our model for occurrent thought.

Christopher Gauker
August 16, 1993

THINKING OUT LOUD

Introduction

THIS BOOK IS AN EXTENDED CRITIQUE of a certain picture of language, namely, this one:

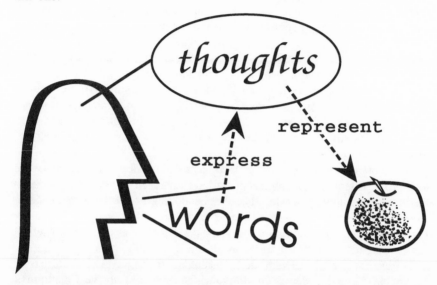

The theory says that the function of words is to *express* thoughts, which in turn *represent* things outside the mind. I call this the *Lockean theory of communication*, because Locke stands out as one of its earliest and most influential exponents.

My view is that, contrary to the Lockean theory, spoken languages are the very medium of our most sophisticated thinking. "Thought" is a term that might be applied to many sorts of mental process. So I do not claim that language is the medium of every kind of thought. I readily allow and even insist that animals and prelinguistic children in many ways *think*. But not every kind of thought is a kind that words might be taken to *express*. I hold that language cannot be *explained* as the expression of thought, because public language is itself the medium of a certain sort of thought, and the sort of thought for which language is the medium is the very sort that might have been cited as that which utterances in public languages express.

If language is the very medium of a certain sort of thought and not merely the means of communicating thought, then some other conception of communication must be put in place of the Lockean conception. The theory of communication developed here is, very roughly, that communication is matter of getting people to *do* things in the course of mainly cooperative interactions. To explain this without lapsing back into the Lockean theory, it is necessary to provide some explicitly non-Lockean account of how communication, so conceived, is possible. Further, it is necessary to identify the proper place for those sorts of things, such as beliefs and meanings, in terms of which the Lockean proposes to explain communication. These are some of the conditions I will try to satisfy.

A great many contemporary philosophical doctrines conspire to make the Lockean theory seem inevitable and to make my thesis seem false. Further, there is no competing perspective on fundamental matters from which the conception of language as a medium for thought might clearly emerge. So the scope of this book is necessarily rather broad, taking in many of the central issues in contemporary philosophy of mind and language.

Locke's own version of the Lockean theory of communication grew out of his interest in prescribing a remedy for merely verbal misunderstandings not resulting from any real disagreement over the nature of things. But, as I argue in chapter 1, "Contra Locke," Locke's own version depends on an unworkable theory of the thoughts, or ideas, that words express. In particular, Locke has no viable theory of the origin of the general ideas that general terms are supposed to express. Contemporary philosophers have managed to retain the Lockean theory of communication while largely abandoning Locke's theory of ideas. Nonetheless, a constant theme of the first, critical half of the book is that the Lockean conception of communication makes it hard to make good theoretical sense of the nature of the thoughts words are supposed to express.

In view of the prevalence of the Lockean theory and the evident attractiveness of the alternative idea, according to which language is the very medium of a certain kind of thought, it is surprising that so little effort has gone into *arguing* for the Lockean conception of communication. In chapter 2, "Communication," I survey a number of motivations for the Lockean theory and argue that none of them is persuasive. It is not enough that words in some sense express thoughts. It is not enough that animals and prelinguistic infants in some sense think. It is not enough that speakers mean something by what they say or that hearers must understand a speaker's presuppositions. On the contrary, it seems that any explanation of how children can learn to communicate in the way the Lockean imagines will presuppose that words can instill beliefs in some way more fundamental than the Lockean theory itself can explain.

According to the Lockean, a speaker's words express the speaker's thought, and there is something about the thought expressed that a hearer has to comprehend in order to grasp the speaker's message. Call this thing that has to be comprehended the *content* of the speaker's thought. But what is this thing called *content*? In chapter 3, "Mental Content," I attempt to reduce the Lockean theory to absurdity through a close examination of this concept of content. In outline, the *reductio* goes like this: If the Lockean theory is correct, then it ought to be possible to explain that speakers speak as they do *because* their words express their thoughts. But what makes it the case that a speaker's thought has a certain content, I argue, is largely just that the speaker's linguistic community uses words in a certain way. And that means that we cannot explain the speaker's choice of words by saying that those words express the speaker's thought.

For many psychologists as well as philosophers, the contemporary successor to the defunct Lockean theory of ideas is what I call *the network theory of concepts*. According to this theory, systems of concepts may be represented as networks of *linked nodes*, and conceptual development may be understood as a process of constructing such networks. In chapter 4, "Conceptual Development," I show that if the network theory is correct, then conceptual development must be guided by what I call *abstraction heuristics*. But this is grounds for criticism, for there is nothing that these abstraction heuristics can be. They can be neither universal principles of rational thought nor species-specific principles of any kind. The reason why we should not think of them as species-specific is that if they were, then our capacity to understand languages of hypothetical species other than our own would be subject to limits that we have no independent reason to acknowledge.

On a more abstract plane, the contemporary Lockean thinks of the thoughts expressed in speech as essentially the theoretical entities governed by certain psychological laws. The existence of such laws is also presupposed by certain accounts of the process by which a person's thoughts may be inferred. The problem is that there are no good examples of the requisite sorts of laws. The most promising candidate is perhaps the *belief-desire law*, which says, roughly, that people will do what they believe will satisfy their desires. In chapter 5, "Psychological Laws," I argue that there is no such law. No normatively *neutral* formulation is a law, because people can learn to do what they *ought* to do. But a normatively *correct* formulation turns out to be nothing more than a few minimal conditions on preference orderings and not at all a suitable paradigm for the psychological laws on which the nomological theory of thoughts depends.

In contemporary versions of the Lockean theory of communication, the theory is tightly bound up with referential semantics. Referential semantics seeks to explain the truth and falsehood of sentence-like representations in terms of reference relations between word-like components and objects in the world. Referential semantics for spoken languages depends on the Lockean theory of communication inasmuch as the reference relation for a spoken language is typically explained in terms of a reference relation for underlying mental representations. Further, referential semantics is an essential component of some contemporary Lockeans' conception of the mental representations, or thoughts, that words express. Thus, if explanation of truth in terms of reference is a mistake, then that is reason to doubt the Lockean theory. In chapter 6, "Reference," I argue against the explanation of truth in terms of reference by disputing the most important accounts of the nature of the reference relation. My critique focuses on the idea that mental representations constitute a partial *map* of reality.

Referential semantics is not easily dispensed with, however, since it seems essential to contemporary conceptions of logic. The logical validity of arguments is defined in terms of what are called *interpretations*, which are best understood in terms of reference relations. This reason for insisting on referential semantics will be undercut if it can be shown that the conception of logical validity in terms of reference relations is mistaken. That is what I try to show in chapter 7, "Validity." I argue that some of the forms of argument that referential semantics declares valid are in fact not valid and that other forms of argument that it declares invalid are in fact valid. This chapter not only further motivates my rejection of referential semantics but also motivates the alternative theory of logical validity that I develop in chapter 12 as part of my constructive proposals.

In explaining communication, it is necessary to explain it in terms of something. Since I reject the Lockean explanation in terms of content and expression, it is necessary for me to develop alternative tools. The alternative tools I intend to employ are what I call *similarity judgments* and *kausal judgments* (with a "k"). In chapter 8, "Similarity Judgments," I explain what kind of thing similarity judgments are and also answer an important objection against explaining fundamental aspects of cognition in terms of them. The objection is that similarity is subjective and consequently cannot be appealed to in any explanation of the possibility of objective judgments. To answer this objection, it is necessary to get clearer about the sort of objectivity in question. Roughly, an objective question is one on which rational subjects who can communicate can be expected to reach agreement. I argue that the usual sorts of reasons to doubt the objectivity of similarity judgments do not succeed and that, on the contrary, similarity judgments are objective in this sense.

My other basic tool, the concept of a kausal judgment, I explain in chapter 9, "Causal Judgments." Basically, a kausal judgment is a judgment to the effect that in the context of a relatively unchanging background, one event *x led up to* a second event *y*. The ability to judge that one thing *caused* another, I argue, can be understood as a refinement of the ability to judge that one thing *kaused* another. In chapter 9 I also take up the question of the sorts of thing that one who has not yet learned a language may be capable of judging to be similar or kausally related. I indicate a criterion of object identity that can be used to identify the objects of a kind of prelinguistic representation, and I explain the representation relation that holds between such prelinguistic representations and such objects. In this chapter I also spell out a number of *principles* of kausal judgment that I will appeal to in chapter 10.

In chapter 10, "Command and Assertion," I return to the subject of language. Here I set out my basic conception of language. According to this, language consists of basically two kinds of utterance: commands and assertions. The function of a command is to make the hearer do something. The function of an assertion is to prepare the hearer to respond effectively to commands. Further, I explain how a simple language, embodying this basic conception of language in its purest form, might be learned. This is where the concepts of similarity judgments and kausal judgments are put to good use. The good thing about this explanation is that it does not presuppose that the learner possesses the very same capacity to conceptualize that language acquisition first makes possible. Further, I explain why it makes sense to think of such a language as usable *intra*subjectively as well as *inter*subjectively.

One of the most conspicuous facts about language is that sentences possess an internal structure. In chapter 11, "Structure and Assertibility," I make a start at explaining this fact by explaining one particular aspect of structure, namely, logical structure. The theory begins with an account of the assertibility of simple assertions (including simple negations) relative to a string of assertions followed by a command. In terms of these assertibility conditions, it is possible to define the assertibility conditions for disjunctions. It then becomes possible to define a primitive kind of logical validity. In terms of this, one can define what I call a *context*, which is a certain sort of set of sentences. Further progress in explicating logical structure can be made in terms of the concept of *assertibility in a context*. In particular, I define the conditions under which conditional sentences, modal sentences, and quantified sentences are assertible in a context.

In chapter 12, "Context Logic," I present a formally precise definition of logical validity in terms of assertibility in a context and explore the consequences of that definition. I argue that the arguments that are valid on this account are those that really ought to qualify as valid. In particular, this account of validity has the right results with regard to the examples wielded against referential semantics in chapter 7. I consider this chapter to be confirmation that the theoretical devices invented in earlier chapters are reflections of reality and not just figments of my imagination.

Up to this point in my positive account of communication, I will have said nothing about the concepts of belief and meaning. To guard against recidivistic Lockeanism, it is necessary finally to assign these their place. In chapter 13, "Interpretation," I argue that *ascriptions* of belief may be usefully characterized as *assertions on behalf of another*. The concept of *meaning*, as Locke saw, arises first in the context of certain sorts of disagreements, ones that do not yield to a straightforward exchange of facts and hypotheses. Talk of a difference in meaning serves conversation as a diagnosis of such disagreements. But it is also possible to explain a person's behavior by citing his or her beliefs and desires, and the possibility of this needs to be explained. Here I explain how belief-desire explanation may be conceived as a reconstruction of partially hidden conversation. I conclude this chapter with an account of the aims and methodology of translation.

This account of *ascriptions* of belief does not seem to answer the question, What *are* thoughts? But as I argue in my final chapter, "Interpretationism," an account of the nature of thought can in fact take the form of a theory of the *ascription* of thought. This view may seem to be a confusion of epistemology and ontology, but I argue that it is not a confusion. Moreover, the theory certainly does not say that a thing has intentional states such as beliefs and desires just in case we find it convenient to attribute such states to it. On the contrary, I distinguish between three grades of intentionality, the *superfluous*, the *merely dispensable*, and the *indispensable*. Human beings really do have the indispensable kind. That is the kind that one indispensably must attribute to them in order to *talk* to them.

There are certain things one might expect a book such as this to do that I do not do. In particular, I do not discuss the extent to which different cultures may have different styles of thinking due to the peculiarities of their languages. I do not deny that there might be such differences, but my concern is with the fundamental functions of languages in general. Whether the differences between languages amount to differences in the psychologies of those who speak them is a question beyond the scope of this book.

Further, I do not try to survey the varieties of nonverbal thinking. I devote two chapters to two kinds of nonverbal judgment (primitive forms of similarity judgment and causal judgment), but these by no means exhaust the possibilities. It is very important to me that there be other sorts of thinking. That there are is my answer to some of the objections against the idea that language is the very medium of *one* sort of thinking. I think it would be good if I had more to say about these other varieties. But since I do not, I will not waste words on the subject.

Part A

DESTRUCTIVE

1

Contra Locke

> When a Man speaks to another, it is, that he may be understood; and the end of Speech
> is, that those Sounds, as Marks, may make known his *Ideas* to the Hearer.—John
> Locke, *Essay* III.ii.2 (1690)

> What matters to successful linguistic communication is the intention of the speaker to
> be interpreted in a certain way, on the one hand, and the actual interpretation of the
> speaker's words along the intended lines through the interpreter's recognition of the
> speaker's intentions, on the other.—Donald Davidson, "The Structure and Content of
> Truth" (1990, 311)

1. As the quotations above illustrate, philosophers who have little else in
common may share a certain very general conception of linguistic communication. I will call this conception of communication the *Lockean theory*, although
Locke's own account is only one of many versions and not even the earliest.
The defining tenet of the Lockean theory is that communication takes place
when a hearer grasps some sort of mental object, distinct from the speaker's
words, that the speaker's words express. This theory contrasts with the view
that spoken languages are the very medium of a kind of thought the most basic
form of which is overt speech.

In this first chapter I aim to do two things. First, I will set forth and criticize
Locke's own version of the Lockean theory. My critique will focus on Locke's
underlying theory of ideas. This will be a useful prelude to what is to come, for
a constant theme of the critical first half of this book will be that the Lockean has
no viable account of the thoughts words are supposed to express. Second, I will
introduce some of the ways in which the Lockean theory of communication
lives on in contemporary philosophy of language and indicate what is at stake in
deciding whether to take the Lockean approach.

Locke's own version of the Lockean theory of communication stems from his
interest in preventing certain sorts of misunderstandings. This interest is well
expressed in the following passage:

> I was once in a Meeting of very learned and ingenious Physicians, where by chance
> there arose a Question, whether any Liquor passed through the Filaments of the
> Nerves. The Debate having been managed a good while, by a variety of Arguments
> on both sides, I (who had been used to suspect, that the greatest part of Disputes were
> more about the signification of Words, than a real difference in the Conception of

Things) desired, That before they went any farther on in this Dispute, they would first examine, and establish amongst them, what the word *Liquor* signified. . . . they were pleased to comply with my Motion, and upon Examination found, that the signification of that Word, was not so settled and certain, as they had all imagined; but that each of them made it a sign of a different complex *Idea*. This made them perceive, that the Main of their Dispute was about the signification of that Term; and that they differed very little in their Opinions, concerning some fluid and subtile Matter, passing through the Conduits of the Nerves; though it was not so easy to agree whether it was to be called *Liquor*, or no, a thing which when each considered, he thought it not worth the contending about. (III.ix.16)

Locke finds that many disputes result in this way from our misunderstanding one another's words, and not from any difference in opinion concerning the nature of things (see also III.xi.7). In order to prescribe a remedy, he must formulate a theory of communication in terms of which he may write out the prescription.

Given Locke's theory of ideas, which has many sources, his theory of communication is a natural response to this need. The main problem Locke sees concerns the signification of general terms, such as "man" and "murder." As Locke sees it, the problem is that a constant relation between words and things may be lacking. If the relation between general terms and the things they stand for is to be made more constant, then it is first of all necessary to understand in what this relation consists. Locke's way of explaining it is to divide it into two parts. The first part is a relation between general words and general *ideas*. The second part is a relation between general ideas and the things they represent (III.i.3, iii.6–13). A single word may be applicable to several particulars—as "man" is applicable to many human beings—inasmuch as it signifies a general idea, which in turn represents those several particulars. This account raises two further theoretical questions: First, what does it take for a word to "signify" an idea? Second, what does it take for an idea to represent several particulars?

Locke offers no explicit account of the relation of signification between words and ideas. He is explicit only about the function of signification: inasmuch as a word signifies an idea, hearers may know that a speaker who uses the word has the idea, and, consequently, speakers may use words to convey their ideas to hearers (III.i.2, xi.5). But Locke has little to say about how these things are possible. He says that words "excite" ideas in hearers (III.ii.6, 8, iii.3, ix.4), which suggests an automatic reaction unmediated by any kind of inference, and he resorts to the plumbing metaphors of "conduits" and "pipes" (III.xi.5). Some role for inference on the part of the hearer seems to be acknowledged inasmuch as Locke acknowledges that hearers may rely on the verbal context to ascertain a speaker's meaning (III.xi.27). Moreover, what Locke calls "common use" is supposed to "regulate the meaning of Words" somehow (III.ix.8; see also ii.4–8, xi.25). In the speaker, on the other hand, the relation between a word and the idea the speaker uses the word to signify is a "voluntary imposition" (III.ii.1). That notwithstanding, no one can ensure that others use the same words to signify the same ideas (III.ii.8).

Regarding the second question, concerning the relation between ideas and things outside the mind, Locke has much more to say. For Locke, an account of the relation between ideas and the world will follow the lines of a theory of the acquisition of general ideas. But in fact Locke offers several not apparently compatible theories of general ideas. One of these theories holds that general ideas are the product of something called *composition*. Another holds that general ideas result from a process he calls *abstraction*. Moreover, Locke has a couple of different ways of thinking of abstraction. So Locke has not just one account of the relation between ideas and the world but several different accounts, and these correspond to different theories of general ideas.

Locke's official position is that general ideas are the product of abstraction (II.xii.1). Composition, on the other hand, produces what Locke calls *complex* ideas. But many complex ideas are also general ideas, and it is clear that Locke often thinks of these general, complex ideas as the product of composition. And so I will treat composition as one of the processes by which Locke explains general ideas. According to the composition theory, the mind's process of forming general ideas begins with its taking in what Locke calls *simple* ideas, such as *solidity* and *whiteness*, which enter the mind through sensation and reflection. These simple ideas are then combined to form general ideas, such as *swan* (II.xxiii.14) or *gold* (III.ii.3). (A middle step, which Locke frequently does not mention, is the formation of certain ideas of powers, such as the power of swimming, which may enter into the general idea [II.xxiii.7].)

Given the composition theory of general ideas, the first step toward explaining the relation between general ideas and things outside the mind must be to explain the relation between simple ideas and things outside the mind. Some of these simple ideas are supposed to resemble the things they represent (II.viii.15). This talk of resemblance and Locke's occasional comparison between ideas and pictures (II.xxix.8, III.iii.7) might encourage an interpretation of Locke as holding that the relation of representation is fundamentally a relation of resemblance. But the explicit exceptions show that this is not so (II.viii.5). The relation that simple ideas in all cases bear to the qualities they represent is a causal relation. Sensory or reflective contact with a thing possessing a certain quality is supposed to cause the corresponding simple idea. Thus Locke's theory of representation might be characterized as a *causal* theory.

In light of the composition of general ideas from simple ideas and the causal theory of representation for simple ideas, one can explain the relation of representation for general ideas as well. General ideas represent all of those particular things sensory or reflective contact with which will cause the simple ideas that compose the general idea. The general idea *swan*, for instance, represents various different swans, because sensory contact with any of them will produce the simple ideas that compose the general idea *swan*. (By this account, a simple idea is a limiting case of general ideas, although a simple idea is not what Locke would call general.)

It is in terms of this composition theory of general ideas that Locke explains his remedy for the misunderstanding of words. In principle, one might prescribe a remedy to the *hearer*, a method by which the hearer might determine what ideas the speaker uses a given word to signify. But that is not Locke's way. Where there is any uncertainty in the signification of words, the remedy lies wholly with the *speaker*. The remedy is a two-stage process. First, words for simple ideas may be explained by showing the hearer something that will produce that idea in his or her mind. Second, words for general ideas may be defined in terms of words for simple ideas (III.xi.13–25). In this way, Locke's explanation of the process of communication serves a regulative function as well as an explanatory one.

As I said, there is also a second theory of general ideas in the *Essay*, which I will call the *abstraction* theory. By a *particular idea* I mean an idea of one particular object, such as a child's idea of its own mother (see Locke's use of the term, II.xi.9 and IV.vii.9). According to the abstraction theory, what enters the mind through sensation is particular ideas in this sense (III.iii.7). General ideas are then formed from these particular ideas by a process of abstraction. Moreover, Locke gives two different accounts of abstraction. According to one account, abstraction is a process of *subtraction*. General ideas are formed by subtracting from particular ideas that which distinguishes them from other particular ideas. For instance, the general idea *person* is formed by leaving out of the ideas of Peter, James, Mary, and Jane "that which is peculiar to each" and retaining "only what is common to them all" (III.iii.6–9).

Alternatively, abstraction is defined as a process "whereby *Ideas* taken from particular Beings, become general Representatives of all of the same kind" (II.xi.9; see also III.iii.11–13). Locke does not clearly explain what this amounts to, but he may have in mind something like Berkeley's theory, according to which a particular idea, while retaining all that makes it particular, is made to do duty in our thinking for a variety of other particular ideas that merely resemble it (Berkeley *Principles*, intro. §16). According to Berkeley, one may draw conclusions about triangles in general by reasoning about a particular triangle inasmuch as the proof may make no mention of the distinctive features of the particular. For Locke, the point would be not so much that our reasoning may be abstract while our ideas remain particular, but that particular ideas may serve us as standards or patterns to which other particular ideas, through their similitude, may be found to agree (II.xi.9, III.iii.11–13).

No doubt Locke would deny that there is any conflict between the composition theory and the abstraction theory. At one point he presents them both in the course of one long sentence:

15

> For observing, that several Things that differ from their *Idea* of *Man*, and cannot therefore be comprehended under that Name, have yet certain Qualities, wherein they agree with *Man*, by retaining only those Qualities, and uniting them into one *Idea*, they have again another and a more general *Idea*; to which having given a Name, they make a term of a more comprehensive extension: Which new *Idea* is made, not by any new addition, but only, as before, by leaving out the shape, and some other Properties signified by the name *Man*, and retaining only a Body, with Life, Sense and spontaneous Motion, comprehended under the name *Animal*. (III.iii.8)

Here Locke describes the idea *animal* as both the product of uniting the ideas of several qualities into one (composition) and as the product of leaving out ideas of certain qualities that distinguish the idea *man* from the idea *animal* (abstraction as subtraction).

These two accounts of general ideas are blended even in the context of Locke's prescription for remedying uncertainty in the signification of words. In concluding his discussion of the utility of definitions, Locke adds one final point, namely, that when it comes to explaining the signification of words "standing for Things, which are known and distinguished by their outward shapes," the true signification is best taught by means of pictures. For instance, we get a clearer idea of the meaning of "ibex" from a picture of the animal than we could get from a long definition (III.xi.25). (This is a point that Locke emphasizes as well in *Some Thoughts concerning Education*, §156.) It is as though Locke were recommending that the signification of a word be taught, not by teaching the pupil the composition of the idea, but by giving the pupil suitable materials from which to abstract.

One ought to beware of a certain specious reconciliation in which it turns out that composition and abstraction are simply inverses of one another. Simple ideas, we might suppose, may enter the mind in either of two ways. First, contact with a particular object may produce a particular idea in which several simple ideas are united. In this case the mind may form simple ideas by abstraction. Second, simple ideas may enter the mind separately, through contact with several objects. In this case, the mind may compose them. On this view, the product of composition is ultimately a particular idea, not a general idea. Such an interpretation squares with some of the things Locke actually says. Where Locke explicitly distinguishes in Book II between combining, by which complex ideas are made, and abstraction, by which general ideas are made, he lists as examples of complex ideas the idea of *a* man, the idea of *an* army, and so on (II.xii.1; see also III.iii.9). Here it seems that the product of composition is a particular idea. The problem is that elsewhere, even later in Book II, Locke is at least as clear that what we produce by combining simple ideas is ideas of *sorts* of substances (II.xxiii.6–7). And in many places in Book III it is absolutely clear that the product of composition is supposed to be a general idea (e.g., III.v.4, vi.30).

Perhaps it will be said that Locke conceived of particular ideas and general ideas as lying on a continuum and that he conceived of both as products of composition. Particular ideas might be, for Locke, as for Leibniz, just maximally specific general ideas. (They will still differ from Leibniz's individual concepts in allowing ideas of place and time as components [see III.iii.6].) By composing simple ideas, we arrive, first, at general ideas. By composing them still further, we arrive at particular ideas. The trouble is that if abstraction is the inverse of composition, then the final output of abstraction must be the basic input to composition, which means that maximally general ideas have to be simple ideas. That is clearly not what Locke thinks. For instance, one of the most general of ideas is the idea *body*. But the idea *body* is not a simple idea. Rather, Locke holds that the idea *body* is a complex idea comprising such simple ideas as *solidity* and *extension* (II.iv.1, xiii.11). Moreover, simple ideas are not maximally general. The simple idea *red* may indeed be general, but an even more general idea is *color*, which according to Locke is not simple (III.iv.16).[1]

Further, this line of thought depends on the assumption that Locke might allow that simple ideas enter the mind in two distinct ways: either united with others in a particular idea or separately from several sources. In the first case, they enter the mind as undifferentiated components of a particular idea that is not, as it enters the mind, evidently complex. Abstraction is then the operation that isolates the several general components in the otherwise undifferentiated whole. Only if simple ideas can enter the mind in this way is there work for the mental operation of abstraction to do. In the second case, a simple idea may enter the mind in conjunction with a number of others with which it composes a particular idea, but as it arrives it is evidently distinct from all of the others. Only if simple ideas can enter the mind separately in this way is there work for the mental operation of composition to do. Otherwise, any general idea could be reached by a process of *partial* abstraction that factored particular ideas into still complex components. (Or at least, any general idea representing something existing could be formed in this way.)

But it is a very strange theory that says that simple ideas enter the mind sometimes in one of these ways and sometimes in the other. The ways of entering the mind at issue here do not require any peculiarly mental mediation, for they are ways of producing the raw materials for the mental operations, such as composition and abstraction. Why, then, would there need to be these *two* ways? What would distinguish simple ideas that enter in one way from simple ideas that enter in the other? Could the idea *red* enter the mind as an undifferen-

---

[1] In fact, the idea *color* is essentially an exception to Locke's theory of general ideas. It is not formed by abstraction from ideas of particular colors such as red and yellow. Since these ideas are simple, there is nothing that could be left out while leaving something behind. Rather, the idea of color "signifies no more, but such *Ideas*, as are produced in the Mind and only by Sight, and have entrance only through the Eyes" (III.iv.16).

tiated part of the idea of a particular apple and requiring to be abstracted, while the idea *blue* entered the mind as a result of contact with an iris but not as an undifferentiated part of the idea of the iris and not requiring to be abstracted? And if there are these two ways, why does Locke not explicitly draw any such distinction?

Because I cannot find any tolerable synthesis of Locke's two theories of general ideas—the composition theory and the abstraction theory—I am simply going to assume that he had two different theories. In any case, this serves my purpose, since my real interest is not so much what Locke's theory of general ideas really was as whether it approximates to anything true. Even if for Locke the two theories were common coin, a contemporary theorist might find inspiration in one but not the other.

2. The main problem with the composition theory is that the sorts of general ideas that Locke thinks can be defined in terms of simple ideas cannot in fact be so defined. Simple ideas, recall, are the type that might enter the mind directly through sensation or reflection. Thus, if the explanation of non-simple ideas in terms of the composition of simple ideas is not to beg the question, the generation of simple ideas through sensation and reflection must be *relatively un-problematic*. By this I do not mean that there is nothing about the process to be explained, but only that the explanatory problem is very different from the problem of explaining general ideas. The difficulty I find is that it does not seem possible to define ideas like *man* and *swan* and *gold* in terms of such relatively unproblematic ideas.

In Locke's own example, the idea *swan* is supposed to be a composition of ideas of white color, long neck, red beak, black legs, whole feet, a certain size, a power of swimming, and a power of making a certain kind of noise (II.xx-iii.14). But the origin of ideas such as *leg* and *swimming* is surely not unproblematic relative to the origin of the idea *swan* itself. A leg is, roughly, a bodily part that supports an animal on a relatively stable place (such as the ground or a tree limb) and facilitates locomotion from one place to another. The idea *leg* is not the sort of idea that might enter the mind directly without aid of the very sorts of cognitive operations, whatever they may be, that might also generate the idea of a swan. Again, Locke defines *man* as a solid, extended substance having life, sense, spontaneous motion, and the faculty of reasoning (III.iii.10). Plainly the ideas *life* and *reasoning* are not unproblematic relative to the idea *man*.

In the example of the swan, Locke speaks as if he were putting together the several pieces of a picture. If that is what the process amounts to, then the component that Locke calls the idea *leg* need not itself be a general idea, namely, the idea *legs in general*, but only an image of a particular colored shape. Locke plainly does think of ideas as like pictures, even if they are not pictures. As I have already mentioned, he thinks that some simple ideas actually resemble the things they represent, and he sometimes uses pictures as at least a metaphor for ideas. But if the product of the composition is like a picture, in all its particularity, then it remains to be explained in what sense the idea produced is the general idea *swan*.

In sum, the composition theory faces the following dilemma: If the product of the composition is truly general, then the component parts, namely, the ideas of the characteristic features of the general type of thing, are not in general relatively unproblematic. If, on the other hand, the product of composition is something like a picture, then the component parts may be unproblematic relative to the whole. But then the generality of the idea is unaccounted for.

Further, I see no prospect of defining a class of simple ideas that might enter the mind through sensation or reflection in the relatively unproblematic way that Locke imagines. Locke would say that if I hold an ice cube in my hand, then through sensation I may receive both the idea *solidity* and the idea *coldness*. Likewise, if I stub my toe against a table leg, I receive both the idea *solidity* and the idea *pain*. This raises two questions: First, how does my mind separate the idea *solidity* from the idea *coldness*? Second, what makes one of the ideas I receive from the ice cube, namely, the idea *solidity*, the same as one of the ideas I receive from the table? Evidently, the answers to these questions will cite some kind of mental process. It is reasonable to doubt whether the mental process that explains the origins of these ideas will be essentially simpler than, or different in kind from, the mental process that explains the origins of other general ideas like *swan* or *gold*.

When people first consider the origin of general ideas, one of the first things that occurs to them is the composition theory. Perhaps this is because they try to get the answer through introspection, and what they find when they introspect is only mental images of things. Or maybe it is because the usual way for a human to make a thing is by building it. Or maybe it is because they focus on the case in which what we communicate is a way of recognizing something and suppose that the way to recognize a thing is through its observable features. Or maybe it is because they rely on the model of definitions conceived as lists of characteristics. Or maybe it is just because Locke's philosophy has seeped so deep into our culture. In any case, the composition theory of general ideas lives on in rarefied form in contemporary work in psychology. This rarefied form needs to be dealt with separately and in its own terms, as I will do in chapter 4. But the composition theory per se is hopeless. The sorts of ideas we want to account for simply cannot be generated through composition.

Consider the abstraction theory, then, where abstraction is conceived to be a kind of subtraction. If we think of a particular idea as like a mental image, then it can seem puzzling how the child might subtract, say, its mother's shape from its image of its mother and still have something left (a color without a shape? a fuzzy shape?). But it is not necessary to think of a particular idea as literally an image, and so I will not settle for any such objection. Still, if subtracting certain ideas from a particular idea of a particular person is supposed to result in the general idea *person*, then either that general idea must have been present in the particular idea all along or it need not have been. If it must have been present, then the origin of the general idea is not explained but presupposed. And if subtraction is a process that generates an idea that was not already present, then subtraction is itself a mysterious process, and nothing is gained by characterizing the generation of ideas as a process of subtraction.

The abstraction theory begs the question equally in the Berkelian version, where abstraction is supposed to be a matter of letting one particular idea stand in for a variety of others. The question then is, Which class of particular ideas is the chosen idea supposed to stand in for? We who already have the general idea *chair* might readily identify the particular ideas of particular chairs that the chosen idea is supposed to represent, but the problem is to explain how someone who does not already have the general idea *chair* is supposed to form it by deciding which particular ideas go together under the type that is to be represented. Why should I allow my idea of my desk chair to do duty in my thinking for my idea of the stuffed armchair in the living room that no one ever sits in and not allow it to do duty in my thinking for my idea of my desk? No straightforward appeal to similarity is going to solve the problem, as I will now explain.

This notion that ideas, or concepts, are groupings of similar objects is another one that seems to stick in people's minds and thwart all deeper understanding. Oftentimes people in the grip of this notion fail at first to distinguish between groups of actual physical objects outside of the mind and what we might call *structures of ideas* of particular objects. But it is generally easy to get them to agree that what they really want is the latter. Ideas are supposed to be components of judgments and manipulable in the mind. Consequently, ideas must be *in* the mind, or at least *mental,* in a way they would not be if ideas were literally groups of objects outside the mind. Still, the source of the notion of similarity that is appealed to is the kind of similarity relation that holds between objects outside the mind.

I do not wish to deny that concept acquisition may begin with a kind of prelinguistic recognition of similarities. On the contrary, I too am going to assign a role to the recognition of similarities. But certain oversimple theories of its role have to be strictly avoided. According to one simple-minded theory, things are classified together if and only if they are judged to be similar, and things are judged to be similar if and only if they are judged to have certain *features* in common. For instance, the first step toward forming the concept *chair* might be to recognize that this object, an emperor's throne, and this other object, a collapsible lawn chair, have certain features in common that this other object, an umbrella, lacks, for instance, the function of being used for sitting. The obvious problem with this theory is that it presupposes that the person doing the classifying can recognize the common features and so has concepts of these common features. For instance, in order to recognize that the throne and

it leaves still unexplained the source or nature of the categories the child is presented with. Why, in light of the differences between the throne and the lawn chair, do they both deserve to be called "chair"? Why, in light of the similarities between the desk chair and the desk, are they not both called "chair"? The strategy we have been exploring is one of supposing that similarity imposes a categorization on the world, but we still have not explained how it does that.

Quite apart from the problem of how the mind gets from particular ideas to general ideas by abstraction, the abstraction theory has still other problems. Recall that the composition theory left us with the difficult task of explaining the origin of simple ideas in some way different from the way we explain the origin of other ideas. If abstraction is not just the reverse of composition—if abstraction is either subtraction from a particular idea that is not already composite or abstraction of the Berkelian kind—then that particular problem about simple ideas is avoided. When I hold an ice cube or see a swan, the idea I receive need not be a composition of ideas that are already distinct but may be an undivided idea of that particular object. But then the question arises, how can I have an idea of a particular object without having ideas of any of its particular qualities, the ideas of which I acquire only by abstraction from my ideas of such particular objects?

Here it may be tempting to say that what makes an idea an idea *of* a particular object is just that it was caused by sensory contact with that object without the mediation of other ideas. This answer is at best incomplete. I have sensory contact with both the coffee cup in my left hand and the pencil in my right hand, but the mereological sum of the coffee cup and the pencil does not cause in me a particular idea of the cup-*cum*-pencil. Moreover, for any idea of a particular thing there will be *many* non-ideas in the chain of causes and effects leading up to that idea. Which one is the idea *of*? So this account clearly does not yet identify the desired relationship between ideas and objects.

Moreover, nothing has been said about the characteristics of particular ideas that distinguish one particular idea from another so that one of these ideas might enter into a process of abstracting general idea A and another might enter into a process of abstracting general idea B. If particular ideas are distinguished from one another by the general ideas that compose them, then abstraction must be just the reverse of composition after all. Alternatively, particular ideas might be simply mental images. In that case, particular ideas might be distinguished from one another, not by their ideational components, but by their observable qualities. As already noted, abstraction as subtraction is utterly mysterious if particular ideas are mental images. But the conception of particular ideas as mental images comports rather well with the Berkelian conception of abstraction, according to which one particular idea is made to do duty for others. It does not help us with the problem of deciding where to draw the boundaries between general classes of things, but it seems to provide a basis for at least the comparison of particular ideas prerequisite to such decisions.

I do not wish to deny that mental pictures play an important role in thought or that imagistic thinking is properly a kind of thinking. When we are trying to figure out how the pieces of a faucet go together, we may indeed experiment in mental imagery before trying to put the actual pieces together. When trying to decide whether a syllogism is valid, we may literally imagine some children all of whom are team members and some of whom are not boys, in order to decide whether some team members are not boys as well (Johnson-Laird 1983). But the qualities of mental images, whatever they are, will rarely be sufficient to generate, by whatever process, the general ideas that those images illustrate. It is quite incredible to think that someone who merely studied a lot of pictures of dogs and cats, including pictures of them doing all sorts of things, would find compelling reason to put a Pekingese and a Great Dane in one group and a bobcat in another. The case for a role for images is even worse when it comes to general ideas like *electron* or *justice*. So the assimilation of particular ideas to mental images does not ultimately help us very much to understand how a particular idea can be the input to a process of abstraction.

The Lockean theory of ideas, I conclude, is a disaster. Indeed, the Lockean theory of ideas has largely been abandoned by contemporary philosophers (but again, see chapter 4). One might have thought that the Lockean theory of communication would hold little attraction apart from the Lockean theory of ideas. For Locke, the reason to think of communication as the conveying of ideas is that then, in light of the relation between ideas and the things that ideas represent, a remedy for miscommunication can be prescribed. Surprisingly, the Lockean theory of communication survives without the theory of ideas.

3. In the rest of this chapter I will do three things. First, I will survey some of the forms in which the Lockean theory of communication has survived apart from the forsaken theory of ideas. Second, I will briefly describe what is at stake in deciding between a Lockean conception of communication and some other. Finally, I will present a brief glossary.

I will use the term *speaker's message* as a generic label for whatever sort of thing a given version of the Lockean theory defines as the mental object speakers express and hearers are supposed to grasp. So my claim is that there are versions of the Lockean theory of communication for which the speaker's message is something other than a Lockean idea.

For instance, I consider Donald Davidson to be a Lockean whose conception of the speaker's message (in the sense defined) is very different from Locke's. Davidson's Lockeanism has not always been a transparent feature of his philosophy. Some of his writings (esp. 1975) can be interpreted as arguing against the Lockean theory; but all along (see 1974) he has conceived of translation as serving to enable the interpreter to infer the speaker's beliefs, and his Lockeanism emerges quite clearly in his later papers, especially when he turns to problems of everyday interpretation, such as seeing past malapropisms (e.g.,

1986b). As the quotation at the beginning of this chapter illustrates, Davidson thinks of the speaker's meaning as an intention, which the hearer is to recognize the speaker to have. Davidson has a great deal to say about intentions (1980), but he nowhere tells us exactly what the content or meaning of an intention is, in the sense of reducing it to something outside the circle of intentionality. On the contrary, he declares himself a foe of certain sorts of reductions (1970, 90). However, whenever Davidson is confronted with a need to explain what such things as satisfaction conditions, beliefs, and intentions are, he answers by sketching a methodology for ascribing such properties (1975, 1977, 1990). So it is fair to say that, for Davidson, what it is for an intention to have a certain content is to be understood in terms of a theory of interpretation.

Other exponents of the Lockean theory of communication may give yet other accounts of the speaker's message. One distinction is between those who think of the speaker's message as an *attitude* toward a proposition in some sense and those who think of the speaker's message as something more like the proposition itself. In either case, various accounts of the relevant attitude and of the nature of the proposition are possible. Some may think of the attitude as simply one of *belief*. The speaker's message in that case is either the belief that p or the proposition p believed. Others may think of the pertinent attitude as an *intention* to get the hearer to believe that p (Bennett 1976, 131). Others may think of the attitude as an intention to get the hearer to believe that the *speaker* believes that p (Grice 1968). Others may think of the attitude as an intention to make the proposition "manifest" to the hearer (Sperber and Wilson 1986, 63). Further, various conceptions of the pertinent proposition are possible too. Some may think of it as some kind of abstract object (a structure of universals, a set of possible worlds) that exists independently of minds but in some way characterizes individual speakers (Lewis 1969, 1975). For instance, the proposition might characterize a subpersonal physical particular in the speaker's brain. Some may think of this internal physical particular, in turn, as a sentence in an inner language of thought (Fodor 1975).

We have seen that Locke gave little attention to the method by which hearers grasp the speaker's message. In contemporary work there has been somewhat more interest in this. Let us say that the condition under which a sentence is true is its *truth-condition*. For instance, the truth-condition of "It is raining" (in English) and "Es regnet" (in German) is that it is raining. According to Davidson, the hearer's grasp of a speaker's message is mediated by the hearer's knowledge of the truth-conditions of sentences of the speaker's language. The speaker's primary intention in speaking is to utter words that will be interpreted by the hearer as having certain truth-conditions (1984a, 271–73; 1986b, 435). What enables the speaker to realize this intention is the hearer's knowledge of the truth-conditions of sentences in the speaker's language. Recursive theories of truth for a language enter into Davidson's account in his characterization of the hearer's knowledge of truth-conditions. Each interlocutor will enter the conversation with a *prior* theory of the truth-conditions of sentences in the other's language but will substitute an *ad hoc passing* theory as the conversation proceeds and idiolects, metaphors, and malapropisms emerge.

Still other accounts of the manner in which the hearer grasps the speaker's message are possible. Davidson explicitly denies that communication depends on conventions (1984a, 1986b), but many others have considered conventions to be important. Moreover, very different accounts of these conventions and their role in communication have been proposed. For instance, according to David Lewis (1975), there are essentially just two conventions, which he calls conventions of *truthfulness* and *trust* in a language. Jerry Fodor, by contrast, thinks of these conventions as *recipes* for communicating specific messages (1975, 106). Still others stress the role of creative hypothesis formation. For instance, Sperber and Wilson (1986, 163–71) argue that the hearer must infer the speaker's intention by inventing hypotheses concerning the speaker's possible intention and then selecting from these by means of a presumption that the speaker is being "optimally relevant."

Perhaps no one will claim that every time a hearer understands a speaker's words there occurs in the hearer a special sort of mental act of inferring the speaker's message. The claim will be at most that the hearer's part is *essentially* a matter of inferring the speaker's message. The idea might be that where there is understanding the hearer must have been able to infer the speaker's message even if no such inference actually took place. Or the idea might be that a hearer must infer the speaker's message whenever the exchange between them is not routine in some sense. Or the idea might be that in theorizing about language we should *suppose* that the hearer constantly infers the speaker's message.

4. Could the Lockean theory, so broadly defined, possibly be false? Yes, it could be, because it requires a possibly false distinction between the thoughts words express and the words that express them. No doubt there are many mental processes that deserve to be called "thought," and so an outright identification of *all* thought with speech would be absurd. What is not so absurd, although the idea has not been taken very seriously recently, is that the sort of thought that one might have believed speech to merely express is only an internal form of that very sort of speech. This is one thing that no version of the Lockean theory can allow. If thoughts of the kind that one might have taken speech to express are themselves simply acts of inner speech, not otherwise essentially different from overt acts of speech, then an overt act of speech cannot be explained by citing a relation (namely, expression) between it and some such thought. Whatever fundamental questions might be raised about the overt acts of speech might be raised as well about the inner acts of speech.

Lockeans commonly concede that in certain ways thought depends on language (Schiffer 1972, 15–16; Bennett 1976, 96). Locke himself acknowledges that words may serve an important mnemonic function (III.ii.2). A Lockean

might also acknowledge that language enables us to hold in mind more complicated thoughts than we could hold in mind without language (Fodor 1975, 84–
85). Further, Lockeans may acknowledge that linguistic behavior might be the
only kind of overt behavior capable of *manifesting* certain sorts of thoughts
(such as "unrestricted existentially quantified beliefs about contingent exis-
tences" [Armstrong 1973, 32, 100]). In addition, a Lockean might acknowledge that certain sorts of thoughts, such as thoughts about Tuesdays, will be
formed only in the context of language-using communities. But none of these
concessions gives up the distinction between the thoughts words express and
the words that express them.

Let us call the sort of mental particular that might, according to the Lockean,
bear the content of a speaker's message *propositional thought*. Now, consider
all the functions in the person or the body that one might have supposed
propositional thought to play (aside from being that which words express).
Next, consider that it might be tokenings of sentences of the person's home
spoken language that play those roles. To conceive of this is to conceive of an
alternative to the Lockean theory. On this alternative, spoken words need no
longer be conceived as signs by which hearers may discover the speaker's
message. Rather, spoken words may themselves function in the hearer as we
conceive certain thoughts to function in the individual mind. Once thinking is
conceived as a kind of inner talking in this way, communication between
persons might even be conceived as a kind of collaborative thinking.

A single language may of course take several forms. The sentences of what I
am calling *spoken* language need not be literally spoken. For instance, the
sentences on this page belong to a spoken language—English—without being
spoken. Likewise, an arrangement of magnetic particles on a computer disk or a
sequence of electrical pulses traveling along a telephone line might belong to a
spoken language. What makes it the case that two forms of a given language,
such as written English and spoken English, are both forms of a single language
is, roughly, that both are actually employed within a single linguistic community and that they have identical grammars and that there is a one-to-one,
meaning-preserving mapping of the words of one into the words of the other. In
consequence of this structural isomorphism, a kind of translation from one form
to another will be possible that does not attend to the context in which a sentence
occurs. For example, we write down what people say and read stories aloud
from books. So one might also require that the community actually practices
such translation.

Now I can explain some of the ways in which one might understand the claim
that spoken languages are the very medium of a certain kind of thought. On any
version, the claim will be, in part, that publicly observable tokens of language—those spoken aloud or written on paper—deserve to be called
"thoughts" every bit as much as those that are not publicly observable. However, different versions may make different claims about the forms of language

that are not publicly observable. On one version, there are no such forms of thought in language. On this view, all forms of the sort of thought for which language is the medium are publicly observable. On a second version, certain types of event in the brain (or, more generally, the central processor) constitute, as writing does, a form of a spoken language. This view will be distinguished from the Lockean theory in that it denies that sentences literally spoken are explicable as the expression of some inner kind of thought and in that it supposes that the forms of such brain writing will vary from person to person according to the language a person uses out loud. Finally, a third way to take the claim is as the claim that while there may be thoughts that do not occur in any publicly observable form, such as speech or writing, they have no physical form whatsoever but nonetheless share the grammar and vocabulary of the spoken language.

The choice between the Lockean theory and the conception of propositional thought as inner speech makes a tremendous difference in how we theorize about language, although the consequences of choosing the latter have never been thoroughly explored. For one thing, it makes a tremendous difference to how we approach the subject of early language acquisition. If we accept a Lockean theory of communication, then we will have to try to see language acquisition as a process in which the child learns to discover speakers' messages and to make its own messages discoverable to others. The challenge will be to show that the cognitive equipment necessary for this kind of learning is available to the child prior to its reaching the level of linguistic development that has to be explained. On the other side, if we accept that spoken language is the very medium of propositional thought, we will have to try to understand language learning without invoking propositional thought.

Further, the choice will make a tremendous difference to how we approach the subject of conversational dynamics. If we accept a Lockean theory of communication, then we may view conversation as a process in which interlocutors keep track of one another's mental state while trying to alter it in various ways. One challenge on this approach will be to show that each participant in a conversation might actually have sufficient access to the mental states of the other and to show this without presupposing that the participants have the sort of understanding of one another that their conversation first makes possible. If, on the other side, we accept that language is the very medium of propositional thought, then the fundamental parameters of conversational appropriateness will have to be determined by something other than states of the interlocutors' minds.

The present issue is commonly mixed up with certain others that I want to distinguish from it. First of all, the conflict between the Lockean theory and its competitors need not be a conflict between mentalism and behaviorism. It is true that many of those who have opposed the Lockean picture in the past have been behaviorists of one sort or another (Mead 1934; Wittgenstein 1953; Sellars

1969; Quine 1975), and some of them have even seemed to espouse a reduction of thought to behavioral dispositions. But it is not necessary to be a behaviorist of any of these earlier kinds in order to deny the Lockean theory. Thoughts for the non-Lockean may be every bit as particular and efficacious as they may be for the Lockean. The question is, what are they?

Second, the issue is not the nature of linguistic *meaning* but the nature of linguistic *communication*. The concept of meaning is one that theorists may place in various relations to the concept of communication. Davidson thinks that a theory of what he calls *literal* meaning may take the form of a theory of truth conditions, which, as we have seen, he thinks of as only part of a theory of communication (1986b; 1990, 312–13). Ian Hacking has argued that Locke himself had *no* theory of meaning on the grounds that Locke had no theory of anything quite like Frege's concept of *sense* (Hacking 1975, 43–53). So I do not want to claim that there is any particular account of the relation between meaning and communication to which all proponents of a Lockean theory are committed. Consequently, the issue is certainly not whether the concept of linguistic meaning can in any sense be reduced to mentalistic concepts such as belief and intention. The issue is how to explain the process of communication. In chapter 13 I will assign a role to the concept of meaning, but this will be something quite remote from the role this concept has usually been supposed to play.

5. Before proceeding, it might be helpful to fix terminology in a glossary. I do not expect these definitions to be fully intelligible apart from some prior acquaintance with Lockean theories of communication (since they lead in circles). Moreover, one ought not to rely on these definitions too slavishly, since the Lockean theory as I understand it is more like a common theme than a definite doctrine. But I will try to adhere to these definitions throughout my critique of the Lockean theory.

Speaker's message: According to the Lockean theory of communication, there is a kind of mental object that a speaker's words normally express and that, when communication is successful, hearers grasp. This mental object is called the *speaker's message* when it is expressed in words.

Grasp: This is the relation that, according to the Lockean theory, holds between a hearer and a speaker's message when communication is successful.

Expression: This is a relation that may hold between a speaker's words and the speaker's message. According to the Lockean theory, its holding normally enables hearers to grasp the speaker's message.

Content: This is something that a speaker's message *has*. The content of a speaker's message is what, according to the Lockean theory, a hearer has to *comprehend* in order to *grasp* the speaker's message. The speaker's choice of words will depend largely on the content of the speaker's message.

Comprehension: This is the relation that holds between a hearer and the content
of the speaker's message when the hearer grasps the speaker's message.

Propositional thought: A propositional thought is a component of a speaker's
message and *bears* the *content* of the speaker's message. Propositional
thoughts have syntactic structure, either intrinsically or extrinsically. The
structure of the sentence that most fully expresses the speaker's message
corresponds in some way to the structure of a propositional thought that bears
the content of the speaker's message. Words can also be said to express a
thought, namely, the propositional thought that bears the content of the
speaker's message.

Concept: This term has two senses. On the one hand, a concept is a component
of a propositional thought. As a propositional thought corresponds to a
sentence, a concept corresponds to a word or phrase. On the other hand,
a concept is a component of a content. As a propositional thought bears a
content, a concept in the first sense bears a concept in the second sense.

Normal: Where in these definitions I say that something is *normal*, I mean that
it obtains in the paradigmatic cases of communication. I am taking for
granted that we all have the ability to recognize these. I would not be able to
define them without prejudging the issue with the Lockean.

For some versions of the Lockean theory, some of this terminology could be
collapsed. At one extreme, speaker's message, propositional thought, and
content might all be one. For other versions it may be important to draw all
these distinctions. For instance, consider a Gricean version according to which
communication is a matter of the hearer's recognizing that the speaker intends
the hearer to believe that *p*. Here we might say that the speaker's message,
which the speaker expresses and the hearer grasps, is the speaker's intention to
bring it about that the hearer believe that *p*. The content, which determines the
speaker's choice of words and which the hearer has to comprehend, is the
proposition *that p*. And the propositional thought is the subpersonal physical
particular in the brain of the speaker that bears the content *that p*.

The term "propositional thought" deserves a bit more commentary. I will use
the term both within and outside of the context of the Lockean theory. Within
the Lockean theory a propositional thought is the kind of thought that words
may be said to express, although not every propositional thought that actually
occurs in some mind will actually be expressed in words. Outside the Lockean
theory I will use the term to refer to a wide variety of mental entities, such as
occurrent thoughts, standing beliefs, long-term and short-term desires, and so
on. I think of propositional thoughts, whether within or outside of the context of
the Lockean theory, as *particulars*. As I will use the term, propositional
thoughts are not universals. They are not the universals that two particular
thoughts having the same content may share, nor are they universals characterizing distinct thinkers. However, in some contexts two distinct propositional

thoughts may *count as* the *same* thought. For instance, if you think that it is time for lunch and I think that it is time for lunch, then, in a sense, we think the same. In such a context, your propositional thought and mine might count as one. Similarly, books are particulars, but two of them might count as the same book in some contexts.

It is sometimes supposed that to speak of a propositional thought's *content* is just to adopt a certain mode of individuating, or counting propositional thoughts. So, for instance, if you think that you are being chased by a bear and I think that I am being chased by a bear, our thoughts may be counted as one thought (since each of us thinks the same thing about himself or herself) or as two (since your thought is about you and mine is about me). Accordingly, it may be said that there are two kinds of content, one kind that your thought and mine share and another kind that distinguishes our thoughts.

Content considered as merely a mode of individuation has to be distinguished from content considered as what, according to the Lockean theory, a hearer must comprehend in order to grasp a speaker's message. If there were contents in the Lockean sense, then propositional thoughts could indeed be individuated in accordance with them. But it cannot be assumed that there is such a thing as content in the Lockean's sense just because we can group thoughts together however we wish. On the contrary, to establish that there is such a thing as content in the Lockean's sense of the term, it is necessary to show that there is something that plays the requisite role in a theory of communication. This necessity will be the crux of my criticism of the Lockean theory in chapter 3.

In order to discourage glib replies to serious criticisms of the Lockean theory, therefore, I will strictly avoid using the term "content" merely as a term for various modes of individuating thoughts. In my usage, it will everywhere be the Lockean term of art defined above. It might be possible to develop a theory of the conditions under which two propositional thoughts count as one (and thus have the same content in the forsworn sense of the word) (e.g., Stich 1983), but I will not develop any such theory in this book.

Finally, I should remark on the two senses of "concept." In the first sense, in which a concept is a component of a propositional thought, a concept is a particular, not shareable between two thinkers. In the second sense, in which a concept is a component of a content, concepts are shareable. In this book I will use the term "concept" in both of these senses. In speaking of concept acquisition, in particular, I will intend to speak of the origin in the mind of a certain particular, but I will normally identify that particular by speaking of the shareable content component that that particular bears.

Sometimes it is said, as if this were interesting, that no two people have exactly the same concept of even ordinary sorts of thing such as reptiles. What people who say this have in mind is that people think about the pertinent sort, for example, reptiles, in somewhat different ways. For instance, they believe different sets of facts about them. By either definition of concepts, this is a confusion. If concepts are components of propositional thoughts in my sense, then since they are particulars, it is trivial that none that is your head is in my head too. If concepts are components of contents, on the other hand, then people must quite commonly have the same concept. For instance, if you tell me, "Some reptiles can swim," and I understand you, then I must grasp the very same concepts that you express with "reptile" and "swim." A theory that held that communication does sometimes take place and is a matter of the hearer's grasping the speaker's concepts but that hearer and speaker share no concepts would be simply inconsistent. Perhaps one could define concepts in such a way that they were neither particulars nor in fact shared, but I doubt that such a conception of concepts would have any utility in any kind of theory of cognition or of language.

2

Communication

1. In this first half of this book I will criticize the Lockean theory in many ways. In some chapters I will question the metaphysical presuppositions of contemporary versions of the Lockean theory. In the next chapter I will even attempt a refutation. But in this chapter I simply question some of the primary motives for adopting a Lockean theory of communication. My objective here is only to make the Lockean theory seem unobvious. Toward the end of the chapter, however, I will raise a more fundamental doubt having to do with language acquisition.

The Lockean theory is often construed as mere common sense or as the deliverance of introspection (Fodor 1975, 103; Sperber and Wilson 1986, 23). But *common sense* is often the alias for an old and mistaken theory, and introspection, we now know, offers no direct insight into the mechanisms of the mind (Nisbett and Wilson 1977). In the unreasoned conviction of some philosophers that the Lockean theory must be true, I think I see the influence of a vernacular shaped by prior theory. Not only philosophers know that words express thoughts and that one can decide whether to speak one's mind or to keep to oneself. Such ways of talking plainly invite a model of hidden mental objects that words merely reveal.

In some sense words express thoughts. We need to distinguish two cases. One case is that in which words spoken by one person are said to express the thought of another person. For instance, if A says, "B thinks that p," then A may be said to have expressed B's thought. The other case is that in which a person's words are said to express that same person's thought. The first sort of case will be no support for the Lockean theory unless the second sort is.

Let us consider, then, whether the fact that a person's words express his or her thought is any support for the Lockean theory. That all depends on what sorts of facts make it correct to say such a thing. The facts that make it correct to say that a person's words express his or her thoughts may be of many sorts. For instance, the fact may be merely that the speaker used those words to make an assertion and was not lying or merely toying with hypotheses or paraphrasing someone else's words. Or the fact may be that the words said to express a thought constitute an out-loud repetition of the very words that the speaker spoke silently to himself or herself. Or those may be the words the speaker decides he or she should have spoken rather than those he or she did speak.

So it is not obvious that a speaker's expressing his or her thought in words is a matter of the speaker's choosing words that might enable the hearer to grasp something distinct from the words that the words merely serve to convey. So the fact that a speaker's words express his or her thought in some sense is no direct support for the Lockean theory. So likewise the fact that a person may use words to express someone else's thought is also no support for the Lockean theory. The more general lesson is that we must not assume that our ordinary ways of talking about language reveal the fundamental entities and relations on which a theory of language must rest.

We sometimes sense that we lack the words to express an antecedently present thought. This is still no reason to believe that we choose our words to match up with something that is not already in words (contrary to Armstrong 1973, 32). When we have this sense that we lack the words, various sorts of things may be going on other than a failure to match. The problem may be that for a moment one knew what to say but then suddenly forgot. Or the problem may be that one has a certain mental image that one cannot well describe. Or certain words may come to mind, but they may be rejected as untrue or prolix or tactless. Or one might find oneself in a position where one ought to have a definite opinion and be unwilling to admit, even to oneself, that one does not.

Certainly there are *nonverbal thoughts*, by which I mean thoughts that do not belong to any public language. The obvious example is animal thought. We say that a dog thinks that a squirrel is in the tree, and that means that "A squirrel is in the tree" expresses the dog's thought. But the dog's thought certainly does not belong to any spoken language. Moreover, there is surely nonverbal thought in language-using humans as well. Clearly our own overt speech is accompanied by an undercurrent of thought that we do not speak. We have to suppose so in order to explain why people speak when they do and why they say what they do. Even when we try to think out loud there is such an undercurrent that we do not speak. So it is hard to believe that this undercurrent consists of words from the very language we speak out loud. Given that nonverbal thoughts exist, is it not reasonable to view words as a means of making such nonverbal thoughts known to others?

To get straight about this, it is necessary to realize that there may be many different kinds of thought. One kind is *propositional* thought, by which I mean a sort of thought possessing a logical form (or logical type) and analyzable into parts (or aspects) corresponding to the words and phrases of sentences. This is the kind of thought that a Lockean will take to bear the content of a speaker's message. In addition to propositional thought, there may be *imagistic* thought. This will differ from propositional thought in ways analogous to the ways in which pictures differ from sentences. Problem solving may be possible not only by forming hypotheses and drawing inferences but also by a kind of mental movie-making. Yet another kind of thought is what might be called, for lack of a better term, *athletic* thought. This is the kind of thought by which split-second decisions are made in athletic competitions. An example would be a tennis player's decision to run from one side of the court to another in anticipation of a cross-court volley. In addition to these kinds of thought, there may be still other kinds that we cannot identify by means of any simple analogies and that we may someday understand in exclusively neurological terms or in ways we have not yet thought up.

To the argument that words must be a means of making nonverbal thoughts known to others I may now give three answers. First, our attributions of thought to languageless animals and prelinguistic children cannot be the basis for any very direct argument for the Lockean conception of thoughts as distinct from but expressible in language. We ought not to say, "We *know* that animals and prelinguistic children have such and such concepts, and so it is plain that language would evolve in order to enable creatures to express thoughts containing such concepts." In fact, if animals and prelinguistic children have concepts, then we certainly do not know what concepts they have. Certainly, we cannot assume, on the basis of our ordinary characterizations of animals' and infants' thoughts, that their thoughts contain concepts that the ordinary words and phrases of ordinary public languages might be used to express. Although we might *say*, "The dog thinks a squirrel is in the tree," we plainly we have no reason to suppose that the dog's thought contains specifically the concept *squirrel*—that the dog conceives of the squirrel *as* a squirrel. Nor is there any other conceptualization, such as *furry moving thing* or *pesky critter*, that we can assume to be the dog's conceptualization of the squirrel. From this alone I do not infer that there are concepts only where there is language, but I do infer that the Lockean is in no position simply to assume that animals and prelinguistic children do have definite concepts.

It is sometimes supposed that we could determine the content of an animal's concepts by finding out what kinds of discriminations the animal can make in the context of learning. For instance, we might find that a pigeon who has been taught to peck when shown slides of trees and not to peck when shown slides of other things will also peck when shown new pictures of trees, which it had not been trained on. From this kind of evidence, Herrnstein (1992) concludes that pigeons are able to *categorize* things according to whether they are trees (or some closely related category). But this is a fallacy. Herrnstein's experimental evidence does not provide any reason to think that the pigeons in any sense mentally group trees or pictures of trees together in such a way as to include unencountered instances. The results are adequately explained by supposing that when the pigeons had to decide whether or not to peck in response to a novel picture, what they decided was whether the novel picture was more *similar* to the earlier pictures that had brought reward than to the earlier pictures that had not brought reward. Moreover, as I explained in chapter 1, these judgments of similarity do not immediately induce a categorization. (For further criticism of Herrnstein, see Gauker 1994.)

My second reply to the argument that words must be a means of making nonverbal thoughts known to others is that the sorts of nonverbal thought that humans and other animals possess may not be serious candidates for the sort of speaker's message that, according to the Lockean theory, any hearer who understands the speaker has to grasp. For instance, a kind of nonverbal thought will not be a serious candidate if it is any kind of *imagistic* thought. No doubt there *are* mental pictures, and words can describe them and, in that sense, express them. When I say that the dog thinks a squirrel is in the tree, my words may express the dog's thought in the sense of describing a scene that the dog imagines (which is not to say that I must *think* that the dog forms such an image). But the fact that words may in this way express mental pictures is no support for versions of the Lockean theory worth taking seriously. In order to understand a speaker's message it is not necessary for the hearer to grasp the speaker's mental picture (unless perhaps that is the topic of the message), and even if the hearer did grasp the speaker's mental picture, that alone would not constitute understanding. For instance, if someone says, "Some reptiles can swim," he or she may communicate with the hearer as perfectly as one could hope for, and yet the hearer may have no idea what the speaker is picturing (snake, iguana, German shepherd) or whether the speaker is picturing anything at all (see Alston 1964, 22–25; and Blackburn 1984, 45–50).

My third reply is that even if we grant that nonverbal thoughts may be propositional, it is not necessary that words be conceived as a means of expressing them. Whether the possibility of nonverbal propositional thought is any support for the Lockean theory of communication will depend on how these nonverbal propositional thoughts are supposed to be related to the languages we speak. One possibility, yielding a version of the Lockean theory, is that spoken languages merely translate, or encode, these nonverbal propositional thoughts. But a second possibility is that the medium of nonverbal propositional thought is only a kind of *proto*language, by which I mean an inner language of thought that, like the spoken language of infants, is too underdeveloped to be exactly translated into any spoken language of adults. In this case, the fact that there is nonverbal propositional thought will be no support for the Lockean theory, for it might still be maintained that public languages are the very medium of the sort of thought that the Lockean mistakenly supposes public languages serve merely to express. The protolanguage might be, as it were, the seed from which a capacity for speaking in a public language grows. Yet what grows from this seed need not be a medium of thought distinct from public language. It might be a capacity to think in public language.

2. Another idea that motivates the Lockean theory is that understanding a person's speech is always a matter of actively interpreting the speaker's meaning. For example, Davidson writes: "The problem of interpretation is domestic as well as foreign: it surfaces for speakers of the same language in the form of the question, how can it be determined that the language is the same? Speakers of the same language can go on the assumption that for them the same expressions are to be interpreted in the same way, but this does not indicate what justifies the assumption. All understanding of the speech of another involves radical interpretation" (1973, 13). Here Davidson seems to conclude that all linguistic understanding, "domestic as well as foreign," involves interpretation on the grounds that the hearer *can* always ask whether the speaker is speaking the hearer's language. However, that conclusion follows only on the additional assumption that the hearer does in fact, or at least ought to, take such a question seriously. Is that so?

It all depends on how we individuate languages. If we individuate languages in such a way that the several members of a rather large linguistic community may all be supposed to speak the *same* language, then the possibility that the speaker is not speaking the hearer's own language will not always be a possibility that the hearer need take seriously. Surely there have been linguistic communities isolated from all others for many decades in which people have lived long lives without ever once having reason to contemplate even the possibility that people elsewhere in the world might speak what would count as a *different* language in this sense. In whatever sense the members of such a community can understand one another without so much as wondering whether they are speaking the same language (as presently individuated), the members of our own linguistic community, interspersed among the members of other linguistic communities, can normally understand one another without raising such a question. It is not necessary to wonder whether someone else is speaking the same language (in the present sense) as oneself until something happens that gives one specific reason to wonder.

But this is not how Davidson tends to individuate languages. According to Davidson, it is almost true that each person speaks his or her own language, since "different speakers have different stocks of proper names, different vocabularies, and attach somewhat different meanings to words" (Davidson 1984a, 277). If we individuate languages in the finer-grained way that this suggests, then there may always be a live possibility that the speaker is not speaking the hearer's own language. But then it is unclear why the fact that we may have to interpret other people in the sense of deciding which of these fine-grained languages they are speaking is a reason to accept a Lockean theory of communication. One cannot assume that interpretation in this case is anything very like understanding a language that qualifies as different from one's own even under the coarse-grained mode of individuation. From the point of view of the Lockean theory of communication, there might be reason to view every novel proper name, every metaphor, and every malapropism as identifying a unique language, but how, conversely, do the facts on which the fine-grained individuation of languages is based motivate the Lockean theory?

Davidson acknowledges that he, like many others, has been influenced by H. P. Grice's analysis of *meaning something by something* (Davidson 1990, 311n).

A simplified version of Grice's analysis for "indicative-type" utterances (similar to Grice's formulation in 1968, 230) is this:

> Utterer U meant that p by uttering x if and only if for some audience A, U uttered x intending
> (1) that A should believe that U believed that p,
> (2) that A should believe that U intended (1), and
> (3) that (1) should be achieved by means of achieving (2).

Grice himself formulated his claims as concerned with meaning. However, Davidson and others (e.g., Sperber and Wilson 1986, 21) have wished to construe his theories as pertaining first of all to communication. (That Grice too thought of his theory as pertaining to communication becomes clear in the later essay "Meaning Revisited" 1989b.) The above analysis does indeed lead very directly to a version of the Lockean theory of communication. Since participants in a conversation almost always mean something p by what they say, this analysis implies that in conversing they almost always intend (1), (2), and (3). Thus, on this analysis, successful conversation depends on the participants' achieving (1), (2), and (3). But achieving (2) means getting one's interlocutor to recognize one's intention to achieve (1). This intention to achieve (1) may be taken as the speaker's message in a version of the Lockean theory.

My objection to Grice's analysis is not that it is psychologically unrealistic or that the concepts being analyzed are somehow more fundamental than the concepts employed in the analysis (cf. Avramides 1989). In particular, my objection is not that our grasp of sentence meaning is epistemologically prior to our grasp of speaker's meaning or that our grasp of speaker's meaning is epistemologically prior to our grasp of a speaker's intentions in speaking (Biro 1979). My objection is only that there is no good reason to believe the analysis in the first place.

A typical Gricean move is this: We are invited to compare a case in which a speaker means something by something to a case in which another agent performs some act without meaning anything by that act. In one of Grice's examples, a man leaves B's handkerchief near the scene of a murder "in order to induce the detective to believe that B was the murderer" (Grice 1957, 381–82). Grice expects the reader to agree that the man did not *mean* by that act that B was the murderer, and in fact that act does seem different from the paradigm case of meaning something by something, namely, candidly saying something out loud. Apparently, a genuine case of meaning something by something must possess some feature that is lacking in the case described. In the case described, the man did not intend that the detective should recognize that he intended that the detective should infer that B was the murderer. Thus Grice concludes that in order for an agent to mean something by something the agent must intend that the audience recognize the agent's intention.

I see no reason to draw this conclusion. One way to draw a conclusion is to generalize from a representative example. If Grice's inference is supposed to be a generalization from the example, then it is utterly fallacious. The fact that a certain thing is both not black and not a raven gives us no reason to believe, no matter how representative that thing might be, that all ravens are black. Likewise, the fact that a certain condition is *unfulfilled* in a case of *not* meaning something by something gives us no reason to believe, no matter how representative the case may be, that that condition is fulfilled in every case of meaning something by something. Another way to reach a conclusion is to draw an inference to the best explanation. But we cannot construe Grice's inference as one of these until we are given some reason to believe that Grice's conclusion *is* a good explanation. (For further examples of this fallacy, see Green 1989, 13– 14, and Clark 1992, 11–14.)

Strangely, many people have been persuaded by Grice's argument, so it would be good to supplement this criticism with some diagnosis of the argument's persuasive power. What puzzles me first of all is why anyone would believe that there really is some definite thing called "meaning something by something" that possesses some real essence that stands in need of analysis and on which the very possibility of language rests. Perhaps people are in part misled by our ordinary ways of talking about language. In various ways, language may be effective or not. When we find that it is ineffective, we have various ways of dealing with that fact. One way is to talk about "meaning." For instance, someone's asking, "What do you mean by that?" might serve as a call for greater specificity, or candor, or elaboration, or disambiguation. Even where there is no real misunderstanding, we can give a trivial answer to the question ("I meant exactly what I said"). Since there is always some potential for misunderstanding and we can always give at least a trivial answer, it may indeed make some sense to say that we always do mean something by what we say. But clearly, the fact that talk of meaning in this way plays a useful role in the conduct of conversations is no reason to base our theory of the process of communication on the idea that for every assertion there is an underlying act of meaning something by something.

My guess is that when we take ourselves to be analyzing the concept of meaning something by something and wind up with Grice's answer, what is going on is something like this: We have in mind certain paradigm cases of candidly saying something in words. We then consider certain other cases in which one agent instills belief in another, and we try to think of some difference between the two that might possibly hold *in general* between candidly saying something and other means of instilling belief. Moreover, our strategy for finding a general difference is to think of the agent as deliberately deciding between two methods of instilling belief. Thus we ask ourselves, in effect, what the man would have had to intend if he had deliberately chosen (*a*) simply telling the detective in words that *B* was the murderer *over* (*b*) leaving the handkerchief at the scene of the crime. A reason for the man to choose (*a*) over (*b*) might indeed be that the man intends the detective to realize that the man intends the detective to believe that *B* was the murderer. Thus we conclude that in general meaning something by something requires that the speaker intend the hearer to recognize the speaker's intention to instill in the hearer a certain belief. If this diagnosis of our acquiescence in Grice's reasoning is correct, then the fallacy lies in the assumption that if a certain state of mind accompanies any deliberate choice of candidly saying something over some other means of instilling belief, then that same state of mind must accompany any act of candidly saying something. This is a mistake, since normally there is no need for any deliberate choice.

One thing that supports my diagnosis is that it is hard to find any clear cases of meaning something by something that do not involve the use of some conventional sign. It is easy to think of cases in which someone "says" something by doing something that is not in any narrow sense an act of speaking in a language. For instance, by clearing one's throat one may "say" that the conversation has taken an unseemly turn. But that is definitely a conventional sign in this context. Some of Grice's followers (Lewis 1969; Bennett 1976) have sought to explain how a language might possibly have originated as a coordination of the sorts of intentions that enter into Grice's analysis of meaning something by something and so have supposed that speakers can mean things by signs that do not already have a conventional meaning. For instance, someone might convey the message that a snake is nearby by making hissing noises and moving his or her hand in an undulating motion (Bennett 1976, 138–39). But in such cases it is not at all obvious that the work is done by Gricean means. The observer may come to believe that snakes are nearby only because the hissing and gestures remind him or her of snakes in a context in which he or she will realize from the looks of things that snakes are a danger.

Something else that might encourage acquiescence in Grice's reasoning is the prior assumption that people must normally speak with some common purpose and that it is necessary to give a theoretically interesting account of that common purpose. But this is something we ought to question along with the Lockean theory of communication, which amounts to a schema for theoretically interesting accounts of that common purpose. I do not deny that people normally speak with some common purpose, but if we do not assume that our account must be theoretically interesting, then our account of the purpose that speakers have in common might be simply that their purpose is to *say something*. (I think this observation suffices to refute the argument in Loar 1981, 239–41.)

I do not think it is obvious that we need a theoretically interesting account of people's common purpose in speaking, but there are indeed many subtle aspects of communication that need to be explained. The greatest attraction of the Gricean analysis, I suspect, is simply that it offers *a* theoretical framework in which some of these things might seem to be explicable. In particular, it promises to explain such "pragmatic" phenomena as presupposition and conversational implicature.

3. We are here approaching a deeper motive for the Lockean theory than any I have considered so far. In order to characterize the order we find in the bits of language we observe, we may have to specify certain *conversational parameters*, as I will call them, that depend on the context of utterance and cannot be determined, even by native speakers, from the speaker's choice of words alone. The question arises, what is the locus of this linguistic order? The Lockean will suppose that the conversational parameters are in some sense recorded in the mind of the speaker and that to follow a conversation we must somehow ascertain what is written there. I will now present three examples.

1. In order to evaluate a universal generalization it is necessary to know the *domain of discourse*. A woman walks into her apartment, which has just been burglarized. She looks around and declares to her friend, "Oh no, everything is gone!" Is what she says true? The walls are still there. The radiators are still there. Most of the dust is still there. So if the domain of discourse includes absolutely everything, then what she said was false. But the TV is gone, the microwave is gone, her jewelry is gone. If the domain of discourse is *portable objects of non-negligible value that had been in the apartment earlier in the day*, then what she says may be true. But what kind of fact is this, that the domain of discourse = X? A Lockean might answer that it is somewhere recorded in the mind of the speaker that the domain of discourse = X.

2. Various sorts of thing go under the heading *presupposition*. Here is an example that has been used to illustrate the referential/attributive distinction (Donnellan 1966). Having just observed Mrs. Green's companion treating her kindly, A says to B, "Her husband is kind to her." A's presupposition, we may suppose, is that Mrs. Green's companion is her husband. The Lockean will hold that it is in some way recorded in A's mind that Mrs. Green's companion is her husband.[1]

3. Finally, let us consider an example of what Grice calls *conversational implicature*. In one of Grice's examples, a teacher writes a letter of recommendation that reads as follows: "Dear Sir, Mr. X's command of English is excellent, and his attendance at tutorials has been regular. Yours, etc." (Grice 1989a, 33). The teacher thereby implies (or "implicates," as Grice says) that the

---

[1] For a list of other parameters in addition to domain of discourse and presupposition, see Lewis 1979. In characterizing his theory of these in a general way, Lewis endorses a Lockean conception. "Conversational score," he says, "is, by definition, whatever the mental scoreboards say it is" (346). However, his treatment of specific conversational parameters is not always perfectly Lockean. For instance, he says that the referent of a definite description depends on salience (348). This kind of ambivalence appears to be common among authors writing about pragmatics. See, for instance, how Green contradicts herself in Green 1989, 20. She says both that the reference of an indexical pronoun is the *intended* referent and that the reference is a "function" of spatiotemporal coordinates of the utterance.

student is not very talented. A Lockean will perhaps hold that this implicature is one of those mental objects, or speaker's messages, that anyone reading the letter would have to grasp in order to understand it.

There is good reason to doubt the Lockean account of these things. If conversational parameters are set by speakers' states of mind, then the initiator of a conversation (or of some turn in a conversation) will always determine what they are. But that does not seem to be the case. Consider the case of domain of discourse. Suppose Tommy walks into Suzy's room while Suzy is counting her marbles and declares, "All of the red ones are mine!" If Tommy gets to decide the parameters, and the domain of discourse he has in mind is the class of marbles in his own room, which do belong to him, then what Tommy says will be true. So if Suzy retorts, "No they're not," then that will have to be deemed a misunderstanding of Tommy. But that seems wrong. Suzy's objection is correct in every way even if Tommy does have his own marbles in mind. It seems, then, that the domain of discourse is the class of marbles in Suzy's room and not the class of marbles that Tommy, the speaker, has in mind.

The Lockean might reply by drawing distinctions between ways of being wrong. Suzy's objection is *justified*, it may be said, even though what Tommy said was *true*. Or Suzy's objection was a correct response to what Tommy *said* but not to what Tommy *meant*. I do not deny that these are important distinctions, but I do not think that they fully insulate the Lockean account of conversational parameters from my counterexample, for we can take it as a question about the truth of what Tommy meant. I grant that from the point of view of an outsider, the dialogue between Tommy and Suzy can be explained without supposing that the domain of discourse is anything other than what Tommy had in mind. But by the same token, from the point of view of an outsider it is not necessary to know what the domain of discourse really is at all. To explain why Tommy and Suzy speak as they do, it is necessary only to know what they *take* the domain of discourse to be. We need to know what the domain of discourse really is only insofar as we wish to take sides in the dispute between them, and determining the domain of discourse is our way of doing so. But surely if we are going to take sides in this dispute, we should side with Suzy, not with Tommy. We should not expect someone like Suzy to try to see through an error like Tommy's. But siding with Suzy by deciding the domain of discourse means deciding that the domain of discourse was the class of marbles in Suzy's room and not the class of marbles that Tommy had in mind.

The Lockean account of presupposition is questionable as well. Suppose that just as Mrs. Green's companion is in the act of doing something that would clearly qualify as an act of kindness, B, indicating Mrs. Green's companion, says to A, "That's Mr. Green over there." A responds, "Her husband is very kind to her." Suppose now that C, overhearing this exchange between A and B, interjects, "But that is not her husband at all!" It is no use for A to protest at this point that he did not really mean—was not presupposing—that Mrs. Green's companion was her husband, but said what he said only on the grounds that he had once heard that Mrs. Green's husband was kind to her. From the context it is clear that *A was* presupposing that Mrs. Green's companion was her husband.

Here the Lockean may grant that the fact that *A* spoke as he did in the context shows that he did presuppose that Mrs. Green's companion was her husband, but he or she may insist that, by the same token, the story shows that *A* did have it in mind that Mrs. Green's companion was her husband. If *A* disavows that presupposition, then that only goes to show that through lying or self-deception or ignorance of one's own mind, it is possible for a person to deny that one had in mind what in fact one had in mind. However, to the extent that the Lockean criteria for having something in mind in the relevant sense simply merge with independent criteria for the attribution of presuppositions, having something in mind ceases to be the sort of thing that a Lockean can fairly cite in explanation of communication.

As for the third case, in which something is "implicated," here I think we have to divide the phenomena. One case is that in which the writer of the letter formulates an explicit strategy for bringing it about that readers of the letter will know that Mr. *X* is not very talented. But that case provides no model for communication in general and thus no support for the Lockean conception of communication. Another case is that in which the letter writer merely writes the most favorable letter he can write while conforming to a policy never to say anything negative about a person. Readers may still infer from the letter that Mr. *X* is not very talented. But this too is no model for communication. We might identify another sort of case as that in which the letter writer writes his recommendation *intending to convey his thought* that Mr. *X* is not very talented. But if intending to convey a thought in this sense were supposed to be the normal accompaniment of assertion, then we would be building a commitment to some kind of Lockean theory into our very taxonomy and so would be begging the question.

The case for a Lockean treatment of these examples is weakened still further by the availability of an alternative. Think of an utterance as a particular event in time and space, and think of the occasion of utterance as a specific course of events, linguistic or otherwise, leading up to it. For any given utterance, there are various ways the conversation might proceed, some of which will be appropriate in light of the occasion and some of which will not. My non-Lockean alternative, then, is to treat a conversational parameter as a *principle of conversational potential*. By that I mean that by identifying a conversational parameter governing an utterance, we in some way specify which sorts of continuations of the conversation would be *appropriate*.

For example, we might explain that to specify the domain of discourse is to say something about the course of conversation that might have been appropriate at the time. Suppose that *A*, upon setting foot in her apartment, exclaims, "Everything is gone!" and *B* replies by asking, "Is the television gone?" If we say that the domain of discourse equals the class of transportable objects of non-negligible value that had been in the apartment earlier, then we are saying, in effect, that a negative answer to this question would be *in*appropriate but an affirmative answer would be appropriate (which is not to say that *B*'s question is intelligent or that *A*'s answer is true).

Further, we might explain that in stating that *A* presupposes that Mrs. Green's companion is her husband we are saying something about the course of conversation that might have been appropriate at the time. Compare these two dialogues:

I. *A*: Her husband is kind to her.
    B: But that's not her husband.
    A: Well, then whoever that is, he's kind to her.
II. *A*: Her husband is kind to her.
    B: But that's not her husband.
    A: Nonetheless, her husband is kind to her.

To say that *A* presupposes that Mrs. Green's companion is her husband is to say that certain dialogues, such as dialogue I, are appropriate and that certain others, including dialogue II, are not.

Finally, in the case in which the teacher "implicates" that his student is not very talented, we might think of the implicature as something that would have been explicitly stated in an explicitly appropriate version of the teacher's letter. A fully and explicitly appropriate letter of recommendation explicitly addresses what is most in question. Where this is not addressed, the reader may infer that what would have been said is something the author might have reason not to say. Inasmuch as the appropriate course for a conversation, or correspondence, to take depends on what would be contained in the explicit version, the specification of conversational implicature, like the specification of domain of discourse or presupposition, may be regarded as a specification of a constraint on the appropriate course of further conversation. Many of Grice's other examples of conversational implicature, but not all, can likewise be viewed as filling lacunae in inexplicit but otherwise appropriate conversations. Grice's Cooperative Principle and its several submaxims can be construed as criteria of appropriateness.

At this point I cannot yet say anything very precise about the nature of appropriateness. The key idea is that in various ways language facilitates cooperative activity. Language makes possible the building of buildings, the exchange of products, the conduct of government, the invention of gadgets, and other activities. Appropriateness, I am assuming, is a matter of whether a conversation facilitates such cooperative activity. Cooperative activity need not be understood as always directed at any very specific goal. Often it may amount only to what we call keeping one another informed. Moreover, speech may qualify as appropriate even when it does not in fact facilitate cooperation if it belongs to a highly determinate type that *normally* facilitates cooperation. Whether the non-Lockean account of conversational parameters as principles of conversational potential is viable will depend on whether this cooperative activity and the manner in which language makes it possible can be understood without invoking the Lockean theory of communication. These are matters to which I will return in part B.

Why should anyone prefer the Lockean conception of conversational parameters as recorded in the minds of speakers over the non-Lockean conception of conversational parameters as principles of conversational potential? One reason might be the idea that principles of change hold universally and that any difference between outcomes must be traceable to differences in initial conditions. So since conversational parameters vary from conversation to conversation, they cannot be principles governing the course of appropriate conversations but must instead be initial conditions. Having concluded this much, it is certainly reasonable to conclude in addition that conversational parameters are states of speakers' minds.

Why, then, should anyone suppose that the principles governing the course of conversation are universal, in which case conversational parameters must be initial conditions? I do not think this is a consequence of any general ontological truth. Perhaps there are universal truths of physics that constrain the possibilities for the universe considered as an arrangement of particles or a bumpy field. It does not follow, of course, that there are universal principles governing conversations considered as sequences of statements, questions, and commands.

Might there be some epistemological advantage if the principles of conversation were universal? This is actually two questions. The first is whether there might be some epistemological advantage to outside observers of a conversation. If the principles of conversation were universal, then observers would not have to work them out anew every time they wanted to explain, or follow, the course of a conversation. But the Lockean account has no advantage on this score, since it requires the observer to work out anew the initial conditions hidden from view in the mind of the speaker. Besides, observers may have a good idea what sorts of principles to look for (domain of discourse, presupposition, and so on). To work out the details they can look at the way the conversation actually goes.

The second epistemological question is whether there might be some epistemological advantage to participants in a conversation. Apparently, a participant in a conversation cannot wait to see how the conversation goes but must know in advance what principles are in effect. If the principles of conversational potential were universal, then the participants could count on their always being the same. Then in order to isolate a range of appropriate responses, the participants would have only to ascertain the pertinent initial conditions, which, since they already obtain, will often be ascertainable somehow.

However, this is not a reason to believe that whatever principles of conversational potential there may be are universal unless the participants in a conversation must in some sense know what the principles are that govern their conversation. That assumption is itself a Lockean prejudice. The Lockean prejudice is to suppose that whatever principles of conversation there may be are *prescriptive* in the sense that participants in a conversation set themselves the goal of conforming to them in order effectively to express their thoughts. So, for instance, the Lockean will suppose that a hearer has a sort of duty to ascertain the domain of discourse that the speaker has in mind and to be sure not to take for granted some other domain of discourse without giving some sign.

The principles of conversational potential are indeed *normative* inasmuch as they specify what is appropriate and serve prediction only insofar as we may assume that speakers speak appropriately. Moreover, speakers may learn to reflect on the principles of conversation, and when they think they have found some, they may strive to conform to them, may teach them to their children, and so on. But the principles, as I conceive of them, map out what is appropriate, not in the sense of defining the sorts of responses speakers require of themselves, but in the sense that they describe the way a conversation must or must not go if it is to be effective. Just as a pair of billiard balls can in some sense conform to the law of conservation of momentum without in any sense knowing that law and a lily can in some sense conform to its own genetic code without in any sense knowing that code, speakers can conform to the principles of conversational potential without in any sense knowing what they are.

4. I turn now from the idea that speaker's message is the locus of linguistic *order* to the idea that it is the source of linguistic *ability*. One of the issues here concerns the *productivity* of linguistic understanding, the fact that at any given time a person is able to understand each of an indefinite number of distinct sentences formed from a fixed vocabulary in accordance with a fixed grammar. To explain this it is tempting to postulate an inner language that serves as the medium of thought and itself has a vocabulary and grammar from which thoughts can be formed corresponding to each of the sentences that can be understood. (This is exactly the rationale offered in Jackendoff 1989, 70–71.) If productivity is explained in this way, a Lockean theory of communication is a natural next step.

The other matter of linguistic ability that may motivate a Lockean theory of communication is language acquisition. Jerry Fodor (1975) has argued that children can learn the extensions of public language predicates only by formulating and testing *hypotheses* concerning the extensions of predicates. One problem they face is that there are bound to be indefinitely many hypotheses compatible with their data. According to Fodor, they must choose between hypotheses on the basis of simplicity. But simplicity is relative to mode of representation, and so these hypotheses must be formulated in some definite language, namely, the language of thought (1975, 39). Having explained language learning in this way, it is natural for Fodor to think of linguistic communication as a process in which the hearer infers the speaker's message from the speaker's words, which the speaker chooses precisely in order to enable the hearer to do this (1975, 103–9). The medium of the speaker's message and the medium of the hearer's inference will be precisely the language of thought that makes language learning possible.

As many have noted, a dubious consequence of the language of thought hypothesis is that for any public language predicate that we are able to learn, we must be able to define its extension by means of the vocabulary of an innate, or at least not-learned, language.[2] Surely the vocabulary of a not-learned language would be confined to such terms as human beings might have had some use for throughout the course of human evolution. So the not-learned language might include words for such qualitative concepts as *green*, such metaphysical concepts as *cause*, and such logical concepts as *or*, but certainly it will not include words for concepts as young or as specific to our culture as *airplane* or *electron*. In chapter 4 I will present and criticize a more general conception of language learning of which Fodor's is an instance. For the moment I will simply point out that Fodor's theory faces much the same problem as Locke's theory of ideas. No one has any idea how to define the extensions of words like "airplane" and "electron" by means of vocabulary that might plausibly be not-learned.

Besides, such explanations of productivity and acquisition only postpone the difficult question, namely, how did a world containing languages, whether inner languages of thought or public languages of speech, evolve from a world without them in the first place? Even if we suppose that the child's language of thought is innate, and thus do not need to explain how it is acquired, a complete theory of the world will still have to explain how this language evolved in a world that did not initially contain it. So if we have no other reason to believe in an innate inner language, then as long as we have no better understanding of how an innate inner language might evolve than we do of how a creature with no sort of language might learn one, we might as well allow that the child starts life without any sort of language and somehow acquires a public language.

Moreover, I find that developmental considerations create a more fundamental doubt about the Lockean theory. If the Lockean conception of communication is correct, a child will learn language by learning how to grasp the speaker's message on the basis of the speaker's choice of words and the context. My more fundamental doubt has to do with how the child might come to be able to do

---

[2] Strangely, Fodor himself (1975, ch. 3; Fodor et al. 1980) has questioned whether many of the concepts our words express are literally defined by means of a family of conceptual primitives. He thinks he can escape the apparent inconsistency in his views by drawing a subtle distinction between definitions and "meaning postulates" (1975, 152), but I do not see how this helps with the problem I am pointing to. In any case, others, such as Jackendoff (1989), have embraced semantic decomposition wholeheartedly.

this. Others before me have questioned whether Lockean theories of communication can make sense of language learning, but I will go a step beyond merely raising the question.[3]

It is fair to assume that if the fluent speakers of a language understand one another's speech by grasping speakers' messages, then the process by which the child learns a first language must likewise involve the grasping of speakers' messages. For the Lockean, the result of learning language is that the child becomes able to grasp fluent speakers' messages more or less correctly most of the time. The process that leads to this product must be one of ever more closely approximating to it. Thus the process must be one in which the child ever more frequently succeeds in latching onto a message ever closer to that which the speaker had in mind. The process must be at least this for the Lockean even if it involves other things as well (such as abstraction from ideas of particulars). Moreover, it is fair to suppose that for the Lockean the process of grasping a speaker's message is a matter of formulating *hypotheses* concerning the speaker's message. In some cases, a hearer may have to *decide* between alternative hypotheses. In other cases, the hearer may be able to leap to the correct hypothesis without having to make any such decision. In either case, the process may also be described as an *inference* in some broad sense.

This conception of language learning as a matter of learning to formulate correct hypotheses concerning speakers' messages raises two questions. First, How does the child invent hypotheses in the first place? That is, why does the child ever consider that when a person makes a sound there might be a message that the speaker is trying to express, and what is the source of the child's hypotheses concerning the content of that message? One can hardly maintain that the child possesses innately a full-blown theory of the mind. However, it is perhaps not out of the question that the child knows innately that there are such things as thoughts and that people's actions, including speech, tend to result from thought. As for the actual content of a speaker's message, if something about the child's immediate surroundings especially interests the child, he or she may assume that the adult is remarking on that. Such egocentric interpretations will often be wrong, but they might be right often enough to get the process of learning language started.

The second, more difficult question is, How does the child acquire the concepts that enter into its hypotheses? In order for the child to hypothesize that someone who says "There are apples in the refrigerator" means *there are apples in the refrigerator*, the child has to possess the concepts *apple* and *refrigerator*.

---

[3] For instance, Loar (1981, 213) raised the question as it pertains to a Gricean theory. Unaccountably, he nonetheless endorses a Gricean theory. An earlier literature (e.g., Aune 1967, 195) readily took for granted that language learning was the main source of a person's conceptual scheme, so that language could not be understood in a theoretical way as the expression of prior conceptualizations. But in the current philosophical and psychological climate that cannot taken for granted.

Where do such concepts come from? I have already dismissed the possibility that they are all not-learned or all definable in terms of not-learned ones. This leaves the possibility that they are learned somehow other than by learning definitions. Conceivably, some of them might be learned independently of language, through the child's own experience of and experimentation in the nonlinguistic world. But many, if not most, of a person's concepts are acquired only as a result of his or her exposure to language (even if they could in principle be acquired independently). *Electron* is an example, but so is *apple*. Our concept *apple* covers various sorts of apples while excluding pears. No doubt the biology of fruit offers good reasons for conceiving of things in this way, but for most of us possession of the concept *apple* is independent of such reasons and cannot be explained without citing the fact that our language contains the word "apple," with its peculiar use.

The mere fact that concepts are acquired through exposure to language is not all by itself a problem for the Lockean theory. The problem, as I will now argue, is that in order to explain how language instills concepts, the Lockean must acknowledge a kind of communication more fundamental than that described by the Lockean theory. My first premise is that the instilling of concepts through language is a *pre*requisite to the child's ability to formulate correct hypotheses concerning speakers' messages. Some concepts, I will allow, may be innate or may be acquired independently of language. Other concepts, such as those that the child learns through explicit verbal definitions, might be acquired only by means of a grasp of some speaker's message. But of those concepts instilled through exposure to language, many will have to be grasped independently of grasping any speaker's message that contains them in order that they may be used in the formulation of hypotheses concerning speakers' messages.

My second premise is that one cannot acquire a concept without acquiring certain beliefs. There may be nothing in particular that one has to believe in order to have a concept, but one cannot have a concept C and believe nothing at all about things considered as C's. For instance, if one has the concept *armadillo*, then one must believe that armadillos are mammals, or that armadillos are reptiles, or that *this* is an armadillo, or that the thing out of view behind the rock is an armadillo, or . . .

My third premise is that a child learning a first language can be expected to succeed in grasping a speaker's message only to the extent that the child shares beliefs with the speaker. Here is why I think a Lockean ought to accept this premise: As far as I can see, no matter how the Lockean might propose to explain the child's ability to grasp the speaker's message, it will turn out that the child must in effect assume that the speaker normally believes the same, with regard to the pertinent situation, as what the child believes. To the extent that this is not so, the child is liable to err in attempting to grasp the speaker's message.

For instance, according to one account of how the child is able to grasp the speaker's message, the child will start with the hypothesis that the speaker believes the same things that the child does and then minimally modify this hypothesis when it leads to predictions that prove false. If this starting hypothesis is regularly mistaken, then minimal modifications also are unlikely to succeed. Alternatively, the child might be supposed to look for correlations of some kind between the speaker's words and states of the world and then assume that the speaker's message represents some state of the world correlated with the speaker's words. Once such correlations have been established, the child might discover on occasion that the state of affairs correlated with the speaker's words does not exist. But in order for such correlations to be established in the first place, the correlated states of affairs will have to be such as the child believes to exist. So since the child will think of those existing, correlated states of affairs in accordance with his or her own beliefs, the method can be expected to succeed only to the extent that the speaker and the child share beliefs.

I should point out that in arguing from what is necessary in order to infer a person's beliefs I do not mean to imply that in fact belief attribution is normally a process of inference. Much ground will have to be covered before I will be in a position to explain how it could be anything else. At present I can only hint at my alternative by saying that in chapter 13 I will argue that belief attribution ought rather to be conceived as a device by which conversation is conducted in advanced kinds of languages. That idea will be explained in a way that does not encourage us to think of belief attribution as the product of inference. Nonetheless, I can argue as I have from strategies for inferring a person's belief inasmuch as the belief attribution required by the Lockean strategy for explaining language learning must be a kind of inference.

By means of these three premises it can be shown that the Lockean theory of communication presupposes a more fundamental kind of communication than the one it describes. By the first premise, the instilling of concepts through exposure to language is a prerequisite to the child's ability to infer speakers' messages. By the second premise, the very process that instills concepts must instill beliefs containing those concepts. By the third premise, the beliefs thus instilled must be largely the same as those of the speakers whose messages the child has to learn to infer. So a prerequisite to the child's ability to infer speakers' messages is that the child's exposure to language instills beliefs like the beliefs of those to whose use of language the child is exposed. Whatever exactly this process of instilling beliefs involves, it deserves to be called a kind of communication, since the beliefs of speakers are transferred to hearers. Thus, the Lockean theory of communication entails that there is a kind of *sub*-Lockean communication as well.

My more fundamental doubt about the Lockean theory may now be expressed thus: Whether or not one believes that there is a process of communication such as the Lockean theory describes, one is forced to concede that there is some other kind of communication in addition. Would it not be reasonable to withhold assent from the Lockean theory until one had a better understanding of this other sort of communication? As long as one does not understand this other sort of communication, one ought to recognize as a live possibility that a theory of this other sort of communication might do all the explanatory work that the Lockean theory was supposed to do.

3

Mental Content

1. My objective in this chapter is directly to refute the Lockean theory of communication. The usual strategy for refutation is to try to show that the meanings of words are in some way more fundamental than the mental objects in terms of which the Lockean theory explains communication. The apparent problem with this strategy as it is usually carried out is that it seems to confuse epistemological priority with ontological priority. From the fact that we learn of people's thoughts by listening to what they say, or that we conceive of thoughts on analogy with overt utterances, or that we may be uncertain how to characterize the thoughts of languageless creatures, it is inferred that language cannot be essentially the expression of thought, as the Lockean contends. But that does not follow. My argument will avoid this fallacy.[1]

The main thing that a theory of communication has to do is explain why people speak the words they speak. For the Lockean, the explanation will be that people normally speak the words they speak because those words express their thoughts. The Lockean need not assume that the speaker's choice of words is always, or ever, deliberate. But in some sense a speaker's objective in speaking must normally be to enable hearers to grasp the speaker's message, and the explanation of the speaker's choice of words must normally be that this is the speaker's objective. I grant that a Lockean theory of communication might serve other purposes in addition to this explanatory purpose. For instance, it might serve the regulatory purpose envisioned by Locke. But it is hard to see how any other such purpose might be best served by a theory of communication that did not also serve this explanatory purpose. (This is not to deny that there might be quite different sorts of explanation of communication in addition.)

It is important to draw a distinction between explaining a given phenomenon in general and explaining a particular instance of that phenomenon. Of course,

---

[1] Biro (1979) can perhaps be charged with this fallacy, although of course his argument is not quite so simple as this. Very roughly, what Biro says is that the behavioral and contextual clues to a speaker's intention could be what we cite in explaining the meaning of a speaker's utterance on a given occasion instead of citing the speaker's intention itself. The Lockean answer to this, I think, should be that attributions of intention may be an ineliminable link in the reasoning by which we infer the speaker's meaning from behavior and context. For another example of the fallacy, see Sellars 1963a, 188, where Sellars, by reminding us that overt linguistic utterances are our model for inner episodes of thought, makes the point that the meaning of overt speech is not to be analyzed in terms of the intentionality of thoughts. Sellars's fallacy is reiterated by Rosenberg 1974, 28.

what explains a particular instance may not explain *every* instance. Moreover, what is explanatory in every instance may not explain the phenomenon in general. For instance, to explain why Otto fell asleep after taking some diphenhydramine, we might cite the fact that diphenhydramine is a soporific. But the fact that diphenhydramine causes sleep is not explained by citing the fact that diphenhydramine is a soporific. Similarly, we must draw a distinction between explaining a speaker's choice of words on a given occasion and explaining speakers' word choice. It is certainly some kind of explanation to say that Otto said "Ich muß schlafen" because he thought he needed to get some sleep and the words "Ich muß schlafen" expressed that thought. But the fact that that may be a good explanation is no reason to believe that in general, or even normally, people speak the words they do *because* their words express their thoughts. Yet it is some stronger claim such as this that the Lockean theory of communication is committed to.

According to the Lockean, people speak the words they do because their words express their thoughts. Any Lockean articulation of this idea will assign a role to something we may call *content*. In the simplest versions, the speaker's message is just the thought expressed, and one message will be distinguished from another only by the content of the thought expressed. In order for such a theory to be at all comprehensive and accommodate imperative and interrogative messages as well as declarative messages, a content will have to be characterized by a mood as well as by a proposition. In other versions—for instance, in Gricean versions—the mood of the speaker's utterance will be determined by the speaker's intention with regard to the content, and not by the content. For instance, the speaker may intend the hearer to form a *belief* having that content and in that case utter a sentence in the indicative mood; or the speaker may intend the hearer to form an *intention* having that content and in that case may utter a sentence in the imperative mood. In any version, one message will be distinguished from another largely by its content. So on any version of the Lockean theory, the following will normally be true: The speaker speaks the words that he or she speaks in part because his or her message has the content it has, and if the hearer succeeds in grasping the speaker's message, that is in part because he or she succeeds in comprehending the content of the speaker's message.

My argument against the Lockean theory will focus on this concept of content. I will argue that the very content of a speaker's message is *relative* to the way the speaker's words are used in his or her linguistic community. That is, there may be two subjects whose thoughts differ in content even though the only difference between them to which that difference might be traced is the way words are used in their communities. But this means that we cannot maintain that speakers normally speak as they do because the thoughts they aim to express have the contents they have. So we cannot explain that speakers normally speak as they do because their words express their thoughts. So the Lockean theory fails to explain communication.

This is a *reductio ad absurdum* rather than a direct argument for the negation of the Lockean theory, because the concept of content that I am employing is the Lockean's and is not anything I need ultimately make good sense of. A theory of communication that does not treat communication as a matter of speakers' expressing thoughts need not entail that there is any such thing as content in the Lockean's sense. Further, for the purposes of my *reductio* I will acquiesce in the Lockean assumption that words express thoughts. For the most part, I will presume a simple version of the Lockean theory in which the message is just the thought, but my argument will apply as well to more sophisticated versions.

2. To complete the argument, I now need to establish that the very content of the thought that a speaker expresses in words is relative to the way those words are used in his or her linguistic community. This will consume most of the rest of the chapter. My argument is very directly inspired by Tyler Burge's argument in his 1979 paper "Individualism and the Mental." Burge's argument has been very influential, but there continue to be many ways to miss the point. In this chapter I will try to strengthen the case for a strong form of Burge's relativity thesis by providing a taxonomy of possible objections and showing why the several species all fail. A crucial premise will be that any account of the nature of thought and its expression must render intelligible the division of epistemic labor that words make possible.[2]

A division of epistemic labor, as I define it, is a social arrangement in which people benefit from the expertise that others possess regarding subjects of which they themselves do not possess an expert understanding. Thus a student may learn about electrons from a physics teacher, an architect may consult with a geologist in designing a house, a person who has arthritis but who does not know exactly what arthritis is can walk into a pharmacy, ask the pharmacist for "arthritis pills," and in that way actually get relief from what ails him or her. My argument will turn on a close examination of this last example, which derives from Burge.

It is necessary to tell Burge's story very carefully, but I will tell it in my own way, which is not quite Burge's. Imagine a pair of doppelgänger, call them Art and Bart, who reside in different worlds but who, as it happens, have been microstructural duplicates of one another since birth. Their senses have been stimulated in exactly the same ways, their bodies have executed exactly the same motions, and exactly the same sorts of electrochemical events have mediated between these inputs and outputs. Both Art and Bart speak a language very

---

[2] I have been struggling with this argument for a long time. An early version occurs in my paper "Language as Tool" (1987b). A second version, which comes close to the version here, was my paper "Mental Content and the Division of Epistemic Labor" (1991b).

like our language, English, and both have heard and spoken sentences containing a word that they pronounce and spell "arthritis." For instance, they may have heard the sentence "Aunt Martha has arthritis in her hands," and they may have spoken the sentence "The pain of arthritis inhibits movement."

The important difference between Art's world and Bart's lies in the way the local medical experts use the word "arthritis." In Art's world, as among the speakers of our own language, the medical experts tend to use "arthritis" exclusively in connection with inflammations of the joints. Moreover, if you ask them, "Is arthritis specifically an inflammation of the joints?" they will generally reply affirmatively. In Bart's world, on the other hand, the medical experts use "arthritis" in connection with a broader class of rheumatoid ailments, including such ailments as might occur in areas of the body such as the thigh. Moreover, if you ask them, "Is arthritis specifically an inflammation of the joints?" they will reply negatively.

As it happens, these differences between the ways "arthritis" is used in their respective communities have not resulted in any difference between their physical constitutions. The sentences they have heard or seen containing this word sound or look exactly alike. In particular, neither has heard any sentence from which he might have drawn a conclusion that he might express by saying, "Arthritis is specifically an inflammation of the joints." So far are they from any such conclusion that under certain counterfactual conditions they might even be disposed to draw conclusions that they would express by saying "I have arthritis in my thigh."

The conclusion that Burge would have us draw is that the thoughts Art expresses when Art uses the word "arthritis" differ in content from the thoughts Bart expresses when Bart uses the word "arthritis." Suppose that each develops a chronic pain in his knuckles and is told by his doctor, "You have arthritis in your hands." Thereafter, Art and Bart go around speaking sentences like "I have arthritis in my hands." The conclusion we are supposed to draw is that the thought Art expresses by means of this sentence is different in content from the thought Bart expresses by means of this sentence.

Here, in outline, is how I think this conclusion may be reached. We may suppose that a good translation of "arthritis" as it is used in Art's language is our own word "arthritis." Our language does not contain a single word that translates "arthritis" as it is used in Bart's community, but we can make one up. Let "*b*arthritis" be the translation into our language of "arthritis" as it is used in Bart's community. Thus, we may accept the premise that

(1) The translation of "arthritis" as it is used in Art's community into our language is "arthritis," and the translation of "arthritis" as it is used in Bart's community into our language is "*b*arthritis."

From (1) it seems permissible to infer that

(2) The best way for Art to express his thought in our language would be "I have arthritis in my hands," whereas the best way for Bart to express his thought in our language would be "I have *b*arthritis in my hands."

From (2) it seems permissible to infer that

(3) Art's thought differs in content from Bart's thought.

The prima facie case for the inference from (1) to (2) is this: Both Art and Bart choose their words deliberately, and there is nothing unusual or inappropriate in their use of those words, and so the translation of their words into our language ought to yield the best way to express their thoughts in our language. Certainly we should not use "barthritis" to express *Art's* thought, because no one around him has ever used a word translatable as "barthritis," and we should not use "arthritis" to express *Bart's* thought, because no one around him has used a word translatable into our language as "arthritis." The prima facie case for the inference from (2) to (3) is that a good way to identify the content of a person's thought is by the words in our language that that person would choose to express it. At least, this is something that should be accepted by the Lockean, whose view is that in normal communication hearers must be able to comprehend the content of the speaker's message on the basis of the words the speaker uses to express it.

One published complaint against Burge is that he confuses the that-clauses in belief-ascriptions with the contents of the beliefs ascribed and consequently infers a difference in the contents of the beliefs ascribed from a difference in the "that"-clauses used in the ascription (Loar 1985, 106; Bach 1987, 271; Bach 1988, 92n). The present argument cannot be dismissed so easily. Throughout I have avoided the use of those "that"-clauses, as in "Art believes *that* he has arthritis," that someone might think could be confused with content. Of course, any critic of the present argument might still think that any persuasiveness the argument has derives from such confusions.

Equally, the argument does not rest on a confusion of *de re* and *de dicto* attributions of thought. On the pertinent *de re* reading of "Art believes he has arthritis in his hands," the word "arthritis" as it occurs in that sentence refers to arthritis, whereas on the *de dicto* reading, the word "arthritis" as it occurs in that sentence refers not to arthritis, but only to a certain aspect or component of Art's thought. If the difference between Art and Bart were supposed to be only the fact that of Art we can say "He believes he has arthritis in his hands," while of Bart we can say "He believes he has *b*arthritis in his hands," then someone might try to resolve the apparent disparity by showing that these attributions must be read *de re* and not *de dicto*. In that case, the difference between these attributions will not all by itself betoken a difference between aspects or components of Art's and Bart's thoughts, but only a difference between the reference of their thoughts. But since I have avoided such belief-ascriptions altogether, that strategy is bound to fail against the argument as I have formulated it.

I believe that resistance to Burge's conclusion sometimes stems from an elementary confusion between *relations* and *relation-dependent properties*. Being the mother of someone is a relation between the mother and her off-spring. Being a lintel is not a relation, but whether a beam of wood is a lintel does depend on whether it is positioned (or apt to be positioned) over a door-way. Now, a thought's having a certain content is certainly not a relation between the thought and any other (nonabstract) entity (even if having a thought is a relation between a thinker and a thought). But clearly the difference be-tween Art and Bart is first of all a difference between their relations to things, namely, Art's being in Art's community and Bart's being in Bart's community. So if one assimilated all relation-dependent properties to relations, one might conclude that this difference between Art and Bart cannot entail a difference between the contents of their thoughts. But this, as I say, is a confusion. A thought's having a certain content is not a relation, but what the argument from (1) to (3) purports to show is that whether a thought has a certain content does *depend* on relations to linguistic communities.

To refute the argument for (3), one must challenge either premise (1) or the inference from (1) to (2), or the inference from (2) to (3). First, consider premise (1). If one conceived of translation as having to represent accurately the contents of the thoughts a speaker expresses by means of the words translated, then of course one could not assume that the correct translation of Art's word "arthritis" differed from the correct translation of Bart's word "arthritis" with-out begging the question whether Art's and Bart's thoughts had the same content. But that's not how translation is to be understood in evaluating (1). The translation in question is what I call *literal* translation. Literal translation is the mode of translation employed in the actual, living practice of translating novels, textbooks, and documents. No doubt the correct literal translation of a word or a sentence depends on the verbal context and even on the author's historical context, literary liaisons, and so on. But literal translation is not so sensitive to the author's level of expertise that it would translate Art's word "arthritis" into some other word than "arthritis" or Bart's word "arthritis" into some other word than "barthritis." In short, I take (1) to be a fairly obvious empirical fact about literal translation. This construal of (1) may increase the burden on the inference from (1) to (2), but that is where I intend the burden to be.

The hard questions concern the inferences from (1) to (2) and from (2) to (3). These are indeed subject to many doubts. Consider first the inference from (1) to (2). Certainly it is not always the case that a speaker's thought is best expressed in our language by means of the sentence of our language that best translates (literally) the speaker's own words. For instance, a person who was confused about the meaning of "acrophobia" might say "I have acrophobia" when what he or she really meant was that he or she had *agora*phobia. Since, we may suppose, this person speaks our language, the best translation of his or her words into our language might be the very words he or she speaks, although the words of our language that actually express the thought would be, instead, "I have agoraphobia." One could deny the disparity by supposing that the speaker speaks a dialect in which the translation of "acrophobia" into our language is "agoraphobia," but this construal might be very implausible. One thing that might count against it is the speaker's intention to speak to us in *our* language. Since the best translation of a speaker's words may thus differ from the best expression of the speaker's thought, the best translation of Art's words might differ from the best translation of Bart's words, as (1) states, even though the best expression of Art's thought in our language is the same as the best expression of Bart's thought in our language, contrary to what (2) states.

Alternatively, one might challenge the inference from (2) to (3). The best way to express a thought, one might maintain, is largely a pragmatic matter having to do not only with the content of one's thought but also with the words available in one's language, the needs of one's audience, and the ends to be achieved in speaking. Conceivably, then, the best expression of Art's thought might differ from the best expression of Bart's thought, as (2) states, not because their thoughts differ in content, as (3) states, but because their different situations call for different expressions.

Such doubts might be seen as sufficient refutation of the argument for (3) on the grounds that these doubts show that the inferences from (1) to (2) and from (2) to (3) are not strictly valid. But at most they show that various inferences *like* the inference from (1) to (2) or from (2) to (3) may have a true premise and a false conclusion. These other inferences must not be confused with the inferences from (1) to (2) and from (2) to (3). Moreover, (1), (2), and (3) must not be confused with any more general claims. That certain other inferences may fail does not show that (1) is not, in light of the details of the case, a good reason to accept (2) or that (2) is not, in light of the details, a good reason to accept (3). The nature of intentionality is too uncertain to allow easy generalizations about the valid inferences concerning thought and language. Since we are questioning fundamentals, and since there is no room for prejudice, the prima facie case for the inference from (1) to (2) and the prima facie case for the inference from (2) to (3) ought to be very persuasive unless very specific challenges to (2) or to (3) can be mounted. Most of the rest of this chapter will be a survey of such challenges. In each case, I will argue, a certain test of adequacy is failed. The test that I will insist must be passed is that of not rendering unintelligible certain transactions between experts and nonexperts.

3. In particular, I want to focus on the question how Art can use the word "arthritis" to purchase an analgesic for arthritis from his local pharmacist. Here are the relevant details: Art's doctor says to Art, "Your hands are afflicted with arthritis." The doctor may say various other things, but Art draws no conclusions that he might express by saying "Arthritis is specifically an inflammation of the joints." (So, as before, Art's counterpart, Bart, has no thought expressible in terms of our word "arthritis.") Later, Art comes across various advertisements, on television and in magazines, in which various products are described with such words as "an analgesic specifically formulated to relieve the pain of arthritis." (Arthritis is too many kinds of thing and has too many causes for there to be any drug specifically formulated to attack it. Nonetheless, an analgesic might be specifically formulated to relieve the pain caused by an inflammation of the joints. This means that it would not be very effective in relieving the pain of *b*arthritis in the thigh.) As a result of these advertisements, Art goes to his local pharmacy and makes a certain request of his pharmacist. For simplicity, let us suppose Art expresses his request rather bluntly thus: "Sell me an analgesic specifically formulated for arthritis!" The pharmacist, we may suppose, responds to this request by selling Art an analgesic specifically formulated for arthritis. Let us suppose, moreover, that Art's pharmacist has an expert understanding of the nature of arthritis so that we need not doubt that some of the pharmacist's thoughts would be well expressed using our word "arthritis."

As I said above, I am going to assume that any account of thought and its expression must render intelligible the division of epistemic labor. The reason to examine such transactions as this one between Art and his pharmacist is that the division of epistemic labor depends on them, so that to render the division of epistemic labor intelligible one must render such transactions intelligible. One could imagine a society embodying a division of epistemic labor in which such transactions did not occur. Legally empowered experts might simply tell nonexperts what to do, and these nonexperts might then be legally bound to do as they were told. Art's doctor might call up Art's pharmacist and tell him to send Art certain pills, and the pharmacist might be empowered to draw payment from Art's account. But that is not how the division of epistemic labor operates in our society, and my assumption is that every good theory of thought and its expression must render the division of epistemic labor intelligible even in a society such as ours.

To render the pharmacist's response intelligible in the sense that I mean, a Lockean must at least display a line of reasoning about the content of Art's thought that gives the pharmacist good reason to sell Art an analgesic specifically formulated for arthritis. One does not have to suppose that the pharmacist would actually think through such a line of reasoning. His response might be, so to speak, routinized. But his routine will be intelligible in the sense that I mean only if it is supportable by a good line of reasoning. To *display* such a line of reasoning means to express it in words, aloud or on paper, in such a way that its persuasive force can be grasped by others without any independent insight into the pharmacist's thought.

For example, the pharmacist might be supposed to reason somewhat as follows:

First step: Art has a request that he expressed by saying, "Sell me an analgesic specifically formulated for arthritis!" Since Art appears to be speaking the same language as I speak, probably the best translation of Art's words into my language is the very words he speaks. So the best way to express his request in my language is, "Sell me an analgesic specifically formulated for arthritis!"

Second step: Since this is the best way to express his thought in my language, the content of his request is that I sell him an analgesic specifically formulated for arthritis.

Third step: Since the content of Art's request is that I sell him an analgesic specifically formulated for arthritis, and I have a good one and I am a pharmacist, etc., I ought to sell him an analgesic specifically formulated for arthritis.

But in fact the Lockean cannot suppose that the pharmacist reasons in just this manner, for the steps of this reasoning closely parallel the steps of the argument for (3). The first step of this reasoning is like the inference from (1) to (2). In both cases there is an inference from a fact about the best translation of the speaker's words to a conclusion about the best way to express the speaker's thought. Further, the second step of this reasoning is like the inference from (2) to (3). In inferring (3) from (2) one assumes that (in the case of Art and Bart, even if not in general) a difference in content corresponds to a difference in optimal forms of expression. Likewise, in the second step of the above reasoning, the pharmacist assumes that he may characterize the content of Art's thought in terms of its optimal form of expression without thereby drawing distinctions between thoughts too finely.

Since it is important to render intelligible such transactions as that between Art and the pharmacist, a fair test of any challenge to (2) or to (3) is to ask whether it preserves the intelligibility of such transactions. I will conclude that a challenge to (2) or to (3) fails this test if it introduces a gap in the pharmacist's reasoning or in our understanding of the pharmacist's reasoning that I cannot see how to fill.

Here are some ground rules. First, the division of epistemic labor will be rendered unintelligible if it turns out that in order to have a good reason to sell Art an analgesic specifically formulated for arthritis the pharmacist must be ignorant of certain facts or believe certain falsehoods. In particular, it must not turn out that the pharmacist's response depends on his ignorance of the real content of Art's thought or on his presuming or pretending that Art has an expert understanding of the nature of arthritis. The division of epistemic labor that depends on such transactions is too useful and too fundamental to our way of life to be regarded as resting on error, even systematic error. Second, the division of epistemic labor will also not be intelligible if it turns out that, in order to have a reason to sell Art an analgesic for arthritis, the pharmacist has to know a great deal about Art's personal history. If the pharmacist knows a lot about Art's personal history, the transaction will not be representative of the sort of transaction on which the division of epistemic labor depends.

A terminological note: I am going to use the term "request" to refer to the type of *thought* that Art expresses by means of his words. I will speak of his *words* not as themselves *being* the request but as *expressing* the request. (In so doing I do not need to acknowledge any real distinction. Remember, this is all part of a *reductio*.)

I want to emphasize that I am not going to argue simply as follows: Art's pharmacist ought to sell Art arthritis pills. Bart's pharmacist ought to sell Bart barthritis pills. But if Art's request and Bart's request have the same content, then they ought to get the same thing. Q.E.D. I am not going to argue in this way because the Lockean need not suppose that the proper response to a request depends on nothing but its content. Instead, I am going to argue that challenges to (2) and (3) introduce a gap in the pharmacist's reasoning that I cannot see how to fill.

4. Specific challenges to (2) will take the form of what I will call *reinterpretation strategies*. In general, a reinterpretation strategy seeks to show that the best way for Art to express his thought in our language is the same as the best way for Bart to express his thought in our language. More precisely, for some noun phrase P other than "arthritis" or "barthritis," the best way for both Art and Bart to express their thoughts in our language would be to say, "I have" $\widehat{\ } P \widehat{\ }$ "in my hands."

One reinterpretation strategy, which I'll call the *phenomenalistic reinterpretation strategy*, holds that P consists of nontechnical vocabulary that refers exclusively to the sorts of entities Art and Bart are both well acquainted with. For instance, P might be "the sort of disease that Aunt Martha has and that tends to inhibit movement." (One can find evidence of this strategy in Fodor 1982, esp. 110–13, and in Peacocke 1983, 196–99, esp. n. 20.) If the phenomenalistic reinterpretation strategy is correct and P is the phrase to be substituted for "arthritis," then the best way for Art to express in our language the request he puts to his pharmacist would be to say, "Sell me an analgesic specifically formulated for" $\widehat{\ } P$. So to pass my test, the proponent of the phenomenalistic reinterpretation strategy has to explain what reason the pharmacist might have to sell Art an analgesic specifically formulated for arthritis if in fact this is the best way to express Art's request.

As I have explained, the division of epistemic labor must not rest on ignorance or error. So we may suppose that the pharmacist realizes that the best way for Art to express his request in his, the pharmacist's, language would be to say,

"Sell me an analgesic for" P. Possibly the pharmacist would have reason to sell Art an analgesic for arthritis if the pharmacist had reason to think that of all possible ailments *exactly* arthritis satisfied the description P, as exactly arthritis satisfies "arthritis." (I will say that *exactly* arthritis satisfies P if and only if arthritis satisfies P and of all possible ailments only arthritis satisfies P.) He might have reason to believe this if P includes "the disease that Aunt Martha has" and he has reason to believe that Art's Aunt Martha has arthritis. But since Art, by hypothesis, knows nothing well expressed by "Arthritis is specifically an inflammation of the joints," P will pick out exactly arthritis *only* in such indirect ways as this. Then, in order for the pharmacist to have reason to believe that exactly arthritis satisfies the description, he will have to be fairly well acquainted with Art's personal history. In that case, as I explained, the transaction will not be representative of the sorts of transactions on which the division of epistemic labor depends.

Conversely, if the pharmacist does not have reason to think that of all possible ailments exactly arthritis satisfies P, then I do not see what reason the pharmacist might have to sell Art a medication formulated specifically for arthritis (rather than, say, mere aspirin). The problem is to explicate a sense in which Art can be construed as *asking* for an analgesic for arthritis if something other than arthritis might possibly satisfy P. Unless the pharmacist can suppose that in some sense Art is asking for an analgesic specifically for arthritis, I do not see that the pharmacist has any good reason to take Art's money in return for one.

Someone might reply that it is not at all necessary that exactly arthritis satisfy P as long as the pharmacist has reason to believe that Art is *referring* to arthritis. This reply may be motivated by the sorts of cases that are supposed to illustrate the referential/attributive distinction (Donnellan 1966). Even though Smith may *say*, "The man in the corner drinking a martini is . . . ," we may know that Smith is *referring* to the man in the corner drinking *water* from a martini glass. Likewise, someone might say, even if the phrase that best expresses Art's request is not "arthritis" but P and the pharmacist has no reason to think that exactly arthritis satisfies P, the pharmacist may have reason to think that Art is *referring* to arthritis.

There is a crucial difference, however, between the case of Smith and the case of Art. Presumably, Smith is able to produce some other name or description that in fact is satisfied by exactly the man in the corner, such as "the man wearing a green tie and now standing in a corner of this room," and from the context we may be able to infer what one of these names or descriptions would be. Even if Smith is merely repeating something she heard from Jones, we may know that Smith has in mind "the man to whom Jones was referring when Jones said . . . ," which may be a description that the man in the corner actually satisfies. In general, the cases that illustrate the referential/attributive distinction are cases in which the speaker uses an incorrect name or description to refer to something but can also produce some correct name or description and in which there is no doubt whether that name or description accurately expresses the speaker's thought. In contrast, if the phenomenalistic reinterpretation strategy is correct, then the pharmacist has no basis for inferring that there is some other expression that Art might produce that exactly arthritis satisfies and that accurately expresses Art's thought. Thus the referential/attributive distinction cannot be used to defend the reinterpretation strategy.

The objection that Art, or his request, might be referring to arthritis, even though it is not the case that exactly arthritis satisfies P, might also be motivated by the sorts of cases leveled against the description theory of reference for proper names and natural-kind terms (Kripke 1972). Even if Jones is unable to say anything about the physicist Murray Gell-Mann that would distinguish Gell-Mann from a dozen other physicists, Jones may succeed in referring to Gell-Mann by using the phrase "the physicist Murray Gell-Mann." Likewise, someone might think, Art might succeed in referring to arthritis even though he is unable to describe arthritis in a way that distinguishes it from other things.

I agree that the case of Jones will be like the case of Art *if* it is allowed that Art's request is best expressed by means of "arthritis" and not P, but this will not help the phenomenalistic reinterpretation strategy, which says that Art's request is best expressed by means of P and not "arthritis." Either the phrase "the physicist Murray Gell-Mann" well expresses Jones's thought or it does not. If it does not, then it is not clear that Jones does refer to Murray Gell-Mann by means of the phrase, and in that case one cannot use the example of Jones to argue that Art may refer to arthritis. If the phrase "the physicist Murray Gell-Mann" does well express Jones's thought, then there is a crucial disanalogy between our interpretation of Jones and the pharmacist's phenomenalistic reinterpretation of Art. The difference is that while we can tell that exactly Murray Gell-Mann satisfies the expression that expresses Jones's thought, namely, "the physicist Murray Gell-Mann," it is not the case that the pharmacist can tell that exactly arthritis satisfies the expression that expresses Art's thought, namely, P.

A second sort of reinterpretation strategy is what I call the *metalinguistic reinterpretation strategy*. According to this strategy, the best expression of Art's thought would merely *mention* the term "arthritis" and not actually *use* it. For instance, one version of this strategy might be to hold that the thought Art expresses by saying "I have arthritis in my hands" would actually be better expressed by the words "My hands are afflicted with the sort of thing my doctor calls 'arthritis.'" (This reply is briefly advanced by Bach [1987, 269], and it is Loar's way of dealing with a related argument due to Putnam [Loar 1981, 159–61].)

According to such a metalinguistic reinterpretation strategy, the best expression of Art's request would be something like

> (*a*) Sell me an analgesic specifically formulated for the sort of thing my doctor calls "arthritis"!

As before, let us suppose that the pharmacist can tell that this is the best expression of Art's request. Since this is supposed to be the best expression of Art's thought, one is justified in taking the expression "the sort of thing my doctor calls 'arthritis'" *very* literally. What satisfies Art's description, "the sort of thing my doctor calls 'arthritis,'" taken very literally, is just whatever Art's doctor would respond to by saying something like "This is a case of arthritis." But surely the pharmacist has no reason to believe that Art's doctor would never misdiagnose a case of arthritis as something else or a case of something else as arthritis. It is little help to substitute the words "the sort of thing my doctor *defines* as 'arthritis'" or "the sort of thing the medical community defines as 'arthritis,'" since the pharmacist presumably has no reason to believe that Art's doctor's definition is so precise and accurate that only arthritis would satisfy it or that there is any one definition that members of the medical community will all accept without qualification.

The problem with (*a*) and its variations is that they express Art's request in terms of the characteristics of particular people. Perhaps one ought to interpret Art's request as expressible thus:

(*b*) Sell me an analgesic specifically formulated for the sort of thing that "arthritis" in our language genuinely refers to!

If (*b*) is truly different from (*a*) and its variations, then the reference relation it mentions must be that word-world relation in terms of which some philosophers of language explain the truth of sentences. It is possible to doubt whether there really is such a relation (see chapter 6), but even if there is, it is hardly obvious what that relation is, and certainly most people do not know. So the transaction between Art and his pharmacist will remain typical of the sort of transaction that has to be rendered intelligible even if we suppose that Art does not know very well what the reference relation is. But in that case, one can imagine a microstructural duplicate of Art whose linguistic community is such that the best translation into our language of "refers to" as used in that community is not "refers to" but something else. Thus anyone disposed to use a reinterpretation strategy to try to block the inference from (1) to (2) will likewise have to reinterpret Art when he utters sentence (*b*). So (*b*) cannot after all be the reinterpretation by means of which the proponent of the reinterpretation strategy may block the inference from (1) to (2).

A more radical metalinguistic reinterpretation might be that Art's request would be best expressed thus:

(*c*) Sell me what you would sell me if my doctor told you, "Sell Art an analgesic for arthritis"!

Notice that this does not have the form "Sell me an analgesic specifically formulated for" $\widehat{\ }P$. Thus (*c*) differs from Art's actual words not only in containing a descriptive phrase in place of "arthritis." Consequently, it is not clear how we might coherently reconstruct the lines of *reasoning* that Art might express with the word "arthritis." In particular, it is not clear how to interpret the reasoning by which Art decides to go to the pharmacy and make his request. What he says might be something like this: "I have arthritis. This advertisement says that this product is specifically formulated to relieve the pain of arthritis. Therefore, I will try to buy this product or something similar." I do not see how any metalinguistic reinterpretation strategy along the lines of (*c*) might reinterpret such lines of reasoning while preserving whatever soundness such reasonings may possess.

No doubt a rational pharmacist would respond to (*a*), (*b*), or (*c*) by selling Art an analgesic for arthritis, but only, I believe, because the thought expressed would normally be treated as equally expressible by means of the sentence "Sell me an analgesic specifically formulated for *arthritis!*"

At this point, one might raise again the question whether the pharmacist really does need reason to believe that of all possible ailments exactly arthritis satisfies the description in the best expression of Art's request. Might not the fact that Art uses the term "arthritis" to express his thought give the pharmacist reason to sell Art an analgesic for arthritis even if the thought that Art expresses is not specifically about arthritis? Certainly there are other cases in which a transaction succeeds by means of terms that one of the participants does not exactly understand but in which we certainly will not identify the content of the speaker's thought by means of those terms. However, I think we will find in all such cases some crucial disanalogy with the case of Art and the pharmacist. I will consider two examples.

Compare, first, the case of a child who walks into a hardware store with a note from his mother that reads "Sell me #8 toggle-bolts." No doubt the shopkeeper would have good reason to sell the child toggle-bolts, but surely we should not conclude that the child is expressing a thought of his own with a content characterizable in terms of "toggle-bolt." There is an important difference, however, between Art and the child with the note. I was careful to make it part of the story of Art that it is he himself who resolves to seek an analgesic for his ailment. His going to the pharmacist is the result of the combination of two causes neither of which would be sufficient by itself, namely, his being told by his doctor, "You have arthritis," and his exposure to certain advertisements for "arthritis" pills. It is fair to tell the story in that way, because the resulting transaction with the pharmacist will still be characteristic of transactions on which the division of epistemic labor depends. The difference, then, is that while the child's mother has given him an entire message, what Art brings from his doctor is only a single word. One can describe Art as bearing a message, but it is a message from no one but himself. While in the case of the child the thought expressed can be attributed to someone else, in the case of Art the thought can be attributed to no one but Art.

Compare then the case of a woman who walks into an oriental grocery store and says, "Give me whatever you call 'kim-chee'!" Notice that the grocer can tell that what he sells to the woman exactly fits the description, since the woman refers to the grocer himself and he calls "kim-chee" what he sells her. By contrast, Art's pharmacist has no reason to believe that of all possible ailments exactly arthritis fits Art's description "the sort of thing my doctor calls 'arthritis,'" and Art has no reason to ask the pharmacist for an analgesic for the sort of thing the *pharmacist* calls "arthritis." So suppose the woman says, "Give me whatever *people* call 'kim-chee.'" Given that we are supposed to take this very literally, it is hard to know how to take it. It could mean "Give me something that most people who use the word 'kim-chee' would call 'kim-chee.'" But if that is how we take it, then the case is plainly quite unlike the case of Art.

5. That is all I have to say about specific challenges to (2). Now let us consider specific challenges to (3). One might hope to block the argument, or at least to render it harmless, merely by distinguishing between *wide* and *narrow* content. Two thoughts may be said to have the same *wide* content if and only if they have the same *truth-conditions*. Art's and Bart's thoughts are clearly not the same with respect to wide content, because they have different truth-conditions. Art's thought will be true only if a certain fact about *Art* obtains, whereas Bart's thought will be true only if a certain fact about *Bart* obtains. Moreover, even those who resist the Burgian conclusion (3) may grant that Art's and Bart's thoughts differ in wide content for yet this further reason: Art's thought will be true of a person x (for instance, Art) if and only if x has *arthritis* in his or her hands, whereas Bart's thought will be true of a person x (for instance, Bart) if and only if x has *barthritis* in his or her hands. However, the objection goes, these differences with respect to wide content do not entail that Art's and Bart's thoughts may not be classed together with respect to some other sort of content, call it *narrow content*. But since, as I explained at the end of chapter 1, content is not merely a mode of individuation, it is not enough just to presume that there *must be* some kind of narrow content. One has to give a fairly specific account of it so that we can see that it is the sort of thing that may play the requisite role in a Lockean theory of communication.

I can think of basically four approaches to narrow content. All four may be found, with no clear distinctions drawn between them, in Ned Block's "Advertisement for a Semantics for Psychology" (1986). Call the first approach the *indexical approach* to narrow content. This approach is inspired by a distinction we have to draw in any case between two ways of counting what is *said* when a speaker uses an indexical expression such as "I" or "that" or "now." Suppose that two English speakers in the same world, Ken and Len, both speak the words "I feel a pain." Clearly, there is a sense in which each says something different from the other, since Ken is talking about Ken and Len is talking about Len. But there is also a sense in which they are saying the same thing, since they speak the same words. Accordingly, we may conclude that there is a kind of content, namely, wide content, such that the thoughts they express with those words have different contents, but also a kind of content, namely, narrow content, such that the thoughts they express with their words have the same content.

I have no objection to the introduction of a distinction between wide and narrow content along these lines, but no reason has been given to think that when Art says, "I have arthritis in my hands," and Bart says, "I have arthritis in my hands," they are expressing thoughts having the same narrow content in just this sense. The reason it seems so clear that when Ken and Len say, "I feel a pain," they are saying the same thing may be just that in this case the best way to express Ken's thought in our own language is the same as the best way to express Len's thought in our language. But in the case of Art and Bart, that is precisely what the argument for (2) shows *not* to be the case.

The second approach to narrow content is the *psychological approach*. Here the idea is that two thoughts may be said to have the same narrow content if they would be classed together for purposes of subsuming psychological states and events under psychological laws. In chapter 5 I will argue that the psychological laws that would be needed are utter fictions, but I do not need to take that for granted here. It suffices to observe that even if there are psychological laws, it is begging the question to assume that Art's and Bart's thoughts will occupy the same place in the psychological taxonomy that those laws generate. If those laws relate the contents of people's thoughts to the meanings of their words, then since the meaning of Art's word "arthritis" differs from the meaning of Bart's word "arthritis," the thought Art expresses might well occupy a different place in the psychological taxonomy than the thought Bart expresses occupies. (See Owens 1987 for a defense of Burge along these lines.)

The third approach to narrow content is the *functional-role approach*. According to this approach, narrow content is the kind of content that two thoughts have in common if and only if they have the same functional role vis-à-vis sensory inputs, behavioral outputs, and other thoughts. Further, functional roles are conceived in such a way that the functional role of Art's thought is the same as the functional role of Bart's. Thus, (3) will be false for narrow content understood in this way.[3] The problem is that narrow content understood in this way is not a kind of content at all, not as content is to be understood in the context of the Lockean theory of communication. The functional role of a thought in the physical mechanisms of the mind cannot be something that a hearer has to comprehend in order to grasp the speaker's message in a success-

[3] In this category I place also Dennett's somewhat different conception of narrow content. According to Dennett (1982), the narrow content of a person's thoughts is a matter of the sort of world in which the organism as a whole would function optimally. This categorization of Dennett's view is fitting because it too makes narrow content unknowable in practice. But I have other objections as well. Since Dennett's measure of optimality is simply potential for survival, he in effect assumes that all creatures desire survival above all else, which is clearly mistaken.

ful episode of communication. This functional role is something we know almost nothing about, although we successfully communicate quite frequently. Still, the identification of narrow contents with functional roles might be preserved if narrow contents are not supposed to be comprehended by hearers qua functional roles. That, as we will see, is how the fourth approach tries to approach the matter.

For lack of a better term, I will call the fourth and final approach to narrow content the *input-output approach*. According to Block's version of this approach (1986), narrow content is a function (in the mathematical sense) from *contexts* onto *referents*. In Fodor's version, narrow content is "*essentially* a function from contexts onto truth conditions" (1987, 53). The idea was probably first put forward by Stephen L. White (1982), who, borrowing heavily from David Kaplan (1989), defines narrow content in a more complex way that takes into account the distinction between indexicals and nonindexical terms like "arthritis." I will focus on Fodor's version.

Thinking of contents in Fodor's way, one is supposed to be able to see that the content of the thought that Art expresses by saying, "I have arthritis in my hands," is the same as the content of the thought that Bart expresses by saying, "I have arthritis in my hands." The one content that these two thoughts have in common is such that in the context of Art's linguistic community any thought having that content is true if and only if the thinker of the thought has arthritis in his hands but that in the context of Bart's linguistic community any thought having that content is true if and only if the thinker of the thought has *b*arthritis in his hands.

Fodor does not explicitly address the question whether anything like (2) is true, but his theory lends itself to the following explanation of why, as (2) states, the best way to express Art's thought in our language differs from the best way to express Bart's thought in our language: In expressing a person's thought, one wishes to use a sentence that has in one's own context the same truth-condition as that person's thought has in the context that person is in. The sentence of our language that, if spoken by Art in *our* context, would have the same truth-condition as Art's thought has in Art's context is "I have arthritis in my hands," whereas the sentence of our language that, if spoken by Bart in our context, would have the same truth-condition as Bart's thought has in Bart's context is "I have *b*arthritis in my hands."

Fodor's conceptualization of narrow content applies only to thoughts that have truth-conditions, such as beliefs and judgments, and does not apply to thoughts that lack them, such as requests. An obvious elaboration to handle requests would be to say that the content of a request is a function from contexts onto *fulfillment-conditions*. Thus, the reason why Art should get arthritis pills and Bart should get barthritis pills is that in their respective contexts the one content that their requests have in common yields different fulfillment-conditions.

But notice, first, that all by itself Fodor's conceptualization of content as a function from contexts onto truth- or fulfillment-conditions presents not the slightest challenge to the inference from (2) to (3). If we think of functions as sets of ordered pairs, then according to Fodor's theory, to say that two thoughts x and y have the same content is to say that for all contexts c and all truth- or fulfillment-conditions t, $\langle c, t \rangle$ belongs to the content of x if and only if $\langle c, t \rangle$ belongs to the content of y. But without a way of deciding whether $\langle c, t \rangle$ belongs to the content of x if it belongs to the content of y, this criterion of content identity does nothing to enable us to decide whether two thoughts actually have the same content. In particular, one cannot infer from this alone that the thoughts of Art and Bart have the same content.

Notice second that all by itself Fodor's conceptualization of content does nothing to explain how the pharmacist might ascertain the fulfillment-condition of Art's request. Merely to say that the content of Art's request is a function from contexts to fulfillment-conditions is not yet to say anything about what those fulfillment-conditions might be in a given context.

Clearly Fodor's answer to the first point would be to join his conceptualization of content to a kind of functionalism. Certainly Fodor (1987, ch. 3) is no friend of functionalism considered as an account of the assignment of *propositions* to mental states or as an account of the truth-conditions of sentences of the form "S believes that p." He thinks that this sort of functionalism leads to holism and thus to the absurd conclusion that no two people are ever in the same intentional state (57). However, he also believes that two mental states will have the same narrow content if and only if they have the same *causal powers*. This is Fodor's functionalism. The case in which $\langle c, t \rangle$ belongs to the content of x if and only if $\langle c, t \rangle$ belongs to the content of y is the case in which x and y have the same functional role (or, as Fodor says, causal powers). Since the thoughts of Art and Bart presumably have the same functional role, those thoughts will have the same content by this criterion.

This is still not an answer to the second point, however. The pharmacist may know that in general the content of any thought is the same as that of any functionally equivalent thought and yet have no way whatever of determining what the truth- or fulfillment-conditions of a given thought are. To see this quite clearly, let us suppose that the pharmacist can learn a lot about the functional role of Art's request, perhaps by asking him pertinent questions. But we are assuming that the functional role of Art's request is the same as the functional role of Bart's request. So the very most the pharmacist can learn from the functional role of Art's request is that its fulfillment condition is either (*a*) that he, the pharmacist, sell Art an analgesic specifically formulated for arthritis or (*b*) that he, the pharmacist, sell Art an analgesic specifically formulated for *b*arthritis.

To decide between (*a*) and (*b*), the pharmacist will have to take account of that which distinguishes Art's context from Bart's context, namely, the way that others in Art's community use the word "arthritis." From the fact that the medical experts in Art's community use the word "arthritis" as they do and the fact that Art has expressed his request using this word, the pharmacist must be able to infer that the fulfillment-condition for Art's request is (*a*) and not (*b*).

Fodor's view is clearly that an account of the conditions under which a given pair $\langle c, t \rangle$ belongs to the content of a given thought will take the form of a theory of reference (1987, ch. 4, esp. 97–98). According to Fodor, a thought is composed of components that are like words in a mental language. These mental words *refer*, although what they refer to may depend on the context in which they occur. If one knew the reference of the mental words that make up a thought, Fodor thinks, then one could infer the truth-conditions of the thought by means of something like a recursive definition of truth. (Of course, one would have to know the logical form of the thought as well.) So Fodor's idea is that the main thing one has to supply in order to specify content is a theory of reference for mental words.

If this is the right approach to content specification, then what the pharmacist needs to know in order to determine the fulfillment-condition of Art's request is the reference of the mental words that make up the request. Presumably, this is where he will want to take into account way "arthritis" is used in their (his and Art's) community. The conclusion he will want to draw from the way the public-language word "arthritis" is used in their community is that "arthritis" refers to arthritis. Let us allow him that conclusion. Then, the pharmacist's problem comes to this: To infer that a *mental-language* word in Art's request refers to arthritis from the fact that Art's *public-language* word "arthritis" refers to arthritis.

Certainly Fodor's own attempt at a theory of reference will not justify this inference. Fodor proposes only a sufficient condition for mental reference, and so it cannot be used to infer that Art's thought does not refer to arthritis. But it also cannot be used to infer that Art's thought does refer to arthritis. One component of the condition that Fodor takes to be sufficient for a mental word "A" to refer to A's is that "All instances of A's cause 'A''s when (i) the A's are causally responsible for psychophysical traces to which (ii) the organism stands in a psychophysically optimal relation" (1987, 126). Consequently, Fodor's account will not solve the pharmacist's problem. The fact that in Art's public language "arthritis" refers to arthritis does not give the pharmacist reason to think that this condition is satisfied. Moreover, the pharmacist will not, in the sort of situation characteristic of the division of epistemic labor, have *any* reason to think that this condition is satisfied. Indeed, it may not *be* satisfied. Art may stand in a psychophysically optimal relation to the *pains* that his arthritis causes even if there is no single word of Art's mental language that Art always tokens when he feels those pains, for he might think that his pains have two different sorts of causes.

Further, it is hard to see how any theory of reference could solve the pharmacist's problem without the help of assumptions concerning the relation between thought and language. In particular, it is hard to see how the pharmacist could infer the reference of Art's thought from the reference of his words without assuming that the content of Art's thought corresponds to the words that best express it. But that is a notion of content that permits the inference from (2) to (3) and is therefore not a kind of narrow content. I conclude that the attempt to introduce a role for the input-output approach to narrow content introduces a gap in our understanding of the pharmacist's reasoning that I cannot see how to fill. Thus the input-output approach to narrow content fails my test.

6. Generalizing from the failure of those specific challenges to (2) and (3) that I have considered, I conclude that any version of the Lockean theory that does not render the division of epistemic labor unintelligible will acknowledge that the very content of a person's thought is relative to the way words are used in that person's linguistic community. More specifically, the division of epistemic labor is intelligible in the context of the Lockean theory only inasmuch as (*a*) the very content of a person's thought is reflected in the best expression of that thought in public language and (*b*) the best expression of a person's thought in public language (even in languages other than that person's own) is relative to the way words are used in that person's linguistic community.

The very content of a person's thought is relative to the way words are used in that person's linguistic community. So we cannot maintain that speakers normally speak as they do *because* the messages they aim to enable their hearers to grasp have the contents they have. But whether a given choice of words will enable a hearer to grasp the speaker's message will depend on the content of the message. So we cannot say that speakers normally speak as they do *because* their objective is to enable hearers to grasp their message. So we cannot say that speakers normally speak as they do *because* their words express their thoughts. So the Lockean theory fails to explain why speakers speak as they do and so fails to do what a theory of communication has to do.

Why exactly does the relativity of content to linguistic community imply that we cannot explain people's choice of words in terms of the contents of their messages? After all, a Lockean may certainly acknowledge that a given speaker's choice of words will depend on how other members of the speaker's community have used words in the past. A speaker may choose certain words on the grounds that those are the words conventionally employed in his or her community to express thoughts such as that which the speaker wishes to express. Acknowledging this introduces no circularity or vicious regress in the Lockean theory (although the Lockean may be challenged to explain how such a convention arises in the first place). Why should the relativity of content to linguistic community be a problem when the relativity of word choice given a content is not?

The answer is this: According to the Lockean, a speaker's objective in speaking is normally to express a message, and whether the words chosen are suited to do this will depend on the content of the message. The Lockean may acknowledge that a speaker's choice of words to achieve this end will depend on other speakers' past uses of words and may acknowledge this because those past uses of words on the part of other speakers may be explained independently in the same way. But the Lockean cannot also allow that content is relative to linguistic community, for in that case the Lockean's very conception of the objective to be achieved would require an independent account of the community's use of words, which is what was supposed to be explained.

Finally, here are some things I have *not* done in this chapter. First, I have not tried to abstract any general principles governing the inference from (1) to (2) or the inference from (2) to (3). Second, I have not claimed that the social relativity of content can always be traced to the division of epistemic labor. Third, I have not claimed that all contextual relativity of content is relativity to *social* context (see Gauker 1987a). Fourth, I have not tried to say in terms acceptable to *me* what conditions there might be on the intelligibility of the division of epistemic labor. The conditions I laid down were formulated in terms of the Lockean theory of communication.

4

Conceptual Development

1. The Lockean theory of communication rests on a conception of thoughts as possessing a certain independence from language. For the Lockean, what we think may, of course, depend on what we are told. Further, the very concepts we form may depend on the meanings of the words in the languages we learn. But for the Lockean, thoughts and concepts must have a nature that is explicable without essential reference to language. Only in that case will it be possible to explain language in terms of thought in the way the Lockean proposes.

Already in two of the preceding chapters the issue has been whether the requisite account of thought is available. In chapter 1, I criticized Locke's own theory—the theory of ideas. In chapter 3, I constructed a *reductio ad absurdum* on the very notion that thoughts have a content of the sort that the Lockean theory requires. Here I will take up the subject yet again. This time the focus will be on a certain conception of concepts now widely accepted both in psychology and in philosophy. This is what I will call the *network theory of concepts*.

The network theory of concepts comprises both a theory of conceptual structure and a theory of conceptual development. According to the network theory of conceptual structure, a person's system of concepts may be represented as a network of nodes connected by links. Versions of the theory may differ in the way they label the nodes and links. In some accounts, the nodes may be labeled with individual words, such as "bird" and "feathers." In such accounts, a link between two nodes might bear such labels as "has" or "is a kind of." In other accounts, nodes might be labeled by whole sentences, such as "Ostriches are birds," or sentence schemata, such as "x is a bird." In that case, a link between nodes labeled "x is a bird" and "x has feathers" might be labeled "implies" or "makes probable to degree 0.9." For simplicity, I will call the things represented by the nodes *concepts*. It should be borne in mind, however, that according to some versions of the network theory, nodes represent whole thoughts or theories.

As we will see, the structure of such a network cannot be the product of experience alone but must evolve in accordance with *abstraction heuristics*, which constrain the varieties of network between which experience must decide. The difficulty I am going to raise for the network theory of concepts concerns the nature of these abstraction heuristics. They cannot, I will argue, be universal principles of rational thought. So if there must be abstraction heuristics, then they must be nonuniversal principles of some sort. But this is problematic too. One way to see that there is a problem is to consider the possibility that there might be intelligent extraterrestrials who speak a language. If abstraction heuristics are not universal but species-specific, then, I will argue, the only extraterrestrials whose languages we could understand would be those who happened to share our own abstraction heuristics. So either our capacity to understand nonhuman languages is limited in this way or the network theory of conceptual development, which requires that there be abstraction heuristics, is mistaken.

My initial objective, then, is to pose a dilemma. Beyond that, I intend to grasp one of the horns of the dilemma. I will raise some doubts about contemporary work on abstraction heuristics, and I will argue that the possibility that we might be able to understand the languages of creatures very unlike ourselves cannot easily be dismissed. Thus my ultimate objective is to pose a challenge to the network theory of conceptual development.

Explicit commitment to the network theory may be found in several places (e.g., Smith 1978; Keil 1981, 1989, 1990; Thagard 1990a, 1990b). In many books and articles one can find figures depicting networks such as I have described. Such figures are seldom used to represent the results of any actual empirical study, however. Rather, they are used to illustrate the author's basic conception of the relations between concepts or of conceptual change. Keil, in particular, uses such drawings to represent and discriminate various patterns of conceptual change. So it might be objected that the network theory does not in any deep way guide the course of research. On the contrary, I believe that the network theory has had a tremendous influence on the course of research.

Much research has had to do with the relations between concepts and the characteristic *features* that people associate with these concepts. (A characteristic feature associated with the concept *chair* might be *people sit in them*.) Consider, for instance, the highly influential work of Eleanor Rosch (Rosch and Mervis 1975; Rosch et al. 1976; Rosch 1977, 1978). One of Rosch's main theses is that there are certain *basic* concepts that are psychologically fundamental in various ways. For Rosch, what distinguishes basic concepts from others is above all their characterization in terms of associated features. (I will say more on this later.) Further, Rosch has advanced certain views on categorization in which the concept of a *prototype* plays a central role. For Rosch, the prototypicality of a prototype is a matter of its relations to the features possessed by the other members of the category.

Douglas Medin, who disputes many of Rosch's views, shares with her the idea that concepts may be understood in terms of characteristic features (Medin 1983; Murphy and Medin 1985; Medin, Wattenmaker, and Hampson 1987; Medin and Shoben 1988). One of Medin's theses is that features that figure in subjects' theoretical generalizations are treated by subjects as particularly important in discriminating between concepts. This idea that features may be associated with concepts by means of theories is one that has generated a great deal of research in recent years. For instance, the main burden of Keil's 1989 book is to show that as children develop, their concepts undergo what he calls a "characteristic-to-defining shift." This means that at early ages children view certain stereotypical features as criterial in deciding whether something should be categorized in a certain way, and at later ages they rely to a greater extent on definitions, which sometimes stem from general theories.

To a large extent, this sort of research, which views concepts almost wholly in terms of their relations to characteristic features, depends on commitment to the network theory of concepts. The objective, broadly speaking, is to describe the structure of relations between concepts and their features. But these features are themselves understood as conceptual items in the mind or at least as represented somehow in the mind. So broadly speaking, the objective is to describe a structure of relations between concepts. If the network theory were not in the background, then research might move in quite different directions. For instance, research might focus on the ways *words* are used in games and problem solving.

The network theory of concepts manifests itself in many other areas as well. It is present in the conception of concepts as constituted by their place in "knowledge frameworks" or "event-scripts" (Abelson 1981; Fivush 1987), an idea that has had a tremendous impact on work in artificial intelligence. The network theory is present also in the conception of the meanings of words as representable as complexes of semantic markers (Jackendoff 1983, 1989), an idea that has had considerable influence in linguistics.

The network theory of conceptual *structure* leads, although perhaps not inevitably, to the network theory of conceptual *development*. According to this theory, the neonate begins life with a system of innate concepts representable by a network such as I have described. The acquisition of further concepts, beyond those that are innate, is a process representable as the addition, and sometimes deletion, of links and nodes in a network. Clearly this conception of development is only the barest schema of what would normally be considered a theory. But as we will see, it is not too schematic to be doubted.

When I say that the network theory is committed to the existence of *innate* concepts and an *innate* network, I mean only that *their origin is not explained by the network theory of conceptual development*. To say that something is innate in my sense is not to say that it is present at birth or that it is universal to the species or even that it is not in some sense learned. So the conceptual or semantic "primitives" that some theorists speak of (e.g., Clark 1973, 102–6; Jackendoff 1983, 112; Jackendoff 1989), as well as concepts that are "triggered" in the sense of Fodor et al. 1980 and even Locke's "sensory ideas" (*Essay* II.i–viii) will all qualify as innate in my sense.

It is true that theories conforming to the network theory of conceptual structure are not always presented as theories of conceptual development. But for several reasons I think one may safely assume that the network theory of conceptual structure is motivated in part by the network theory of development. First, most of the current literature descends from an earlier body of literature in which a developmental thesis is quite explicit (e.g., Quine 1960, ch. 1; Quine 1969; Clark 1973; Rosch et al. 1976; Tversky 1977). Second, although the network theory of conceptual structure plainly suggests a network theory of development, few who work with a network theory of conceptual structure go out of their way to disavow the network theory of development.[1] Finally, if the process of development cannot be explained in terms of networks, then it is unlikely that the outcome of the process will be usefully characterizable in such terms. In any case, the network theory of conceptual development, and not the network theory of conceptual structure, is the immediate topic of this chapter.

In practice, network theories often amount to the old idea, which we found to be one of several strains in Locke, that concepts are analyzable in terms of features that are perceptually or developmentally more basic and that acquiring a concept is a matter of learning the analysis. Few hold that concepts are classically *definable*, but many still seem to hold that concepts are analyzable in some other way. The most glaring problem with this sort of view is that there are no good examples. The characteristic features we might list for the concept *bird*, such as *wings* and *feathers*, are not more basic than the concept *bird* itself. Concepts such as *square* and *blue* might be more basic, but the concept *bird* will certainly have no analysis in terms of concepts like these. In general, the components of any analysis that might be proposed stand equally in need of analysis themselves.

But this objection is not general enough to cast doubt on the network theory per se. If it is granted that some concepts are developmentally more basic than others, then it is conceivable that some sort of network theory of conceptual development might be worked out that does not imply that individual concepts have *analyses* in terms of features. So I will try to take as the object of my critique a merely conceivable version of the network theory that is better than the crude sort of theory that is usually advanced.

Against the theories of concepts that I am examining here it has sometimes been argued that they do not make good sense of the *identity* of concepts between several thinkers (see Rey 1983, 1985; and Kobes 1989). I do not deny the validity of such a strategy, but it is not the strategy I will pursue here. Concepts in my sense are particulars, those components of propositional thoughts (in my sense of the term) that correspond to words (see chapter 1). The theory I am criticizing is a theory of how concepts in that sense grow in the mind. Although a Lockean might like to put the network theory to use in

---

[1] Carey 1982 questions whether the theory of development has been experimentally supported but expresses no serious doubt about its truth. Armstrong, Gleitman, and Gleitman (1983) question whether the developmental thesis is true, but they view their doubts as pertaining to the theory of structure as well.

explicating the notion of content that figures in the Lockean theory of communication, the network theory does not itself directly solve any problems about how content in the Lockean sense might be assigned to concepts so conceived. Nor is it an answer to any questions about content considered merely as mode of individuation.

2. Exponents of the network theory of conceptual development tend to think of language learning as a process in which the child discovers a connection between the concepts in his or her network and the words of the language. Some go so far as to argue that early word learning is a process in which children find words to *match* certain concepts that they possess antecedently (Nelson 1974; Clark 1977). But most would grant that concept acquisition, even if it is a process distinct from word learning, is a process that goes hand in hand with word learning. Which concepts people acquire depends largely on which words they have to learn. Almost no one would acquire the concept *electron* who did not have to learn the word "electron" or some synonymous term of another language. This holds even for the concept *dog*. Few who possess the concept *dog* could explain why dachshunds and Great Danes are both dogs, while wolves are not. Most people's possession of the concept *dog* cannot be explained apart from the fact that they have learned a language with a word like "dog" with its peculiar use. So any theory of conceptual development, even from the perspective of a Lockean theory of communication, will have to include a theory of word learning.

What has to be explained above all is how the child, on the basis of a finite number of exposures to a given word in a finite variety of contexts, learns to use that word and to respond to it more or less appropriately in *novel* contexts. On the one hand, the child has to generalize beyond the sorts of contexts in which he or she has observed the word's being used. Thus, although the child may never have seen a frog indoors before, the child learns, without being told, that a frog indoors is called a "frog." On the other hand, the child must not overgeneralize. Although the child may never have been told that a footstool is not called a "chair," the child may never make the mistake of calling a footstool a "chair" in, for instance, a context in which the child is called upon to count the number of "chairs" and has to decide whether to count a footstool. How does this ability to use words appropriately in novel contexts come about? No doubt children's uses of words are not always appropriate. Mistakes are made. But eventually most of us reach a stage where we reliably, though not infallibly, use words appropriately in novel contexts. How?

So far this is not a very definite question. It is not obvious that such a question will arise for every account of cognitive development. A definite problem of this kind does, however, confront the network theory of conceptual development. According to the network theory, conceptual development is representable as the addition or deletion of links or nodes in a network. So in order to explain how exposure to language facilitates the acquisition of certain concepts, a network theory has to explain how the changes wrought by exposure to language can be represented as changes in the network that represents the child's concepts. In outline, the answer has to be that the uses of words depend on certain relations between words and networks (or whatever networks represent in the mind). Consequently, the child's use of a word will be explicable in terms of certain *semantic relations*, as I will call them, between the word and the network representing the child's concepts.

Thus we may distinguish between networks according to the uses of words that the network would generate. Let us say that a network is *compatible with the child's experience with a given word* just in case the following condition holds: If the word stood in the requisite semantic relations to that network, then the child's uses of that word would conform to at least those precise uses of that word that the child has *actually encountered*. Further, let us say that a network is *appropriate to a given word* just in case the following, different condition holds: If the word stood in the requisite semantic relations to that network, then the child would reliably use the word appropriately even in *novel* contexts.

Not every conceivable network compatible with the child's experience with a given word will be appropriate for that word. That is, for some conceivable networks compatible with the child's experience with a given word, the child would not reliably use that word appropriately in novel contexts even if the word stood in the requisite semantic relations to that network. The reason is that, given any specific network theory, we would find that for any limited course of experience, we could conceive of networks that survived all tests of appropriateness provided by that course of experience but would fail further tests of appropriateness that lie outside that course of experience. In short, the tests of appropriateness will inevitably go beyond the precise uses of the word in question that the child has actually encountered. In terms of the network theory of conceptual development, then, the question we began with may be reformulated thus: Given that the child's experience with a given word does not all by itself determine a network appropriate for that word, how does the child manage to select a network appropriate for that word?

In outline, the solution has to be that there are constraints on the child's selection of a network beyond the constraint that the network must be compatible with the child's experience with words. These further constraints may be explicit rules formulated in an inner code, or limitations inherent in the architecture of the organism as a whole, or anything in between. They may select from a range of networks generated as candidates, or they may ensure that certain sorts of network are never even considered. Let us call these further constraints, whatever their nature, *abstraction heuristics*. Thus, the success of the network theory of conceptual development will depend on whether suitable abstraction heuristics can be identified. Please notice that while I have introduced the notion of abstraction heuristics as the network theorist's solution to a problem about word learning, I have defined abstraction heuristics as constraints on networks and not as constraints on languages.

3. What literature there is on abstraction heuristics often deals with them in a very abstract manner without saying specifically what the content of the heuristics might be (e.g., Keil 1990). One can, however, find a number of attempts to say something specific. Here I will not attempt a comprehensive review of these. However, I would like to say a little about each of the main ideas in order to discourage confidence that psychology is well on its way to discovering the abstraction heuristics that the network theory requires. The point will not be merely that the abstraction heuristics that have been proposed are not sufficient. The point will be that each is either question-begging, ill-defined, or probably false.

Some of the proposals simply beg the question of concept formation. For instance, Markman argues that children employ what she calls the *taxonomic assumption*. This is the assumption that nouns "refer to objects that are taxonomically related," such as a poodle and a collie, rather than to objects that are "thematically" related, such as a dog and dog food (Markman 1989, 36). She produces some very interesting data, but she simply takes for granted that children know what sorts of taxa nouns can stand for and makes no attempt to explain how children might form their taxonomic groupings and distinguish them from thematic groupings. Consequently, the claim that children obey the taxonomic assumption completely begs the question.

Another of Markman's claims is that children tend to assume that words have mutually exclusive extensions (Markman 1987; Markman and Wachtel 1988; Markman 1989; see also Grandy 1987). This assumption can make it hard for children to learn words for relatively superordinate categories such as "animal," but it is helpful when they are trying to learn the meanings of words like "dog" and "cat." Elsewhere I have criticized her arguments (Gauker 1991a), but for present purposes let us suppose that her conclusion is correct. Still, in order to *apply* the mutual exclusivity assumption, the child must already have a fairly good grasp on the nature of the groupings nouns may stand for. Otherwise, the mutual exclusivity assumption will do nothing to prevent a child from assigning words to wildly idiosyncratic concepts, since no matter how incongruous, by our lights, the membership of a given set is, it is an easy thing to find some mutually exclusive and equally incongruous set. So apart from other constraints, the mutual exclusivity assumption does no work whatsoever.

Clearly, the abstraction heuristics we seek will have to deal with more than merely certain relations *between* concepts. In addition, the child's abstraction heuristics will have to address the characteristics of the world that its concepts are supposedly used in representing. How the child's concepts might depend on the character of the environment is a question Eleanor Rosch and her colleagues attempted to answer in the mid-1970s. Rosch's claim was that "categories tend to become organized in such a way that they mirror the correlational structure of the environment . . ." (Rosch and Mervis 1975, 575). These words have echoed through the literature ever since.

One problem with Rosch's work is that she nowhere states her thesis very precisely. Sometimes the claim is that there are certain categories that qualify as *basic* and that these maximize something called "cue validity" (Rosch et al. 1976, 385; Rosch 1977, 29). Basic categories are categories that are supposed to be psychologically and developmentally primary in various ways. Cue validity has to do with how well the characteristic features of the type of thing in question indicate membership in the category. Against the thesis that basic categories maximize cue validity, Gregory Murphy (1982) and Douglas Medin (1983) have argued that this implies that basic categories are always the broadest, most superordinate categories of all, which is clearly false and clearly not what Rosch intends. The reason the thesis implies this is that no matter how well a given characteristic indicates membership in a given category, it will always indicate membership in any superordinate category at least as well. Thus if *wings* is a valid cue for *bird*, it must be just as valid for *animal*. I think this criticism misses the target, because the "characteristic features" that are supposed to contribute to a category's cue validity are only those that all, or almost all, of the members have in common. Almost all birds have wings, but not nearly all animals do. Unfortunately, this defense of Rosch undermines any attempt to use the cue validity criterion in accounting for conceptual development. It means that the child cannot form categories by maximizing cue validity, since the child cannot know what counts as a characteristic feature until the child knows the pertinent category.

If we take seriously Rosch's talk of "correlational structure," then perhaps we might formulate Rosch's developmental thesis thus: Some categories, the natural ones, are categories all or most of whose members tend to have all of a number of features that tend to go together in the world (as do wings and feathers), and given a choice between supposing that a word stands for *such* a category and supposing that it stands for a category that does not have this property, people prefer to suppose that it stands for such a category. (Rosch's idea is developed in this way in Medin 1983 and in Medin, Wattenmaker, and Hampson 1987.) Let us call this the *correlated-features heuristic* for concept formation.

The problem I find in the correlated-features heuristic may be formulated as a dilemma: Either we are very liberal in calling something a *feature* or we are not. Suppose we are liberal. In that case, wildly unnatural categories will satisfy the heuristic as well as intuitively natural categories. For instance, consider the category that consists of all birds and all bananas. All (or almost all) members of this category have both of the following two features: (1) being either (*a*) winged or (*b*) the color of a banana; (2) being either (*c*) feathered or (*d*) shaped like a banana. Assuming that any overlap between the class of winged things

and the class of banana-colored things is negligible and that any overlap between the class of feathered things and the class of banana-shaped things is
negligible, the correlation between (1) and (2) is bound to be either as high as
the correlation between (*a*) and (*c*) or as high as the correlation between (*b*) and
(*d*). (See the appendix to this chapter.)

Suppose, on the other hand, that we are not so liberal in deciding what to call
a feature. Suppose we require features to be in some sense *natural*. In that case,
we face all over again the problem of defining the abstraction heuristics by
means of which natural concepts are acquired. Suppose instead that we confine
the pertinent features still further, to those that correspond to *innate* concepts.
In that case, it is plainly doubtful whether any ordinary concepts satisfy the
correlated-features heuristic at all, since it is doubtful whether the requisite
correlations can be defined exclusively in terms of innate concepts. Such concepts as *wings* and *feathers* certainly will not count as innate.

In any case, the thesis that Rosch's data actually support is none of these.
What her data (in Rosch et al. 1976) actually show is only that there are certain
concepts that are in various ways more fundamental to our thinking than others.
These, again, are what Rosch calls "basic categories." To emphasize that our
topic is something in the mind, I will call them basic *concepts*. Rosch offers no
usable definition of basic concepts. (Her definitions are always like this: "[T]he
basic categorization is the most general and inclusive level at which categories
can delineate real-world correlational structures" [Rosch et al. 1976, 384].)
Rather, certain concepts turn out to be especially important in a wide variety of
tasks, and these are the ones she calls basic. (She speaks of "converging
operational definitions" [Rosch et al. 1976, 385].) Nevertheless, the facts by
which she most frequently identifies basic concepts are these: Subjects will list
a relatively large number of characteristic features of instances of basic concepts. Thus, for the concept *chair*, which is supposed to be basic, subjects will
list such things as *can sit in it*, *movable*, and so on. However they will list far
fewer features for the instances of concepts that are superordinate to the basic
concepts (as the concept *furniture* is to the concept *chair*), and they will list few
additional features for concepts that are subordinate to the basic category (as
dining-room chair is to *chair*).

I have no quarrel with the claim that certain concepts are basic in Rosch's
sense or even with her claim that words for these concepts are among the
earliest words learned (Rosch et al. 1976, experiment 11). However, from these
facts alone one can derive no useful abstraction heuristics by means of which
children might form concepts and assign concepts to words. In particular, the
child will gain nothing by supposing that the words he or she hears express basic
concepts. To see that this is so, notice that whether a concept is basic is entirely
relative to the language being used to express the concept. In English, as it
stands, the concept *chair* is basic because we have a word that expresses the
concept *chair*, namely, "chair," and we do not have a single word that expresses

the concept *chair-or-sofa*. But if we lacked a word meaning *chair* and instead possessed a word "chofa," meaning *chair-or-sofa*, then the basic concept would be *chair-or-sofa* and not *chair*. Since basicness is relative to language in this way, a child undertaking to learn a first language will not be able to tell which concepts are the basic concepts and so will have no use for a heuristic that tells him or her to assume that words express basic concepts.[2]

In discussing the principles of conceptual development, Rosch also endorses an account due to Amos Tversky (Tversky 1977; Rosch 1978). Tversky's hypothesis is that the natural categories are those that maximize something he calls *category resemblance*, which is a function of the pairwise similarities between members of the category. As Tversky himself points out (1977, 349), if category resemblance is simply *average* pairwise similarity between members, then the most natural categories, by this criterion, will always be the *least* inclusive categories, and if category resemblance is simply the *sum* of the similarities between members, then the most natural categories will be the *most* inclusive categories. Tversky's way of effecting a compromise is to divide the sum of the pairwise similarities by a factor that is a decreasing function of the number of category members.

Tversky's idea can be criticized in several ways. First, he defines similarity as a function of shared and distinctive features but does not explain what a feature is. Thus we can pose a dilemma like the one I put to Rosch. Second, it is very doubtful whether the naturalness of a category in general depends directly on its size. Perhaps in some cases we have a concept of X's just because we come across so many X's. But surely the best way of dividing a domain into categories does not in general change just because we add to the domain a number of objects *exactly* like some that are already present. Third, in order to allow that the naturalness of a category depends not only on what is in it but also on which, of those things present in the classification problem are not in it, Tversky has to treat similarity as a function of context. He says that the salience of a feature, which figures into the calculation of similarity, depends on its "diagnosticity" (342). But what matters most about context is how things are classified. As Tversky himself says, "[T]he diagnosticity of features is determined by the classifications that are based on them" (343). So Tversky's account of classification in terms of similarity is circular. In response, one might concoct various

---

[2] Rosch et al. (1976) explicitly argued that the primacy of basic level categories is *not* dependent on language. Experiments 8 and 9 of that study purport to show that children are better skilled at sorting by basic-level categories. From the fact that the children in these experiments did not correctly use the "names" of these categories in explaining their categorizations, Rosch et al. conclude that their results are "not simply due to difference in knowledge of names for basic and superordinate level categories" (419). But the experiments in question demonstrated only that of two levels of classification *chosen by Rosch et al.* the children were better skilled at the lower-level classification. Their data certainly do not show that of all possible classifications children are most skilled at classification according to precisely that level that Rosch calls basic. So my claim that basicness is language-relative is in no way contradicted.

ways of letting naturalness be a function not only of similarities and dis-similarities within a concept's extension but also of the similarities and dis-similarities between the extensions of concepts. But Medin has shown that such proposals fail on both a priori and empirical grounds (Medin 1983; Medin, Wattenmaker, and Hampson 1987).

4. The failures in attempting to specify definite abstraction heuristics inspire me to look for some more general argument to show that there can be no abstraction heuristics of the right sort and thus that the network theory of conceptual development, which depends on there being abstraction heuristics, is mistaken. My first step will be to argue for the following disjunctive conclusion:

> Either (i) the network theory of conceptual development is mistaken or (ii) the only creatures whose languages we can understand are those who happen to share nonuniversal abstraction heuristics with us.

I am segregating off this much of my total argument because I think that this much might be accepted even by proponents of the network theory. But after arguing for this disjunctive conclusion, I will support (i) by raising doubts about (ii).

I begin by asking, What sort of principles might abstraction heuristics be? I am not asking about the physical realization of abstraction heuristics—whether they are features of overall architecture or are instead messages in the brain—but about their status as principles. One answer, which I will reject, might be that they are universal principles of rational thought. For present purposes I define a *principle of rational thought* (not necessarily *universal*) as any princi-ple conformity to which promotes the construction of a *true and useful* repre-sentation of reality. By a *universal* principle of rational thought, I mean a principle that any possible creature or machine must conform to in order to perform well in the construction of a true and useful representation of reality. I do not need to assume that there really are such principles, but if there are, examples might include the principle that one ought not to believe both that *p* and that not-*p* and the principle that one ought not to generalize from a biased sample.

Alternatively, abstraction heuristics might conceivably be *non*universal prin-ciples of rational thought. Not all principles of rational thought need be univer-sally necessary for rational thought. Some may pertain only to creatures whose sense organs are of a certain sort or whose memories are organized in a certain way, or they may pertain only to beings who already have certain specific beliefs or think in accordance with certain other principles. For instance, hu-man beings might be less likely to become confused when their theories and conceptual networks possess a certain sort of simplicity. In that case, the principle that one ought to prefer theories and networks possessing that sort of simplicity might be a principle of rational thought for human beings. But if what makes this a good rule for human beings is that humans have certain physiological limitations, then since the physiological limitations of other intelligent creatures might be quite different, we cannot expect that they too ought to prefer hypotheses and expositions possessing simplicity of the same sort. Thus, this principle of rational thought might be specific to human beings.

Another alternative is that nonuniversal abstraction heuristics might be what I call *natural conventions*. By *convention* I mean a regularity in behavior or thought that is beneficial to the agent who conforms to it but that would not be any more beneficial than any of a number of other regularities if others in the agent's community did not also conform to it. An example is driving on the right-hand side of the road. As things stand, doing so is beneficial (in most places), but there would be no special benefit in doing so if other people did not also do so. By a *natural* convention I mean a convention that an agent is innately disposed to conform to. To say that a disposition is *innate* is to say, roughly, that the agent's possession of it is not dependent on the agent's having any very specific course of experience. (So here I am not using the term "innate" to mean what I said I meant in speaking of innate concepts and networks.) Mating rituals in certain species of birds might be examples of natural conventions.

A possibility that we have to consider is that the abstraction heuristics required by the network theory of conceptual development are natural conventions. Abstraction heuristics might be beneficial to agents who have them inasmuch as agents who have them use and respond to words in novel contexts in ways that others in their community regard as appropriate, and there may be no other benefit that these agents derive from these heuristics that they could not equally derive from any number of other heuristics. In that case, innate abstraction heuristics will qualify as natural conventions in my sense. Some natural conventions might even qualify as nonuniversal principles of rational thought.

If contemporary network theorists were forced to say whether they thought of abstraction heuristics as universal principles of rational thought or as nonuniversal principles of some sort, such as natural conventions, what would they say? Some of them, I think, such as those who stress that human cognition is the product of evolution and that evolution may generate a variety of different solutions to problems of adaptation (e.g., Keil 1981, 217), would opt for natural conventions. This answer, moreover, is consonant with the strong forms of nativism that permeate current psychology. But some of the proposed constraints would have to be viewed as universal principles of rational thought. Above I explained why I am unable to make sense of Rosch's idea that concepts "mirror the correlational structure of the environment." But whatever it means, it sounds like something that, if it is true of *any* system of concepts, ought to be true of *every*.

The first step toward the disjunctive conclusion I am aiming at is to argue that abstraction heuristics are not universal principles of rational thought. Suppose, for a *reductio*, that abstraction heuristics are universal principles of rational thought. In that case, the range of networks conducive to a true and useful representation of reality must be much narrower than the range of networks compatible with the child's experience. Otherwise, these abstraction heuristics will not adequately constrain the development of a network. Unfortunately, the range cannot be narrow enough. That, I think, is a lesson that can be drawn from more than thirty years of philosophical debate concerning a number of related problems, including Goodman's "new riddle of induction" (Goodman [1955] 1983, ch. 3), Quine's thesis of the indeterminacy of translation (Quine 1960, ch. 2), and the Kripke-Wittgenstein puzzle about rule-following (Kripke 1982).

The lesson that has emerged is that no concept is intrinsically unsuitable to serve as a component in some true and useful representation of reality.[3] To show this, it is not necessary to give any general account of the true and the useful. Examples will suffice. Consider, for instance, the concept of a *blork*, which I define as follows: x is a *blork* if and only if x is either a wooden coat hanger or a plant with edible roots. Well, here is a true belief of mine—a true representation of reality—containing the concept *blork*: my belief that some blorks grow in Idaho. This is true because potato plants grow in Idaho and potato plants are blorks. This belief might even prove to be a *useful* representation of reality if, for instance, I am hungry in Idaho. Knowing that blorks grow in Idaho and that I am in Idaho, I may realize that one place to look for something to eat is in the ground. (There is no danger of my trying to eat the blorks hanging in the closet.) This means that if abstraction heuristics are universal principles of rational thought, then abstraction heuristics will not prevent the child from supposing that the words he or she hears express concepts as incongruous, by our lights, as the concept *blork*. In other words, abstraction heuristics will not prevent the child from using words in ways that others will regard as very strange, which is what they were supposed to do. I conclude that abstraction heuristics are not universal principles of rational thought.

Someone might reply that not all concepts are equally conducive to good *inductive* reasoning and that in that respect they are not equally useful. For instance, there are few *general* truths that we might infer from data conceptualized by means of the concept *blork*. From the fact that several particular blorks in a certain region of the world grow in the ground, it would be a mistake to infer that *all* blorks in that region grow in the ground (since some might be wooden coat hangers). To this I reply that, while the concept *blork* might have little inductive value in a system of concepts otherwise like our own, it is not obvious that it would have no inductive value in some system of concepts in

---

[3] I have to acknowledge exceptions in certain paradoxical concepts, such as the concept of the set of all sets not members of themselves (Russell's paradox).

many other ways different from our own. For instance, if in place of concepts like *grows in the ground* we employed concepts like *grows in the ground or hangs in the closet*, it might well be safe to generalize from facts about particular blorks.

Or someone might reply that the problem with the concept *blork* is that it lacks simplicity. But in what sense is it not simple? The idea may be that in some sense definable in terms of links and nodes *blork* is more remote from conceptual primitives than, say, the concept *plant*. But this will not shield the idea that abstraction heuristics are universal principles of rational thought unless *blork* is bound to be equally remote from conceptual primitives in all rational creatures, and I do not see why that should be supposed to be so.

Perhaps a case could be made for the universal complexity of the concept *blork* if it could be shown that the class of blorks is objectively heterogeneous in a way that would discourage any rational being from supposing that some word stood for that class. But what is objective homogeneity? Do the classes we regard as natural have it? The class of plants, for instance, includes things as diverse as redwoods, lichens, and flowering vines. Perhaps the answer will be that objective homogeneity may be explained in terms of objective similarity. But I have already argued in chapter 1 that similarity cannot be the sole basis for classification. Still less may we suppose that similarity will lead any rational creature whatsoever to classify things in the same way that we do. The kinds of similarity that matter to us may not be the kinds that matter to others.

Alternatively, it might be supposed that the members of a natural category possess a certain *theoretical* unity. For instance, there may be good biological reasons to classify the various kinds of plants together, whereas there is no such reason to classify things with edible roots together with wooden coat hangers. My answer to this proposal is that although the theories that provide this unity may be the products of rational thought under certain conditions, they cannot themselves qualify as universal principles of rational thought. There is indeed a lively research program devoted to showing that children's theories of things play a role in their acquisition of concepts (Murphy and Medin 1985; Mervis 1987; Carey 1988; Keil 1989). But children's theories cannot qualify as universal principles of rational thought.

I should emphasize that I am not saying that it is arbitrary whether we think with concepts like *plant* and *coat hanger* or instead think with concepts like *blork*, and I am not saying that rational creatures are equally as likely to form the one sort of concept as they are to form the other. On the contrary, I agree that it is unlikely that rational creatures would classify plants with edible roots together with wooden coat hangers while excluding all other things. I will have my own explanation of this fact at the end of chapter 8. But this will be an explanation unavailable to any sort of network theorist. In particular, the explanation will not be that only the one sort of concept is likely to result from universal principles of rational thought.

I conclude that the abstraction heuristics demanded by the network theory of conceptual development cannot be universal principles of rational thought. If there are abstraction heuristics at all, then they must be *non*universal principles of some sort. But we have already seen that if the network theory of conceptual development is true, then there must *be* abstraction heuristics of some sort. Thus to reach the disjunctive conclusion I am aiming for, it will suffice to show that if abstraction heuristics are nonuniversal and learning a first language depends on abstraction heuristics, then the only creatures whose languages we can understand are those who happen to share nonuniversal abstraction heuristics with us.

5. Imagine a race of intelligent extraterrestrials—I will call them *Martians*—who may or may not share abstraction heuristics with us. Would we be able to understand the Martian language if language learning depended on nonuniversal abstraction heuristics? To deal with this question, I first need to say something more about what I mean by *understanding* a language. Above all, I assume, understanding the Martian language means being able to distinguish between appropriate and inappropriate uses of the Martian vocabulary in the sense of "appropriate" introduced in chapter 2. I cannot precisely define "appropriate," but it is the sort of thing that Martians too have to learn when they learn their language, and at least one sort of appropriateness is what abstraction heuristics are supposed to enable them to learn.

That we are able to *understand* the Martian language does not imply that we are able to *translate* all of the Martian language. For example, if their sense organs are different from ours, Martians may have words that we cannot translate for perceptual qualities that we cannot perceive. But even where translation fails, we may exhibit understanding through our explanations of the conditions under which the Martian vocabulary is appropriate (as described in our own language, of course). For instance, we may explain that such and such a configuration of filaments on the Martian head is a word for a quality that the Martians perceive when they rub up against an object that has an acidic surface.

The question is not whether we could learn to understand the Martian language easily or whether we could learn to speak it fluently. The problem might be that any direct translation of a Martian sentence into English would be so long and complicated that the only way for us to get a handle on what the Martian was saying would be to rewrite and rearrange a paragraph-length or even book-length chunk of the Martian's thought. Or the problem might be that what the Martian treats as an intuitively obvious one-step inference is comprehensible to us only after we have interposed a lot of further steps between the premises and the final conclusion. But none of these difficulties would constitute failure to understand in the sense I mean.

To understand the Martians in the sense I mean, it is certainly not enough to be able to *predict* what they will do. If we know how the Martians are wired, then, perhaps with computers to help us with complex computations, we could predict what the Martians will do wholly on the basis of our knowledge of how electrical and chemical signals are transmitted through their bodies from their sense organs to their limbs. Even if this were so, it would not all by itself count as understanding them in the sense I mean. Martians may make mistakes, and so to understand the Martians it will be necessary to be able to tell when they are saying what they ought to say and responding to language in the ways they ought to do and to distinguish these cases from their mistakes. For instance, we would want to be able to recognize that a certain word means *plus* even if in that case we must interpret a certain Martian as saying that 256 plus 378 is 624 (the right answer is 634).

Now, the first proposition I need to establish is this:

(*a*) If learning a first language depends on nonuniversal abstraction heuristics and understanding a given Martian language is nonetheless a possibility for us, then we must have some access to the Martian abstraction heuristics independent of our understanding of the Martian language.

To see that this is so, observe that there are two possibilities: Either (i) we must acquire our understanding of the Martian language much as, according to the network theory, young Martians do, namely, by working out an underlying network on the basis of experience and guided or constrained by abstraction heuristics, or (ii) we can do it some other way.

If the correct alternative is (i), then (*a*) clearly holds. I do not say that we would need complete access to the Martian abstraction heuristics before we could begin to make progress in understanding the Martian language, but I do suppose that every advance in understanding their language would be attributable to some gain in access to their abstraction heuristics. Notice that (*a*) does not say that the abstraction heuristics must always be *discovered*. If we just happen to share abstraction heuristics with a given species of Martian, then we may have all the *access* to the Martian abstraction heuristics that we need without even being able to say what our abstraction heuristics are.

Consider, then, the possibility that we might understand the Martian language without access to abstraction heuristics. I, for one, certainly will not deny that that is a possibility. But likewise I doubt that there are such things as abstraction heuristics at all. We will have an objection to (*a*) only if we can explain how it can be that, on the one hand, young Martians, in learning a Martian language, must rely on certain abstraction heuristics, to which they have native access, while, on the other hand, *we* can learn to understand the Martian language *without* any kind of access to those abstraction heuristics. To explain this, we need to explain what difference there might be between the young Martians and us such that they are forced to rely on abstraction heuristics, while we can do without them.

Someone might suggest that the crucial difference is that we already possess a language, while the young Martians have yet to learn one. Thus we might be able to learn the Martian language by drawing analogies between their language and our own, whereas the young Martians are forced to rely on abstraction heuristics. I do not wish to deny that we might rely on such analogies. But I do not see how we might succeed in understanding the Martian language through such analogies if the young Martians must rely on nonuniversal abstraction heuristics and we have no access to their abstraction heuristics. For if the way words are used depends on nonuniversal abstraction heuristics and we happen to be dealing with Martians who do not share ours, such analogies are bound to be misleading. In relying on analogies with our own words, we will treat the Martian language as if it were generated by such abstraction heuristics as generate ours. So if the Martian language is in fact generated by some other abstraction heuristics, we will persistently make mistakes.

Or someone might suggest that the important difference between us and the young Martians may be just that we may know much more about the world. In particular, we might learn a lot about Martian physiology, which might help us to understand Martian languages. Or a scientific understanding of the objects the Martians talk about might help us out. I do not wish to deny that our knowing a public language might put us in a position to know much more than any creature who has not yet acquired a public language. But again, if learning a first language depends on nonuniversal abstraction heuristics, then I do not see how that extra knowledge might enable us to understand the Martian language unless by giving us access to the abstraction heuristics. Knowledge of Martian physiology might enable us to predict Martian behavior, but, as I have explained, an ability to predict their behavior does not immediately entail an ability to understand their language. Our knowledge of the nature of things might enable us to decide what groupings of things are in some sense dictated by nature. But if learning a first language depends on nonuniversal abstraction heuristics, as opposed to universal principles of rational thought, then there is no reason to expect that the Martian language will reflect these natural groupings.

The second proposition I need to establish is this:

(b) If abstraction heuristics are nonuniversal and we do not happen to share the Martian abstraction heuristics, then in order to discover the Martian abstraction heuristics, we will need some independent means of understanding the Martian language.

If abstraction heuristics are nonuniversal and we do not happen to share their heuristics, then to discover the Martian abstraction heuristics, we will have to study the Martians. But what kind of study would reveal to us their abstraction heuristics? The only kind I can think of would involve first gaining some understanding of the Martian language. If we knew something about the appropriate uses of words in the Martian language, then from this knowledge we might make inferences concerning the kind of network that would generate such uses. From there we might make inferences regarding the kind of abstraction heuristics that would generate such networks. But if we did not already possess some understanding of their language, then I do not see how we could begin to get a grip on their networks. The best we could do is prune away those networks incompatible with the linguistic behavior we observe in the Martians. But that, as we have seen, will not suffice to determine a network that reliably generates appropriate uses of words.

Someone might object that we could discover the Martian abstraction heuristics through a study of Martian physiology. It is commonly supposed that every individual psychological entity, such as an individual feeling or thought or even abstraction heuristic, must be identical to some subpersonal entity somewhere in the nervous system or at least to some identifiable physical characteristic of the organism as a whole. However, little thought has been given to the question how the identifications could actually be worked out. How, in particular, could we distinguish the Martian abstraction heuristics from everything else that goes on in the Martian brain (or whatever serves for a brain in Martians)? I do not see how we could do that without some independent grasp on the Martian language, and if we must have that, then (b) is not contradicted. (For further discussion of the general problem of drawing psychophysical identifications, see Gauker 1988.)

Or someone might think that we could in principle discover the Martian abstraction heuristics through consideration of the demands placed on their kind by their native environment. But in that case, as far as I can see, we will have to think of these abstraction heuristics as consequences of some more general principles together with the initial conditions provided by the Martians' environment. But these more general principles would have to be either universal or nonuniversal. If they are universal, then as far as I can see, they would have to be principles of rational thought, which I have already considered. If these more general principles are nonuniversal, then there is still no reason to doubt (b).

If in order to discover the Martian abstraction heuristics we must have some independent understanding of the Martian language, then our access to the Martian abstraction heuristics cannot be independent of our understanding of the Martian language. So from (a) and (b) it immediately follows that if abstraction heuristics are nonuniversal and learning a first language depends on abstraction heuristics, then the only creatures whose languages we can understand are those who happen to share nonuniversal abstraction heuristics with us.

I can now draw the disjunctive conclusion I have been aiming for:

(1) If the network theory of conceptual development is true, then learning a first language depends on abstraction heuristics.

(2) Abstraction heuristics are either universal principles of rational thought or nonuniversal principles of some sort.

(3) Abstraction heuristics are not universal principles of rational thought.

(4) If abstraction heuristics are nonuniversal and learning a first language depends on abstraction heuristics, then the only creatures whose languages we can understand are those who happen to share nonuniversal abstraction heuristics with us (from (a) and (b) above).

(5) Either (i) the network theory of conceptual development is mistaken or (ii) the only creatures whose languages we can understand are those who happen to share nonuniversal abstraction heuristics with us (from (1)–(4)).

6. My next objective is to support the first disjunct of (5) by casting doubt on the second disjunct. I want to cast doubt on the network theory by casting doubt on the notion that we must share nonuniversal abstraction heuristics with any creature whose language we could understand. But I cannot *show* that the network theory is false because I cannot *show* that there is no such restriction on the languages we can understand. All I aim to do is to point to a prima facie reason to conclude that there is no such restriction and then to argue that this apparent reason holds up under criticism apart from the network theory of concepts.

Suppose we went to the Martians' planet and observed for a long while the things they do. They hunt the local pterodactyls, repair their bodies after injury, build deep underground cities, and travel to neighboring planets in flying saucers. In the course of all this, they emit various detectable signals. It appears to us that these signals have something to do with their success at their several enterprises. How is it, for instance, that when they are building a large structure and one of them picks up one end of a long steel girder, another one simultaneously picks up the other end? This apparently is no coincidence but has something to do with the fact that as the one picks up his end of the girder a certain pattern of lights appears on his belly.

These sorts of language-mediated transactions would exhibit dependencies of linguistic behavior on environment and of nonlinguistic behavior on linguistic behavior. That the one Martian picks up his end of the girder depends on the linguistic behavior of the other. With a little imagination, anybody ought to be able to concoct elaborate examples of such dependencies. I think that it ought to seem prima facie plausible to everyone that by studying these dependencies we could in principle learn to understand the Martian language. Prior commitment to the network theory of concepts might be reason to deny this, but if there is no other reason to deny it, then it ought to diminish the plausibility of the network theory. I will acknowledge one possible limitation below, but I see no reason, apart from the network theory of conceptual development, to accept that a mismatch of abstraction heuristics might completely prevent us from understanding the Martian language.

When I say we might *in principle* be able to understand the Martian language, I do not mean that understanding it would be easy. As I have already explained, the question is not whether we could learn to understand the Martian language easily or learn to speak it fluently. Moreover, the process of acquiring whatever understanding we might have might be long and difficult. If the Martians speak to one another in radio waves, we might have to build special instruments to record their speech in a form that we can observe. If their handwriting is very tiny, we might have to look at it through microscopes. Moreover, we might require their cooperation. They might have to take us to their planet, or show us films of the place, because that is where the sorts of things and the sorts of situations they mostly talk about may be found. They might have to teach us by, for instance, holding up various objects, or by exhibiting various actions, and then telling us what they are called. They might have to allow us to observe them doing things while engaged in speaking more simply than they normally would. Moreover, the entire project might require more time and resources than humankind would ever be willing to devote to it.

My claim is not that we might be able to understand the Martian language wholly on the basis of the internal structure of their signals. Certainly we would have to look very closely at the Martians' nonverbal responses to verbiage and at the environmental conditions under which they speak. I once had an argument with a philosopher who thought it should be possible for me to work out a translation of Turkish from the conversation of Turkish philosophers talking about philosophy at a cocktail party. My position is nothing like that. I acknowledge that we might be unable to understand a language spoken by creatures who long ago had completely automated their world and ceased to speak of practical affairs at all and ceased even to be able to conduct practical affairs by means of language. If one were trying to get a handle on Turkish, then the marketplace, where people are asking for things and handing things over, would be a better place to go than a cocktail party. Likewise, I would not expect that we could get any grip on the language of the Martians if we could not observe them using it to *do* things.

Someone might object that there might be Martian concepts that we are forever cut off from precisely because we do not have the Martian physiology and, in particular, lack the Martian sense organs. As I have already acknowledged, we might, in consequence of such differences, be unable to *translate* the Martian language. It does not follow that we would be unable to *understand* the Martian language in the sense I explained. Still, someone might object that for lack of the Martian physiology we would be unable even to understand it in the sense I mean. It is an old question in philosophy whether a human being blind since birth can understand what "red" means. To get straight about this, a distinction has to be drawn between understanding and sensation. A blind person can understand what "red" means, because he or she can know everything there is to know about the color red and can know that "red" expresses the property that he or she knows these things about. What a blind person cannot do is *see* the color red. Likewise, we might be able to understand the Martian vocabulary even if we are unable to perceive the qualities that that vocabulary expresses.

Another objection I have heard is that the Martian language might simply be too *complicated* for us to understand. If that is an objection to the idea that we could learn to understand the Martian language easily or that we could learn to speak it fluently, then, again, it is irrelevant. If the point is that complication might prevent understanding altogether, then the objection is relevant but unpersuasive. Some things that human beings understand quite well, at least collectively, such as the computer programs that manage the various NASA systems, are very complicated. Other things that human beings fully expect to understand one day, such as the way DNA guides ontogeny, are probably even more complicated.

Another possible objection is that the Martians may be too *advanced* for us. If their science and technology are far more advanced than ours, then they may have theories and words that are in no way expressible in our own language. We could not simply *tell* Shakespeare what an electron is, except in the very inaccurate and misleading way we explain such things to children. Before we could explain to him what an electron is we would have to educate him in some rudimentary physics. We might stand to the Martians as Shakespeare stands to us; thus, we might be unable simply to *say* in our own language what certain terms of the Martian language mean. But this is not an objection to the claim that in principle we could come to understand their language, for in principle we might be able to acquire the necessary background theories. In the course of acquiring these, we might have to augment our own language with new theoretical terms. But all of that is quite consistent with my claim that in principle we would be able to understand the Martian language. If at first they are too advanced for us, we might become more advanced ourselves.

Still, might we not stand to the Martians as *chimpanzees* stand to us? There are chimpanzees who can do impressive things with symbols (Savage-Rumbaugh 1986). But no chimpanzee is ever going to understand the word "electron." Somehow we humans are able to know more about the world than the chimpanzees could possibly know. Analogously, it seems, there might be creatures who are able to know things about the world that we could not possibly know, whose language we might be unable to understand. I do not know whether this is true, but I am willing to concede the point. So I concede that we might be unable to understand the language of Martians who are intellectually superior to us. (This is the limitation I mentioned earlier.) But this is no defense of the network theory of conceptual development. Even if there were such things as nonuniversal abstraction heuristics, I see no reason to think that the class of language-speaking creatures who are not intellectually superior to us would be included in the class of creatures who shared abstraction heuristics with us.

If there are creatures who have a language that we cannot even in principle come to understand because we do not share their abstraction heuristics, then this is a most unique kind of necessary ignorance. There are indeed many things of which we must remain ignorant. There are things lost in time that leave no mark on the present, or so far away that we can never reach them, or so small and ephemeral that if we can tell where they happened, we cannot tell how fast. But the case of our supposed ignorance of other languages due to our lack of the requisite abstraction heuristics is unlike any of these other cases. In this case, the ignorance is not supposed to be due to our inability to make the relevant observations: we can fully describe the linguistic behavior of the Martians. Rather, the ignorance is supposed to be due to our inability to make the requisite generalizations. That very uniqueness means that we should be reluctant to concede such a kind of necessary ignorance without a very persuasive reason. The fact that recent psychology is committed to a theory that has this consequence ought not to be persuasive enough.

7. After introducing the network theory of conceptual development, I argued that it entails the existence of what I called abstraction heuristics. After pointing out that psychology is not making much headway in identifying suitable abstraction heuristics, I argued that either the network theory of conceptual development is mistaken or the only creatures whose languages we can understand are those who happen to share nonuniversal abstraction heuristics with us. Finally, I argued that we should not readily concede that the only creatures whose languages we can understand are those who happen to share nonuniversal abstraction heuristics with us. I conclude that the network theory of conceptual development, though barely the schema of a theory, ought to be resisted.

Proponents of the network theory have wanted to construe my argument as an attempt to show that conceptual development is impossible. Since conceptual development is clearly possible, any such argument would have to be mistaken somewhere. So in closing this chapter I want to emphasize that while the network theory encompasses a great deal, my critique does not evidently extend much beyond it and certainly does not extend to the very possibility of conceptual development.

First, the term "abstraction heuristic," as I have been using it, has no clear meaning apart from the network theory. For that reason alone it should seem unobvious that if my argument works, then it works as well against any theory of conceptual development. Second, the network theory of concepts rests on a more or less Lockean conception of the relation between thought and language, and I think the objections I have raised against the network theory may in fact be avoided if we adopt a distinctively non-Lockean perspective on the relation between thought and language.

From a non-Lockean perspective, public languages may be conceived as the very medium of a certain kind of thinking, and possession of a concept may be mastery of a word. While conceding that words in some sense express thoughts (see chapter 2), we might deny that it is theoretically useful to conceive of the function of words as the expression of thought. Rather, spoken language might be conceived as a device by which we control our environment and even ourselves, and our explanation of how this device works might not be that words express thoughts.

From this perspective, conceptual development will be possible if language learning is possible. It is true that even if we think of language in this non-Lockean way, we may have to countenance certain innate structures or dispositions that first enable a creature to learn a language spoken by members of its species. But since learning a word will not be a matter of matching a word to a general concept, these innate characteristics need not be *abstraction* heuristics. The innate characteristics that make learning a first language possible may vary widely from species to species. Yet if in all cases language serves a function of environmental and self control, then it may be possible for someone who has mastered one language to learn to understand another one by discovering the ways in which that other language performs its function.

Appendix

In this appendix I show that if we are liberal in defining features, then unnatural categories can easily be defined that pass the correlated-features test as well as natural categories. I begin with a definition and a theorem of probability.

DEFINITION. I define the *correlation between features f and g* Cor(f, g) as $\Pr(x$ is f and x is $g)/\Pr(x$ is f or x is $g)$, that is, the ratio of cases in which something is both f and g to the cases in which something is one or the other (inclusive).

THEOREM. If either $\Pr(p$ and $r) = 0$ or $\Pr(q$ and $s) = 0$, then either Cor((p or r), (q or s)) $\geq$ Cor(p, q) or Cor((p or r), (q or s)) $\geq$ Cor(r, s). *Proof.* Suppose (i) Cor((p or r), (q or s)) $<$ Cor(p, q) and (ii) Cor((p or r), (q or s)) $<$ Cor(r, s). Case 1: $\Pr(p$ and $r) = 0$. By algebra and the laws of probability, (i) implies Cor(r, s) $<$ Cor(p, q). By algebra and the laws of probability, (ii) implies Cor(p, q) $<$ Cor(r, s). But this is a contradiction. So our supposition must be mistaken. Case 2: $\Pr(q$ and $s) = 0$. Similarly, we derive a contradiction. *End of proof.*

Now, suppose that $C1$ is a category every member of which is both $f1$ and $g1$, and suppose $C2$ is a category every member of which is both $f2$ and $g2$. Suppose, moreover, that $C1$ passes the correlated-features test by virtue of a high correlation between $f1$ and $g1$ and that $C2$ passes the correlated-features test by virtue of a high correlation between $f2$ and $g2$. Let $C = C1 \cup C2$. If we are liberal in defining features, then two features possessed by every member of C are (a) being $f1$ or $f2$ and (b) being $g1$ or $g2$. So to show that C passes the correlated-features test either as well as $C1$ does or as well as $C2$ does, it will suffice to show that Cor((*f1* or *f2*), (*g1* or *g2*)) ≥ Cor(*f1*, *g1*) or Cor((*f1* or *f2*), (*g1* or *g2*)) ≥ Cor(*f2*, *g2*). By the *theorem*, this will be so provided that either Pr(*x* is *f1* and *f2*) = 0 or Pr(*x* is *g1* and *g2*) = 0. This proviso limits the generality of the result, but it also helps to ensure that *C* is a category that we would regard as unnatural.

5

Psychological Laws

1. The issue of psychological laws arises for the Lockean in at least three ways. First, as I noted in chapter 2, one motive for the Lockean theory of communication may be the idea that linguistic order might be locatable in the domain of the speaker's message. If we consider just the words that people speak, there may seem to be so little order among them that we might despair of explaining a speaker's choice of words solely on the basis of the order we find among them. Think, for instance, of the words in an impressionistic poem. If we could discern the thoughts that stand behind those words and the laws of psychology governing those thoughts, then we might hope to explain the words. So the Lockean might believe in psychological laws in the hope of devising such an account of linguistic order.

Second, the Lockean theory of communication rests on the assumptions that there is such a thing as a speaker's message and that there is a kind of thought that can bear the content of a speaker's message, which the hearer must comprehend in order to grasp the speaker's message. In chapters 3 and 4 I questioned whether we can really make sense of the requisite conception of thought. But I have yet to consider one way of trying to do so. That way is to say that the thoughts postulated by the Lockean theory are, in essence, just whatever certain psychological laws make them out to be. To say what such thoughts are is simply to spell out the laws that govern their behavior. More precisely, a given sort of propositional thought might be defined as *the* sort of state s such that $T(s)$, where T is a statement of the laws and s is a variable that stands in place of the usual expression for the sort of propositional thought to be defined.[1] I do not suggest that any Lockean must conceive in this way of the thoughts words are supposed to express, but it is how many Lockeans do conceive of them.

Third, the issue of psychological laws arises for the Lockean in the context of theories of interpretation. By *interpretation* (in the context of the Lockean theory) I mean the process by which an observer infers the thoughts that a person is thinking—his or her beliefs and desires, broadly speaking. To explain this third way in which the issue of psychological laws arises, it is necessary for me to say something more than I have said so far about theories of interpreta-

---

[1] For details, see Lewis 1970. Given an infinity of propositions p, there is an infinity of beliefs that p to be defined. I have never understood how an account of definition such as Lewis's might work when there are infinitely many entities to be defined. (Loar's attempt to solve the problem [1981, 61–62] seems to me not to work.) But I will not make that an objection.

tion. Therefore, I will begin this chapter with a brief survey of some of the most important theories of interpretation. This will enable us to see how a Lockean might be drawn to a conception of interpretation as resting on psychological laws. I will then take up the question whether the requisite psychological laws can actually be found.

2. A good place to begin a history of recent theories of interpretation is Quine's theory of radical translation, as presented in chapter 2 of *Word and Object* (1960). Quine is no Lockean. His theory of translation is not overtly committed to a Lockean theory of communication. But subsequent, more overtly Lockean theories can be viewed as reactions to prior theories, and Quine is a primary root at the bottom of a tree of such reactions. Since Quine is no Lockean, detailed criticism of his theory lies beyond the purview of this book. I would nonetheless like to indicate why the Quinean approach is not a viable option for me.

Suppose one came upon an alien culture whose language had never before been translated into one's own native language. Suppose, moreover, that there was no one who was bilingual both in this alien language and in some antecedently translated language. How could one translate the alien language? One could perhaps proceed by immersing oneself in the alien culture and assimilating the language as a child might do. But suppose one wanted to proceed by deliberate data collection and inference making. The problem of radical translation, as Quine understands it, is to describe a method for doing so.

The discussion of Quine's theory has focused mainly on the thesis of the *indeterminacy of translation*, which Quine took to be a consequence of the methodology he describes. Many who have written about this have apparently taken for granted that Quine's methodology is essentially sound but have tried to show that indeterminacy is not a consequence (e.g., Kirk 1986). My own view is that the methodology is very far from sound and that there is no point in discussing the problem of indeterminacy apart from a better methodology.

The problem with the methodology is twofold. First, the data on which the translation is supposed to be based consist of sensory stimulations. A necessary (but not sufficient) condition for the translation of the sentence s of L into a sentence s' of language L' is supposed to be that the same sorts of sensory stimulation *prompt assent* to s among speakers of L as prompt assent to s' among speakers of L'. Consequently, no language spoken by any race of creatures whose sense organs differ radically from the human sort will contain any sentence that translates the English sentence "This rock contains iron." I think that is a patently unreasonable conclusion.

The second problem is that Quine's methodology entirely ignores the effects of a speaker's words on other members of the speaker's linguistic community. It is no part of the conditions Quine lays down on translation that the effect that a sentence of L has on the behavior of speakers of L must be somehow the same as the effect that its translation into L' has on speakers of L'. It is as though Quine held that the function of language in the community would be wholly a consequence of the association of a sentence with conditions that prompt assent to it and of its logical links to other sentences of the language. (For a helpful account of the philosophical biases that led to Quine's theory of translation, see Solomon 1989.)

An early offshoot of Quine's theory of radical translation was Davidson's theory of radical "interpretation." According to Davidson, translation, and interpretation more generally, is above all a matter of constructing an "empirical theory of truth" for the subject's language. By studying speakers of L, we are to confirm hypotheses of the form, "s is true in L (in context c) if and only if p." Such sentences are called *T-sentences*. The empirical theory of truth for L will be a theory that implies a T-sentence for each sentence s of L. To the extent that the T-sentences implied by the empirical theory of truth are those we can confirm independently by studying speakers of L, the empirical theory of truth will be confirmed. With an empirical theory of truth in hand, we will be able to interpret a subject on the basis of what he or she says by determining the conditions under which what he or she says would be true.

A crucial question, on this theory, is, How are we to confirm T-sentences? Basically, Davidson's answer (1973, 1977) is that we are to look for *correlations* between the types of sentences uttered and the circumstances under which the utterances took place. If Karl, a speaker of German, utters, "Das Haus brennt," when and only when he is standing in the presence of a burning house, then that will be evidence for the T-sentence

> "Das Haus brennt" is true in German in a given context if and only if a house is burning in that context.

Clearly we need not *accept* any T-sentence on the basis of any such correlation apart from a comprehensive theory of truth for the language. But if such correlations are to be the empirical basis for such a theory, then such correlations must independently *support* some T-sentences, considered as hypotheses, more than others. How might a correlation between utterance type and circumstance type support one T-sentence more than another?

Part of Davidson's answer is that we must interpret *charitably*. We must assume that what a speaker says tends to be true under the circumstances correlated with the utterance. I do not doubt that interpretation must be charitable in some sense (I will be more specific in chapter 13), but charity cannot be the only constraint on interpretation. We might interpret Karl as speaking exclusively truths by interpreting him as speaking exclusively truths of arithmetic. It just so happens that whenever Karl sees a burning house, he feels like reminding everyone that $2 + 2 = 4$, which is, of course, true under the circumstances. One such additional constraint is our desire for simplicity in our theory of truth for the language. Moreover, Davidson has held all along that a theory of truth for a language must take into account independent constraints, grounded in decision theory, on what speakers of the language might be taken to believe (1974), and, as we saw in chapter 1, Davidson has sought in his later writings (1986b, 1990) to take into account speakers' intentions in speaking. Further, he holds that we must also exercise some kind of principle of charity, or assimilation of others to ourselves, in attributing desires as well as in attributing beliefs (1986a).

Many of Davidson's critics have focused on his formulation of the principle of charity as enjoining us to maximize the *truth* of the beliefs we interpret a person as having (e.g., Goldman 1989). Under certain circumstances, they point out, we definitely do not expect a person to believe the truth. This does not seem to me a very weighty objection. Davidson has always recognized that there will be other constraints, such as those I have just listed. These other constraints, together with the principle of charity, might, as far as these objectors can tell, yield plausible interpretations. In particular, satisfying these further constraints may well entail ascription of a great deal of false or even irrational belief.

The real problem, it seems to me, is that these various constraints require grounding in some more fundamental conception of the aims of interpretation. The need for such a grounding will become especially clear as we pile up subordinate constraints. But we ought also to ask for a deeper rationale for the fundamental constraint of charity. Exactly why should interpretation be charitable? One reason offered by Davidson (e.g., 1967) is that we can interpret a speaker's words as having any meaning we like provided we are willing to make commensurate attributions of belief. Thus, if our interpretation of a speaker's words is to be constrained within acceptably narrow limits, our attributions of belief must likewise be constrained *somehow*. But it does not follow that they need to be constrained by a principle of charity rather than by some other principle, such as a principle of maximizing absurdity. So this rationale for charity get us nowhere.

Another rationale is Davidson's oft-repeated contention (e.g., 1973) that disagreement is intelligible only against a background of agreement. Only where there is much agreement can we understand the meanings of the words that express *dis*agreement. One good thing about this way of stating a rationale for charity is that it explicitly addresses the possibility of alternatives to charitable interpretation. The problem with uncharitable interpretations is that if the theory of the world that we attribute to a person differs in many fundamentals from our own, then our interpretation, like that theory, will be unintelligible to us. Still, this rationale leaves unanswered the question, What is this intelligibility that is possible only against a background of agreement? That is my primary objection to Davidson's approach to interpretation.

One result of the criticism of Davidson's conception of charity in interpretation has been that some philosophers have come to think of charity in interpretation as essentially an assimilation of the subject to oneself rather than as a presumption of true beliefs. This conclusion leads some of them to the *empathic model* of interpretation (see Goldman 1989, where it is called the *simulation theory*). The basic idea is that we attribute beliefs and desires by starting with the hypothesis that the other person believes and desires what we ourselves would believe and desire if we were in that other person's position, and then we modify this hypothesis in light of our observations of that other person.

My first problem with the empathic model of interpretation is that I do not see how it can fail to beg the question. In imagining ourselves in the other's place, either (*a*) we imagine observing *ourselves* saying and doing what the other says and does or (*b*) we imagine looking out at the world from where the other stands. If (*a*), then we need a method for inferring the thoughts of our imagined self. If (*b*), then already in imagining ourselves in the other's place we must assume that the other has certain propositional, or at least conceptual, thoughts, for we must imagine *perceiving*, from where the other stands, that such and such is the case. We cannot simply imagine having certain nonconceptualized images and ask, If I had these images, what would I think? If I cannot take any propositional thoughts as premises, then *what I would think* can only mean whatever occurs to me when I perform the experiment. But that might be anything, and not something I should expect the other thinks. When I perform the experiment, I may be thinking that there is a stone in my shoe, but this is not a thought I should attribute to the other. Or else I am relying on some kind of general theory and not arguing by analogy with my own case at all. Our attributions might not be so arbitrary if we were to attribute what we would think given that we perceive that such and such is the case, for then we might attribute those thoughts we would have reason to think. But then we must assume that the other has those same perceptions, those same perceptually based propositional thoughts, on which our reasoning is based. It is hard for me to see how there might be a method for ascertaining that the speaker had these propositional thoughts that was not already a method for ascertaining the propositional thoughts we were supposed to be inferring.

My second doubt about the empathic theory is this: In supposing that we understand the empathic theory, we are supposing that we understand *what thinking is* in the interpreter. The thought of the interpreter about things other than interpretation is a given, and, given that, we go on to explain how the interpreter interprets. But now let us consider this thinking in the interpreter that we take for granted. What is it? On pain of infinite regress, we cannot explain what it is by explaining that it is what we arrive at by means of the empathic method. Suppose we explain it in some other way. Then a more fundamental theory of interpretation than the empathic theory would be a theory that explains our basis for attributing the sort of thing that we have explained in this way. So the empathic theory cannot be a fundamental theory of interpretation, but at most an account of an expedient that is permitted within the framework of our fundamental account.

Proponents of the empathic model question Davidson's methodology for interpretation but do not question the assumption that radical interpretation, that is, the sort of interpretation "from scratch" envisioned by Quine and Davidson, is possible. Others, such as Fodor and Lepore, question whether radical interpretation is even possible (1992, ch. 3). In part, their reason for doubting this is that they question whether the child's problem in language learning ought to be thought of as a problem in radical interpretation. Children may rely on innate dispositions or assumptions that the radical interpreter cannot, as radical interpreter, take for granted. But part of their reason is also that they think of interpretation as a matter of applying our knowledge of psychological laws rather than as a methodology governed by mere methodological precepts such as the principle of charity (152–53). If we knew the psychological laws, then we could infer a person's belief and desires by figuring out which beliefs and desires stood in law-governed relations to the person's sensory stimulations and overt behaviors.[2] This is reason to doubt the possibility of radical interpretation, since there might be limits on our capacity to interpret "from the outside" in this manner. On this view, it might be impossible to know what people are really thinking without knowing what is going on in their brains (77–81).

3. Thus the Lockean may be led, through consideration of the nature of interpretation, as well as through consideration of the nature of thought and communication, to the conclusion that there must be definite psychological laws. For all of these reasons, then, it is relevant to my critique of the Lockean theory to consider whether there really are any psychological laws of the requisite sort. I cannot show positively that no such laws are possible, but I think it is highly doubtful that there are just because there are no good examples or even any good example sketches. My primary objective in this chapter will be to argue that the most common example, which I will call the *belief-desire law*, is not a good example at all. Nothing like it is a law of the sort that the Lockean requires.

Perhaps there is a tendency to reason that there must be psychological laws somewhat as follows: (1) Psychology is the science of the mind. (2) Sciences describe laws. (3) Therefore, there are psychological laws. The main flaw in this argument is the premise that in general sciences seek laws. There are laws in physics, and physics may in many ways be the best example of a science, but one simply does not find in other paradigmatic sciences, such as biology, the kind of laws one finds in physics. The laws of physics take the form of mathematical equations of quantities. There are equations in biology, such as equations relating population growth to genetic variability, but I know of none that are believed to be universally true under all conditions, let alone lawlike.

---

[2] This conception of interpretation as a matter of applying principles of "folk psychology" is widely accepted among developmental psychologists studying the ways in which children interpret other people (see, e.g., Wellman 1991).

Philosophers since Hume have tended to think of natural laws as statements to the effect that whenever *A* happens, *B* will happen. But I know of no such laws in physics or biology. The law of gravity, for instance, does not say that any two bodies having certain masses will accelerate toward one another at a certain rate depending on their distance, for the law of gravity does not say that no other force will come along and prevent it. Moreover, such laws are not what physics and biology are about. The law of gravity is actually a very good example of what physics is about, and it is not the sort of law that philosophers have envisioned. So the example of the other sciences should give us no reason to expect such laws in psychology.

All parties acknowledge that the requisite psychological laws are not already known, but those who believe in them tend to believe that considerable progress has already been made toward discovering them. I see no cause for such optimism. If, as I argued in chapter 4, we ought to be thoroughly skeptical of the dominant approach to the study of conceptual development, then next to nothing is widely known about conceptual development. But conceptual development is fundamental. So we can have little confidence in any theory of cognition that has ever been put forward.

In general, when we are dealing with a complex body of interrelated phenomena, our confidence in theories concerning any part must be low pending a better understanding of the rest. But conceptual development is a particularly crucial missing link in our understanding of cognition. Here is why: It is fair to say that cognition is largely a kind of discovery and that discovery, at any level, is some kind of process comparable to inventing and testing hypotheses. Whenever we search for something we have lost, we form several hypotheses about where it might be. To anticipate our competitor's next move, we form several hypotheses about his or her overall strategy. If we conclude that lunch caused our stomachaches or that insider trading caused the leap in stock prices, these will be merely the best of the hypotheses we can come up with. In general, very little can be concluded on the basis of observations alone. By and large, ampliative inference involves the confirmation and disconfirmation of hypotheses. So to understand much about cognition we have to understand hypothesis generation. But hypothesis generation is tightly bound up with conceptual development.

The connection is not just that hypotheses contain concepts, so that the hypotheses we can form will be limited by the concepts we possess. The connection is even more intimate than this in two ways. First, conceptual development is largely a matter of learning to generate plausible hypotheses. To acquire the concept *dog* is to learn to generate plausible hypotheses concerning dogs. Someone who thinks that a dog might have stolen his car probably does not know what a dog is. Moreover, acquiring the concept *dog* is in part a matter of learning to recognize dogs as dogs. But as we have seen, we cannot think of this recognition as fundamentally an inference from antecedently recognized features (because the characteristic features are not in general more basic). To be able to recognize a thing as a dog is to be able to *hypothesize* that something is a dog when and only when it is one. This will look wrong to anyone who thinks of a hypothesis as a guess, but a hypothesis is not a guess. It will look wrong to anyone who thinks of recognition as an unmediated response to a sensation, but recognition is not that.

Second, hypothesis generation is very frequently the first step toward the invention of a novel concept. When Moritz Traube hypothesized that yeast contained a substance that would promote fermentation as well as the living cell itself does, he took a large and important step toward the invention of the concept *enzyme*. When Johnstone Stoney concluded that the unit of electric charge must be a particle, he essentially invented the concept *electron*. When some prehistoric hominid hypothesized that if he accepted some pretty seashells in return for his corn, he would be able to trade those pretty seashells for some arrows, he took a step toward inventing both money and the *concept* of money.

For these reasons, we cannot expect to understand hypothesis generation apart from conceptual development. My critique of the network theory of conceptual development notwithstanding, someone might think that work in artificial intelligence has made great strides toward an understanding of hypothesis generation. No doubt one can write special-purpose computer programs that generate appropriate hypotheses in the course of problem solving. For instance, one might write a program that guesses numbers between 1 and 10. First it guesses 1, then it guesses 2, and so on. It is easy to get the idea that what humans do is like what these computer programs do, only a lot more complicated and versatile. If that is right, then my doubts should be dismissed as simply due to ignorance of the programs we humans use in thinking.

But the comparison overlooks an important difference. Half of all freshmen will object that computers cannot really think because what computers do is all "preprogrammed." In a way, that is my objection too (but what I have in mind is not any kind of free-willism). Contemporary artificial intelligence programs rely on a database of very specific information concerning the task domain and on a large number of subroutines or specialized functions of one sort or another, each one specifically designed to handle some contingency that the programmer has foreseen. In other words, they rely on a great deal of innate knowledge. Insofar as computers hypothesize, they rely on a great deal of innate knowledge concerning the hypotheses pertinent to the tasks they are programmed to perform. This innate knowledge goes beyond what can plausibly be ascribed to humans. Unlike current computer hypothesizing, human hypothesizing cannot be understood as a matter of drawing hypotheses from an innate store. So it is doubtful whether we can usefully think of the hypothesizing that humans do as like whatever hypothesizing computers can do.

People who work in artificial intelligence will vehemently deny this, but they are hardly unbiased observers. Consider, as a case in point, Allen Newell's

SOAR (1990). Newell would have his readers believe that SOAR is a model of the most basic cognitive operations. No doubt SOAR has some important virtues over other systems (such as minimizing the need for conflict resolution), but it is not hard to see that at several junctures Newell has simply bestowed on SOAR the knowledge it needs to complete its task. (Shultz 1992 concurs in this opinion.) First, knowledge about the problem space is given in the form of knowledge of certain procedures. For instance, if the goal is a certain arrangement of blocks, SOAR knows innately to try moving blocks or taking one block off another. That kind of knowledge may seem to be so basic that it is entirely correct for Newell to treat it as innate. The problem is that when SOAR is set to tasks of other sorts, it is not obvious that the innate knowledge it has to be supplied with will be equally basic. Second, knowledge of the current state is given, as if acquiring that knowledge were not every bit as much a problem as the problems Newell sets for SOAR to solve. Third, knowledge of what problem space to move to in the face of an impasse also appears to be given (although Newell does not explain how this is done).

4. Perhaps it is unfair to focus on hypothesis generation, which may be the worst case for believers in psychological laws. But what is the best case? Oftentimes an extensive discussion of psychological laws is conducted without any serious examples at all (e.g., Devitt 1990). But there is one idea that crops up again and again. I will call it the *belief-desire law:*

   Ceteris paribus, people do what they believe will satisfy their desires.

Many people seem to think that some such thing is true. Here is some evidence:

> If z desires q, believes doing A now leads to q, has no desire that overrides the desire that q with respect to A, and believes z-self able to do A, then z wills to do A now. (Loar 1981, 90)

> The knowledge level . . . has a law of behavior, namely, if the system wants to attain goal G and knows that to do act A will lead to attaining G, then it will do A. This law is a simple form of rationality—that an agent will operate on its own best interests according to what it knows. (Newell 1990, 48–49)

> Folk psychology is a network of principles which constitutes a sort of common-sense theory about how to explain human behavior. . . . The theory asserts, for example, that if someone desires that p, and this desire is not overridden by other desires, and he believes that an action of kind K will bring it about that p, and he believes that such an action is within his power, and he does not believe that some other kind of action is within his power and is a preferable way to bring it about that p, then *ceteris paribus*, the desire and the beliefs will cause him to perform an action of kind K. (Horgan and Woodward 1985, 197)

Then by virtue of what I would think of as a vulgar, vernacular, psychological law, the operation of which is the reason for the introduction of the concepts of believing and wanting, we get our first psychological law for the creature or type of creature in question. This is that for any particular object X and for any feature F and for any activity or type of behavior A, if the creature C believes that the object X both has the feature F and is nearby, or within reach, and that things of type F are suitable for activity A, then the creature wants to A with respect to object X. . . . We might then invoke a second psychological law for this creature. . . : that for any type of activity A, if a creature C, wants to A with respect to some particular object X, and if it is not prevented in one or another of a set of ways that might or might not be listable, then creature C does produce the activity A with respect to X. (Grice 1989b, 285)

Now I want to question the belief-desire law, which is apparently regarded as the best case by many of those who believe in psychological laws. I am going to argue that, apart from a prior commitment to the existence of psychological laws, there is no reason to believe that the belief-desire law as I have defined it or anything remotely like it is true. From this I conclude that those who believe in psychological laws have no good examples to offer whatsoever.

Many of these authors recognize that one cannot maintain simply that people do what they believe will satisfy their desires, and so they qualify this basic idea in various ways. Many guarantee themselves escape by adding a *ceteris paribus* clause. Horgan and Woodward have built many of their qualifications into their statement of the law but still give themselves a "*ceteris paribus.*" Grice adds on the same page that the law is "to be thought of as corrigible, modifiable and *ceteris paribus* in character" (1989b, 285). Loar explains that such laws are part of a common-sense theory subject to displacement by a theory with better scientific credentials (1981, 77–78). I want to begin by considering what "*ceteris paribus*" could possibly mean here, because the right way to object to the belief-desire law will depend on how that phrase is taken.

I am going to take for granted that all of the above formulations of the belief-desire law, if taken at face value without invoking the *ceteris paribus* clause, are subject to straightforward counterexamples. What is wanted is a reading of the clause that will insulate some formulation from all counterexamples without trivializing it. The literal translation of the Latin is "other things being equal." But things are never equal, and so what is needed is some nonliteral reading. According to one nonliteral reading, "*ceteris paribus*" means simply *provided nothing prevents it*. But that is a trivializing reading. If I jump through the window, then I will fly, *provided nothing prevents it*.

Perhaps, the words "*ceteris paribus*" may be thought of as a placeholder for some definite statement of further conditions, which may or may not be known already but in principle could be discovered or at the very least exist and are stateable. One might imagine that these conditions can be stated in the vocabulary of what is called common-sense psychology, or one might hold that the vocabulary of some more fundamental science must be employed (Schiffer 1991). Alternatively, the words "*ceteris paribus*" may be taken to mean *normally*, which in turn may be taken in a variety of ways. Here are several ways of reading "If *Fx*, then *normally Gx*":

The statistical interpretation: The ratio of *actual* cases of *Fx*-and-*Gx* to *actual* cases of *Fx* is high.

The frequency interpretation: In an infinite sequence of cases of *F*, the ratio of cases of *Fx*-and-*Gx* to cases of *Fx* will converge to a high value.

The biological interpretation: If *x*'s subpersonal faculties are all behaving in accordance with their biologically proper functions, as determined by natural selection, then its being that case that *Fx* is sufficient for its being the case that *Gx*. (Compare Millikan's use of the term "normal" in her 1984.)

To explain yet another way of taking the *ceteris paribus* clause, I first need to introduce the idea of a *scientific successor concept*. What we take for granted about H_2O is not exactly what people took for granted about water two centuries ago. Just for that reason, there is a sense in which the concept *water* is not identical to the concept H_2O (which is not to deny that there is also a sense in which they are the very same concept). The concept H_2O, we might say, is the *scientific successor* to the concept *water*. Likewise, the concept *mean molecular kinetic energy* is the scientific successor to the concept *heat*. Perhaps *psychosis* is the scientific successor to *insanity*. Similarly, the concepts *belief* and *desire* might someday have scientific successors, although it is an open question what they would be. The concepts H_2O and *kinetic energy* figure into laws of nature, it might be said, whereas *water* and *heat* do not. Still, generalizations in terms of *water* and *heat* may have the status of approximations to those in terms of H_2O and *kinetic energy*. Similarly, the scientific successors of *belief* and *desire* might figure into laws of nature, whereas *belief* and *desire* do not, and yet generalizations in terms of *belief* and *desire* might qualify as approximations to those that will be formulable in terms of their scientific successors. The function of the *ceteris paribus* clause, from this point of view, is to remind us that the generalization it qualifies is only this kind of approximation to the truth.

What all of the readings of "*ceteris paribus*" considered so far have in common is that they aim to accommodate a belief-desire law that describes how people literally do behave. Call these *descriptive* readings of the *ceteris paribus* clause. But there is another sort of reading of the *ceteris paribus* clause, according to which its function is to indicate that the statement it qualifies pertains only to certain ideal cases that may or may not be fully realized in nature. Thus, in the belief-desire law, the *ceteris paribus* clause might indicate that only people who possess a certain ideal rationality can be expected to do what they believe will satisfy their desires. Call this the *ideal* interpretation of the *ceteris paribus* clause.

The ideal interpretation of the *ceteris paribus* clause need not render the belief-desire law vacuous or even useless. If we knew what ideally rational people would do given that they had certain beliefs and desires, then we might be able to explain or even predict what actual, less than ideally rational agents will do by *supposing* that they are ideally rational. They may approximate to the ideal closely enough that such an explanatory strategy sometimes works. And yet there may be no way to substitute a more accurate descriptive statement of how people choose, for there may be no definite way to characterize the entire variety of ways in which people fall short of the ideal.

In outline, my argument against the belief-desire law is as follows: First, on every descriptive reading the belief-desire law is false because people do *not* do as they ought but can do as they ought. So at most the ideal interpretation of the *ceteris paribus* clause is acceptable. But second, we have no account of the ideal that can serve in the ideal interpretation of the *ceteris paribus* clause.

It is obvious that people do not always make decisions as well as they might. Human decision making has been extensively studied by psychologists (e.g., Nisbett and Ross 1980), who have made some very interesting discoveries. One can argue about the extent of people's irrationality. For instance, one can try to show that some things that seem to be irrational make much more sense in a natural, as opposed to a clinical, setting or viewed from a broader perspective. But these are not issues I need dwell on, since it is in any case clear that people do not make decisions as well as they might. For instance, people buy extended warranties on their automobiles even when those warranties have an expected monetary value far below what they cost. When I say that they *might* do better, I do not mean anything very difficult: I mean that a certain sort of instruction (not necessarily mere verbal instruction and not necessarily in a formally instructional setting and not necessarily delivered on purpose by other people) would result in their actually doing better. The evidence for this is that some people who have had such instruction actually do better.

Thus, no descriptive interpretation of the *ceteris paribus* clause is going to insulate the belief-desire law from counterexamples. If the law we formulate in terms of a *ceteris paribus* clause interpreted descriptively is true of those who make decisions as they ought, then it will not be true of those who do not. In other words, if it is true of those who do not decide as they ought, it will not be true of those who do. The problem is not that the belief-desire is not true of everyone. The *ceteris paribus* clause precludes our requiring that it be. The problem is, rather, that in view of the fact that people can learn to do as they ought and can also fail to do as they ought, the belief-desire law, however formulated, can cease to be true of *most* people or perhaps even of anyone.

The obvious reply to this argument is that we have to take a broader perspective and look at decision theory in the context of a theory of learning. Perhaps we could formulate a unitary belief-desire law if we had a psychological theory in terms of which we could distinguish between those who decide as they ought and those who do not and in terms of which we could explain how a person learns to decide as one ought. But if the only answer to my objection were one that, like this answer, took for granted that we might be able to work out a comprehensive system of psychological laws governing learning, then the example of the belief-desire law could not be used to motivate belief in psychological laws. That the example of the belief-desire law fails to motivate belief in psychological laws is all I intended to show.

Let us abandon, then, all descriptive interpretations of the *ceteris paribus* clause and consider instead the ideal interpretation. Here it is not necessary to have a single law that correctly describes all or even most people, but only a single ideal to which all people, insofar as they are understandable in terms of beliefs and desires or other types of propositional thought, must approximate. Call this *the ideal of rational decision making*. The problem with this answer is that when we consider what this ideal might be, we find that we are ineluctably drawn to an ideal that does not serve our purposes at all. This is not at all obvious, but it is what I will try to show.

5. Say that a rule is *definite* to the extent that following it yields a clear, specific choice of action. Say that a rule for decision making is *right* to the extent that the decisions it yields are *correct*. Say that a rule is *explanatory* to the extent that the actions of people who approximate to the ideal might be explained in terms of the rule. I will argue that there is a trade-off between definiteness, rightness, and explanatoriness in the ideals of rational decision making. I know of no ideal that possesses all three.

A fairly explanatory but clearly unsatisfactory ideal would be the following rule: *Do what you believe will satisfy your desires*. This is no doubt the rule that inspires confidence in the belief-desire law. The problem with this rule is that it seldom yields a definite and right decision. The rule can be improved by means of some of the qualifications added to the belief-desire law by the various authors quoted above, but these are far from adequate. Usually there are a number of things that one desires to some extent, and what one chooses to do depends not only on which of these one desires most but also on the likelihood of their being achieved. One might aim for something one desires less if one has a better chance of getting it. So at the very least our rule has somehow to take into account probabilities and preference orderings.

Very definite but again quite unsatisfactory rules can be defined wholly in terms of probabilities and preference orderings over outcomes. For instance: *Do what will give the top-ranked outcome the highest probability*. But such a rule is very far from right. If my top-ranked outcome is that I win the Pennsylvania lottery, this rule would counsel me to spend everything I have on lottery tickets. Another such rule is the *maximin rule: Take that action such that the worst possible consequence is better than the worst possible consequence of any alternative action.* But such a decision rule is also subject to easy counter-examples. For example, one would readily risk the loss of an additional penny in exchange for a strong chance of an extra million dollars.

No rule defined solely in terms of probabilities and preference orderings is going to be right in general. Suppose you are hungry and I offer you a choice between Plan A and Plan B. On Plan A, I simply give you a ham sandwich. On Plan B, we flip a coin, and if the coin comes up heads, you get a turkey sandwich; if it comes up tails, you get a peanut butter sandwich. This example is contrived to be simple, but it is not unrepresentative of everyday decision making. We often have to consider that our actions may have a variety of outcomes and have to consider the likelihood of each one. Suppose you prefer the turkey over the ham, and the ham over the peanut butter. In that case, it is not obvious whether you should choose Plan A or Plan B. What you ought to do depends not only on your preference *ordering* but on the distance between your desire for the turkey and your desire for the ham and the *distance* between your desire for the ham and your desire for the peanut butter.

Let u, for *utility,* be a function that assigns to each outcome a number representing its desirability. If u(turkey) $-$ u(ham) $<$ u(ham) $-$ u(peanut butter), then you should take the guaranteed ham rather than risk getting peanut butter. But if u(turkey) $-$ u(ham) $>$ u(ham) $-$ u(peanut butter), then you should take the fifty-fifty shot at the turkey sandwich. You should be indifferent between Plan A and Plan B if u(turkey) $-$ u(ham) $=$ u(ham) $-$ u(peanut butter), that is, if u(ham) $=$ $.5u$(turkey) $+$ $.5u$(peanut butter). In general, if you rank a over b and b over c, you should be indifferent between a guarantee of b and a gamble in which the only possible outcomes are a and c if and only if $u(b) = (prob(a) \times u(a)) + (prob(c) \times u(c))$.

What the above meditation suggests is that we might try to define a concept of utility and then adopt the following decision rule: *Choose that plan that has the highest utility.* Call this the *utility rule.* The problem with this, I will argue, is that there is no adequate concept of utility. For any definition of utility that we might propose, the utility rule either fails to be definite or fails to be right or fails to be explanatory.

Suppose, for instance, that we think of utility as a measure of expected *happiness.* In other words, utility might be a measure of the happiness that a given prospect would bring, or in the case of a gamble over prospects, a weighted average of the amounts of happiness that the several possible, mutually exclusive outcomes would bring, where each weight is the probability of that outcome. But what is happiness? If we give any very definite account of this, then the utility rule is bound to be wrong. For any very definite account of happiness, we will find that people do not always prefer happiness. Sometimes they sacrifice their own happiness for the happiness of others, or for the sake of duty, or for the sake of beauty. Moreover, we cannot always object that such people's preferences are irrational or in other respects less than ideal. We can avoid this problem by failing to define happiness very definitely, but then of course the utility rule will lack definiteness.

Suppose instead that we think of utility as simply a measure of preference. Toward defining this conception of utility more precisely, let $L(p, x, y)$ stand for a gamble with probability p of outcome x and a probability $(1 - p)$ of outcome y. Define a *lottery* as follows: Where $o_1, o_2, \ldots, o_n$ are *basic outcomes* (like the sandwiches in the example), say that (i) every basic outcome is a *lottery*; (ii) if L_1 and L_2 are lotteries, then $L(p, L_1, L_2)$ is a lottery; and (iii) nothing else is a lottery. Now we can define a *utility scale* for agent A and basic outcomes $o_1, o_2, \ldots, o_n$ as a function u from lotteries to real numbers satisfying the following three conditions:

> For all lotteries x and y,
> (a) $u(x) > u(y)$ if and only if A prefers x to y,
> (b) $u(x) = u(y)$ if and only if A is indifferent between x and y, and
> (c) $u(L(p, x, y)) = pu(x) + (1 - p)u(y)$.[3]

If utility is merely a measure of preference, then any assignment of numbers to lotteries that satisfies this definition will qualify as a measure of utility. In other words, any utility scale is a measure of utility. It should be noted that a utility scale is relative to a given preference ranking over a given set of lotteries defined relative to a given set of basic outcomes and thus that a utility scale is relative to a given decision problem.

From now on, let us assume that utility is merely a measure of preference in this sense, and let us suppose that the utility rule calls for the maximization of utility in just this sense. In this case, the utility rule is no doubt quite definite. However, its rightness can still be questioned, and what is more serious, it is highly unexplanatory.

Consider first whether the utility rule is right. From an external perspective we can certainly question the rightness of the utility rule because we can question the rightness of the agent's preferences. For instance, we can question

---

[3] This definition may not be entirely general. If we think of the objects of preference as propositions, then condition (c) says, in effect, that the probability of a disjunction between x and y where x and y are mutually exclusive and exhaustive is a function of the probabilities and utilities of the disjuncts. However, one might expect that the probability of a disjunction with mutually exclusive disjuncts would *in general* be a function of the probabilities and utilities of the disjuncts, not only when the disjuncts were exhaustive. A theory of utility that satisfies this expectation is that developed by Richard Jeffrey (1983). Except for one problem, my argument could equally well be cast in terms of Jeffrey's theory. The problem is that at one point I am going to assume that we can state necessary and sufficient conditions on preference orderings under which utility assignments can be made and that for Jeffrey's theory there lacks an uncontroversial set of such conditions (Jeffrey 1983, 149). That fact is no comfort to the believers in the belief-desire law, however. To the extent that necessary and sufficient conditions for the existence of a utility function are unclear, the concept of utility is not understood.

whether the agent ought to prefer watching a sitcom on TV over doing his or her homework. But the rightness we are looking for is only that which we need in order to give what I am calling an *ideal* intepretation to the *ceteris paribus* clause, and so it is not obvious that such an external perspective is the right perspective for purposes of judging the rightness of a decision rule.

The rightness of the utility rule can be questioned even without taking any such external perspective. Another reason to question it is the Ellsberg paradox (Ellsberg [1961] 1988). Here is a simple version: You have before you two urns, urn I and urn II. You know that urn I contains fifty red balls and fifty blue balls. You know that urn II contains one hundred balls, some of which are red and some of which are blue, but you do not know the proportion. Say that *betting on red from I* means that you adopt a course of action (accepting a bet) in which you will draw a ball from urn I, where if you draw a red ball you win $100 and if you draw a blue ball you win nothing (and lose nothing). Likewise *betting on blue from I* means that if you draw a blue ball from urn I you win $100 and if you draw a red ball you win nothing. *Betting on red from II* and *Betting on blue from II* are defined similarly. Many people, including myself, would prefer betting on red from I over betting on red from II and would prefer betting on blue from I over betting on blue from II. These preferences reflect a preference for knowing what one is getting into or pessimism about unknown probabilities and can hardly be regarded as irrational. But this combination of preferences is impossible wherever there exists a utility scale for these courses of action, as I will now show.

Suppose that there exists a utility scale for these courses of action. Then by clause (*a*) of the definition of a utility scale, a preference for betting on red from I over betting on red from II will entail that betting on red from I has a higher utility than betting on red from II. Suppose, moreover, that these courses of action can be represented as lotteries. Then by clause (*c*) of the definition, the probability of drawing a red ball from urn I must be regarded as greater than the probability of drawing a red ball from urn II (since the utility of a given number of dollars is the same no matter which bet yields it). In short:

(1) A preference for betting on red from I over betting on red from II implies that the probability of drawing red from I is greater than the probability of drawing red from II.

Similarly,

(2) A preference for betting on blue from I over betting on blue from II implies that the probability of drawing blue from I is greater than the probability of drawing blue from II.

So if there exists a utility scale for these courses of action given these preferences, then the probability of drawing a given color from I is always greater than the probability of drawing that color from II. But since red and blue are mutually exclusive and exhaustive in either case, the probability of red and the probability of blue must in either case sum to 1. So the probability of drawing a given color from I cannot always be greater than the probability of drawing that color from II.

If one has these preferences, then, as one rationally might, then something is wrong. The problem might be treated in either of two ways. First, we might conclude that there is no utility scale for these courses of action given these preferences. Alternatively, we might conclude that the objects of one's preferences—the courses of action between which one has to decide—are not adequately represented as lotteries of the form $L(p, x, y)$. In either case, the utility rule is certainly not right. If there is no utility scale at all, then the utility rule does not yield a *correct* decision, because it does not yield *any* decision. If the courses of action in this case are not adequately represented as lotteries, then the utilities we might assign to these actions represented as lotteries do not form an adequate basis for decision. The point here is not merely that people's preferences are not always measurable on a utility scale—which is certainly true inasmuch as people's preferences often are not rational—but that people's preferences may not be measurable on a utility scale even when they are rational.

But now I want to set aside such doubts about the rightness of the utility rule. Let us suppose that it correctly defines an ideal of rational decision making. Still, I will argue, the utility rule is thoroughly unexplanatory. That this is so emerges when we consider the conditions under which a person's preferences can be measured on a utility scale.

By a *theory of utility* I mean a list of nonnumerical conditions on preference orderings that are jointly necessary and sufficient for the existence of a utility scale. A person's preferences in a given decision problem will be measurable on a utility scale if and only if these conditions are satisfied by that person's preferences. A theory of utility in this sense was first put forward by von Neumann and Morgenstern (1944). Let "xPy" mean that the agent prefers x to y, and let "xIy" mean that the agent is indifferent between x and y. Then a simple version of the von Neumann–Morgenstern conditions (not quite the same as the originals) is as follows:[4]

Ordering: Every lottery is ranked, I is symmetric, P is antisymmetric and incompatible with I; P and I are transitive; and if xPy and yIz then xPz, and if xPy and xIz then zPy.

Continuity: For all lotteries x, y and z, if xPy and yPz, then there is some number a such that $0 < a < 1$ and $yIL(a, x, z)$.

Better Prizes: For all lotteries x, y and z, if $0 < a \leq 1$, then xPy if and only if $L(a, x, z)PL(a, y, z)$.

---

[4] This version of the von Neumann–Morgenstern rationality conditions is a modification of Resnik's version (1987). I have substituted the final condition for a less general one and have eliminated some consequent redundancy.

Indifference between Equivalents: If x and y represent the same distribution of probabilities over basic outcomes, then xIy. (For example, $xIL(1, x, y)$ and $L(ab, x, y)IL(a, L(b, x, y), y)$.)

Call these four conditions the *V-M rationality conditions*. These conditions are all clearly necessary conditions on the existence of a utility scale (since they follow from the definition of a utility scale). But they are sufficient as well. Provided only that the V-M rationality conditions are satisfied, it is possible to construct a utility scale for the given set of lotteries. A simple method is to choose a top-ranked lottery A and give it the value 1; choose a bottom-ranked lottery B and give it the value 0; and give every other lottery the value n just in case the agent is indifferent between it and $L(n, A, B)$. Using just the above four conditions, it can be proved that the function so defined satisfies the definition of a utility scale.

I have gone into such detail because I want it to be quite clear that the utility scale does no essential work. The necessary and sufficient condition for the existence of a utility scale is that all lotteries be ranked in accordance with the V-M rationality conditions. But that means that the utility rule has an equivalent formulation that does not mention utility values at all, namely: *Rank all lotteries in accordance with the V-M rationality conditions and choose the available lottery that you prefer over all other available lotteries.* Call this the *V-M formulation of the utility rule.* Where the adequacy of the utility rule is in question, we may consider the V-M formulation just as well.

What the V-M formulation of the utility rule makes quite clear is that the utility rule is highly unexplanatory. It does this by demonstrating that the utility rule begs all of the important questions that we need to answer if we are to explain why people choose as they do. Suppose that we know how the agent conceives of the lotteries between which he or she has to choose. Then the ideal of rational decision making, whatever it may be, ought to explain at least why the agent chose one lottery rather than another. The only explanation yielded by the supposition that the agent approximates to the ideal of the utility rule is that the agent preferred that lottery to all other available lotteries in a preference ordering conforming to the V-M rationality conditions. But that is hardly any explanation at all!

Perhaps this explanation would not be so vacuous if a person's preferences could be read directly off some feature of his or her observable behavior. If preferences could be read directly from a person's words or past choices, then the utility rule might qualify as explanatory inasmuch as it told us what to look at in predicting a person's choices. For instance, if we could always suppose that an agent preferred what he or she had *said* he or she preferred, then we could explain, "The reason Fred chose A over B is that Fred *said* he preferred A over B." Or if preferences could be read directly from a person's past choices, then we could explain, "The reason Fred chose A over B is that Fred *always* chooses A over B." But if it is true that a person tends to choose what he or she prefers (if that is how we are understanding "preference"), then it is not true that a person's preferences can be read directly off of his or her words or past behavior.

Alternatively, the utility rule would not be so vacuous as an explanation of a person's choices if a person's preferences were an enduring feature of a person's character. But that is not true either. A person who prefers A over B today may prefer B over A tomorrow in view of changes in circumstance or changes in appetite. The more or less enduring features of a person's character relevant to explanation of that person's choices are that person's *values*, by which I mean the criteria by which he or she decides which of two things he or she prefers. If we want to explain a person's decision making, what we need to understand is what his or her values are and how he or she mobilizes these values in forming preferences. Does the agent value pleasure over virtue, beauty over wealth, quantity over quality? Is the agent altruistic or egoistic, moral or amoral? When an option ranks high on one dimension of value but ranks low on another, how does the agent resolve that sort of multidimensional scaling problem? What strategies does this person employ to avoid encountering a conflict between his or her several values? These are questions that the utility rule does not help us with at all. (For further criticism along these lines, see Pettit 1991.)

Notice that I did not say that citing the V-M conditions is entirely unexplanatory. It may happen on rare occasions that someone notices that his or her preferences are not transitive or in some other way do not conform to the V-M rationality conditions. For this to happen in the way I mean, it is not even necessary that the agent conceives of the problem as a failure to conform to certain general rules. Rather, he or she may observe that he or she prefers x to y and y to z but is indifferent between x and z and decide that that *makes no sense*. Inasmuch as the need for this kind of correction is often a live prospect, our explanations of the agent's choices may be enhanced by citing the utility rule, with its implicit or explicit reference to the V-M rationality conditions. But I think this falls far short of the explanatory power envisioned for the belief-desire law.

Why is there so much confusion about this? Why do people think that people's behavior can be explained by citing the utility rule? The answer, I suspect, is that they do not bear firmly in mind what we know about utility. They tend to think of utility as like money. Quantities of money are measurable quite apart from people's preferences. So in the case of a certain money-hungry sort of person, it might be genuinely explanatory on certain occasions to say that he or she prefers the action with the highest expected *monetary* value. Similarly, if it turns out that sensual pleasure is measurable independently of people's choices (by means of examining brain states, perhaps), then the actions of a certain sort of person might be explained on occasion by saying that he or she chooses the action with the highest expected *pleasure* value. But of course these explanations in terms of money and pleasure do not generalize. To generalize, one has to substitute the concept *utility* for the concepts *money* and *pleasure*. This substitution, as we have seen, spoils the explanation.

The utility rule, I conclude, is not the explanatory ideal of rational decision making that we are looking for. Consequently, we still have no rule for decision making that is definite, correct, and explanatory. But I assume that a rule of decision making would have to have all three of these properties if it were to serve as an ideal of rational decision making that the Lockean could cite as a psychological law in accounts of the nature of communication and thought or in a theory of interpretation. So the favorite example of those who believe in psychological laws utterly fails to live up to the demands the Lockean theory would place on it. So I think we should have little confidence that there are any psychological laws of the sort that the Lockean needs.

6

Reference

1. Why is the sentence "John is smart" true? A common answer is that "John" refers to some object o, "is smart" refers to some set S, and o belongs to S. In taking up the subject of reference, what I want to talk about is exclusively the sort of relation that figures into this sort of explanation of the truth of a sentence. Thus, the ostensive reference that consists in literally pointing at something and the kind of reference we are speaking of when we ask, "To whom were you referring a moment ago?" will be excluded if they are are not also the sort of relation that figures into the explanation of truth.

The relevance of the topic of reference to the question of the relation between thought and language is this: If there is anything right about the account of truth just illustrated, then reference must be, as I will say, a *real* relation. But if reference is a real relation, then it must be possible to explain in some way what reference really is. But any such account of reference is going to have to explain reference in terms of something else. Quite commonly, the necessary theory of reference is given in terms of thought. Thus an apparently important feature of language, namely, reference, is explained in terms of thought. So it will be difficult to hold both that reference is a real relation and that language is the very medium of a certain kind of thought. And it will be natural to explain other matters of language, such as communication, in terms of thought as well.

For some theorists, there is this further connection: If communication is to be explained as a matter of the hearer's comprehending the content of the speaker's message, then the nature of this *content* must be explained. For many theorists the concept of content is bound up with the concept of reference that figures into the explanation of truth. Content is that which together with circumstance yields reference (see chapter 3). More generally, content is something the comprehending of which enables one to determine the reference. The viability of these versions of the Lockean conception of communication, then, depends on the possibility of explaining what reference in this sense really is.

Here is what it means to say that reference is a real relation. Consider the following four pairs:

⟨the name "Socrates," the man Socrates⟩
⟨the sortal "chair," the set of chairs⟩
⟨the adjective "rouge," the set of red things⟩
⟨the sortal "basketball," the set of daffodils⟩

Is there some relation that holds between the members of the first pair, between the members of the second pair, and between the members of the third pair, but *not* between the members of the fourth pair? If so, does that same relation hold between indefinitely many other pairs that we can begin to list, but cannot finish listing, after the pattern of the first three, and yet not hold between indefinitely many other pairs that we can list after the pattern of the fourth? If so, and not otherwise, then reference is a real relation. I say that reference considered as a real relation holds between *indefinitely* many pairs like the first three because even after we have finished listing every word of every language that has ever been employed anywhere in the universe, we can go on to invent new names and new predicates, as many as we wish.

Here is why reference must be a real relation if truth is to be explained in terms of it. In proposing to explain truth, our assumption must be that truth is a real property. Thus, truth is a property that distinguishes a sentence such as "The earth is the third planet from the sun" and indefinitely many other sentences from a sentence such as "The earth is larger than the sun" and indefinitely many other sentences. So if truth is explicable in terms of reference, then reference must be a real relation. Only if reference is a real relation, distinguishing indefinitely many pairs from indefinitely many pairs, will we be able to cite it, in the manner illustrated above, in distinguishing indefinitely many true sentences from indefinitely many that are not true.

What could such a relation really be? Some philosophers are content to say that reference is a *primitive*. (I have heard this many times in conversation.) This is supposed to mean that we may cite it in explanations of things but it is not itself in need of explanation. We may identify the relation of reference by means of examples and in the same way explain the word "reference" to those who do not know English or do not know the philosophical usage. But no more is needed, because reference is a concept that anyone who reflects on language and communication will immediately recognize.

This is unacceptable. Outside of the theory of intentionality broadly defined, I know of nothing that is likewise regarded as absolutely primitive, that is, utterly inexplicable even in principle. One might as well say that *weight* is a primitive. Everyone knows what weight is, but the nature of weight calls for explanation nonetheless. The weight of an object *o* relative to a reference body *b* (normally the earth) is the gravitational force that *b* exerts on *o*. The terms of this explanation can be explained in turn. It is true that we cannot go on explaining the terms of our explanations, explaining the terms of *those* explanations, and so on, without eventually circling back. This means that no one can stand in need of such explanations of everything and that teaching cannot consist exclusively of such explanations, but it does not mean that there must be conceptual primitives. Reference, in particular, stands very much in need of explanation. It is necessary to explain what reference is, because it is not even obvious that such a relation exists. Some people might think that it is just intuitively obvious that reference is a real relation, but I do not know why I should accept their intuitions.

Perhaps they are thinking of the act of *pointing*. Pointing at something is certainly a real relation between the person who points and the object pointed to. So if we think of reference as like pointing, then it will seem intuitively obvious that reference is a real relation. Perhaps some words do function like pointed fingers, to draw the audience's attention in a certain direction. So-called indexicals, such as "that" and "I," might be such words. But if we think of referring as very like pointing, then referring will not be the fundamental word-world relation in terms of which we explain truth. The words in the sentence "Electrons have negative charge" do not literally point to their referents.

Or perhaps those who find the reality of reference just obvious are thinking of the fact that there is sometimes a perfectly good answer to a question like "Who were you referring to when you said . . . ?" But it is not obvious that reference in this sense is something in terms of which we can explain truth. When we answer the question, "Who were you referring to?" we know that we are to give some other description that better serves the listener's needs. If such talk of reference can be wholly explicated in terms of its role in mediating linguistic exchange in this way, then the fact that we speak of reference in this way will be little reason to believe in a relation of reference that explains truth.

If reference is a real relation, then it ought to be possible to spell out a *theory* of reference that explains to us what reference really is. So now I will survey some of the main ideas on which philosophers have hoped to construct theories of reference in order to decide whether any of them holds any promise. The upshot is going to be that, quite apart from any doubts about the Lockean theory, none of them holds any promise whatsoever. I will not attempt any sort of *reductio ad absurdum* on the very idea of reference.[1] Nor do I intend to develop a comprehensive critique of all the theories of reference that have ever been taken seriously.[2] I will merely try to say what I think is the main internal problem for each of the main ideas. In this way I hope to convey my despair

---

[1] Putnam (1980) has tried to construct such a *reductio*, but I think his argument is well refuted by Lewis (1984) and Devitt (1984). It is noteworthy that in a more recent exposition of the argument (1989) Putnam responds to Devitt not by articulating his *reductio* but simply by criticizing Devitt's own positive theory. This confirms my suspicion that the only viable way to criticize the reference idea is to criticize all substantive theories of reference that are put forward.

[2] One important type of theory that I will pass over without comment, except for this note, is that represented in Stampe 1979; Millikan 1984, 1986, 1989; and Dretske 1986, 1988. This is an approach that attempts to explain representation in terms of function, and function in peculiarly biological terms. My main problem with these sorts of theories is that I do not see how they might possibly account for representations beyond the sort that these authors attribute to lower organisms. For Dretske, the problem is that his learning theory extends only that far. For Millikan, the problem is that it is hard to believe that every representation has a biologically proper function in her sense. Millikan has an answer to this (1989, 291–94), but I do not understand it.

over the prospects for a theory of reference considered as a real relation. At the end I will indicate how we might conceive of reference other than as a real relation.

2. One theory of the reference relation, with which I will be brief, is the *description theory of reference*, associated with Frege ([1892] 1952) and Searle (1958). This is specifically a theory of the reference of proper names. According to the description theory, the reference of a proper name is explained by the fact that the proper name is associated with a certain description or with a loosely connected bundle of descriptions. Many believe that this theory was decisively refuted by Kripke (1972), who posed a variety of objections. Whether Kripke's objections are persuasive or not, the description theory cannot serve as the theory of reference we are seeking, since it presupposes an account of the reference of descriptions. The reference of "Franklin" might be whatever satisfies the description "the inventor of bifocals," but this explains the reference relation between "Franklin" and Franklin only on the assumption that we understand the reference relation between the word "inventor" and inventors and between the word "bifocals" and bifocals. A historical question I cannot answer is why the reference of proper names has been considered more problematic than the reference of predicates.[3]

A product of Kripke's criticisms of the description theory was the *causal theory* of reference, which has been brought to its fullest development by Michael Devitt (Devitt 1981; Devitt and Sterelny 1987). According to this theory, the utterance of a name refers to a certain object just in case the utterance is connected with that object by the right sort of *chain of events*. This theory is a departure from the description theory, because it turns out that the right sort of connection between a name and its referent might obtain without there being any uniquely identifying description associated with the name.

The problem posed by this causal theory is to say what the "right sort" of chain of events is. In order to solve this problem, Devitt and Sterelny (1987) advance what they call a *descriptive-causal* theory of reference, according to which the reference of a term depends on associated predications as well as on a chain of events leading from the term to the reference. The function of the predicates is to identify which of all the things that lie on the chain of events leading up to the utterance of the name is the referent. Thus the name "Nana" may refer to a whole cat and not just the head of a cat or a time-slice of a cat because a predicate such as "cat" or "animal" or "whole object" is associated with the name.

Along these lines, Devitt and Sterelny attempt to account for the reference of

---

[3] In the case of Russell at least (e.g., in [1912] 1959), part of the explanation is that the mind was supposed to be directly acquainted with universals, which could be treated as the referents of (some) predicates, whereas the mind could not be directly acquainted with the referent of a typical proper name.

predicates as well and thus to avoid begging the question in the way the pure description theory did. But in the case of predicates, as much as in the case of names, they cannot explain reference solely in terms of chains of events leading from referents to utterances, but must appeal also to associated predicates. Thus their account of the reference of any predicate will presuppose an understanding of the reference of some other predicate. So, as Devitt and Sterelny themselves admit (1987, 75), they do not have a comprehensive theory of reference at all.

A theory of reference that focuses first of all on predicates and sortals is what I will call the *correlation theory*. The basic idea is that a predicate F refers to a type of object O just in case that type O is the broadest class of objects such that we can say that O's reliably cause occurrences of F. It is quite clear to all that no such theory will directly account for the reference of spoken words. There is clearly no such relation of reliable causation *directly* between our words and their referents. Rather, any such theory will be first of all a theory of the reference of inner, mental representations that might be supposed to stand in the requisite causal relations. The reference of spoken words might then be explained, in Lockean fashion, as deriving from the reference of mental representations.

Fodor's theory of reference (1987, ch. 4), mentioned in chapter 3, is a theory of this sort. Fodor thinks of the theory as applying in the first instance to observation terms (in the mental language) such as RED and HORSE, and he basically ignores the fact that these observation terms can also be used in predictions and speculations and internal commands, and not only in reporting immediate observations. (In Fodor's usage, capitalized expressions refer to mental representations, and the English word chosen is supposed to indicate the meaning of that mental representation.) The theory applies first of all to observational applications of observation terms, because it is these that we can most readily suppose to be reliably caused by the sorts of things they refer to. Fodor believes that ultimately the theory does apply to other terms, such as PROTON, although in these other cases the causal pathways to the referents are less direct. In these other cases the causal pathway may include a number of mental representations, which intervene, as premises for inferences, between certain observations and certain conclusions that contain the term in question. Fodor thinks of his theory as providing only a sufficient condition, and not a necessary condition, for reference, but of course it is important that it be plausible that his theory gives a sufficient condition that is sometimes actually satisfied.

Any such theory faces at least these three problems:

1. Sometimes we misperceive things. So for any predicate F, referring to a class of things O, there is a class of things M, including things that do not all belong to O, such that M's more reliably cause occurrences of F than O's do. Fodor has tried to deal with this by means of his theory of *asymmetrical*

dependence, but this has been effectively criticized by Baker (1989), Godfrey-Smith (1989), Maloney (1990), and Seager (1993).[4]

2. Consider again how Fodor proposes to accommodate the fact that not all meaningful terms refer to observable types of objects. (I suppose that in somewhat the same way he would deal with the fact that even terms for observable types are not always used to report observations.) If O is not an observable type of thing, what kind of causal connection will there be between objects of that type and whatever mental term may refer to that type? Fodor's idea is that in such cases the causal connection is mediated by a chain of *inferences* that begins with observations. These observations may not be observations of O's as such (for example, protons) but may be observations of circumstances indicative of the presence of O's (for example, vapor trails). The trouble is that an essential kind of inference, namely, ampliative inference, requires *hypotheses*, and these hypotheses are often not themselves *inferentially* connected with observations. This is not to say that these hypotheses come from nothing, but their causation may be indefinitely heterogenous, in which case it is pointless to look for a theory of their causation as such. So it is not clear how one might specify the conditions under which one could expect the sort of inference to take place that Fodor's theory requires. And it is important to specify the conditions under which it should take place, because it certainly will not always take place, even given suitable sorts of observational inputs, and the fact that it does not always take place should not imply that the term in question has no reference.

3. The correlation theory explains reference in terms of reliable causation. But what does it mean to say that O's reliably cause occurrences of F? I suppose that this means at least that (i) leaving aside misperceptions and other misapplications of F, an occurrence of F will always have an O among its causes. But does it mean also that (ii) if an O is present to the senses (or, as Fodor says, if an O causes psychophysical traces to which the organism is in an optimal relation), then it will probably cause an occurrence of F? Suppose (ii) is *not* entailed. In that case, every term (to which the theory applies) will refer to the class of all objects whatsoever, since for any term F the broadest class of objects O such that (i) is true is the class of all objects whatsoever. This is not problem 1 all over again, because it does not depend on the fact of misapplications of terms. Suppose (ii) *is* entailed. Then whenever I am looking at a rectangle, a mental

---

[4] Fodor 1990 contains a reply to Baker. But in this later paper Fodor employs a notion of *nomic dependence*, which he makes no attempt to define. What he says about nomic dependence is just what one might say about representation. For example, the nomic dependence of "cat" on the occurrence of small dogs in bad lighting is dependent on the nomic dependence of "cat" on cats just because the use of "cat" to refer to small dogs depends on the use of "cat" to refer to cats. Far from stating any substantive theory of representation, Fodor merely dresses up a number of platitudes about representation in the language of nomic dependence. The criticisms by Baker and the others all succeed as well as they do only inasmuch as their authors suppose that Fodor has some definite kind of relation in mind other than representation as such.

representation must very probably occur in me meaning something like, "There's a rectangle." So when I am looking at a brick wall consisting of hundreds of rectangular bricks, I must think in response to each one, "There's a rectangle." That might not be so implausible if we think of the mental representation as something like a *sensory* response to the brick wall or even if we think of it as something like a sensory response of which we are in some sense aware. When I look at a brick wall, it is indeed possible for me to be aware of all the bricks that I am seeing. But a sensory response, even one of which I am aware, is not itself a predication. It is not a classification of something *as* something. So it is not the sort of representation for which we are trying to find a reference relation.

Perhaps the problem with the correlation theory is that it attempts to account for reference piecemeal. That is, it attempts to explain the reference of a word without taking into account the relation between that word and other words. A theory of reference that attempts to avoid this error is Davidson's (1977). Davidson comes as close as anyone to denying that reference is a real relation without denying it altogether. His theory begins with his conception of empirical theories of truth, which I briefly explained in the previous chapter. According to Davidson, reference is to be understood as a theoretical relation postulated in the course of developing an empirical theory of truth for a language. In terms of reference one may state a finite number of axioms from which an infinite number of T-sentences may be inferred. For instance, from the fact that "Socrates" refers to Socrates and "snub-nosed" refers to the class of snub-nosed things and that in general a sentence of the form "x is F" is true in English if and only if the thing that x refers to belongs to the class that F refers to, it follows that "Socrates is snub-nosed" is true in English if and only if Socrates belongs to the class of snub-nosed things, that is, he is snub-nosed. According to Davidson, we understand everything there is to understand about reference in L in understanding the role the concept of reference plays in such a theory of truth for L.

It is important to distinguish between Davidson's theory of reference and what Davidson would call a theory of reference *for L*. Davidson's theory of reference is what I have explained in the previous paragraph. A theory of reference *for L*, by contrast, is a product of the interpretation of L. A theory of reference for L might, if the vocabulary of L is finite, be merely a *list* that tells us, for each nonlogical constant of L, what the constant refers to. If Davidson's theory of reference were confused with such a theory of reference for L, then it might seem unclear whether reference on Davidson's theory is a real relation at all, for a finite list of nonlogical constants and their referents would not qualify as a theory of reference considered as a real relation. In fact, Davidson intends to be a realist about reference (even if his account of it might strike some as instrumentalistic).

On Davidson's conception of reference, there must be some way to confirm the *T*-sentences apart from an independent account of reference. His account of this is the account of the confirmation of empirical theories of truth that I sketched in the previous chapter in discussing his theory of interpretation. Thus my doubt about Davidson's theory of reference is the same as my doubt about his theory of interpretation. The theory seems to rest on some more fundamental conception of the nature of interpretation that is not explained. My doubt about Davidson's conception of reference is whether we will find any place left for a conception of reference as a real relation when we have finished explaining that more fundamental conception.

3. There is a long tradition in philosophy of trying to understand linguistic representation by means of an analogy with cartographical representation (Wittgenstein [1921] 1963; Sellars 1963d, 1979; Rosenberg 1974). This has seemed to be a useful strategy inasmuch as the relation between maps and what they map seems fairly easy to explain. Roughly, if one were to enlarge a map (according to a certain projection), then the map could be laid over the terrain that it maps in such a way that each point on the map would actually lie above the point on the terrain that it represents. With the advent of cognitive science, this conception of representations as like maps has been latched onto by many as a way of understanding *mental* representation. One virtue of this approach is that, unlike some of the approaches to reference considered so far, it seems to acknowledge that the reference of one representation depends on that representation's relation to others. A mark on a map successfully represents a given point on the terrain only if the mark on the map stands in relations to other marks on the map that the corresponding points on the terrain stand in to one another.

No one supposes that mental representations are very like maps. For one thing, mental representations change over time as a result of changes in the environment. An improvement over the map analogy might be an analogy to a computer simulation of the weather. A computer simulation of the weather represents the weather by virtue of some kind of *structural isomorphism* between what goes on in the computer and what goes on in the atmosphere and at the surface of the earth. Similarly, one might suppose, the mind performs *computations* on *symbols*, and these computations are *isomorphic* to processes in the world. This isomorphism determines a mapping from the symbols onto things in the world, and this mapping is the reference relation. Call this the *isomorphism theory of reference for mental representations*. Theories of this sort have been proposed by a large number of authors representing various disciplines, including Palmer (1978), Haugeland (1985), Cummins (1989, ch. 8), Newell (1990, §2.3), Perner (1991, ch. 2), and Gallistel (1992).

Before I can criticize the isomorphism theory of reference, I must try to define it more precisely. To this end, I need to say something more about the relation between truth and reference. As I illustrated at the start of this chapter, the truth of a sentence is supposed to be explicable in terms of the reference of its constituent terms. Here are some examples:

- "The earth is larger than the moon" is true because "the earth" refers to an object o_1, "the moon" refers to an object o_2, and "is larger than" refers to a set of pairs S and $\langle o_1, o_2 \rangle \in S$.
- "John is smart" is true because "John" refers to an object o, "is smart" refers to a set S of one-tuples, and $\langle o \rangle \in S$. (Notice that for uniformity with the previous case, I now say that "is smart" refers to a set of one-tuples, not that it refers to a set of objects.)
- "All pangolins are mammals" is true, because "pangolins" refers to a set S_1, "mammals" refers to a certain set S_2, and $S_1 \subseteq S_2$.
- If "Every boy loves some girl" were true, then that would be because "boy" referred to a set S_1, "girl" referred to a set S_2, "loves" referred to a set of pairs S_3, and if any object o_1 were such that $\langle o_1 \rangle \in S_1$, then there would be an object o_2 such that $\langle o_2 \rangle \in S_2$ and $\langle o_1, o_2 \rangle \in S_3$.

Each of these explanations is wholly structural. That is to say, given the referents of each of the nonlogical terms, the truth of the sentence depends only on certain set-theoretic relations between them. (Logical terms are terms like "all" and "not." Nonlogical terms are terms like "John" and "mammal.") For instance, the truth of "All pangolins are mammals" does not depend on the fact that it is specifically mammals that "mammals" refers to, but only on the fact that whatever "mammals" refers to, the set that "pangolins" refers to is a subset of it.

Here I have assumed that the reference of a singular term is an object and that the reference of an n-place predicate is a set of n-tuples. The theory of reference could be formulated differently. For instance, one might suppose that the reference of a predicate is a *property* (where properties are conceived as different from sets). So for instance, the reference of the predicate "is green" would not, in this case, be the set of (one-tuples containing) green things, but the property of *being green*. I believe that the ensuing discussion could be reformulated to suit any of the usual approaches, but for definiteness I will continue to assume that a term refers to either an individual object or a set of n-tuples.

One important fact that I have not mentioned so far is that reference is relative to certain *parameters*. For instance, reference is relative to *time of utterance*. Thus, the set of things that the tensed predicate "is now hungry" refers to at time t is the set of (one-tuples containing) creatures that are hungry at t, and not the set of (one-tuples containing) creatures that are hungry at some other time. That is why "John is now hungry" and "John is not now hungry" may both be true, at different times. Further, reference is relative to other features of the context of utterance, such as who is speaking. Thus "I am sick" may be true if said by John but not true if said by Mary, because when John says it, "I" refers to John, and when Mary says it, "I" refers to Mary. In addition, reference is usually supposed to be relative to *possible world*. Thus, we may say that "Possibly p" is true in the *actual* world if p is true in some *possible* world. By a *parameter* I mean a specification of all the various variables to which reference is relative. For instance, a parameter may specify a time, a speaker, and a world. (As I have explained it, reference is a parameter-relative relation between *words* and things, not between *utterances*, i.e., tokens of words, and things. But a token of a word may also be said to refer to what the word refers to at the parameter pertinent to that token. Accordingly, I need not try to be careful about the type/token distinction in what follows.)

If the truth of a sentence is explicable in terms of reference, then we should find that a possibly different class of sentences consists of those that *would have been* true if the basic vocabulary of the language had referred to different things. For instance, given that "John" refers to some object o, "is smart" refers to some set S, and o belongs to S, we may conclude that "John is smart" is true. But if "John" had referred to this chair and "is smart" had referred to the class of sparrows, then since this chair is not a sparrow, "John is smart" would be false. Thus we are led to the concept of *truth on an interpretation*. By an *interpretation*, I mean a parameter-relative assignment of objects to terms that mimics the reference relation in the sense that if the term refers to a single object, then the interpretation assigns a (possibly different) single object to that term, and if the term refers to a set of n-tuples, then the interpretation assigns a (possibly different) set of n-tuples to that term. Suppose, further, that the meanings of the logical terms of L are fixed. We may conclude that if reference explains truth (at a parameter), then likewise an interpretation determines a class of sentences that would be true (at a parameter) if what that interpretation assigns to each term were what that term actually referred to (at that parameter). We may say that those sentences are true on that interpretation (at that parameter).

Now I can define what I mean by a *model* for a set of sentences. A *model* for a set A of sentences of L, at a parameter, is an interpretation of L such that at that parameter every member of A is true on that interpretation. (So a single interpretation, which makes an assignment for each parameter, may be a model for a given set of sentences at one parameter but not at another.) Now, the advocate of the isomorphism theory of reference for mental representations is going to assume that mental representations are structured like sentences in a mental language of some kind. So we may likewise speak of a model for a set of *mental representations* at a parameter. Further, the advocate of the isomorphism theory of reference for mental representation is going to assume that each belief is tokenwise identical to some mental representation. So we may assume that a set of beliefs is a certain set of mental representations. So we may likewise speak of a model for a set of beliefs at a parameter.

Let a *history of belief* for a given thinker be a sequence $\langle B_1, B_2, \ldots, B_n \rangle$ of sets of mental representations such that (i) for each B_i in the sequence, the membership of B_i consists of the thinker's beliefs at a certain moment in time i, and

(ii) every change in what the thinker believes may be represented as a transition from some B_i to B_{i+1}. Define a *dynamic model M* for a given history of belief as an interpretation such that for all i, $0 < i \leq n$, M is a model for B_i at the parameter pertinent to B_i (that is, in the thinker's world, at the time of B_i, and so on). Although the thinker may at one time believe that he is hungry and at a later time believe that he is not hungry, M may be a model for both of these beliefs, since they are associated with different parameters.

I do not suppose that the proponent of the isomorphism theory of reference would expect to find an isomorphism between a thinker's beliefs and the world if that thinker's beliefs were wildly mistaken. The proponent of the isomorphism theory might say that to the extent that the beliefs we would attribute would be false, it is doubtful whether the creature in question has beliefs at all. Alternatively, the isomorphism theorist might say that these false beliefs, even among mostly false beliefs, do qualify as beliefs, but only by virtue of their formal, or structural, relations to the beliefs of someone else whose beliefs are mostly true. But consider the special case of an ideal thinker whose beliefs are always exclusively true beliefs. Call such a thinker a *true believer*. If a true believer is possible, then the isomorphism theory of reference must apply to the mental representations of such a creature. If the isomorphism theory of reference fails in this case, then it fails altogether. So if a true believer is possible, it is fair to confine our attention to such a case. One might question whether a true believer is really possible. Will not any finite mind be subject to error if sensory inputs are misleading? Perhaps. But that does not mean that a true believer is impossible. It only means that a true believer can only be found in an environment that is well suited to his or her belief-forming dispositions.

Now I can state the isomorphism theory of reference for the mental representations as it pertains to true believers: *the reference relation is a dynamic model for the history of the true believer's beliefs.* Here is why this theory deserves to be called an *isomorphism* theory of reference: If the reference relation is a dynamic model for a history of belief, then the syntactic properties of beliefs (conceived as representations in a mental language) correspond to certain select set-theoretic relations between referents. For instance, if any belief at a parameter w has the form "All F are G," then $M(w, F)$ must be a subset of $M(w, G)$. (Technically speaking, however, this is not an isomorphism, because two different mental words might have the same reference. It is not even a homomorphism, for even if every pertinent set-theoretic relation between referents corresponds to some syntactic property of the set of *truths*, not every pertinent set-theoretic relation between referents need correspond to a syntactic property of *beliefs*.) Notice that this account of the isomophism theory of reference gives it a head start by allowing that the logical terms of the language of mental representation are identifiable, and their meanings determinable, quite apart from the determination of the reference relation.

Now I can state my initial criticism of the isomorphism theory of reference

for mental representations. It is that indefinitely many wildly incorrect interpretations of the thinker's language of mental representation will qualify as
dynamic models for the history of the true believer's beliefs. For instance, if in
fact Chicago is the referent of a certain mental designator a, then some dynamic
model of the believer's history of beliefs will assign to a the Pacific Ocean. If in
fact the class of chairs is the referent of a certain mental predicate F, then some
dynamic model of the believer's history of beliefs will assign to the mental
predicate F some subset of the class of green things. Say that the *domain* of an
interpretation is the set of objects from which the interpretation draws in assigning objects to mental designators and in forming n-tuples assigned to mental
predicates. Let π be a one-to-one function from the domain of M into some set
of objects (not necessarily the same as the domain of M). If x is an individual
object, say that $\Pi(x) = \pi(x)$, and if x is a set of n-tuples, say that $\Pi(x) = \{\langle y_1, y_2,$
$\ldots, y_n \rangle \mid \langle z_1, z_2, \ldots, z_n \rangle \in x$ and $\pi(z_1) = y_1, \pi(z_2) = y_2, \ldots,$ and $\pi(z_n) =$
$y_n\}$ (that is, the set of n-tuples that results from simultaneously substituting $\pi(z)$
for z wherever it occurs in x). Then if M is a dynamic model for a thinker's
history of beliefs, then so is ΠM (where $\Pi M(x) = y$ if and only if $\Pi(M(x)) = y$).
This is a consequence of the fact that the explanation of truth in terms of
reference is "wholly structural" in the sense I explained above. What it means is
that the isomorphism theory of reference so badly underdescribes the reference
relation that it cannot count as a theory of reference at all.

   The isomorphism theorist might reply that an integral feature of the isomorphism theory is the idea that the *processes* by which beliefs change correspond
to processes in the world. Let us try to characterize this idea more precisely.
What a person comes to believe at time $t + 1$ will depend on at least two factors,
namely, what the person believed at time t and the person's sensory inputs at t.
So let us think of the process of belief change as a function Rev from beliefs and
sensory inputs into beliefs. Since a person's beliefs may depend on *any* of his or
her sensory inputs, we should think of the sensory input to Rev as in some sense
complete. Of course, there is no guarantee that if a person's beliefs are exclusively true and that person then has additional sensory experiences, then that
person will continue to believe only truths. Again, some sorts of experiences
may be misleading. But we may perhaps suppose that certain types of sensory
input will not be misleading relative to a given set of prior true beliefs and that in
that case the output of Rev will again be a set of exclusively true beliefs.

   Say that a set of beliefs B_j is a *revision* of a set of beliefs B_i if and only if either
(i) for some sensory input σ that is not misleading relative to B_i, $Rev(\sigma, B_i) =$
B_j, or (ii) for some revision B_k of B_i and some σ not misleading relative to B_k,
$Rev(\sigma, B_k) = B_j$. Say that the *belief tree* for a given thinker is a set Θ of sets of
beliefs such that (i) there is exactly one set of beliefs in Θ such that every other
member of Θ is a revision of that one (the root) and (ii) if B_i is a member of Θ
and σ is a set of sensory inputs that is not misleading relative to B_i, then $Rev(\sigma,$
$B_i)$ is a member of Θ as well. In other words, a belief tree represents all of the

various possible histories of belief that a true believer might follow, in accordance with *Rev*, given different possible histories of sensory experience. (I am assuming that a true believer's possible histories are represented by a unique belief tree and thus that for each true believer there is at most one set of beliefs with which that believer might begin, namely, the root. If that is not correct, then we might define a *belief forest* as a set of belief trees and continue the argument with belief forests in place of belief trees.)

Say that a *branch* of a belief tree is a subset of a belief tree such that (i) that subset contains the root of the tree and (ii) for each set B_i in the subset there is exactly one set B_j in the subset such that for some σ not misleading relative to B_i, $Rev(\sigma, B_i) = B_j$. If B_i is a member of a given branch in a belief tree, and $Rev(\sigma_1, B_i) = B_j$ and $Rev(\sigma_2, B_i) = B_k$ and $B_j \neq B_k$, then B_j and B_k do not both belong to that branch. In other words, the branches of a belief tree divide where *Rev* yields different sets of beliefs from a single set of beliefs given two (or more) different sensory inputs. Since σ_1 and σ_2 are both supposed to be complete, they cannot both be actual. So different branches belong to different possible worlds. In other words, if a given branch describes a thinker's history of belief in a given possible world, then any other branch can describe that same thinker's history of belief only in some other possible world.

Define a *branching dynamic model M* for a given belief tree as an interpretation such that for all belief sets B_i in the tree, M is a model for B_i at every parameter pertinent to B_i. Because different branches describe different possible worlds, if belief sets B_j and B_k belong to distinct branches, then the parameter at which M must be a model for B_j must be distinct from the parameter at which M must be a model for B_k. If a belief set lies on the intersection of two branches, then there are two parameters pertinent to it, corresponding to those two branches, and M must be a model for that belief set at both parameters.

An improved version of the isomorphism theory as it pertains to true believers may now be stated as follows: *The reference relation is a branching dynamic model for the true believer's belief tree.* This version expresses the desired additional constraint, namely, that the processes by which beliefs change must correspond to processes in the world, for the belief tree, taken as a whole, represents the processes by which the true believer's beliefs change. More precisely, it represents those processes insofar as given nonmisleading sensory inputs, those processes preserve truth. We need not represent those processes insofar as given *misleading* sensory inputs, they do not preserve truth, for when they do not preserve truth, they do not correspond to processes in the world. We need not represent those processes insofar as given *non*-misleading sensory inputs, they do not preserve truth, for, by hypothesis, a true believer does not form beliefs in that way.

This second version of the isomorphism theory does indeed meet my earlier objection. Here we cannot object that if M is a dynamic model for a history of beliefs, then so is ΠM, for not every dynamic model of a true believer's history of beliefs represents the reference relation for the true believer's beliefs. In order to qualify as a representation of the reference relation an interpretation must be a *branching* dynamic model. Nonetheless, an exactly parallel objection can still be made. Suppose that M is a branching dynamic model for the true believer's belief tree. Then so is ΠM. So again the theory does not put a significant constraint on the reference relation.

Perhaps a proponent of the isomorphism theory will try to strengthen the requirements on the process of belief revision. The process, it might be said, must not only preserve truth given nonmisleading sensory inputs. Rather, the changes in the world to which the changes in belief correspond must instantiate *laws of nature*. But on any plausible conception of laws of nature this requirement is simply too strong. Suppose I believe that there is no dog behind me. Then I seem to hear a dog bark behind me (that is, I have an auditory experience like that which would be caused by a dog barking behind me), and I come to believe that there is a dog behind me. This is quite reasonable. It is the sort of transition that ought to be an instance of *Rev* if any is. But is it a law of nature that whenever I seem to hear a dog barking behind me there will be a dog behind me? Surely not.

Here is a different reply: The sets into which most of these branching dynamic models will map the predicates of the mental language will be completely unnatural, indefinitely Goodmanesque groupings of things, whereas what the isomorphism theorist means to say is that a reference relation is determined by an isomorphism between mental representations and *natural* groupings. But what is a natural grouping? Loose talk about "carving nature at the joints" is no answer! Loose talk about "real properties" or "properties in the world" is no answer either. If S is a set, then why should the property of belonging to S not qualify as a "real property"? Even if it is not the case that for *every* set there is some one property such that that set is *the* set of things possessing that property, some properties will characterize some very heterogenous sets. Being green is a property. So is being six-sided. So is not being six-sided. So is being either green or not six-sided. And so on. So even if we confine ourselves to sets defined by properties, there will be enough sets to define some very nonstandard models. In chapter 1, I explained why it will not do to try to define natural categories as those whose members are objectively similar. The only general way I know of to define the natural categories is to define them as those that we are disposed to represent. But that is not an answer that we can use when we are trying to appeal to natural categories in order to constrain a theory of representation.

A different way of conceiving of the natural categories is to conceive of them as the categories that emerge in the course of doing science. They are the types that we must postulate in order to make scientific sense of the world. I would not try to show that this way of conceiving of the natural categories begs our question. By the same token, natural categories so conceived are not the only ones we must recognize in order to identify the reference relation. On any very narrow understanding of "science," such categories as *green* and *house* will not qualify. And if "science" is interpreted so broadly that every natural category is a scientific category, then a question that arises with the same force as the question we started with is, What is a scientific category?

In denying that we can appeal to a distinction between natural and unnatural groupings in a theory of reference, I am by no means denying that any such distinction can be objectively drawn. But an adequate account of categorization, I hold, is impossible apart from a theory of language and communication. So the distinction between natural and unnatural categories must be drawn in light of a theory of language and communication as well. That the distinction can only be drawn in this way is not something I am assuming at this point, but it is something I want to state at this point so that the reader will not misunderstand my intentions.

Another overly easy reply to my objection is that in order to qualify as the reference relation, an interpretation may assign to mental designators only those objects that stand in certain relations to those designators in addition to the isomorphism. But it is certainly not enough to say that the things that the mental designators refer to must be things in the thinker's environment that the thinker *interacts* with (see Pylyshyn 1984, 44). One has to say how the reference relation depends on interactions with the environment. Otherwise my objection will still go through. For instance, one might say that the things that mental representations refer to must be causes of the mental representations that refer to them. But in fact that particular theory is either vacuous or false. One can certainly think of things that do not very directly cause one's thoughts. For instance, I can think of the carbon atoms in the table on which Thomas Jefferson signed the Declaration of Independence. I cannot demonstrate a priori that no such constraints will do the job, but I very much suspect that the search for such constraints will only lead to one of the sorts of theories I have already surveyed and set aside (such as the correlation theory).

Perhaps it has been obvious all along to all proponents of the isomorphism theory of representation that smallish systems of representations could be placed in various isomorphisms to objects in the world. But I suspect that some have imagined that for very large systems, such as might make up a mind, the alternatives would be limited to a few definite kinds all but one of which could then be ruled out by adding a few additional constraints on the theory. For instance, we might rule out a purely numerical interpretation of the system by requiring that the system causally interact with the objects that it represents. The significance of my spelling out of the objection is that it makes quite clear that mere isomorphism in the intended sense, no matter how large the system, does almost nothing to pin down the reference relation. So a few trivial constraints in addition to the requirement of isomorphism are not going to suffice to determine a reference relation for mental representations either.

As I noted at the start of this discussion of the isomorphism theory of mental representation, its attraction is that it seems to be supported by an analogy with computer simulations, such as computer simulations of the weather. Now that we have seen how the isomorphism theory fails, we can accept the following account of the difference between a computer simulation and a mind (I do not think this stands as an objection all by itself): A computer simulation of the weather is no such thing apart from our capacity to interpret it. Unless the program is run and the output is displayed in a form that we can read, such as numbers in a table with headings in English or weather maps on a screen, then the program is at most a *potential* simulation. But a mind, as proponents of the isomorphism theory conceive of it, is supposed to be something that can be said to represent the world quite independently of anyone's *taking* it to represent the world.

4. If truth is to be explained in terms of reference, then reference must be a real relation. If reference is conceived to be a real relation, then a theory of reference, considered as a real relation, is necessary. But I despair over the prospects for such a theory of reference. So I am inclined to think that it is a mistake to think that truth is explicable in terms of reference. But how could it fail to be? We need some kind of alternative.

An alternative is to give a *metalinguistic* theory of truth and reference. To understand what this means, consider the distinction between explaining what an *electron* is, on the one hand, and explaining what the logical operation of *disjunction* is, on the other. An explanation of the nature of electrons will involve explaining the relations they bear to other basic particles and how these particles and their relations together result in the grosser properties of matter. An explanation of disjunction, by contrast, will be an explanation of the function of the English word "or" and words that in other languages function in the way "or" does in English. Thus the explanation of disjunction is metalinguistic in the sense that while the question about disjunction is not immediately phrased as a question about words, the answer can only take the form of an explanation about words. In the same sense, our theory of truth and reference might be metalinguistic. In place of explaining truth per se, we will explain something about the word "true." In place of explaining reference, we will explain something about the word "refers." In both cases, what we will explain is how sentences containing the word may be correctly used.

Here, for instance, is a very simple and probably inadequate metalinguistic theory of truth. The theory says that what we have to understand about truth is just the valid inference rules governing the use of the word "true," and they are as follows: 1. From p infer "p is true." 2. From "p is true" infer p. This particular metalinguistic theory of truth is one version of the "redundancy theory of truth," which was put forward by F. P. Ramsey ([1927] 1965), although he did not formulate it in quite this way. Other varieties of metalinguistic theory have been discussed in the literature as well.[5] One problem with the redundancy theory is that it rests on an unexplained notion of a valid rule of inference, and the usual way of explaining validity is in terms of truth (see chapter 7).

It is pointless to try to develop a metalinguistic theory of truth and reference apart from some broader conception of the nature of language. Only in the context of some broader conception will it be possible to say what sort of the thing the *correct use* of a word is, and thus only in such a context will it be possible to explain the correct use of words such as "true" and "refers." Further, only in the context of that broader conception of language would it be possible to answer the various objections to taking a metalinguistic approach. In part B, I will try to provide some of the basic elements of an alternative conception of language, but I will not go so far as to develop a metalinguistic theory of truth and reference.

In endorsing the metalinguistic approach, I do not deny that there are word-world relations. *No doubt there are word-world relations.* For instance, my catching a glimpse of a moose in the forest may make me say, "Yow, there's a moose!" My own positive account of language in part B focuses very directly on certain sorts of word-world relations. What I deny is only that any of those word-world relations is a relation of reference in terms of which truth might be explained. Moreover, I do not even deny that every sort of relation that might be called "reference" is truly a relation between words and the world. But none of those real reference relations is a relation in terms of which truth might be explained.

In giving up the idea of explaining reference as a real relation, however, I am indeed giving up on the idea of explaining what the pairs ⟨"Socrates," Socrates⟩, ⟨"chair," chairs⟩, and ⟨"rouge," red things⟩ have in common that the pair ⟨"basketball," daffodils⟩ lacks. If we ask what the first three of these pairs have in common that the last one lacks, then the answer, I am suggesting, is really *nothing*. Assuming that our theory of reference must be metalinguistic, the most we will be able to say is that such *sentences* as "'Socrates' refers to Socrates," "'rouge' refers to red things," and so on, have something in common.

---

[5] A different sort of metalinguistic theory is Grover's prosentential theory (Grover, Camp, and Belnap 1975), which Brandom (1984) has attempted to extend to reference. One problem with this is that it does not give a very satisfactory account of the truth of sentences in languages other than the language of the prosentence. The simple theory stated here may be usefully compared with Paul Horwich's (1990) theory of truth and reference. The main difference between Horwich's theory and the theory stated here is that while the latter theory is metalinguistic in my sense, Horwich resists the metalinguistic construal of his theory of truth (as concerned not with the nature of truth but with the word "true"). The problem with that resistance is that it forces him to take the position that a theory may be infinitely long. In logic it is commonplace to refer to infinite sets of sentences as "theories," but these are not theories in the sense of something one might defend against objections. For further metalinguistic approaches to reference, see Hill 1987 and Gauker 1990b, 438–39.

7

Validity

1. I have two reasons for including a chapter on the nature of logical validity. First, the usual conception of logical validity indirectly lends support to the Lockean conception of communication. That is because theories of reference, as I explained in chapter 6, lead to the Lockean theory, and one of the main sources of the idea that the concept of reference must play some kind of foundational role in our understanding of language is a certain venerable theory of logical validity. My second reason is that one of the main features of my alternative conception of language is a new theory of logical validity, which I present in chapter 12 and which disagrees with the usual conception of validity. My theory of validity is new not only in that it defines validity in novel terms but also in that it validates a different class of arguments from the usual. As preparation for my own theory of validity, therefore, it is necessary in this critical half of the book to criticize the standard conception of validity. In light of my first reason for discussing validity, the first thing I need to do is explain how adoption of the usual theory of validity commits one to a conception of reference as a real relation. For both of my reasons, I will then try to undercut this conception of reference by criticizing that theory of validity. (This discussion presupposes familiarity with elementary logic.)

In what I call *standard semantics*, the validity of arguments is defined in terms of *parameter-relative interpretations* of the language. A *parameter* is a set of indices of some kind. In the standard semantics for modal logic, a parameter will include a possible world; in tense logic, a parameter will include a time; and in the logic of demonstratives, a parameter will include a context of utterance (which in turn may contain several factors). An *interpretation* of the language L is a function the inputs to which are pairs consisting of a parameter and either an individual constant (name), a predicate, or a sentence of L. In other words, an interpretation is a parameter-relative assignment of things to individual constants, predicates, and sentences of L. (For simplicity, I am ignoring other sorts of expression, such as function terms.) To each individual constant at a parameter, an interpretation assigns an individual object from a given domain for that interpretation. To each n-ary predicate at a parameter the interpretation assigns a set of n-tuples of objects from the domain. Further, to each sentence of L at a parameter, an interpretation assigns a *truth-value*. This assignment of truth-values to sentences at a parameter is defined inductively using the grammatical sentence-forming operations of L. The basis for the induction is the assignment of individuals to individual constants at a parameter and sets of n-tuples to n-ary predicates at a parameter. The upshot is that the truth-value an interpretation assigns to a sentence at a parameter is a function of what that interpretation assigns to the individual constants and the predicates at that parameter. The sentences said to be *true on an interpretation* (at a parameter) are those to which the interpretation assigns the value *Truth* (at that parameter).

The standard semantical definition of validity may now be given as follows: An argument in language L is *valid* if and only if for every interpretation I of L and every parameter w, if all of the premises are true on I at w, then the conclusion is true on I at w as well.[1] The usual definition of validity for classical first-order logic omits to mention the parameter w, since it plays no role in that kind of logic, but of course it can be added as a useless frill.

For later use, let us observe here that as a consequence of the inductive manner in which interpretations are defined, every standard semantics will have the following property: For any two interpretations I and J, if for every sentential component c of a sentence s and every parameter w, c is true on I at w if and only if c is true on J at w, then likewise s is true on I at w if and only if s is true on J at w. To express this property in a simpler fashion, define an *intension* as a function from the parameters into truth-values. Then we may think of an interpretation as a function from sentences into intensions, and the property that every standard semantics will have is that the intension assigned to a sentence must be a function of the intensions assigned to its sentential components.[2]

Suppose we think of the standard semantical account of validity as the right way to define validity for the formal languages under study and think of those formal languages as approximating to natural languages, which are what ulti-

---

[1] This is not quite general enough for my purposes. I wish to define standard semantics in such a way that many-valued logics may also qualify as varieties of standard semantics. To generalize, say that a standard semantics defines a valid argument as one such that for every interpretation I of L and every parameter w, if all of the premises have *designated values* on I at w, then the conclusion has a designated value on I at w as well.

[2] Some theories might have to be reformulated if they are to be viewed as varieties of standard semantics as here defined. Moreover, I am using "intension" in a broader sense than usual. David Kaplan (1989) defines an *intension*, which he also calls a *content*, as a function from possible worlds (or possible worlds and times) to extensions (truth-values in the case of sentences) and thinks of an interpretation as assigning to each formula what he calls a *character*, which is a function from what he calls *contexts* to contents. This distinction between contents and characters is important to him for purposes of drawing various semantic distinctions. But each of the sorts of validity that he defines can be formulated in terms of intensions in my sense. The general schema for definitions of validity (for sentences) in terms of intensions (in my sense) is this: p is a valid sentence if and only if it is assigned the same intension on every interpretation, namely, the intension that yields Truth at every parameter. This is equivalent to Kaplan's definition of validity in the logic of demonstratives (547) if parameters are contexts in his sense (543). It is equivalent to Kaplan's definition of validity in the "neo-traditional" sense (549) if parameters are pairs consisting of a world and a time.

mately interest us. In that case, we will suppose that validity in natural languages too may be understood in terms of interpretations that postulate relations between elementary vocabulary items and objects or sets of n-tuples of objects in a domain. And in that case it seems to me almost inevitable that we will suppose that for any natural language L there is one special interpretation, call it the *intended* interpretation, such that truth in L on that interpretation (at w) is truth *simpliciter* in L (at w). The intended interpretation will be *the* interpretation such that (i) the domain includes every actual individual (and, in some versions of standard semantics, every *possible* individual as well) and (ii) what the assignment assigns to each name and predicate (relative to w) is what that name or predicate *really refers* to in L (at w). Standard semantics, we may say, is committed to there being an intended interpretation for L that *represents* the reference relation as it pertains to L. In this way, standard semantics is committed to the idea that truth in a language L may be defined in terms of the reference relation as it pertains to L.

In short, it seems to me almost inevitable that the reference relation as it pertains to a given language will be viewed as a special case of the sort of interpretation in terms of which truth on an interpretation is defined. But why is this almost inevitable? The answer is that otherwise there will be no way to explain why the account of validity in terms of truth on an interpretation should be thought of as explaining what a valid argument really is. The reason to think that the explanation of validity in terms of truth on an interpretation captures validity per se is this: What a valid argument really is is an argument having premises the truth of which in some sense guarantees the truth of the conclusion without regard for the meaning of the nonlogical words.[3] The definition of validity in terms of truth on an interpretation is supposed to capture this idea by telling us that the truth of the premises guarantees the truth of the conclusion no matter how we vary the interpretation of the nonlogical terms, that is, the assignment of objects to names and of sets to predicates. But varying the assignment can be thought of as abstracting from the meaning only if we think of one such assignment as *giving* the meaning (in some sense of "meaning"). The only way I can think of to understand such an assignment as giving the meaning is to think of it as assigning to each name and predicate what it really refers to.

Moreover, what standard semantics is committed to is a *real* reference relation. The reference relation required by standard semantics is not the sort of

---

[3] I do not need to suppose that this captures, even in an imprecise way, every kind of logical validity. For instance, the following argument is valid in some sense but not in the present sense: "x is red; therefore, x is colored." I need only suppose that the present characterization captures *formal* validity, since that is the only kind that standard semantics is supposed to define. Etchemendy (1990) has argued that this conception captures no kind of validity, but close inspection of his argument reveals that he makes the questionable assumption that the identity sign must be a logical term.

thing that might be fully explained by means of the sort of metalinguistic account that I gestured toward at the end of the previous chapter. If reference as it pertains to a given language is represented as a standard semantical parameter-relative assignment of individuals to individual constants and of sets to predicates, then an account of reference must tell us, for any given language, which such parameter-relative assignment represents the reference relation for that language, that is, which assignment is the intended interpretation. But a metalinguistic account of reference would not do that, as I will presently explain.[4]

Of course, we should not expect a theory of reference to enable us to define a predicate that holds of just those predicates that belong to their own extension, for then we could define a predicate that holds of just those predicates that do not belong to their own extension, which leads to Russell's paradox. Moreover, by a result due to Tarski (see Enderton 1972, 228–29), the truths of arithmetic are not decidable. So for any language that includes the language of arithmetic, we cannot expect an account of reference to yield an algorithm by which, for any given sentence of that language, we could decide whether that sentence was true or not.

Further, we should not expect an account of reference to identify the reference relation for a given language in the sense of explicitly telling us which individuals belong to the extensions of all of the predicates and which individuals the names refer to. If our theory of reference did that, then we could use it as a substitute for empirical research. To decide whether any given sentence in the language was true, we could simply check the referents of its constituent terms. Since we should not expect a theory of reference to be a substitute for empirical research, we should not expect to identify the reference relation in *that* sense.

Still, we might expect a theory of reference to provide, for any given language, a *description* that only the reference relation as it pertains to the language satisfies, and in this sense it might tell us which standard semantical assignment represents the reference relation as it pertains to the language. My claim is that a metalinguistic account of reference will not in this sense tell us which standard semantical assignment represents the reference relation. The question is whether a metalinguistic account of reference for L could succeed in specifying which of all possible assignments of objects and sets to terms of L is the reference relation for L. The answer, I will argue, is *not in general*.

To begin, I think we can agree that we do not discover truths by inspecting reference relations (or at least this is not the main way). So we may rule out some assignments by confining the reference relation as it pertains to L to those

---

[4] Field (1972) argued that what I am calling *standard semantics* rested on what I am calling a *real reference relation*. He did not argue in the very general way that I argue here against the idea that a metalinguistic account of reference might suffice for purposes of standard semantics.

assignments of objects and sets to nonlogical constants of L on which the sentences of L that we independently take to be true turn out true. In short, we may confine our attention to those assignments that belong to interpretations that are models for our theory of the world as formulated in L. However, as we saw in chapter 6, any set of sentences that has at least one model is bound to have more than one. So more than one assignment is going to satisfy this condition. If this were the only condition the reference relation had to satisfy, reference would be wildly and inevitably indeterminate. So there must be more to a theory of reference than this.

Thus our question becomes whether a metalinguistic account of reference would suffice to isolate the reference relation as it pertains to L from all the *unintended* models of our theory of the world as formulated in L. In order to address this question, we need to distinguish between the primitive vocabulary of L and what we might call the *primitive referrers* of L. Roughly, the primitive vocabulary of L consists of those vocabulary items of L that cannot be generated (either alone or as part of some longer expression) by applying the formation (grammatical) rules of L. The primitive referrers of L, on the other hand, are those vocabulary items of L to which a standard semantical interpretation makes some assignment (not on the basis of some recursion). The primitive referrers need not in general be included in the primitive vocabulary. For instance, we might have a language in which an infinite number of individual constants (primitive referrers) were generated by concatenating the letter "a" with one or more apostrophes.

If there are only finitely many primitive referrers in L, then perhaps a purely metalinguistic account of reference will suffice to isolate the intended interpretation. If there are only finitely many primitive referrers to which referents need be assigned, then a specification of the reference relation as it pertains to L could take the form of a mere *list* of sentences of the form "x refers to y," and to decide whether any such sentence belonged on our list we could perhaps apply our metalinguistic account of reference, our account of the conditions under which sentences of that form are correctly used. On the other hand, if the number of primitive referrers in L is infinite, then no metalinguistic account will suffice for specification of the intended interpretation, for no such theory will say in a general way what it takes for a term of L to refer to an object or a set. Granted, by applying our account we might rule out some of the possible assignments. Whenever we find by that account that we are licensed to assert that t refers to a, we may rule out all assignments in which something other than a is assigned to t. But if the number of primitive referrers in L is infinite, such a procedure will never isolate a unique assignment.

So the question whether we can have both standard semantics and a metalinguistic account of reference becomes the question whether we need to countenance any language containing an infinite number of primitive referrers. Perhaps there is no real need to countenance languages having an infinite primitive *vocabulary*, and maybe there would be something fundamentally unlearnable about such languages. But if we think of reference as a standard semantical assignment of a privileged sort, then it is hard to see how we can escape from even *considering* languages containing an infinite number of primitive *referrers*. Consider languages containing a name for each natural number (formed, of course, from a finite vocabulary). Or suppose that the best theory of adverbs does *not* treat the reference of expressions of the form VERB + ADVERBIAL-PHRASE as an explicable function of the reference of VERB and the reference of ADVERBIAL-PHRASE or that the reference of verb phrases of the form "believes that *p*" cannot be treated as an explicable function of the reference of component parts drawn from a finite stock.[5] In these cases we would have to allow for an infinite number of primitive referrers. So if we want to hold on to standard semantics and want to be able to contemplate these theoretical contingencies, we will have to hold out for an account of reference as a real relation as opposed to merely a metalinguistic account of reference.

2. If I am right that one of the main sources of commitment to a real reference relation is standard semantics, then the belief in the reality of reference can be criticized by criticizing standard semantics. That is what I will now do. But since I want to criticize the belief in reference *by* criticizing standard semantics, I am not going to criticize standard semantics by raising further doubts about reference. Instead I will argue that standard semantics yields the *wrong logic*. That is, the set of arguments that are valid according to the standard semantical account is not the set of arguments that are valid in fact.

My strategy will be to identify a number of patterns of inference that in some cases cannot be accommodated in any standard semantics and in others merely have not been. It is important to consider a fairly large number of cases. Any one of my counterexamples can be rationalized away. In those cases where I claim that a certain pattern of inference *cannot* be accommodated in a standard semantics, it is possible to doubt whether the pattern of inference *ought* to be accommodated. In those cases where I merely point out that a certain pattern of inference *has not been* accommodated in a standard semantics, it is possible to doubt also whether it cannot be. It is only the cumulative effect of these many examples that ought to persuade one that something is surely wrong with standard semantics.

The principle of substitutivity. Standard semantics obeys a principle of substitutivity, which says that if an argument is valid, then the argument that results from uniformly substituting complex sentences for atomic sentences must also be valid. (This definition is not quite as general as it could be. By imposing

---

[5] For instance, "*S* believes that it is raining" might be analyzed as "*S* believes *x* and *x* is a that-it-is-raining," where "is a that-it-is-raining" is an unanalyzable (which is not to say inexplicable) predicate. In that case, there is bound to be an infinite number of such predicates.

certain conditions on the choice of variables, we could allow also the substitution of complex subsentential formulae for simple subsentential formulae in quantified sentences.) Consider, for example, the following valid argument:

If John is clever then John will act.
It is not the case that John will act.

It is not the case that John is clever.

Since this is valid, the principle of substitutivity tells us that the following argument must also be valid, as surely it is:

If all fish fly then all cats swim.
It is not the case that all cats swim.

It is not the case that all fish fly.

Here we have substituted the complex sentences "All fish fly" and "All cats swim" for the atomic sentences "John is clever" and "John will act."

Here is why the principle of substitutivity holds for any standard semantics: Consider how substitution of complex sentences for atomic sentences might turn an argument Σ into an invalid argument Θ. Making the substitution would have to open up the possibility of an interpretation I and a parameter w such that all of the premises of Θ were true on I at w but the conclusion of Θ was not true on I at w. Now consider the intensions that I assigns to the sentences of Θ that were substituted for atomic sentences of Σ. There is bound to be an interpretation J such that for each of the replaced atomic sentences s in Σ, J assigns to s exactly the intension that I assigns to the complex sentence that replaces it in Θ. (Here is where we make use of the assumption that the components for which we substitute are atomic.) But as I explained above, in any variety of standard semantics the intension that an interpretation assigns to a sentence s is wholly determined by the intensions that the interpretation assigns to each sentential component of s. So if I is a counterexample to Θ, then J must likewise be a counterexample to Σ. Thus, if Σ is valid, then so is Θ.

So if the principle of substitutivity is false, then the standard semantical approach is mistaken. Here, then, is a counterexample to the principle of substitutivity. If p and q are atomic, then the following form of argument, modus tollens, is surely valid:

(A)   If p then q.
      It is not the case that q.

      It is not the case that p.

However, modus tollens is not in general valid. Here, for example, is an invalid instance of modus tollens:

(B)   If I am going to be in Cincinnati on Friday, then it is necessarily possible
       that I will be in Cincinnati on Friday.
       It is not the case that it is necessarily possible that I will be in Cincinnati on
       Friday.
       _____

       It is not the case that I will be in Cincinnati on Friday.

I take the first premise of (B) to be a logical truth. Or to put the point in a less
philosophically loaded way, I take it to have by virtue of logic alone whatever
property must be preserved by valid arguments. This is so because if *p* actually
holds, then it logically follows that *p* is necessarily possible. (This statement
should not be taken as an unqualified endorsement of the rule of conditional
proof.) How could it be that *p* is actually the case and yet it is possible that it is
not even *possible* that *p*? So (B) will be invalid if the conclusion does not follow
from the second premise alone. But it does not. What the second premise says is
that it is possibly necessary that I will *not* be in Cincinnati on Friday (that is, I
may have to be out of Cincinnati on Friday). From that it does not follow that I
will not be in Cincinnati on Friday. So since (B) results from substituting
complex sentences for *p* and *q* in (A), which is valid when *p* and *q* are atomic,
substitutivity fails.

   Someone might object that (B) is not a genuine instance of modus tollens
because the terms "necessarily" and "possibly" are used in different senses in
the two premises. But I do not see why they have to be interpreted in that way. It
is true that one can define concepts of modality on which the first premise is a
logical truth just in case the conclusion follows from the second premise alone.
For instance, this will be the case on any of the standard accounts of necessity
and possibility stated in terms of possible worlds (see below). But that does not
contradict my claim that there is a univocal reading on which both the first
premise is a logical truth and the conclusion does not follow from the second
premise.

   Alternatively, someone might object that (B) appears to be a counterexample
to modus tollens only if one misreads the scope of "necessarily" in the first
premise. "Necessarily" could be read as having narrow scope and pertaining
only to the consequent of the conditional or it could be read as having wide
scope, so that the first premise is equivalent to "Necessarily, if I am going to be
in Cincinnati on Friday, then it is possible that I will be in Cincinnati on Friday."
The argument will be an instance of modus tollens only if "necessarily" has
narrow scope. But only if "necessarily" has wide scope, it may be said, will it
appear that the first premise is a logical truth, even where the conclusion does
not follow from the second premise alone.

   To escape this diagnosis, it is necessary to show that the first premise is a
logical truth even if "necessarily" has narrow scope. Let us then assume narrow
scope and consider the equivalent formulation, "If I am going to be in Cincin-

nati on Friday, then it is not the case that I may have to be out of Cincinnati on Friday." This is not subject to the scope ambiguity in the original. Nonetheless, it is a logical truth, for in any context in which it is assertible that I am going to be *in* Cincinnati on Friday, it is deniable that it *might* turn out that, on the contrary, I *have* to be *out* of Cincinnati on Friday. One thing I am assuming here is that in evaluating the validity of an argument, when one comes to evaluating the conclusion (for truth or assertibility or whatever), one must not lose sight of the premises, and thus one must take the premises for granted. Bearing in mind that one is taking the premises for granted, one asks about the conclusion. So let us take for granted that I will be in Cincinnati. Given that we are making such an assumption, it is certainly deniable that I may have to be *out* of Cincinnati.

Against this last defense, it might be said that "I am going to be in Cincinnati on Friday" and "I may have to be out of Cincinnati on Friday" are consistent. I may have to be out of Cincinnati on Friday, since I am expecting an invitation to fill in for the secretary of state in Friday's peace negotiations. But in fact, my plane will be grounded by terrorists opposed to the negotiations. My response to this is that, no, these two sentences are not consistent. One might *say*, "I may have to be out of Cincinnati on Friday," if one does not know that one will be in Cincinnati, but one cannot consistently maintain both that one will be in Cincinnati on Friday and that one may have to be out of Cincinnati on Friday. If I say, "I will be in Cincinnati on Friday," and someone replies, "But you may have to be out of Cincinnati on Friday," then that reply will qualify as a *challenge* to my assertion. I will discuss this sort of challenge further under the heading "the principle of inconsistency."

Here is another apparent counterexample to modus tollens for complex substitutions. In the 1980 U.S. presidential race, Reagan, a Republican, won the election; Carter, a Democrat, came in second; and Anderson, a Republican running as an independent, came in third. Now consider:

(C) If a Republican will win, then if Reagan does not win, then Anderson will win.
It is not the case that if Reagan does not win, then Anderson will win.

It is not the case that a Republican will win.[6]

I take for granted that in some sense the premises are "good," while in the same sense the conclusion is not "good." The first premise is good, since Reagan and Anderson were the only Republicans in the race. The second premise is good, since Carter, not Anderson, was the runner-up. But the conclusion is not good

[6] I owe this example to Vann McGee (1985). I do not share McGee's doubt about the validity of the modus ponens version of the argument: "If a Republican will win, then if Reagan does not win, then Anderson will win. A Republican will win. Therefore if Reagan does not win, then Anderson will win." The conclusion will look wrong only to one who forgets that it is being assumed in the second premise that a Republican will win.

because in fact Reagan won and he was a Republican. The "good" conclusion would be only that either a Republican will not win or Reagan will win. The question for standard semantics is whether we can explain the sense in which these things are so, while maintaining that the argument is really valid. If not, and we must therefore conclude that (C) is really not valid, then this will be a further counterexample to substitutivity.

Someone might question whether (C) is really an instance of modus tollens, for it might be objected that the embedded conditional in the first premise is just the material conditional, whereas the conditional in the second premise is some stronger kind of conditional. To see why this is wrong, consider this alternative counterexample: (1) If a Republican will win, then it is not the case that even if Reagan does not win, then Anderson still will not win. (2) Even if Reagan does not win, then Anderson still will not win. (3) Therefore, it is not that case that a Republican will win. Here the embedded conditional in (1) plainly cannot be a material conditional. If it were, then (1) would mean that if a Republican will win, then Reagan will not and Anderson will, which is not what it means.

If substitutivity fails for a given conception of validity, then it will not be possible to construct a proof theory of the usual sort corresponding to that conception of validity. That is, we will not find a system of axioms and inference rules such that all and only the arguments derivable by means of those axioms and inference rules qualify as valid. To traditionalists, that will seem like a very weighty reason to insist on substitutivity. But apart from tradition and standard semantics, I do not see why we should expect to be able to construct a proof theory that captures the logic of natural languages. It is enough to have a precise and simple definition of validity formulated in terms that are explicable by means of a more comprehensive theory of language.

The principle of equivalence. I will say that two sentences are *equivalent* if and only if each can be validly inferred from the other. Every standard semantics will conform to a principle of equivalence, which says that if p and q are equivalent and the result of substituting q for p in r is s, then r and s must be equivalent as well. In standard semantics, equivalent sentences will have the same intension. So the principle of equivalence is another consequence of the principle that the intension that an interpretation I assigns to a sentence s is wholly determined by the intensions that I assigns to the sentential components of s.

The principle of equivalence is also subject to counterexample. I take it that the following two sentences are equivalent:

(a)   If switch A is thrown, then the motor will start.
(b)   Either switch A is not thrown or the motor will start.

Probably no one will deny that (b) follows from (a). Someone might deny that (a) follows from (b) on the grounds that (a) implies some kind of connection between the switch and the motor, while (*b*) does not. But on the contrary, whatever kind of connection is implied by (*a*) is implied by (*b*) as well, and I do not see how (*b*) could possibly be acceptable while (*a*) was not. (This does not mean that I hold that "If *p* then *q*" and "Either not-*p* or *q*" are in general equivalent. I deny it.)

Consider, then, the following sequence of inferences:

(1) If both switch *A* and switch *B* are thrown, then the motor will start.
(2) So, either switches *A* and *B* are not both thrown or the motor will start.
(3) So, either *A* is not thrown or the motor will start or *B* is not thrown or the motor will start.
(4) So, either if *A* is thrown then the motor will start or if *B* is thrown then the motor will start.[7]

I take it that both the inference from (1) to (2) and the inference from (2) to (3) are uncontroversially valid. By the principle of equivalence, the inference from (3) to (4) is valid too. So the inference from (1) to (4) is valid. But that is a mistake. From the fact that *A* and *B* are jointly sufficient, it surely does not follow that one or the other must be sufficient alone. So the principle of equivalence is mistaken. Here is another counterexample: "Not (not-*p* or *q*)" implies *p*. So if the principle of equivalence were correct, then "Not (if *p* then *q*)" would imply *p* too (at least in the case where *p* and *q* are atomic). But clearly it does not.

Here is a counterexample to the principle of equivalence that involves modal operators instead of conditionals. Surely, if it is possible that it is possible that I will leave the house, then it is possible that I will leave the house. In general, "Possibly possibly *p*" implies "Possibly *p*." So since the converse certainly holds also, "Possibly *p*" is equivalent to "Possibly possibly *p*." On the other hand, "Necessarily *p*" does not imply "Necessarily necessarily *p*." For example, suppose it is necessary that I not leave the house. Suppose also that the only reason it is necessary that I not leave the house is that I have decided not to leave the house and necessarily do what I have decided to do. But it was not necessary for me to decide not to leave the house, and I could now change my mind. So it is not necessary that it be necessary that I not leave the house. But these results contradict the principle of equivalence, for given the principle of equivalence and the equivalence of "Possibly possibly *p*" and "Possibly *p*," we can prove that "Necessarily *p*" implies "Necessarily necessarily *p*" as follows:

(1) Necessarily *p*.
(2) Not possibly not *p*. *From (1)*
(3) Not possibly possibly not *p*. *From (2) by the principle of equivalence*
(4) Necessarily not possibly not *p*. *From (3)*
(5) Necessarily necessarily *p*. *From (4)*

---

[7] I owe this example to Adams (1965), although Adams does not use it as a counterexample to the principle of equivalence.

So there is something wrong with the principle of equivalence. (At steps (2), (4), and (5) I am taking for granted the usual interdefinability of necessity and possibility.)

The principle of inconsistency. According to standard semantics, two sentences p and q are inconsistent if and only if for every I and every parameter w, p and q are not both true on I at w. We may assume that if p is not true, then "not p" is true. So any standard semantics conforms to a *principle of inconsistency* according to which if p and q are inconsistent, then p implies "not q."[8] But I claim that there is a kind of inconsistency for which the principle of inconsistency is mistaken.

Clearly the inference from p to "Not possibly not p," that is, "Necessarily p," is invalid if p is contingent. By the principle of inconsistency, then, p and "Possibly not p" must be consistent if p is contingent. Still, there is a sense in which p and "Possibly not p" are inconsistent even if p is contingent. If one party says to another, "It is going to be a nice day," and the other party replies, "But it is possible that it is *not* going to be a nice day," in a way that will be inconsistent with what the first party says. It will be a *challenge* to what the first party says. Or again, if someone says, "It is going to be a nice day," but then looks up at the sky, hesitates, and says, "But it may not be a nice day," then that amounts to his or her changing his or her mind or at least casting doubt on what he or she first said.

This inconsistency between p and "Possibly not p" cannot be dismissed as merely a *pragmatic* inconsistency like the pragmatic inconsistency between asserting that p and asserting, "I do not believe that p." A pragmatic inconsistency between two assertions is representable as an explicit inconsistency between the sentences that express what one implies in making the assertions. There is a pragmatic inconsistency between asserting that p and asserting, "I do not believe that p," because in asserting that p one *implies*, in a sense, that one believes that p. So if the inconsistency between p and "Possibly not p" is merely a pragmatic inconsistency, then there must be a pair of explicitly inconsistent sentences other than p and "Possibly not p" that express what one implies in asserting that p and "Possibly not p." I do not see what those other sentences might be.

It might be said that where "It is possible that not p" is a challenge to p, that is because the speaker who asserts that p *implies* that *necessarily p.* But this is implausible. If someone says, "It is going to be a nice day," he or she may or

---

[8] In the usual sorts of many-valued logics it is not true that if p is not true, then "not p" must be true. However, what is true in the usual many-valued logics is that if p does not have a designated value, then "not p" does have a designated value. So if p and q are said to be inconsistent only if for every I and every parameter w, p and q do not both have a designated value on I at w, then even these many-valued logics conform to the principle of inconsistency. Granted, not every many-valued logic will assign "not p" a designated value whenever p has an undesignated value.

may not acknowledge that, furthermore, it is *necessarily* going to be a nice day. And even if he or she will *not* acknowledge that it is necessarily going to be a nice day, "It *may not* be a nice day" will be a challenge. If some *one* person says both *p* and "Possibly not *p*," then it might be said that that person implies both "I do not doubt that *p*" and "I doubt that *p*." In that case, the apparent inconsistency between *p* and "Possibly not *p*" might be attributed to the explicit inconsistency between these two implications. But this explanation will not work in general. There is an apparent inconsistency even when it is one person, *A*, who says *p* and *another* person, *B*, who says, "Possibly not *p*." But there is no inconsistency between "*A* does not doubt that *p*" and "*B* doubts that *p*."

Someone might grant that "It is possible that not *p*" is a challenge to *p* and yet deny that it is the business of logic to explain such relations. "The sun is shining" is also, in a sense, a challenge to "It is going to rain," and yet we should not expect logic to tell us why that is so. But I think we should expect a different sort of explanation in the former case than in the latter. The challenge in the former case is clearly a function of the meaning of the words "possible" and "not." This means that within certain limits we will have the same challenge regardless of the content of *p*.[9] We cannot likewise formalize the challenge between "The sun is shining" and "It is going to rain," and so it is not a challenge that we should expect a logical theory to explain.

One could accept my claim that *p* and "Possibly not *p*" are in a way inconsistent without denying that in the sense of inconsistency that standard semantics aims to define, they are consistent. So my claim is not a direct challenge to standard semantics. But I think the example should cast some doubt on standard semantics as long as this other kind of inconsistency is not accounted for in the context of standard semantics.

The logic of necessity and possibility. The most widely accepted theory of the logic of the operators "necessarily" and "possibly" and their kin, such as "may" and "must," is the *possible-worlds theory.* According to this theory, a sentence of the form "Necessarily *p*" is true *at a possible world w* if and only if *p* is true at *every* world *accessible* from *w*, and a sentence of the form "Possibly *p*" is true *at a possible world w* if and only if *p* is true at *some* world *accessible* from *w*. Validity, moreover, is defined in the usual standard semantical fashion, with possible worlds serving as what I above called parameters. Criticisms of the possible-worlds theory will not immediately qualify as criticisms of standard semantics, since conceivably other sorts of theories of necessity and possibility might be constructed within the framework of standard semantics. But criticisms of the possible-worlds theory give us reason to seek an alternative ac-

---

[9] I say "within certain limits" because we should not expect that "It is possible that not *p*" will be a challenge to *p* for every *p*. For instance, "It is possible that it is not possible that it will rain" does not likewise seem to me to be a challenge to "It is possible that it will rain."

count of necessity and possibility, which, we ought to recognize, may turn out not to be a variety of standard semantics.

We have already collected a certain amount of evidence against the possible-worlds theory. For instance, the inconsistency of p and "Possibly not p" examined in the previous section contradicts standard possible-worlds semantics. Even if a kind of possible-worlds semantics could be devised that did not contain the principle of inconsistency, it would still entail the consistency of p and "Possibly not p," for a world at which "Not p" holds may very well be accessible from a world at which p holds.

Moreover, one of the arguments against the principle of substitutivity contained an argument against the possible-worlds theory. Any version of the possible-worlds theory must treat the accessibility relation as symmetric or not. If accessibility is symmetric, then both

(a) p implies "Necessarily possibly p," and
(b)   "Possibly necessarily p" implies p.

If accessibility is not symmetric, then both

(c) p does not imply "Necessarily possibly p," and
(d)   "Possibly necessarily p" does not imply p.

For example, suppose accessibility is symmetric. Then, I claim, (b) "Possibly necessarily p" implies p. To see this, suppose p is false at w. Suppose also that v is an arbitrary world accessible from w. Since accessibility is symmetric, w is accessible from v. So "Necessarily p" is false at v. But v was arbitrarily chosen. So what goes for v goes for any possible world accessible from w. So "Possibly necessarily p" is false at w. So if "Possibly necessarily p" were true at w, then p would have to be true at w. So "Possibly necessarily p" implies p. Likewise, if accessibility is *not* symmetric, then (c) p does not imply "Necessarily possibly p." To see this, suppose that there are just two worlds w and v, that p is true at w and p is false at v, and that v is accessible from w and from itself, but that w is not accessible from v. This situation can arise if accessibility is not symmetric. In this case, while p is true at w, there is a possible world, namely v, accessible from w such that p is not true at any possible world accessible from v. So p does not imply "Necessarily possibly p." But in the argument against the principle of substitutivity we saw that, on the one hand, p does imply "Necessarily possibly p," contrary to (c), and, on the other hand, that "Possibly necessarily p" does not imply p, contrary to (b). So accessibility must be both symmetric and not symmetric, which is impossible.

Moreover, accessibility must be either transitive or not. If accessibility is transitive, then both

(a)   "Necessarily p" implies "Necessarily necessarily p," and
(b)   "Possibly possibly p" implies "Possibly p."

If accessibility is not transitive, then both

(c)   "Necessarily p" does not imply "Necessarily necessarily p," and
(d)   "Possibly possibly p" does not imply "Possibly p."

The problem is that in one of the arguments against the principle of equivalence we saw that, on the one hand, "Possibly possibly p" implies "Possibly p," contrary to (d), but that, on the other hand, "Necessarily p" does not imply "Necessarily necessarily p," contrary to (a). So accessibility must be both transitive and not transitive, which is impossible.

The logic of subjunctive conditionals. The most widely accepted theory of the logic of conditionals is that due to Robert Stalnaker (1968) and David Lewis (1973b). Stalnaker's and Lewis's theories differ somewhat, but both can be loosely characterized thus: Imagine a space of possible worlds in which a smaller distance between worlds corresponds to a greater similarity between them. Then a subjunctive conditional of the form, "If it were the case that p, then it would be the case that q," is true in a given possible world w if and only if the nearest world to w in which p is true is a world in which q is true. Stalnaker, but not Lewis, holds that this works for indicative conditionals as well (Stalnaker 1975). Lewis holds that indicative conditionals have the truth-conditions of the material conditional.

Criticisms of the Stalnaker-Lewis approach to the logic of conditionals do not immediately impugn standard semantics. Maybe some better theory of the conditional could be formulated in the framework of standard semantics. But since the Stalnaker-Lewis approach to the logic of conditionals is the best I know of in the framework of standard semantics, criticisms of the Stalnaker-Lewis approach do cast doubt on the viability of the standard semantical framework.

The great virtue of the Stalnaker-Lewis approach to conditionals is that it ensures that the following form of argument is invalid:

> *Strengthening of the Antecedent*
> If it were the case that p, then it would be the case that q.
>
> ───────────────
>
> If it were the case that p and r, then it would be the case that q.

For example, the following argument is invalid:

(D)   If this match were struck, then it would light.

───────────────

If this match were first dipped in water and then struck, then it would light.

Suppose that the nearest possible world in which this match is struck (p) is a world in which the match lights (q). Still, as illustrated in figure 7.1, the nearest

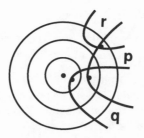

Figure 7.1

world in which this match is *both* dipped in water (*r*) and then struck (*p*) may be farther away and not within the realm of those in which the match lights (*q*).

The problem with the Stalnaker-Lewis approach is that it also invalidates the following venerable form of argument:

> *Hypothetical Syllogism*
> If it were the case that *p*, then it would be the case that *q*.
> If it were the case that *q*, then it would be the case that *r*.
>
> _____
>
> If it were the case that *p*, then it would be the case that *r*.

As illustrated in figure 7.2, the nearest *p*-world may be a *q*-world, and the nearest *q*-world may be an *r*-world, and yet the nearest *p*-world may not be an *r*-world. But it is hard to believe that there is really anything wrong with this form of inference.

The rationale for rejecting hypothetical syllogism along with strengthening of the antecedent is twofold. First, Stalnaker and Lewis claim to find counterexamples to hypothetical syllogism. Here is one that they both use:

(*E*)   If J. Edgar Hoover had been a Russian, then he would have been a Communist.

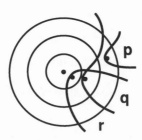

Figure 7.2

If J. Edgar Hoover had been a Communist, then he would have been a traitor.

If J. Edgar Hoover had been a Russian, then he would have been a traitor.

But I do not find such counterexamples persuasive (for some more, which I also find unpersuasive, see Bonevac 1987, 275). The problem with (*E*) is not that the conclusion does not follow from the premises. The problem is simply that the premises are not assertible together. What makes the first premise of (*E*) assertible is the background assumptions that

(*a*)   Hoover was a fervent defender of the interests of his nation, and
(*b*)   Almost every Russian who in Hoover's time fervently defended the interests of his or her nation was a Communist.

What makes the second premise assertible is the background assumptions that

(*c*)   Hoover was FBI director, and
(*d*)   Any Communist FBI director in Hoover's time would almost certainly have been a traitor.

But in light of

(*e*)   No FBI director in Hoover's time was likely to be a Communist,

(*a*), (*b*), and (*c*) imply that it is unlikely that Hoover was a Russian. And in light of

(*f*)   Any fervent defender of the interests of his nation is unlikely to be a traitor,

(*a*), (*c*), and (*d*) imply that it is unlikely that Hoover was a Communist. But the first premise is assertible only in a context where we are not assuming that Hoover was not a Russian, and the second premise is assertible only in a context where we are not assuming that Hoover was not a Communist. It is going to be hard to tell a story in which both premises are assertible.

This defense of hypothetical syllogism takes certain things for granted, for example, that a subjunctive conditional is assertible only where we are *not* assuming the negation of the antecedent. Here is a general rationale for this assumption: In evaluating an indicative conditional, "If *p* then *q*," the questions of interest are primarily whether or not *p* and whether or not *q*. On the other hand, in evaluating a subjunctive conditional, "If *p* were the case, then *q* would be the case," the question of interest is whether a certain relation holds between *p*'s being the case and *q*'s being the case. But *p* and "not *p*" jointly imply any *q* whatsoever. So in a context governed by the assumption that "not *p*," the subjunctive conditional cannot express any special relation between *p*'s being the case and specifically *q*'s being the case. So where the subjunctive conditional has a point, the context must not be governed by the negation of the antecedent. In other words, the negation of the antecedent must not be presupposed.

This assumption runs contrary to what is often said about subjunctive conditionals, namely, that they "presuppose" the falsehood of the antecedent (e.g., Lewis 1973b, 3; Green 1989, 73). That is why subjunctive conditionals are sometimes called *counterfactuals*. I think that is a big mistake. Suppose a labor union is engaged in a contract dispute and one of the union leaders calls up the members of the local chapter and asks each of them the following question: "If there *were* a strike, *would* you honor the picket line?" Anyone who says yes means thereby, "Yes, if there *were* a strike, then I *would* honor the picket line." Must either the person asking the question or the person answering in the affirmative presuppose that there will be no strike? No, quite the contrary. The purpose of asking is to find out how much support there would be for a strike, and if there is enough support, then there definitely will be a strike, and both the speaker and hearer may know these things. In asking the question it is irrelevant whether there will indeed be a strike, for the question is clearly a question about the respondent's disposition. More generally, I would say, subjunctive conditionals concern matters of principle rather than matters of categorical fact. Past-tense examples seem to offer a stronger case for the presupposition of the negation of the antecedent. Suppose that after the contract dispute has passed, someone says, "If there had been a strike, then Smith would have honored the picket line." Here it is very tempting to say that the speaker must be presupposing that there was no strike. But I think that even that is a mistake. To see that it is, suppose that distant history is at issue and it is hard to know whether there was a strike. Still, one might express oneself this way if the issue were Smith's principles and not whether Smith did in fact cross any picket lines.

I think I can explain how it comes to be supposed that in asserting a subjunctive conditional one presupposes the negation of the antecedent. In asserting a subjunctive conditional not only must one not presuppose the negation of the antecedent, as I have already said, but in addition one must not presuppose the antecedent itself. Here is why: If we were presupposing the antecedent, then we could skip over the conditional itself and move straight to the consequent. So the idea that in asserting a subjunctive conditional, one must presuppose the negation of the antecedent is a confusion of *presupposing the negation of the antecedent* with *not presupposing the antecedent*. What is correct is that the antecedent itself must not be presupposed.

The second reason why Stalnaker denies the validity of hypothetical syllogism is that it seems to imply almost all by itself the validity of strengthening of the antecedent thus:

(1)   If p then q.   *Premise*

----

(2)   If p and r, then p.   *Tautology*
(3)   If p and r, then q.   *By Hypothetical Syllogism from (1) and (2)*

(Lewis uses the subjunctive version of this to argue that hypothetical syllogism is invalid for subjunctive conditionals [1973b, 32].) My way of undercutting this argument consists of two steps. First, I want to argue that strengthening of the antecedent is in fact valid for indicative conditionals. But I agree that it is invalid for subjunctive conditionals. So, second, I want to argue that when this argument is reformulated for subjunctive conditionals, the line corresponding to (2) is no longer a tautology and does not validly follow from the line corresponding to (1).

First, then, I claim that strengthening of the antecedent is in fact valid for indicative conditionals. Consider, for instance, the indicative version of (D):

(F)   If this match is struck, then it will light.

If this match is dipped in water and then struck, then it will light.

Anyone who thinks this is invalid is probably evaluating the conclusion apart from the premise. The premise says that striking the match is *sufficient* for the match's lighting. Where that is presumed to be so, it must also be presumed that striking the match after dipping it in water will also be sufficient. The reason it is so easy to lose sight of the premise when evaluating the conclusion is that the conclusion raises the prospect that the match will be dipped in water first, and a context in which that is a live prospect is probably not a context in which striking the match will be regarded as sufficient for the match's lighting.

This defense of the indicative version of strengthening of the antecedent is not likewise a defense of the subjunctive version. As I have already explained, in asserting a subjunctive conditional, we must not presuppose the negation of the antecedent. So suppose that we do presuppose that the match will not be dipped in water. Then we must also presuppose that it is not the case that the match will be both dipped in water and struck. So the subjunctive version of the conclusion, namely, "If this match were first dipped in water and then struck, then it would light," will not be assertible. Yet the subjunctive version of the premise, namely, "If this match were struck, then it would light," might still be assertible, for we might not presuppose that the match will not be struck.

Second, then, I claim that the subjunctive version of (1) through (3) is not valid. The subjunctive version is this:

(1')   If p were the case, then q would be the case.   *Premise*

(2')   If p and r were the case, then p would be the case.   *Tautology*
(3')   If p and r were the case, then q would be the case.   *By hypothetical syllogism from (1') and (2')*

The reason this argument fails is that (2') is *not* a tautology and does not follow from (1'). I have already given the reason in contrasting (D) and (F). Suppose that we are presupposing that r is not the case. Then (2′) is not assertible. But (1′) might be assertible nonetheless.

The Stalnaker-Lewis theory has a number of other extremely dubious consequences. One is that the following form of argument turns out be be invalid:

> *Contraposition*
> If p then q
>
> _____
>
> If not q then not p.

As a counterexample to contraposition, Lewis offers us the following (1973b, 35):

(G)   If Boris had gone to the party, Olga would still have gone.

_____

If Olga had not gone, Boris would still not have gone.

If Olga wants to catch up with Boris but Boris is trying to avoid Olga, then the premise might be true even if the conclusion is false. But it is doubtful whether this is really an instance of contraposition at all. Both the premise and the conclusion contain the word "still," and there is a live possibility that the logic of "If p then *still* q" is not the same as that of "If p then q." In particular, "If p were the case, then q still would be the case" seems to allow the presupposition of q but not the presupposition of "not p." So the premise of (G) might allow us to presuppose that Olga went, but the conclusion of (G) will not allow this.

Another dubious consequence of the Stalnaker-Lewis theory is that the following form of argument turns out to be invalid:

(H)   If it were the case that either p or q, then it would be the case that r.

_____

If it were the case that p, then it would be the case that r, and if it were the case that q, then it would be the case that r.

The premise seems clearly to say that under either of two conditions, p or q, r will hold. In that case, if p holds, r will hold, and if q holds, r will hold. As far as I know, Stalnaker and Lewis have no counterexamples to (H). Ellis (1979, 51) points out that the invalidity of (H) seems inescapable if strengthening of the antecedent is to be invalid. From "If p then r" we seem to be able to infer "If (p and q) or (p and not q), then r," and from this, by (H), we seem to be able to infer "If p and q, then r." My answer to this is that the inference from "If p then r" to "If (p and q) or (p and not q), then r" has little to recommend it.

Universal instantiation. Everyone who takes a course in elementary logic learns a rule of inference called *universal instantiation*, which says that from a universally quantified statement of the form "Everything is F" one may infer any instance of the form "x is F." But universal instantiation is a perfectly ridiculous rule. "Everyone has seen an airplane" does not imply "Socrates has seen an airplane." When the burglary victim from chapter 2 walks into her apartment and exclaims, "Everything is gone!" what she says does not imply that every last speck of dust is gone. In standard semantics, an interpretation is relative to a *domain*, but that is not an answer to the present point, since universal instantiation is nonetheless valid for every instance in the language.

One kind of standard semantics is so-called *presupposition-free logic* (or just *free logic*). In free logics universal instantiation is not valid. But neither is the rule of existential generalization, which says that from "*x* is *F*" one may infer "Something is *F*." In order to infer "Something is *F*" in free logic, one must have not only "*x* is *F*" but also a premise asserting the existence of *x*. One rationale for denying the validity of ordinary existential generalization is the idea that fictional entities have names and that to say that "Something is *F*" is to imply that something that exists is *F*. I myself see no reason to deny the validity of existential generalization. In any context in which we are assuming, for some individual constant *x*, "*x* is *F*," we may assume as well "Something is *F*." In any context where we are assuming "Santa Claus lives at the North Pole," either because we really believe it or because we are pretending to believe it, we may assume as well "Something lives at the North Pole." In any case, this rationale for free logic is not my rationale for denying the validity of universal instantiation. Not only instances containing names of fictions fail to follow from universal generalizations. "Socrates" names something real, but "Socrates has seen an airplane" does not follow from "Everyone has seen an airplane." Another rationale for free logic stems from quantified modal logic (Garson 1983), but this also does not address the present concern.

What we need is some kind of restriction on universal instantiation that leaves existential generalization unrestrictedly valid. I cannot show that this is impossible in the context of standard semantics. But as far as I know, this kind of logic has never been developed in the context of standard semantics, and that fact ought to cast further doubt on the viability of standard semantics.

In chapter 12, I present a formally precise account of validity subject to none of the objections I have raised here against standard semantics. However, it is a semantics in which the concept of an interpretation in the standard semantical sense plays no role. Consequently, it gives us no reason to believe in reference. And it rests on a thoroughly non-Lockean conception of communication.

Part B

CONSTRUCTIVE

8

Similarity Judgments

1. The widespread acceptance of Lockean conceptions of communication during the past twenty years is bound up with the demise of behaviorism in psychology. The problem with behaviorism was not so much that it refused to postulate mental mechanisms or that it postulated too few of them but that as long as terms like "conditioning" and "analogy" remained reasonably clear in meaning, not much of interest in intelligent behavior could be explained in terms of them. Behaviorism may have been propped up by a faulty empiricist philosophy, but its demise probably had less to do with the failure of its philosophy than with the failure of its explanations of behavior.

Since behaviorism began to crumble, all sorts of mental mechanisms have been dreamed up to fill the void. We have conceptual networks, prototypes, mental imagery, mental models, production systems, PDP (parallel distributed processing) networks, and more, and each type is touted by its investigators as the fundament of cognition. What all of these theories have in common is that the mental mechanisms postulated are conceived as operating on representations of one kind or another. As far as I know, everyone working in cognitive science today is working under the assumption that intelligent behavior is the product of *thoughts about the world.*

One might well question whether it is necessary to explain intelligent behavior as the product of anything that might qualify as a representation of the world. Alternatively, we might try to explain it directly in neurophysiological or, more generally, physical terms. But the brain is a very complicated organ, and it is very hard to sort out what is going on in there. If we are to have any hope of sorting out the neurological processing, we will need to have some preconceptions about what those neurological processes might add up to. Thus the conception of cognition as a process over representations might have a utility even if what we ultimately seek is an understanding of the mechanical structure of the brain.

One of the things that cognitive scientists hope to explain, of course, is language. So they aim to explain language in terms of representational states. But in a sense language too represents. Given that we are going to postulate representations in terms of which we will explain language, it may seem inevitable that we will cite the representational powers of those representational states in explaining the representational powers of language. It is a short step from this conclusion to a Lockean theory of communication. So anyone who denies the Lockean conception of communication is likely to be accused of being a behaviorist.

I am no behaviorist. I share with the cognitive scientist the aim of providing an explanation of language that lends itself to replacement by a wholly neurophysiological account. In pursuit of that aim, I am willing to postulate certain representational states, which will serve as placeholders for elements of the future neurophysiological theory. However, I will to resist every step beyond that in the direction of a Lockean theory of communication. How I can do this cannot be made fully intelligible in advance, but two observations seem especially important. First, what I aim to explain about language above all is not the representational powers of language but how language makes things happen. Regarding such things as truth and reference, I endorse a metalinguistic account, as I explained in chapter 6. In consequence, I do not need to locate the representational powers of language in the theoretical entities I postulate in the course of explaining language.

Second, there are going to be definite limits on the kinds of representational state I postulate. Language, I assume, is highly adaptive. Even in highly novel sorts of environments, such as the environment around a superconducting supercollider, intelligent life finds ways of using language to get things done. There may be kinds of knowledge beyond that contained in sentences, for there may be kinds of knowledge that require a nonlinguistic (for example, pictorial) medium. Further, there may be questions that we know we will never answer. But we cannot foresee an end to the innovations in language that will enable things to be said that could not be said before and that qualify as discoveries about the world. In contrast, the types of representational state that I will postulate in explanation of language will be very limited in variety.

Since I do seek a link to the physical, the representational states I postulate and cite in my explanation of language must qualify as *cognitive entry points*. To qualify as a cognitive entry point, a type of representational state must satisfy two criteria: First, other fundamental cognitive operations must be explicable in terms of it. Second, its possibility must be explicable in neurophysiological terms. In this and the next chapter I am will characterize two sorts of representational state that might qualify as cognitive entry points in this sense, namely, similarity judgments and what I will call kausal judgments (with a "k"). These are the representational states that I will cite subsequently in my explanation of language.

There is reason to expect similarity judgments to qualify as cognitive entry points. In all sorts of ways similarity judgments appear to be fundamental elements of cognition. In particular, it seems likely that they are involved in language learning. As I argued in chapter 1, it would be a mistake to think that we form concepts simply by mentally grouping together things we judge to be similar. And so it would be a mistake to think that similarity judgments play their role in language learning by yielding concepts that we may learn to express in words. Nonetheless, we may expect similarity judgments to play a role in language learning inasmuch as learning the correct use of a word or a sentence may involve judging two circumstances of use to be more similar to one another than to some other.

Second, similarity judgments, more than some other things, may seem to have identifiable nonmental roots. That is, there is perhaps some prospect of explaining in neurophysiological terms what a similarity judgment amounts to in the brain. As a first step, we might find that similarity judgments are rooted in discriminatory responses at the behavioral level, and then, as a second step, we might find that these discriminatory responses at the behavioral level are rooted in discriminatory responses at the neurological level. In conjunction with these steps, we might try to construct models of the neurological mechanisms responsible. Here there may already have been some progress, since one of the cognitive operations that artificial PDP networks seem particularly well suited to perform is that of deciding which of two inputs is most similar to a third.

There seems, however, to be a good reason to doubt whether fundamental operations will be truly explicable in terms of similarity judgments. Ultimately, what we wish to explain are intelligent activities that we hold to standards of objectivity. For instance, we might wish to explain the capacity to make objective *judgments*. But similarity seems so subjective. If we were to explain such fundamental cognitive operations in terms of similarity judgments, then the subjectivity of similarity judgments might infect these other cognitive operations, so that their objectivity had to be denied. In that case, we would have to deny either the objectivity of fundamental cognitive operations or the explanation of these in terms of similarity judgments.

My objective in this chapter is to defend similarity judgments against the charge of subjectivity. I will not try to show that all similarity judgments are in fact objective, but I will try to show that they may often enough be objective enough to serve as the cognitive entry points we seek. Before I can define the problem more precisely and try to solve it, however, I must first say something about competing conceptions of objectivity and then identify the sort of similarity judgment in question.

2. The important question before us is not so much whether similarity judgments are objective in some sense but whether we can in fact appeal to them as we might like in explanations of fundamental cognitive operations. Nonetheless, the threat takes the form of a doubt about the objectivity of similarity judgments. So I wish now to set out some possible conceptions of objectivity. This will enable me better to explain some of the moves I will make in discussing the objectivity of similarity judgments. Beyond merely presenting these conceptions of objectivity, I will make some evaluative remarks against some of them and on behalf of another. However, this should not lead the reader to assume that the doubts about the objectivity of similarity judgments or my answer to those doubts directly depend on the conception of objectivity that I favor. The question whether the arguments that follow rest on any one of these conceptions of objectivity is complex. I will return to it at the end of the chapter.

The root of the philosophical concept of objectivity is perhaps *mind-independence*. As Peirce says, "[W]e may define the real as that whose characters are independent of what anybody may think them to be" ([1878] 1934, 266). Thus Santa Claus *is* just what the story of Santa Claus, supported by people's collective thinking about Santa Claus, says he is; whereas the stories we tell about quarks could prove to be very mistaken. However, mind-independence is first of all a criterion for the objective reality of *particulars*. It is not obvious how mind-independence might serve as a criterion for the objectivity of *judgments*.

One way to try to apply the concept of mind-independence as a criterion for the objectivity of judgments is to define an objective judgment as a judgment concerned with mind-independent *facts*. Since an objective judgment may be false, we do not wish to define an objective judgment as one that *corresponds* to a mind-independent fact. Nonetheless, we might conceive of an objective judgment as a judgment belonging to a certain *sort* that includes but is not limited to judgments that correspond to mind-independent facts. Objective judgments, we might say, are judgments that are *supposed* to correspond. Call this the *correspondence conception* of objectivity.

The correspondence conception faces many problems. One problem is to make sense of the requisite notion of *fact*. For instance, are there negative facts, such as that this paper is *not* blue? If so, how can there be negations without minds? If not, how are we to explain the objectivity of negative judgments? The more serious problem, however, is to make sense of the requisite correspondence relation. Presumably, if we could explain the nature of the requisite correspondence relation, then likewise we could explain the nature of the reference relation discussed in chapter 6. There I surveyed the most important sorts of theories of reference and found them all wanting. Accordingly, I cannot adopt the correspondence conception of objectivity.

A different way to apply the idea of mind-independence in an account of the objectivity of judgments is to say that a judgment is *objective* if our evaluation of it as true or false may proceed without regard to the question whose judgment it is and to say that a judgment is *subjective* if our evaluation of it as true or false must have regard for the question whose judgment it is. In other words, a judgment is subjective or objective according to whether the truth-value we attribute to it ought to be or need not be relative to the judging subject *S*. Call this the *intersubjective conception* of objectivity.

A subjective judgment, on this conception, is neither true nor false *simpliciter* but only true or false *for S*. One must be careful, however, not to confuse the relative evaluation of a judgment with the evaluation of a relative judgment. My judgment that vanilla tastes better than chocolate is subjective. It is neither true nor false *simpliciter* but only true or false *for me*. But my judgment that vanilla tastes better than chocolate *to me*, which is an example of what I mean by a *relative judgment*, may be perfectly objective and may be true or false *simpliciter*. The use of the phrase *true for S* in this characterization of the intersubjective conception should not suggest any sort of vapid relativism. One needs to recognize that the truth of judgments is relative to many things, including domain of discourse, time of utterance (or time of judgment), direction of motion (in judgments concerning comings and goings), and so on. Relativity to the judging subject, in the relevant sense, is just another one of these.

The intersubjective conception is probably not entirely wrong, although many hard questions remain to be answered. How can a judgment fail to be objective, as presumably it may, if everyone happens to agree with it? If we accept a judgment on the authority of an expert, why does that not make the judgment subjective? The main problem with this conception of objectivity, for my purposes, is that it is not very helpful as a *criterion* for objectivity. It is not an account of objectivity that draws a connection between the concept of objectivity and other concepts on which we have some independent grasp so that we might use our account of objectivity to help us decide whether a given judgment is objective.

Practically speaking, the distinction between subjective and objective judgments concerns the matter of how to react to apparent disagreements. The question is, In the face of an apparent disagreement, shall we press on and try to reach an agreement, that is, a point at which we make the same judgment, or shall we be content to disagree on the grounds that no agreement is possible? Practically speaking, an objective question is, roughly, a question on which people ought to be able to reach agreement, and an objective judgment is an answer to such an objective question. (This is a conception of objectivity familiar from Kant's *Prolegomena* §18.)

But this is barely a start. To characterize an objective question as a question on which people ought to be able to agree is to say almost nothing until one characterizes the conditions under which such agreement ought to be possible. A wide spectrum of answers is possible. At one end of the spectrum the answer is that agreement ought be possible on objective questions when two people both know what is objectively the case. In other words, the account of objectivity in terms of agreement just begs the question. At the other end of the spectrum the answer is that there are no special conditions under which people ought to be able to agree on objective questions. In other words, there is no such thing as objectivity.

According to the view I wish to put forward, there is such a thing as objectivity, and it is not question-begging to characterize an objective question as one on which people ought to be able to reach agreement. That is because a substantive conception of the conditions under which agreement on objective questions ought to be possible can be developed. In particular, two conditions can be imposed: First, we should not expect two people to be able to reach agreement unless they are both *rational* in some sense. They must both be ready and able to accept whatever conclusions reason (in some sense) dictates. (Of course, introducing the concept of rationality raises some big questions in turn.) Second, we should not expect two people to reach the same conclusion unless they can *communicate* with one another. One reason for this is that they must be able to share their data. Another reason is that the conclusions they reach will depend on the hypotheses that occur to them, and so we can expect them to reach agreement only if they can communicate their hypotheses to one another.

Such considerations inspire the following definition:

> An *objective question* is a question such that if any two creatures are ideally rational and are able to communicate with one another, then in principle they ought to be able to reach agreement in their answers to that question.

Notice that this does not say that rational, communicative creatures will always be able to reach a *true* answer to an objective question. Nor does their answer need to be a real *solution*. The answer they agree on may be simply, "We don't know." By "reaching agreement" I mean arriving at the same judgment. Thus, an *objective judgment* may be defined as any judgment that answers an objective question. Call this the *agreement conception* of objectivity.

Two sorts of doubt may be raised against the statement that if any two creatures are ideally rational and are able to communicate with one another, then in principle they ought to be able to reach agreement in their answers to objective questions. The first is whether the statement is true. The second is whether it can serve as an explanation of the nature of objectivity.

Regarding the question of truth, the words "ideally," "in principle," and "ought" are likely to block any direct refutation. Nonetheless, it might be possible to question whether the statement correctly captures a relation between rationality and objectivity. In answer, I think it is fair to say that it would be *good* to regard rationality and objectivity as related in this way. Rationality and objectivity are normative ideals, and so in deciding what relation obtains between them it is relevant to consider what relation it would be good to recognize between them. It would be good to regard rationality and objectivity as related in this way because rationality considered as something that, together with communication, ought to lead to agreement on objective questions is a useful and just ideal. It is a useful ideal because it will lead us to reflect critically on our own ignorance and our own inferences. If we aspire to such rationality and do not too quickly dismiss difficult questions as purely subjective, then we will be motivated to undertake such critical reflections in the face of disagreement with others whose thinking seems to succeed. Moreover, it is a just ideal, because when our own opinions withstand scrutiny, it will lead us to locate our criticisms of those who disagree with us in their inferences and their knowledge of the "facts" rather than in their personal tastes or cultural background.

The second question was whether we can really *explain* objectivity as what those questions have that any two ideally rational thinkers who can communicate ought in principle to be able to agree on. The doubt about this is that when we attempt to explain what rationality is we might be forced to rest our account on a prior conception of objectivity. For instance, we might find ourselves defining a rational thinker as one who has a reliable method for finding true answers to objective questions. But in fact I do not think we will have to circle back to objectivity in this way as long as we do not require a transcendental account of reason valid for all creatures capable of apprehending the world. The alternative is to study the thinking of people who think well and to try to construct concrete models that do as they do. Here there will be many points at which we will speak of relations between the mind and the rest of the world, but none of these relations need be the correspondence relation needed to underwrite the correspondence conception of objectivity. Further, it will be necessary to apply some conception of successful thinking, but that may be conceived as thinking that is effective in bringing about desirable ends rather than as thinking that corresponds to reality.

3. I now turn to the question of the form of the sort of similarity judgment at issue. At first one might suppose that the judgments at issue had simply the form

(1) x is similar to y.

But this ignores the fact that two things may be similar in one respect but dissimilar in some other. So we might consider instead judgments of the form

(2) x is similar to y with respect to R.

But this still fails to acknowledge that similarity, even in a single respect, comes in degrees. Thus, a better representation of the form of judgment that interests us would be

(3) x is more similar than y to z with respect to R.

But what does "with respect to R" mean? Apparently its role is to specify the *type* of property in question. For instance, *shape* is a type of property. *Square* and *circular* are properties that belong to that type. *Color* is another type of property. Thus we may say, "x is more similar than y to z with respect to shape, but y is more similar than x to z with respect to color." Beyond this, however, I do not know what "with respect to R" means. I can substitute other phrases, such as "on the basis of R" or "judging by R," but these are no more helpful to me. In each case we seem to speak of some second-order dyadic relation between the monadic property type R, on the one hand, and a nonrelative triadic similarity relation, on the other, and I do not know what either of these relations is supposed to be.

So I would like to get rid of all such phrases. I can think of two ways to do so.

One is to specify the R-type property that makes x and z alike and y different. Thus, instead of (3), we might consider judgments of the form

(4) x and z are both F, and y is not F

(where F is an R-type property). I will call judgments of form (4) *predicative similarity judgments* (since they merely affirm certain predications and deny others). The other way to eliminate phrases such as "with respect to R" is to suppose that the relata of the similarity relation are not in fact x, y, and z but rather x's R, y's R, and z's R (for instance, x's shape, y's shape, and z's shape). Thus:

(5) x's R is more similar than y's R to z's R.

I will call judgments of form (5) *aspectual similarity judgments* (since the aspects of objects, not the objects themselves, are compared).

Predicative and aspectual similarity judgments fare differently on the dual tests of explanatory power and objectivity. We do not need to question the objectivity of predicative similarity judgments. They may be every bit as objective as judgments of the form "x is F" and "y is not F." The problem with predicative similarity judgments is whether they might have the desired explanatory power. For instance, one might have hoped to explain in terms of similarity judgments how people learn how to use words appropriately. But one cannot explain that a person learns to use "F" by means of similarity judgments to the effect that x and z are both F and y is not F, since in that case a person would have to be equipped with a concept corresponding to every word that had to be learned.

It might appear that learning the use of the word "F" might be explained as resulting from predicative similarity judgments concerning the *characteristic features* of F-things. For instance, if the characteristic features of F-things are G and H, then the relevant sort of judgment might be,

(6) x and z are both G and H, and y is either not G or not H.

The trouble with this theory is that it implies that the child possesses a battery of *elementary* concepts by means of which he or she might define the extension of any predicate that he or she can learn, namely, the concepts of the characteristic features of things. These elementary concepts in turn must be either innate or acquired in some other way. But it is hard to believe that all of the words that people are able to learn to use appropriately, such as "electron," are definable by means of concepts possessed innately. If, on the other hand, the elementary concepts are supposed to be acquired somehow, then we might likewise explain the acquisition of the concept of F-things, and the introduction of the concepts G and H will be unnecessary. As I pointed out in chapter 1 and again in chapter 4, it is doubtful whether concepts of the characteristic features of things are often more elementary developmentally than the concepts of the things that have those features. For instance, the only shape that is characteristic of dogs is dog-shape, and the concept *dog-shape* is not more elementary than the concept *dog*.

The situation with aspectual similarity judgments is just the opposite. Without begging the question, one could perhaps cite aspectual similarity judgments in explaining how people learn to use words appropriately. For instance, if the learner knows that x is called "triangle" and y is called "square," then he or she might know to call z a "triangle" inasmuch as x's shape is more similar than y's shape to z's shape. This explanation presupposes that the person can cognize the shapes of x, y, and z, but it does not presuppose that he or she can cognize them *as* triangles and squares. This is not at all the theory of language learning that I will put forward in chapter 10, but for present purposes it will serve as an illustration of the idea that without begging the question one might cite aspectual similarity judgments in explaining language learning. By contrast with predicative similarity judgments, the problem with aspectual similarity judgments is that one might question their objectivity. If x's R, y's R, and z's R all differ from one another in any way, then one person might find x's R more similar than y's R to z's R, while another person might find y's R more similar than x's R to z's R. What is to show that one judgment is right and the other one wrong?

I do not in fact see any way to rescue the explanatory power of predicative similarity judgments. However, I do think I can make a case for the objectivity of aspectual similarity judgments. Thus I will take our subject to be the explanatory power and objectivity of *aspectual* similarity judgments.

4. The problem with which this chapter is concerned may now be formulated thus: On the one hand, we hope that fundamental cognitive operations might be explicable in terms of (aspectual) similarity judgments. On the other hand, it is doubtful whether (aspectual) similarity judgments are objective. *This doubt seems to undermine our hope.*

To show that there really is a problem here, the first thing I need to do is show that if similarity judgments are not objective, then fundamental cognitive operations cannot be explained in terms of similarity judgments. I will try to show that if similarity judgments are not objective, then, in particular, *word learning*, that is, learning the appropriate uses of words, cannot be explained in terms of similarity judgments. Here is a simple argument for this. Call it *the argument for the requirement of objectivity*:

(1) If words are learned through similarity judgments and similarity judgments are not objective, then the judgments expressed by means of those words are not objective either.

(2) Some of the judgments expressed by means of words that are learned through similarity judgments are themselves objective.

(3)   So if similarity judgments are not objective, then words are not learned through similarity judgments.

The conclusion (3) is just a deductive consequence of (1) and (2). Step (2) will certainly be accepted by anyone who expects to make serious use of similarity judgments in explaining the learning of words such as "dog" and "chair." The reason is that judgments such as "Dogs are animals" and "This is a chair" will certainly have to count as objective if any judgments are to count as objective. The questionable step is (1).

Step (1) may be defended by means of an example. Suppose that learning the word "chair" depends on similarity judgments. For example, learning how to use the word "chair" might entail judging that a given object is more similar than something called a "desk" to some third thing called a "chair" with respect to function. (This is the same oversimplification that I said we could accept for present purposes.) Suppose also that the question arises whether some object o should be called a "chair," that is, whether o is a chair. If learning how to use the word "chair" depends on similarity judgments in this way, then the question whether o should be called a "chair" will likewise depend on the question whether o is more similar to certain things, for instance, those things anteced- ently said to be "chairs," than to others. So if the pertinent similarity judgments are not objective, then it may not be possible for rational creatures who can communicate to reach agreement in their judgments regarding those sim- ilarities. So it may not be possible for rational creatures who can communicate to reach agreement in their judgments whether o should be called a "chair." In that case, the judgment that o is a chair will not be objective. Generalizing from this example, we may conclude that (1) holds.

Still, our hope of explaining fundamental cognitive operations in terms of similarity judgments will not be spoiled, and the objectivity of similarity judg- ments will need no defense, unless some definite reason to doubt the objectivity of similarity judgments can be produced. Here then is what I will call *the argument against the objectivity of similarity*: Consider the three polygons in figure 8.1. I myself judge that the shape of a is more similar than the shape of b

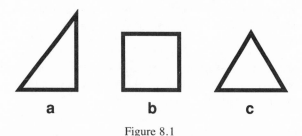

Figure 8.1

to the shape of c. Conceivably, however, someone else might judge that the shape of b is more similar than the shape of a to the shape of c. Suppose that this other person and I are both rational and are able to communicate. How might we resolve our disagreement? I might point out to my interlocutor that a and c both have three sides and b has four. My interlocutor might point out to me that b and c are both equilateral and a is not. We need not doubt the objectivity of such questions. On all such questions we may, let us suppose, agree. Yet it seems that we might continue to disagree over the similarity of the shapes. In that case, the similarity of the shapes is not an objective question, and our judgments concerning it are not objective judgments. Similarly, the objectivity of any other similarity judgments may be denied. Q.E.D.

We have to be careful to distinguish between two ways in which two parties might differ in their similarity judgments. One difference, which I will call the *strong* difference, might be that given three objects x, y, and z and some definite aspect R, one party maintains and the other denies that x's R is more similar than y's R to z's R. Another difference, which I will call the *weak* difference, might be that the two parties spontaneously (without cueing or suggestion) choose different aspects of things by which to judge similarities. Neither difference strictly implies the other, but I suppose the strong difference makes the weak difference very likely, which is why I call it *strong* and the other *weak*.

The only kind of difference in similarity judgments that casts doubt on the objectivity of similarity judgments is the strong difference, for only disagreement signals subjectivity, and the weak difference is not really a disagreement. A human being might spontaneously choose color as an aspect with respect to which he or she will judge similarities. An intelligent extraterrestrial, on the other hand, might have nothing like human vision and be altogether unable to see color. The extraterrestrial, I assume, might nonetheless be able to *detect* color with special instruments, and so if the extraterrestrial were asked to judge the similarities of things with respect to color, he might, with difficulty, be able to do so. And if he did so, his judgments might agree with those of the human being. So the weak difference is no challenge to objectivity.

In reply to the argument against the objectivity of similarity judgments, someone might protest that there is simply no one proposition on which I and my interlocutor disagree. What I assert and my interlocutor denies seems to be that the shape of a is more similar than the shape of b to the shape of c. But, in fact, it may be said, what I mean to maintain is only that a and c have the same number of sides and b has a different number of sides. My interlocutor does not deny that but merely asserts that b and c are both equilateral and a is not. But this objection works only by substituting predicative similarity judgments for aspectual similarity judgments, whereas my topic is the objectivity of aspectual similarity judgments.

One way to try to defeat the argument against the objectivity of similarity might be to argue that if two people disagreed over similarities, then in fact there would be a way for one of them to persuade the other. The method need not be very simple. It might involve waiting to see who in the long run best succeeds in making sense of the world as a whole. But this cannot be one's answer to the argument if one expects to maintain that similarity judgments play a fundamental role in cognition. If one supposes both that the parties to the disagreement can decide between themselves who in fact has made the best sense of the world and that similarity judgments are fundamental to cognition, then one must also presuppose that similarity judgments are objective.

My strategy for defending the objectivity of similarity judgments will focus instead on the matter of communication. I think I can show that to the extent that two people disagree in their similarity judgments, communication will be hindered and in extreme cases will be impossible. This will not demonstrate that all similarity judgments are objective, but it will block the above argument against the objectivity of similarity. It will show that one cannot simply *assume* that rational creatures who can communicate might disagree in the manner described. But if we cannot assume that two rational creatures who disagree in their similarity judgments can communicate, then we will not find the sort of failure to agree that indicates subjectivity.

5. One thing I will take for granted is that in order for two people to communicate, each must be able to anticipate how the other will use words in labeling objects. By *labeling* I mean an overt use of a word by means of which the language user indicates that a given object falls within the extension of the word. For instance, if someone points to an apple and says, "That is an apple," that action is an act of labeling the apple with the word "apple." I do not need to define more precisely what it takes to *indicate* that an object falls within the extension of a word, because the principle that communication depends on an understanding of labeling will hold true even on fairly narrow construals of such indication. I do not claim that in order to understand one another at all, any two speakers must be able to predict one another's labeling with perfect accuracy. I acknowledge, and even insist, that understanding precisely how an agent will use a word as a label is not necessary and not even sufficient for understanding what the word means as used by that agent (see chapter 3). However, other things being equal, one will be better able to communicate with people whose labeling one can better predict.

In some cases, predicting another's labeling behavior may be easy. Having observed Jacques label three different chairs "chaise," one considers the question whether he would also label a certain fourth chair "chaise." The problem is that the fourth chair is somewhat different from the other three. It is made of steel or has a pedestal instead of four legs. This difference may raise a doubt whether Jacques will also label this fourth chair "chaise." Despite such doubts, one might find that one never goes wrong in assuming that Jacques will label all and only chairs "chaise."

Sometimes one may find that one's predictions prove correct, and sometimes not. But sometimes, moreover, one may find that one has little reason to make any definite predictions at all concerning another person's labeling behavior. In that case, as much as in the case in which one's predictions all fail, communication will be thwarted. What I aim to show is that to the extent that two people disagree in their similarity judgments, each will have little reason to make any particular predictions regarding the other's labeling behavior. I will try to reach this conclusion by generalizing from a representative example. For ease in exposition, I will assume that I am the one trying to make the predictions, and for the sake of comparison, I will start with the case of a person who judges similarities as I do.

To begin, consider Alice, who finds herself in a room full of wooden blocks of various shapes and sizes. Her task is to sort these blocks into a number of piles and to label each pile however she pleases. I will assume that the label on a pile may be understood as a label for the blocks in the pile. After watching her sort the blocks for a while, it appears to me that she has chosen to sort the blocks by color. All the green blocks are in a pile labeled X, all the red blocks are in a pile labeled Y, and so on. In other words, for each of her labels w, there is a color c, such that the most plausible hypothesis is that Alice will put a block in the pile labeled w, that is, will label a block w, if and only if the block has the color c.

Now we bring a green tetrahedron into the room. Relative to the situation, this is a novel sort of object. There had been no green tetrahedrons in the room before. Where is Alice going to put it? Plainly the prediction dictated by my most plausible hypothesis is that she will put it in the pile of green blocks. Other predictions would be dictated by other hypotheses. For instance, if I hypothesized that the label on the green pile is a label for *nontetrahedral* green blocks and that the label on the red pile is a label for blocks that are red *or tetrahedral*, then I would predict that Alice would put the green tetrahedron together with the red blocks. This and indefinitely many other hypotheses are compatible with the observations I had made prior to the introduction of the green tetrahedron, but they are all far less plausible. So I am strongly warranted in predicting that Alice will put the green tetrahedron in the pile of green blocks.

Compare now the case of a Martian who faces this same task of sorting the blocks under labels of his own choosing (never mind how we get him to do it). Let us suppose that I have studied very carefully the many properties of the blocks, including their weight, texture, emission of infrared radiation, and so on. Moreover, let us suppose that the Martian has eyes that are very like human eyes, that they are sensitive to the same band of electromagnetic radiation, and so on. Suppose, however, that even after the Martian has sorted a large number of blocks I still cannot discover any obvious principle by which he might be sorting. For instance, the best I can do for one of his labels is to suppose that it is a label for blocks that are either large, nonyellow cubes or medium-sized and green.

Again, we introduce a novel green tetrahedron. It is medium-sized (let us suppose), and so my most plausible hypothesis dictates that the Martian will put it into the pile of blocks that are either large, nonyellow cubes or medium-sized and green. However, there are other hypotheses that are barely less plausible but would dictate a different prediction. For instance, a hardly less plausible alternative is that the label on the aforementioned pile is a label for blocks that are either large, nonyellow cubes or medium-sized, green, *and nontetrahedral*. If that is right, then I ought to predict that the Martian will *not* put the green tetrahedron in that pile. Since this alternative is hardly less plausible, I can have little confidence in my prediction that the Martian will put the green tetrahedron into that pile. I am not strongly warranted in making any particular prediction concerning the Martian's labeling of the green tetrahedron.

There may be some temptation to suppose that the difference between the case of Alice and the case of the Martian is merely a matter of how much evidence we require. To get an interpretation of the Martian that as strongly warrants expectations regarding his response to the green tetrahedron as our interpretation of Alice warrants expectations regarding *her* response to the green tetrahedron, perhaps we simply need more evidence. However, this misses the point of focusing on novel situations. No matter how much evidence we collect, there will always be situations that count as novel inasmuch as we have not observed the subject's responses to them. So while collecting more evidence might enable us to decide between our above two hypotheses concerning the Martian's sorting behavior, there will always be further choices between hypotheses that have not yet been decided in this way. But any decision between hypotheses concerning Alice's or the Martian's sorting behavior entails a decision concerning her or his responses to novel situations, for any general hypothesis will have consequences for novel situations as well as for familiar situations. So the difference between Alice and the Martian will not disappear as we collect more evidence.

In drawing the lesson from my comparison of Alice and the Martian, I am going to assume that the way they sort the blocks is an expression of the way they judge similarities. Thus if Alice or the Martian puts blocks x and z together in one pile and puts block y in some other pile, that is because there is some aspect R such that Alice or the Martian, as the case may be, judges that x's R is more similar than y's R to z's R. This does not mean that their concepts or their uses of words are products of similarity judgments in the simple way I argued against in chapter 1. My assumption is only that the propensity to label things that their sorting behavior exhibits somehow goes hand in hand with a disposition to judge that the things that are labeled in the same way are in some respect more similar to one another than to things not so labeled. If the argument against the objectivity of similarity judgments can be blocked on the assumption that Alice's and the Martian's sortings express their similarity judgments, then the argument against the objectivity of similarity judgments may rightly be rejected by anyone who supposes that similarity judgments may be cited in explanations of fundamental cognitive operations.

Further, I assume that the similarity judgments that lead Alice to sort as she does are such as I too might make. She sorts as she does because for any two blocks in a given one of her piles, she judges that the colors of those two blocks are more similar to one another than either is to the color of any block in any other pile, and I concur with her on this. However, the similarity judgments that lead the Martian to sort as he does are not such as I too might make. This is shown by the fact that the Martian sorts in a way that I would not and in a way that I am not even sure I understand.

From the story of the Martian as I have told it, we may infer that the difference between the Martian and me is the strong difference, as defined above, and not merely the weak difference. My assumption in telling the story was that I had looked far and wide for hypotheses that might explain the Martian's sorting behavior. Among the hypotheses I had considered was that the Martian judges similarities with respect to aspects of things that I myself would not spontaneously choose as a basis for sorting. But for any aspect R, either I could not explain his sorting behavior in terms of judgments of similarity with respect to R or I found that he and I disagreed on questions of similarity with respect to R.

So we have found that I am able to anticipate the labeling performed by a human being who agrees with me on questions of similarity (in the sense that I may have reason to accept a definite hypothesis), but I am unable to anticipate the labeling performed by a Martian who disagrees with me on questions of similarity. The generalization I wish to draw is this: To the extent that two creatures disagree in their similarity judgments, neither will be able to anticipate how the other will use words as labels for objects. I think that this generalization is valid, as generalizations go, because the instances on which it is based are representative of the situation we would face in trying to understand the labeling behavior of a creature whose labeling behavior we did not already understand fairly well. In particular, the fact that in this example the problem was to anticipate the labeling of a novel object is representative. Novelty is pervasive.

The conclusion that I have been aiming for may now be drawn. We have just seen that two creatures will be unable to anticipate one another's labeling to the extent that their similarity judgments disagree. But as I explained, they will be able to communicate only to the extent that they are able to anticipate one another's labeling. So to the extent that two creatures disagree in their similarity judgments, they will be unable to communicate. As I explained, this conclusion undercuts the argument against the objectivity of similarity judgments.

In arguing for this conclusion I have made certain assumptions about what is plausible. Although I cannot here address the topic of plausibility in a general way, I would like to say what I take the source of this plausibility to be. I take it that, other things being equal, a given hypothesis qualifies as more plausible than another to the extent that it possesses greater *imitability*. Greater imitability in a hypothesis means that if we accept it as a solution to a given problem, then when we face further theoretical problems, we will be in a better position to identify solutions that are uniquely most similar to the hypotheses we have already accepted. Both in Alice's case and in the Martian's, I considered two hypotheses. In Alice's case I said that the one hypothesis was far less plausible than the other, whereas in the Martian's case I said that the one hypothesis was *hardly* less plausible than the other. This is so because if we interpret Alice as sorting the blocks by color, then we will know very well how to interpret her if on some later occasion we find that all of the blocks in a given pile have the same *shape*. But suppose we interpret her as grouping together the nontetrahedral green blocks and as grouping together the red-or-tetrahedral blocks. Then, if on some later occasion we find that she has sorted the blocks so that all of the blocks in a given pile have the same shape, we will face a wide variety of hypotheses all about equally similar to the hypothesis that on the earlier occasion she was grouping together the nontetrahedral green blocks. So our hypothesis concerning Alice is much more plausible than its competitors in the sense that it is more imitable than its competitors. In contrast, none of the hypotheses that we might put forward to explain the Martian's groupings is going to give us much guidance if on some later occasion we again have to try to figure out the principles by which the Martian is sorting things.

I wish to emphasize the modesty of my refutation of the argument against the objectivity of similarity. I certainly have not shown that all similarity judgments are objective. On the contrary, two rational people who are unable even in principle to reach agreement on an isolable range of questions of similarity might yet be able to communicate provided their similarity judgments do not diverge too widely overall. I do not need to show that all similarity judgments are objective, because the possibility that some are subjective does not undermine our hope of explaining fundamental cognitive operations in terms of similarity judgments. Even if we wish to cite similarity judgments in explaining the learning of words by means of which objective judgments are expressed, we do not need to suppose that all similarity judgments are objective; at most we need to suppose that those we cite are. So I do not need to show, and I do not believe, that any disagreement in similarity judgments whatsoever would prevent communication.

This concession leads to the further objection to the objectivity of similarity judgments that since total agreement in similarity judgments is not necessary for communication, communication may be possible even though no similarity judgment is totally objective. Consider a community of three rational people A, B, and C. There are three pairs of people to consider, A and B, B and C, and A and C. Suppose that each pair agrees on two-thirds of the questions of similarity that arise in their community and that this is enough agreement to enable them to communicate with one another. But suppose also that each pair disagrees on a distinct third of the questions of similarity (that is, a third that is disjoint from the thirds that the other two pairs disagree on). Suppose also that their disagreements are irresolvable. This means that no similarity judgments are objective, since there is none on which any two rational creatures who can communicate must be able to reach agreement. If the ability to communicate requires agreement on five-sixths of all questions of similarity, then a similar argument can be constructed by considering a community of four in which each of the six pairs of members disagrees on a distinct sixth of all questions of similarity. If still greater agreement is required, consider a still larger community.

The best way to answer this sort of objection, I think, is to distinguish *degrees* of objectivity. To this end, we may first distinguish several *dimensions* of objectivity. One dimension is the *probability* that two arbitrarily chosen agents possessing a certain degree of rationality might be able to reach at least a certain level of agreement in their answers to a given question. Another dimension is the *degree of rationality* that would ensure a certain probability of reaching at least a certain level of agreement. A third dimension is the *level of agreement* such that agents possessing a certain degree of rationality would have a certain probability of being able to reach at least that level. To every question there will correspond a *surface* of points in this three-dimensional space. Degrees of objectivity might then be defined in terms of the convexity of this surface. (See figure 8.2.) A highly objective question might be defined,

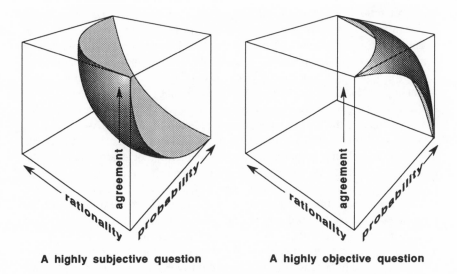

A highly subjective question   **A highly objective question**

Figure 8.2

roughly, as a question on which agents with only a moderate degree of rationality can nonetheless very probably reach a high level of agreement. In practice we could never actually assign such degrees of objectivity, but even so, the
idea of such degrees may be used, as follows, to answer the present argument
against the objectivity of similarity.

In this account of degrees of objectivity, the pertinent probability is the
probability that any pair of subjects from a given community will be able to
reach a given level of agreement. Thus this account relativizes objectivity to a
community. Objectivity *simpliciter* is objectivity relative to the community of
all rational creatures who might possibly exist. The argument from the case of
Alice and the Martian can be taken to show that two creatures will be able to
communicate only if questions of similarity have a certain degree of objectivity
relative to a community consisting of just those two. It follows that in any
community in which every member can communicate with every other, similarity judgments cannot have less than that same degree of objectivity relative
to the community. So the present objection cannot show that similarity judgments possess less than that same degree of objectivity *simpliciter*.

Granting that similarity judgments have only a certain limited degree of
objectivity will not undermine our hopes of explaining fundamental cognitive
operations in terms of similarity judgments unless an argument can be constructed to show that for purposes of explaining fundamental cognitive operations, similarity judgments must have a *greater* degree of objectivity. They may
not need it if, for instance, what we hope to explain is word learning and the
judgments expressed by means of the words so learned are not totally objective
either.

6. I now return to the topic of objectivity in order to determine the extent to
which my argument rests on the agreement conception of objectivity. To begin,
I would like to point out that the doubt about the possibility of explaining
fundamental cognitive operations in terms of similarity judgments cannot easily be formulated without raising questions about objectivity. At first sight it
might appear that the argument for the requirement of objectivity can be reformulated as an argument for the requirement of the possibility of agreement. The
major premise of the reformulated argument would state that if word learning
depends on similarity judgments, and rational creatures who can communicate
may be unable even in principle to reach agreement on questions of similarity,
then they may also be unable even in principle to reach agreement in judgments
expressed by means of those words. However, I think that any persuasiveness
this reformulated argument might have would derive from the original version
formulated in terms of objectivity. The reason is that if the possibility of
agreement among rational creatures who can communicate were not normally
necessary for objectivity, then there might be no reason to hold that the judgments expressed by means of words learned through similarity judgments must
offer the possibility of such agreement.

Nonetheless, one might wonder whether the argument for the requirement of objectivity rests on the agreement conception of objectivity. It is true that the argument I gave in defense of (1), the first premise in the argument for the requirement of objectivity, depended on the agreement conception of objectivity, but that dependence was not essential. Partisans of other conceptions of objectivity would be able, I believe, to construct analogous defenses of (1). For instance, a partisan of the correspondence conception might argue for (1) as follows: If learning how to use the word "chair" depends on similarity judgments, then the question whether o should be called a "chair" is going to come down to the question whether o is more similar to certain things, for instance, those things antecedently agreed to be chairs, than to others. But if similarity judgments are not objective, then there is no sort of fact for them to correspond to. So if the question whether something should be called a "chair" depends on a question about similarity, then there is no sort of fact for the judgment that something should be called a "chair" to correspond to. In that case the judgment that o is a chair will not be objective. So the answer is no, the argument for the requirement of objectivity does not depend on the agreement conception of objectivity.

A second question is whether the argument against the objectivity of similarity judgments rests on the agreement conception of objectivity. Notice that the thesis about objectivity on which that argument rests is just this: (*a*) *If* a question of similarity is objective, *then* it ought to be possible for rational creatures who can communicate to reach agreement in their answers to that question. The argument then proceeds to conclude that questions of similarity are not objective on the grounds that rational creatures might not be able to reach agreement. But (*a*) is not yet the agreement conception of objectivity, for that claims, in addition, that (*b*) if a question of similarity is *not* objective, then there might be ideally rational creatures able to communicate who would be *un*able to reach agreement on that question. Moreover, one could accept (*a*), even both (*a*) and (*b*), while denying the agreement conception, according to which (*a*) and (*b*) amount to an *analysis* of objectivity. As an analysis, (*a*) and (*b*) might be thought to beg the question by relying on a conception of rationality that in turn has to be explained in terms of objectivity. So, no, the argument against the objectivity of similarity judgments does not directly depend on the agreement conception of objectivity.

Nonetheless, (*a*) does seem to be a thesis that partisans of other conceptions of objectivity might wish to reject. No matter what conception of objectivity one favors, one ought to agree, I think, that no kind of rationality that we can hope to possess is guaranteed to reach the *truth*. But a partisan of the correspondence conception of objectivity might maintain in addition that no kind of rationality that we can hope to possess is guaranteed to generate *agreement* on objective questions. Objective judgment, it might be said, aims at correspondence with reality, but there are many equally good but largely incommensurable ways of aiming at correspondence. So since the argument against the objectivity of similarity presupposes (*a*), the agreement conception of objectivity seems to underlie that argument.

Ultimately this is not right, however. Partisans of the correspondence conception may deny that the possibility of agreement among rational creatures who can communicate is strictly necessary for objectivity, but they can hardly deny that the possibility of reaching agreement is normally an important criterion of objectivity. If it regularly happened that ideally rational creatures who could communicate were simply unable, despite their best efforts, to reach agreement on simple questions concerning similarity, then even a partisan of the correspondence conception would be compelled to concede, perhaps by an inference to the best explanation, that similarity judgments were not objective. So the upshot is that the argument against the objectivity of similarity does not depend on the agreement conception of objectivity.

A third question is whether my argument in defense of the objectivity of similarity judgments rests on the agreement conception of objectivity. That depends on how strong a conclusion one aims to draw. The argument against the objectivity of similarity claimed that two creatures might be perfectly rational and able to communicate and yet quite unable to reach agreement on questions of similarity. My defense amounted to arguing that significant disagreement in similarity judgments renders communication impossible. The argument for that conclusion did not explicitly mention objectivity at all and does not rest on any particular conception of objectivity.

But one might wish to draw a stronger conclusion from my argument than merely that a certain argument against the objectivity of similarity judgments fails. One might wish to conclude, in addition, that similarity judgments are indeed objective. That further conclusion can be had if and only if we add something like the agreement conception of objectivity. Without an agreement conception of objectivity, the agreement in similarity judgments guaranteed by the ability to communicate might be regarded as merely agreement in subjective judgments. But given the agreement conception of objectivity, my conclusion that the ability to communicate entails agreement in similarity judgments implies that such similarity judgments are objective.

7. Finally, I want to clear up an apparent inconsistency between what I said in chapter 4 and what I have said here. In chapter 4, I argued that with certain exceptions we should be able to understand (but not necessarily translate) any language. Here, however, I seem to acknowledge certain limits on our capacity to understand other languages. I have argued that we can understand only those languages spoken by creatures who judge similarities more or less as we do. In erecting this limitation on our capacity to understand other languages, perhaps I seem to acknowledge the possibility of a language beyond that limitation, a language unintelligible to us because its speakers judge similarities very differently from the way we do.

On the contrary, I do not acknowledge any languages beyond the limit. Instead, I accept the consequences of my argument and deny that the Martian I have described in this chapter really speaks a language. I have been assuming all along that Alice's and the Martian's sorting behavior is an expression of their labeling. So the oddity in the Martian's sorting behavior, by our lights, would be reflected in an equally odd use of words. But such an odd use of words would be unintelligible to us. So by the assumption that we would be able to understand the Martian language if there were one, the Martian does not speak a language after all. (This is not a "transcendental" argument, because the crucial premise, namely, that we could translate [almost] any language, is not something that I can be said to *know* in the requisite sense.)

Here someone might object that it could happen both that some "language" was as unintelligible to us as our Martian's sorting behavior and yet that that "language" genuinely facilitated an advanced technology. In that case, surely, we should grant that the Martians have a language despite its unintelligibility to us. I grant that a "language" that facilitated an advanced technology would really be a language. But I deny that creatures whose so-called language was as unintelligible as the sorting behavior described in this chapter could conduct an advanced technological society by means of such a "language." Unless these Martians are highly superior intelligences (an exception I have already acknowledged), we should in principle be able to learn to understand their language by studying the ways in which it facilitates their cooperative enterprises.

Here then is why not all systems of classification are equally natural. Not all of them are such as might be exhibited in a language. For some systems of classification, if the "words" of a "language" referred to the classes of such a system, then those "words" would not be learnable and would not facilitate communication, and so the "language" to which they belonged would not really be a language. That is the problem with a concept like *blork*, which I discussed in chapter 4. To the extent that the classes in a classification scheme are gerrymandered after the fashion of the class of blorks, the words of a language cannot refer to such classes. However, this distinction between natural and unnatural categories is not a distinction to which the Lockean, or the network theorist, may appeal in explaining the origin of our concepts, for it is a distinction that rests on an independent conception of the function and possibility of language. I do not say that words cannot stand for certain sorts of categories because those categories are unnatural. Rather, I say that certain categories are unnatural because they are not the sort of categories that the words of languages might stand for. (A Lockean can say that too, provided he or she does not then rest his or her account of language on a prior conception of natural categories.)

9

Causal Judgments

1. The ultimate goal of this, the second part of this book is to present a theory of communication. That theory is intended to accommodate the fact that languages arise in worlds that do not already contain languages and are learned by creatures who do not already speak a language. Accordingly, in the next chapter I will present my account of the basic function of language and then explain how a very simple language might be learned. That explanation will turn on two basic cognitive abilities: the ability to form the sort of similarity judgment discussed in chapter 9 and the ability to form a second sort of judgment, to be discussed in this chapter. This second sort is related to judgments of cause and effect but is not full-fledged causal judgment. It is only the *protoform* of causal judgment.

The protoform of causal judgment, I will argue, is what I will call *kausal* judgment. A kausal judgment is a judgment to the effect that a certain three-place relation obtains between three things. I will call this relation the *kausal* relation. The relata of the kausal relation are a *background*, an *action* and another *action*. An action is an event consisting in an *agent's* doing something. An agent is an *object*, (not necessarily a *thinking* object) and the agent's *doing* something is a *change* of some kind in the agent. Roughly, a kausal relation holds between a background and two actions just in case the background is relatively unchanging, and the first action leads up to the point in time and space where the second action begins.

It should be plausible, I think, that learning is largely a matter of learning cause-effect relations. Thus the plausibility of a theory of language learning in terms of kausal judgments would be enhanced if it could be shown that kausal judgments are in some sense the foundation of the concept of causality. In that case, they would share in the significance that, quite independently of any theories of language, we recognize causal judgments to have. So one thing I will do in this chapter is argue that kausal judgments are, as I will say, the *protoform* of causal judgments.

In order to judge that a certain relation obtains, it is necessary to represent the relata in some way. My twin objectives of explaining language learning in terms of kausal judgments and of showing kausal judgments to be a protoform of causal judgments place certain limits on the sort of account I may give of the representations of the relata. Namely, there must be ways of representing the relata that do not depend on the prior possession of a language or on a prior grasp of cause-effect relations. So another thing I will do in this chapter is argue that this sort of representation is possible.

I should emphasize that the main objective of this chapter is *not* to develop an analysis or theory of causality. Rather, I will take for granted that the reader recognizes a certain kind of causality, which I will call *agentive* causality, and I will appeal to this prior, undefined conception of causality in discussing the relation between kausal judgments and causal judgments. However, the theory of causal judgments that will emerge from this might indeed encourage a certain approach to the subject of causality per se. So at the end of the chapter I will briefly consider the prospects for developing a theory of causality in this way.

Although I do not propose to explain what causality is, it is nonetheless necessary for me to say something about the kind of causality at issue here. *Cause* is said in many ways. Suppose I drop a stone and it falls to earth. What is the cause of the stone's falling? Is my letting go the cause? Is the force of gravity the cause? Is the earth, which is the source of the gravitational field, the cause? Obviously, each of these in its own way can be the cause. Some philosophers have been inclined to conclude from this that causality is just *be*causality. In other words, a cause is just whatever we might cite in an explanation of why something happened. But this is a little like saying that food is just whatever we may cite in answering the question, "What's for dinner?" What we would like is some kind of guidance. We might like to know what food is so that we may decide what we can eat. Similarly, we might want to know what causes are so that we may know what we may cite in explanation. On the other hand, the example of the stone shows that there are indeed various kinds of causality. So what I need to do is say what kind I am interested in.

The kind of causality I am interested in is what I will call *agentive* causality. In agentive causation, an object, called the *agent*, does something—changes in some way—which causes a change in some other object. For example, one billiard ball collides with another billiard ball, causing the second to move. Or a gas furnace heats the house. In this case, the agent is the furnace, the action is the lighting of the burner, and the object acted on is the house, conceived of as including the space that heats up. The agentive cause in the example of dropping a stone is the person who lets go of the stone. The earth does not actually do anything to cause the stone to fall (such as reaching out and grabbing it). The gravitational field is just a background condition under which letting go of the stone can cause it to fall.

Agentive causality in this sense has some claim to being the fundamental, or paradigm, case of causality. Other kinds of causal relation can often be seen as extensions of agentive causality. The concept of agentive causality can be extended by viewing things as agents or events as actions that would not ordinarily be conceived as such. For example, a toxic waste dump might not ordinarily be considered an agent, and raising the incidence of leukemia in a population might not ordinarily be considered an action. But if we think of things this way, then we might think of the fact that the toxic waste dump caused an increase in the incidence of leukemia in the surrounding population as an instance of agentive causality. Having applied the concept of causality in this fashion, we might then retain the conceptualization in terms of causality while altering the ontology. For example, we might think of the cause as a person's *living near* the toxic waste dump and think of the effect as that person's *experiencing a higher risk* of developing leukemia than he or she would experience otherwise. In this way we might arrive at conceptions of causality other than agentive causality.

2. I have said that the protoform of the causal judgment— the agentive causal judgment—is the *kausal* judgment. Kausal *relations* may be defined as follows:

Given background B, x's F-ing *kauses* y's G-ing if and only if
   (i)   background B is relatively *unchanging* during the course of x's F-ing and y's G-ing,
   (ii) x's F-ing begins *prior* to the beginning of y's G-ing and continues at least until y begins to G, and
   (iii) when y begins to G, y is *in the place* where x is F-ing.

For example, if one billiard ball strikes another on an otherwise empty table and the second ball then begins to move, that is a kausal relation. If a person lets go of a stone while everyone else stands still and watches, and the stone then begins to fall, that is an example of a kausal relation. If a telephone rings in an otherwise eventless room and a person picks up the receiver, that too is a kausal relation (assuming that we can think of the ringing as taking place where the person begins to act). Of course many non*causal* relations will be kausal relations as well. For instance, if a telephone rings and while it is ringing an egg rolls off the table, that might be a kausal relation too. Where x's F-ing kauses y's G-ing, I will say that x's F-ing is the *kause* and y's G-ing is the *effekt*.

A little more should be said about the background to a causal relation. One question is how great a volume of space is encompassed by the background. I think of it as roughly the volume of space that can be perceived by someone while witnessing x's F-ing and y's G-ing. So if the agents whose actions stand in a kausal relation are bacteria viewed under a microscope, then the background might be just the region around them that can be seen through the microscope. Similarly, when I say that the background to a kausal relation is "relatively unchanging," I mean that no events of roughly the same scale as x's F-ing and y's G-ing take place. What these clarifications show is that the concept of a kausal relation is very anthropocentric.

My explanation of kausal *judgment* will be simply that it is a judgment to the effect that a kausal relation obtains. However, I will not now try to say what a *judgment* is. Instead I will rely on the reader's intuitive sense of the concept of judgment in order to try to get an explanation of language going. Having done so, I will be able in chapters 13 and 14 to say what such things as beliefs and judgments really are and to distinguish them from the kind of theoretical entity that I am postulating here and calling judgment. I acknowledge that in attempting to pin down this concept of a kausal judgment I am alternating rather freely between the mental and the nonmental. Kausal relations between nonmental events were identified in terms of human perceptual capacities, and kausal judgments were then identified in terms of kausal relations. This kind of alternation between the mental and the nonmental will be a persistent and necessary, but not vitiating, feature of this chapter.

Causal judgment, I conjecture, may be a refinement of kausal judgment. In principle, it might be possible to confirm this conjecture through experimental work with children. But as far as I know, the necessary sort of experimentation has never been done. Partial confirmation may perhaps be found in studies reported by Bullock, Gelman, and Baillargeon (1982). These experimenters found that children as young as three years will judge that the spatially more proximate event is the cause of a later event. They also found that children do not necessarily identify the temporally more proximate event as the cause, which is a finding not helpful to my case. But it is hard to draw definite conclusions, since the studies that tested the relevance of spatial and temporal proximity relied on children's verbal responses to determine whether they judged something to be a cause, and these verbal responses cannot be relied on as indicators of the child's cognitive processes.

So, rather than relying on empirical studies, I will try to lend plausibility to the suggestion that kausal judgments are the protoform of causal judgments by explaining how the capacity to make *kausal* judgments might be transformed into a capacity to make *causal* judgments. To say that one sort of judgment is transformed into another is to say, roughly, that a certain sort of learning exploits the capacity to make the one sort in order to instill the capacity to make the other sort. Unfortunately, I do not have the theory of learning that I would need in order fully to explain how kausal judgment is transformed into causal judgment. But it should be plausible that the processes that, according to my account, must occur in the subject might indeed take place without the subject's possessing extraordinary intelligence or much prior knowledge.

It might be confusing to characterize *kausal* judgment as becoming *causal* judgment, since kausal relations are not causal relations and one would expect a kausal judgment to be something responsive specifically to kausal relations and a causal judgment to be something responsive specifically to causal relations. It should be borne in mind that the transformation is not a matter of a particular occurrence's having been at a particular time a kausal judgment and then at some later time becoming a causal judgment. What I am talking about is, rather, the transformation of a capacity. The capacity to make kausal judgments becomes, through some kind of learning, the capacity to make causal judgments. To avoid confusion on this score, it might be helpful to introduce a third term,

schmausal judgment, and to characterize the capacity to make schmausal judgments as initially a capacity to make kausal judgments and as becoming a
capacity to make causal judgments. But I will decline this extra helping of
jargon. Or it might be helpful to think of kausal judgments and causal judgments as a certain kind of event in the brain. Then the claim that kausal
judgment becomes causal judgment might be understood as the claim that this
type of brain event starts out meaning *kausality* and comes to mean *causality*.
But I will eschew this device as well.

Many causal relations are not kausal relations. So one thing that has to be
explained is how it comes about that a creature learns to judge that given a
certain background, x kauses y when in fact, x causes y but does not kause y.
There are at least three main kinds of cases, which I will treat by means of
examples:

1. *Simultaneous causation.* In Kant's famous example, the sinking of a ball
into a pillow causes a hollow to be formed in the pillow. Contrast two cases: (*a*)
The ball is dropped from some height above the pillow. (*b*) The ball is already in
contact with the pillow when it is released. In (*a*), the fall of the ball is indeed a
kause of the hollow formed in the pillow. In (*b*), however, the fall *causes*, but
does not *kause*, the hollow, because the effect commences as soon as the cause
does. But there is an obvious similarity between the two cases. Since the cause
in (*b*) is so similar to the kause in (*a*), some sort of analogical inference might
lead to the judgment that in case (*b*) too the fall kauses the hollow. In this way
the capacity to form kausal judgments might come to better approximate a
capacity to form causal judgments. (A rule for the necessary sort of analogical
inference will be formulated as the principle of kausal transference below.)

2. *Causation amid activity.* Many causal relations will fail to be kausal
relations just because the causes and effects take place in a very active environment and not against the relatively unchanging background that kausal relations
require. Suppose that billiard ball A strikes billiard ball B at a moment when
many other balls are in motion on the table as well. This fails to be a kausal
relation, because the action of A on B does not take place against a relatively
unchanging background. Nonetheless, the sequence of events involving A and
B will be very similar to other sequences of events involving similar billiard
balls against a relatively unchanging background, that is, one in which no other
balls are in motion. Thus kausal judgments in these other cases might result,
again by a kind of analogical inference, in a judgment to the effect that A's
motion kauses B's motion as well.

3. *Interaction.* Suppose that two billiard balls, A and B, are in motion toward
one another. After the collision, both are again in motion, in opposite directions. Here neither the motion of A nor the motion of B is, strictly speaking, a
kause. However, this case can easily be assimilated to a kausal relation by
thinking of the pair of balls as one agent prior to the collision and as a distinct
agent afterward. The kause is then the motion of the two of them prior to the

collision, and the effekt is the motion of the two of them afterward. Suppose a smaller (less massive) billiard ball strikes a larger (more massive) billiard ball at rest. In that case, the smaller ball rebounds from the larger and also sets the larger in motion. The resistance of the larger, we would like to say, causes the rebound of the smaller, but, as far as the naked eye can see, the larger did not do anything. From some Galilean frame of reference the larger ball too is in motion prior to the collision, but I would not expect an understanding of Galilean frames to precede the grasp of simple causal relations. Nonetheless, a causal relation might be recognized here by an assimilation of this case to cases in which both balls are in motion.

In some cases, in order to find a kausal relation where we find a causal relation, we may have to consider things more as they appear rather than as we know them to be. What we know about a stove is that the space around it begins to heat up as soon as the stove itself does. There is no action, in this case, leading up to the effect, which is what is required for a kausal relation. But from an unenlightened point of view, the stove's heating the room does appear to be a kausal relation, since a space around the stove large enough for us to sit in does not become noticeably warmer until some time after the stove itself has warmed up.

So much for causal relations that are not kausal relations. Now let us consider kausal relations that are not causal relations. Here what has to be explained is how it comes about that a creature learns not to judge that x kauses y when in fact x does kause y but does not cause y. In outline, the explanation is this: Kausal relations that are not causal relations will seldom be anticipated by analogical or any other sort of reasoning. So one may learn to distinguish between cases in which the relation is causal and cases in which it is merely kausal by learning to distinguish between cases in which one might have anticipated that x would kause y and cases in which one could not have anticipated that. A judgment to the effect that x *predictably* kauses y is a closer approximation to a causal judgment than a judgment merely to the effect that x kauses y.

For example, suppose that just as I am hanging up the telephone, the doorbell rings. If nothing else is going on at the same time, then hanging up the telephone *kauses* the doorbell to ring. But of course hanging up the telephone does not *cause* the doorbell to ring. By the same token, I would not have anticipated that hanging up would kause the doorbell to ring. There may have been occasions in the past when hanging up the phone was immediately followed by the ringing of the doorbell, but there were surely many more, equally similar to the present occasion of hanging up the phone, in which it was not. So I would not anticipate that hanging up the phone would kause the ringing of the doorbell on this occasion. Moreover, when the doorbell does ring, I may well recognize (in some sense) that I would not have anticipated that the doorbell would ring. And so, while I may judge that hanging up the phone did indeed kause the doorbell to ring, I may also judge that hanging up the phone did not *predictably* kause the doorbell to ring. This judgment to the effect that one thing did not predictably kause another approximates to a causal judgment.

This solution creates another problem, since not all causes predictably cause their effects. The sound of an acorn hitting the roof may cause a sleeping dog to wake up, but we could not have predicted that. (Even if we could not have predicted the causal relation, we may be fairly confident of it after the fact, for the effect may require some explanation in terms of observable events, and the cause cited may be the only viable candidate.) The solution is to introduce a further transformation. Strange as it may sound, a capacity to make judgments of predictable kausality may be transformed into a capacity to make judgments of unpredictable causality. The case of the acorn's waking the dog is similar to other cases of kausality that are indeed predictable. Thus, by a kind of analogical reasoning again, the same sort of judgment may come to be made in this case as well. I acknowledge that in appealing to similarities in this way I am merely hoping, without real evidence to back me up, that the objective similarities that on this account would have to obtain in order for us to learn to judge causal relations as well as we seem to do really do obtain. But they might.

It is noteworthy that on this theory of our knowledge of causes, we require an environment that is highly cooperative. Causes must frequently be kauses. Otherwise judgments of similarity will not lead us to recognize the causal relations that are not kausal relations. This means that causal interactions must frequently take place against a relatively unchanging background. If the world were indeed, in James's phrase, a blooming, buzzing confusion, we would never sort it out. Moreover, the salient, memorable kausal relations must frequently be causal relations. Otherwise, kausal relations would not have the predictability that enables us to discover causal relations.

3. While I can postpone consideration of the nature of judgment, I cannot likewise postpone consideration of the nature of the representations of the objects of such judgments. In order to judge that a certain relation holds between two or more things, it is necessary to be able to represent those things somehow. So in order to form a kausal judgment, it is necessary to be able to represent a relatively unchanging background and to represent the actions of agents. It it not necessary to be able to represent every possible background or every possible action, but it is necessary to be able to represent those that stand in the kausal relations one can represent in a judgment. Given that kausal judgments are to be cited in explaining both language and causal judgments, the question arises whether it is possible for a person to represent backgrounds and actions in sufficient variety without already possessing a language or a grasp of causal relations.

There are two sorts of reasons to think that the requisite kind of representation is a possibility. The first is that we can see more or less a priori what sort of things might be represented prior to language and a grasp of causal relations.

Objects moving across a relatively unchanging background often have what I will call *kinematic cohesion*. For example, imagine a pink circle moving across a solid blue background. We can think of this pink circle as a continuous sequence of pink-circles-at-a-moment. The many pink-circles-at-a-moment make up one persisting pink circle because their locations in space and time form a continuous path. Suppose, however, that each next pink-circle-at-a-moment is somewhat redder than the one before. In that case, the object may be preserved, but its qualities have changed. Similarly, it may gradually become larger. The identity of the pink circle across these changes in place, color, and size illustrates what I mean by kinematic cohesion. The things representable prior to language and a grasp of causal relations might be things individuated by the criterion of kinematic cohesion.

I cannot define kinematic cohesion. In lieu of a comprehensive definition, one might hope to define at least the paradigm case of kinematic cohesion and then illustrate some of the ways in which kinematic cohesion might diverge from the paradigm case. But even that is not so easy if one is ignorant, as I am, of the ways in which representations of objects individuated by kinematic cohesion might be physically realized in the brain. So what I will do instead is explain by analogy how one might define the paradigm case of kinematic cohesion. To define it properly, one would want to define it in terms of relations between mental states, which, provided certain conditions are met, would constitute *representations*. I will not do that, but I will define it in terms of relations between *photographs* of objects. I intend this to serve as an illustration of the way in which kinematic cohesion might be defined in terms of mental states.

Say that a *landscape* is a three-dimensional arrangement of photographable objects at a given time. Say that a *perspective* on a landscape is a position and orientation of a camera with respect to the landscape. In a familiar way, each photograph is a certain sort of projection of the landscape onto a rectangular sheet of paper. Call this the *photographic projection*. Each region on the photograph corresponds to a region in the landscape consisting of the surfaces of things in the landscape that are projected onto that region of the photograph, and many regions of the landscape correspond to regions in the photograph. (But not all regions of the landscape correspond to regions of the photograph. Only those "visible" to the camera do.)

Consider a temporally ordered sequence of landscapes. Consider a sequence of photographs of those landscapes from a given perspective. Consider a sequence R of *regions* in those photographs, one per photograph. I will say that R is a *paradigm case of kinematic cohesion* in the sense that pertains to regions of *photographs* if and only if (a) excluding regions in the sequence R, every region in every photograph is qualitatively indistinguishable from the region at the same location (relative to the borders) in every other photograph, and (b) for all r and r' in R, if r' is the temporally next member of R after r, then r and r' are spatially and qualitatively indistinguishable (to the naked eye), and (c) there are r and r' in R such that r and r' are spatially or qualitatively distinguishable. Condition (a) ensures that the depiction of the background is unchanging. Condition (b) ensures that any change is very gradual. Condition (c) ensures that something happens.

Now that the paradigm case of kinematic cohesion in the sense that pertains to regions of *photographs* has been defined, it is possible to define the paradigm case of kinematic cohesion in the sense that pertains to *objects* thus: A sequence of regions of landscapes constitutes a paradigm case of kinematic cohesion in the sense that pertains to objects if and only if there is some paradigm case of kinematic cohesion in the sense that pertains to regions of photographs such that each member of the sequence of regions of landscapes corresponds (in accordance with the photographic projection) to a region in the sequence of regions of photographs (and the temporal order of the landscapes is the same as that of their corresponding photographs). Now, in fact this definition is not the one we want, but the one we want would be like this one except that the definition would be given in terms of brain-states and not in terms of photographs.

Suppose the requisite definition given. Still, there will be instances of kinematic cohesion, as I conceive of it, beyond these paradigm cases. For instance, kinematic cohesion does not always require a spatiotemporally unbroken path. For instance, the pink circle might, as we would say, "disappear behind" a black triangle and emerge from the other side, provided that the moment of reappearance is the one we would expect on the basis of the rate of travel up to the moment of disappearance. Further, the unchanging background is not necessary either. It is quite possible for two concurrent sequences to possess kinematic cohesion if they do not cross paths. Moreover, they may even cross paths if they clearly look different and neither object changes as their paths cross. But even where paths cross, qualitative changes of some kinds will preserve kinematic cohesion. In the paradigm case, a kinematically cohering object is moving or changing in some way against an unchanging background. Perhaps the most important way in which a kinematically cohering object may differ from the paradigm case is that it may also exist at rest, in an unchanging state. The idea is that while it may first come to be represented when it is changing against an unchanging background, once it is representable, it is representable even at rest.

Kinematic cohesion, whatever exactly it turns out to be, is not intended to be a necessary and sufficient condition for genuine object identity across time. Two distinct objects might kinematically cohere. For instance, a kitten might disappear behind a flower pot, and its sibling might then emerge from the other side. Two temporal stages of a single object, such as a caterpillar and a moth, might fail the test of kinematic cohesion (relative to rather course measure of graduated change). Kinematic cohesion is, however, intended to be a valid approximation to object identity, at least across relatively short periods. In the normal sort of environment in which learning takes place, kinematic cohesion might often enough serve as an accurate test of object identity. It might be accurate often enough to serve as a basis for learning some important relations between objects.

And yet there is some hope of defining kinematic cohesion in such a way that it is often a reliable test of object identity but without appealing to causal relations. We cannot in general understand object identity apart from a grasp of cause-effect relations. If two qualitatively indistinguishable billiard balls, A and B, collide head-on, A being the one moving from left to right, then after the collision we will know that A is the one moving from right to left, not the one moving from left to right. We know this because of what we know about how billiard balls interact. But even if we ignore such causal tests of object identity, we will often not go wrong. So there is some hope that the test of kinematic cohesion will often enough not go wrong even if it is defined without regard for causal relations.

Moreover, there is some hope of distinguishing the representation of kinematic cohesion from the sort of classification that depends on language. Certainly the recognition of kinematic cohesion can be thought of as a kind of classification. It is a classification of the several temporal stages of a thing as stages of one thing. But that does not mean that the mental mechanisms employed in recognizing kinematic cohesion are the same as thoses involved in recognizing a dachshund and a sheepdog as both dogs or even in recognizing two pink circles as both pink circles.

If these hopes for the concept of kinematic cohesion can be fulfilled, then it might be possible to explain what sorts of things may be represented in kausal judgments prior to the acquisition of language. The representations of kauses and effekts will be representations of things, or *agents*, the identity of which is given by the criterion of kinematic cohesion, and these things will be represented as changing in various ways. We may think of such representations as a kind of sequential trace, or map, of the object across space and time that in some way registers the changing character of that object. This trace may have several aspects or dimensions, corresponding to the several aspects of the acting agent that it represents. Inasmuch as the trace is itself variable along its length, the trace may represent the object as changing in various ways—in position, shape, and color. Inasmuch as it functions in cognition as a single trace, it may qualify as a representation of *one thing*.

The second reason to expect that there might be the sorts of representations necessary for kausal judgments is empirical. In a series of very interesting studies conducted by Elizabeth Spelke (1985, 1988, 1990) and others, it has been demonstrated that infants as young as four months possess some sort of awareness of objects as enduring individuals. Infants this young can be studied by means of *preferential-looking methods*. Infants are repeatedly afforded the same visual, auditory, or tactile stimulus until they grow disinterested in it and

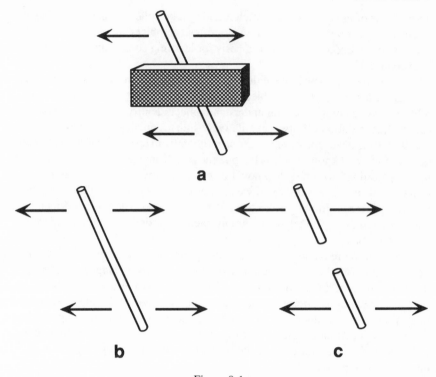

a

b   c

Figure 9.1

stop attending to it when it appears. When this happens, the infants are said to have *habituated* to the stimulus. They are then afforded another stimulus in some way different from the first. If habituation generalizes, if, that is, the infant shows little interest in the second stimulus, then that is evidence that the infant regards it as much the same as the first one. If, on the other hand, the infant spends time studying the new stimulus, then that is evidence that the infant regards the new stimulus as different from the preceding one.

For example, in one study (Spelke 1985, 326–30; 1988, 200–202), infants were first shown a display consisting of a rod that moved back and forth behind a stationary block (fig. 9.1,a). After they had become habituated to this, the subjects were shown a second display. For half of the subjects, the second display consisted of a single rod moving in the same manner as the rod in the first display had moved (fig. 9.1,b). For the other half of the subjects, the second display consisted of two shorter rods moving in unison (fig. 9.1,c). The gap between the two rods in this second display was such that the first display too might have consisted of such a synchronized pair of rods, with the gap between them hidden by the block. The result was that infants in the second group tended to look longer at the display of two short rods than the infants in the first group tended to look at the single rod. Spelke concludes that infants perceived the complete shape of the partly occluded rod in the first display. (I omit mention of a number of subsidiary studies designed to rule out alternative explanations.)

It is difficult to state the general conclusion to be drawn from such studies. Spelke's own conclusion is that such experiments show that infants possess an "object concept" (1988, 227). I have no objection to this way of putting the point as long as it is not supposed to mean that prelinguistic children have a concept of objects in the same sense in which an adult who has mastered the English word "object" has a concept of objects. The difference is not just that adults know more about objects or understand them better. The difference is that in mastering English the adult participates in a kind of thinking entirely foreign to creatures that do not, or do not yet, possess a language. The danger in speaking of an infantile object concept is that one will suppose that there might likewise be an infantile dog concept or an infantile chair concept, and having made such assumptions, one might find the Lockean theory of language very tempting.[1]

In order to draw conclusions from Spelke's studies, what we need is the concept *representation-of-one-thing*. With that, we could then interpret the results of the preferential-looking studies as determining the spatio-temporal and qualitative boundaries of the things that are represented by such representations-of-one-thing. For instance, what the study employing the block and the rod shows is that in the infants' representations of the display, the rod was represented by a single representation-of-one-thing rather than by two distinct representations-of-one-thing. In other words, the preferential-looking

---

[1] Unfortunately, Spelke's own attempts to draw general conclusions are marred by a confusion of representations in the mind and the things outside of the mind that are represented. This confusion is revealed in the way she characterizes her studies as concerning "the organization of the visual world into objects" (1990, 42) or as concerning the ways in which "visual arrays are organized into objects" (1990, 53). Obviously, elements of the visual field are not literally parts of the objects seen, since the visual field is in the mind, and the objects in question are not. More importantly, this confusion is apparent in her attempt to state general "principles of object perception" (1990, 48ff.). For instance, the *cohesion principle* states that "two surface points lie on the same object only if the points are linked by a path of connected surface points" (1990, 49). If this means simply that surface points of a single object are always connected by surface points of that same object, then it is true but tells us nothing about the criteria by which the infant decides whether two surface points are connected by surface points. If, on the other hand, the cohesion principle means that two points in the *visual* field corresponding to surface points a and b on objects are perceived as points on the same object only if those two points in the visual field are connected by points in the visual field corresponding to points perceived as connecting a and b, then it is simply false. The visual field representing the occluded rod contains two points that correspond to two ends of a rod and are perceived to be at two ends of a single object, but those points in the visual field are not connected by a series of points *in the visual field* corresponding to points on the *occluded* portion of the rod.

studies can be used to help us define a mapping of individual representations onto individual things of the infantile ontology. If Spelke's studies converge with my other, a priori considerations, then we will find that the things represented by representations-of-one-thing are things individuated by the criterion of kinematic cohesion.

Still, it might be possible to doubt whether the Spelkean representations-of-one-thing were representations of a sort that might figure into prelinguistic similarity judgments and kausal judgments. But I think there is reason to believe that they might. The reason to postulate such representations-of-one thing in the first place is to explain the results of preferential-looking studies. But looking times, it is assumed, correlate with subjective novelty. Novelty, in turn, is naturally interpreted in terms of similarity judgments. So it is reasonable to suppose that the similarity judgments that interest us lie on the same mental plane as the Spelkean representations-of-one-thing.

4. Encouraged by these a priori and empirical considerations, I conjecture that there is a kind of representation available for the formation of kausal judgments prior to the discovery of causal relations and prior to the acquisition of language. I will call these representations *reflections*. Reflections, I will assume, may have several aspects, corresponding to various aspects of the things they represent. For instance, a reflection of a ball in motion may have an aspect corresponding to the ball and an aspect corresponding to the motion. A reflection of a man throwing a ball may have an aspect corresponding to the motion of the man and an aspect corresponding to the ball thrown. Call these aspects of reflections *reflection-aspects*. Call the corresponding aspects of the things represented *object-aspects*.

The a priori and empirical considerations just reviewed encourage the postulation of such representations because they encourage the idea that we might in principle make good theoretical sense of the relation of representation involved. That is, we might make sense of the relation of representation that is supposed to hold between reflections and the things they represent and of the relation of correspondence between reflection-aspects and object-aspects. If we had the requisite account of kinematic cohesion, then we could proceed to make sense of these relations roughly as follows:

First, let us say that one object-aspect α is *wider* than another object-aspect β just in case whenever an object or arrangement of objects has β, then necessarily it has α as well. So, for instance, the aspect of being colored is wider than the aspect of being red. The aspect of something's being in motion is wider than the aspect of something's moving from left to right. Here, then, is the schema of a definition of the correspondence relation between reflection-aspects and object-aspects: A reflection-aspect *corresponds* to an object-aspect if and only if that object-aspect is the widest object-aspect such that under conditions C sensory contact with kinematically cohering objects possessing that object-aspect would *always* cause the occurrence of a reflection possessing that reflection-aspect. (Here, I acknowledge, I am using the concept of causality in a fairly uncritical way.) To get an actual theory of correspondence out of this schema, one needs to specify the conditions C. I cannot do that, but I can indicate what sort of conditions they are: the subject is awake and paying attention, the object is in full view, and so on.

Reflections, I will assume, come in several varieties, including *impressions*, *envisionings*, and *background reflections*:

An *impression* is a reflection caused by an action or background such that each of its several reflection-aspects corresponds to an object-aspect that the cause actually possesses. The thing represented by an impression is the cause that has such aspects. (By definition, then, impressions do not misrepresent their objects.)

An *envisioning* is a reflection that occurs in the absence of anything possessing the object-aspects corresponding to its several reflection-aspects. When an envisioning occurs, the sort of thing possessing the corresponding object-aspects is said to be *envisioned*. The sort of thing represented by an envisioning is the sort of thing envisioned.

A *background reflection* is a reflection representing a relatively unchanging arrangement of objects. A background reflection too may be either an impression or an envisioning.

A background reflection as just defined is not to be confused with the unchanging areas surrounding a region that I spoke of in defining kinematic cohesion. Rather, a background reflection is a level of representation one notch above the representation of individual kinematically cohering objects. It is a representation of a number of kinematically cohering objects arranged in a certain way. I am going to assume that such representations too are possible prior to language and a grasp of causal relations. A background reflection need not be a representation of all objects before the senses. Instead, it may be a representation of one particularly salient object, or it may even be a representation of a certain event's *having happened*.

In philosophical definitions it is dangerous to say "always" as I have done in defining the correspondence between aspects of reflections and aspects of things they represent. It may be doubted whether it is truly possible to specify the conditions C where the correspondence is defined by such an "always." This might be a problem if the correspondence at issue were supposed to be a natural kind, but it is not. It belongs to the merely dispensable category of things that we use as a hook to get into the real nature of things, which in this case is a neurological nature. So we can accept "always" as a regulative ideal that we are unlikely to achieve in practice. This would not be a credible idealization, however, if we were not so circumspect in the sorts of thing we expect to be represented by reflections. We could not, for instance, expect any feature of a reflection to correspond to the feature *being a dog*. No matter how carefully we specified conditions *C*, we could not expect to find any reflection-aspect such that being a dog was the widest object-aspect such that under conditions *C* the presence of an object possessing that aspect would *always* cause a reflection possessing that reflection-aspect. This is why we confine our attention to things individuated by the criterion of kinematic cohesion.

This last observation is a reminder of my criticisms in chapter 6 of what I called the correlation theory of reference. Here it may appear that I am ignoring my own critique in introducing a relation of representation between reflections and objects. The theory of reference that the present theory of reflections most resembles is what I called in chapter 6 the correlation theory. But a quick review of the objections I raised against that theory shows that they do not apply as well to the present account of representation by reflections. (1) Reflections do not misrepresent. Impressions represent actual things, but do not misrepresent them. Envisionings do not represent actual things at all and so cannot *mis*represent them. (2) Reflections are not components of and are not generated by general hypotheses, and so there is no problem of explaining the representation relation in case they are. (3) The problem with the idea that the referent is the sort of thing that causes the representation was that then there would be more predications going on in the mind than can plausibly be supposed to go on. But a plethora of reflections is not so doubtful. When I look at a brick wall consisting of hundreds of bricks, then if I am aware of all of them, as I may be, there really may occur in me a reflection of each.

The general reason why representation by reflections escapes the problems I raised for reference is that reflections are nothing like general terms or concepts. It is not merely by reflecting something that a person may be credited with conceiving of something as something. To conceive of something as falling under a concept is to conceive of it as belonging to a certain type. To form a judgment containing a reflection of, say, a pink thing is not yet to conceive of that thing as belonging to a certain type, the pink things. Nor do the several *aspects* of reflections qualify as concepts, for the same reason. Reflections and their aspects do not function as classifications. On the present theory, subjects are not presumed to judge, of each of several things, that it belongs to a certain class, namely, that represented by a given reflection.

So a reflection is not a predicate or a concept. But a reflection is not like a *name* either, at least not as philosophers of language like to think of names. It is not a rigid designator. Envisionings are not names, because they represent no particular thing at all. Nor are they vacuous names, like "Pegasus," because impressions, which do represent particulars, are not names either. Impressions are not names, because the judgments in which they figure would not have been false if some other individual possessing all the represented object-aspects had been substituted for the individual that in fact is represented. Further, reflections are not names, because the judgments containing them do not bear the logical relations to other judgments that they would bear if reflections were names. For instance, the judgments that x kaused y and that x kaused z do not create a disposition to judge or an obligation to accept that some one thing kaused both y and z.

It is important to understand that in ascribing a similarity judgment or kausal judgment to a person I am not ascribing to that person the concepts that I use in describing the objects that are judged to be related. The risk is that if I say something like "S judges that the girl's letting go of the ball kaused the ball to fall," then I will seem to be assuming that S has the concepts, *girl*, *ball*, *letting go*, and *falling*, which I will not want to assume. A kausal judgment is a representation that involves, as parts as it were, representations of the objects of judgment. But in *ascribing* a kausal judgment one need not actually describe those component representations or even mention them in any way. Rather, one describes or in some way refers to (yes, I can use that word) the objects of judgment themselves, for instance, a girl and a ball.

On the other hand, in ascribing a kausal judgment, one may, if there is a reason, describe the objects of judgment in a way particularly suited to the character of the judgment ascribed. More precisely, if we are speaking of judgments "in language," then one may choose words that describe the objects of judgment in the way they are described by the words in the judgment. And if we are speaking of judgments that are not "in language," judgments containing reflections and not descriptions, then one may still try to describe the objects of judgment with words that *refer* to the object-aspects to which aspects of the component reflection-aspects *correspond*. In this case, let us say that our ascription is *determined* by the character of the reflections.

Let us suppose that we would like to ascribe kausal judgments that are determined, in this sense, by the character of the subject's reflections. One problem is that we do not really know what sorts of object-aspects are the ones that reflection-aspects correspond to, since, for one thing, we do not even know what kinematic cohesion is exactly. And even if we did know this, we might not have any very easy way to describe them in ordinary English. Nonetheless, we can pretend. Let us suppose that we have added the necessary vocabulary. Call the result *augmented English*. I will use an *angle-bracket notation* to form descriptions in augmented English that are to be understood as determined by the character of the subject's reflections.

Thus, if I write an expression with angle brackets such as "$\langle B \rangle$" or "$\langle \alpha_1, \alpha_2, \ldots, \alpha_n \rangle$," that is to be understood as a description in augmented English of the sort of thing represented by a given reflection. If I write something like "S judges that given background $\langle B \rangle$, $\langle \alpha_1, \alpha_2, \ldots, \alpha_n \rangle$ kauses $\langle \beta_1, \beta_2, \ldots, \beta_n \rangle$," that is to be understood as stating that in the mind of S there obtains a certain relation between reflections amounting to a kausal judgment, and those reflections represent $\langle B \rangle$, $\langle \alpha_1, \alpha_2, \ldots, \alpha_n \rangle$, and $\langle \beta_1, \beta_2, \ldots, \beta_n \rangle$, where "$\langle B \rangle$," "$\langle \alpha_1, \alpha_2, \ldots, \alpha_n \rangle$" and "$\langle \beta_1, \beta_2, \ldots, \beta_n \rangle$" are expressions of augmented English determined, in the sense defined above, by the character of the reflections that are components of the kausal judgment ascribed.

Where a bracketed expression such as "$\langle \alpha_1, \alpha_2, \ldots, \alpha_n \rangle$" contains several component expressions such as "α_1" and "α_2," those component expressions are to be understood as referring to several object-aspects to which several aspects of the component reflection correspond. Where only a single letter occurs between brackets, that does not mean that the reflection does not have several aspects corresponding to several aspects of the sort of thing represented; it only means that I have no reason to distinguish between those several aspects. In particular, reflections of backgrounds may also have distinguishable aspects, but normally I will not have occasion to exploit this fact and so will usually write only "$\langle B \rangle$."

The bracket notation is to be understood in the same way in ascriptions of similarity judgments. Here, however, a further point needs to be made. The similarity judgments that concern us, recall, are aspectual similarity judgments. An aspectual similarity judgment is a judgment to the effect that a certain aspect of one thing is more similar to that same aspect of some second thing than to that same aspect of some third thing. Accordingly, the full form of an ascription of a similarity judgment using the bracket notation will be: "S judges that $\langle \alpha_1, \alpha_2, \ldots, \alpha_n \rangle$ is more similar than $\langle \beta_1, \beta_2, \ldots, \beta_n \rangle$ to $\langle \gamma_1, \gamma_2, \ldots, \gamma_n \rangle$ with respect to i." This form of ascription, then, presupposes that in ascribing a similarity judgment to S using the bracket notation for the relata, each numerical subscript i corresponds to a particular generic type of aspect of the things represented by the pertinent reflections. For instance, the subscript "2" might correspond to shape, in which case α_2, β_2, and γ_2 would represent shapes, namely, the shapes of $\langle \alpha_1, \alpha_2, \ldots, \alpha_n \rangle$, $\langle \beta_1, \beta_2, \ldots, \beta_n \rangle$, and $\langle \gamma_1, \gamma_2, \ldots, \gamma_n \rangle$, respectively. Where an ascription of a similarity judgment is not relativized in this way to aspect, the similarity judgment is understood to be a judgment of similarity with respect to *overall appearance*.

Associated with every reflection of a background or of an event in a background will be a set of envisionings that I will call the *action class* for that reflection. Roughly, the action class for a given reflection will consist of envisionings of events that are feasible in such a background or of events that might lead up to such a background, or the action class might consist of envisionings of other background conditions in which a given background impression might be embedded. For instance, the action class associated with a reflection of a bird sitting on a wire might include an envisioning of a bird taking flight from the wire, or it might include an envisioning of a bird landing on the wire. The action class surrounding the envisioning of a door might include an envisioning of objects on the other side of the door. It is important that the action class for a given reflection might include envisionings of actions that the subject himself or herself can perform in the reflected circumstance. For instance, the action class associated with someone's reflection of a cup on a table might include an envisioning of his or her picking up that cup. In what follows, it will be helpful to think of a member of an action class as consisting of both an envisioning of a background and an envisioning of an event in the background.

In introducing this concept of an action class there is some danger of begging important questions. Important questions will certainly be begged, and the apparatus of comparative, three-place similarity judgments will be rendered superfluous, if the contents of an action class are supposed to be determined by an absolute, two-place similarity relation between the objects of reflections. I think it is fair to assume that mental operations other than similarity judgments generate the contents of action classes. I wish to remain noncommittal concerning the intrinsic nature of reflections, but for purposes of illustrating the present point, let us think of them as like images. Images are subject to transformations of certain sorts. For instance, they can be rotated. Their parts can be rearranged. If reflections were images, then the processes that generate an action class might be such as these transformations. The processes that generate an action class might be learned or improved through learning. The process of learning to generate an action class might be guided by success and failure at the tasks that depend on action classes, such as playing games or learning language. Beyond this I cannot say much more about the production of action classes. That is a definite weakness in my theory. My inability to say more is a consequence of my ignorance of the sorts of nonverbal thinking that I have been insisting on all along but have been unable to identify.[2]

In terms of the action class surrounding a given reflection we may define judgments of *absolute similarity*:

Say that S judges that $\langle B_1, \alpha \rangle$ is *absolutely similar to* $\langle B_2, \beta \rangle$ relative to $\langle B_3, \gamma \rangle$ if and only if, if A is the action class associated with $\langle B_3, \gamma \rangle$, then $\langle B_1, \alpha \rangle \in A$, and for all $\langle B_4, \delta \rangle \in A$, S judges that $\langle B_1, \alpha \rangle$ is not less similar than $\langle B_4, \delta \rangle$ to $\langle B_2, \beta \rangle$.

In short, an absolutely similar action or background is a *most* similar member of the action class.

5. I am now in a position to introduce three important principles of kausal judgment that I will put to use in the next chapter. The first is the *principle of*

---

[2] By now it should be quite clear to all students of cognition that there is indeed a kind of thinking that may be usefully, even if misleadingly, characterized as imagistic (e.g., Finke 1989). The reason I am not going to place greater emphasis on current research into mental imagery is that I think it should be fairly clear already that the study of mental imagery would be very useful in the further development of the psychological ideas in this book and because I have nothing original to say about mental imagery.

kausal transference. This comes in two versions. The *forward* version is as follows:

Suppose that the following conditions hold:
S judges that under $\langle B_1 \rangle$, $\langle \alpha_1 \rangle$ kauses $\langle \beta_1 \rangle$.
S judges that $\langle B_2, \alpha_2 \rangle$ is absolutely similar to $\langle B_1, \alpha_1 \rangle$ relative to $\langle B_2 \rangle$.
S judges that $\langle B_2, \alpha_2, \beta_2 \rangle$ is absolutely similar to $\langle B_1, \alpha_1, \beta_1 \rangle$ relative to $\langle B_2, \alpha_2 \rangle$.
In that case, the following will hold:
S judges that under $\langle B_2 \rangle$, $\langle \alpha_2 \rangle$ kauses $\langle \beta_2 \rangle$.

In short, like kauses under like circumstances have like effekts. Judging in accordance with the forward version of the principle of kausal transference will enable the subject to judge in advance that a certain kause will have a certain effekt and thus, in a sense, to *anticipate* that effekt.

The second version of the principle of kausal transference is the *backward* version:

Suppose that the following conditions hold:
S judges that under $\langle B_1 \rangle$, $\langle \alpha_1 \rangle$ kauses $\langle \beta_1 \rangle$.
S judges that $\langle B_2, \beta_2 \rangle$ is absolutely similar to $\langle B_1, \beta_1 \rangle$ relative to $\langle B_2 \rangle$.
S judges that $\langle B_2, \alpha_2, \beta_2 \rangle$ is absolutely similar to $\langle B_1, \alpha_1, \beta_1 \rangle$ relative to $\langle B_2, \beta_2 \rangle$.
In that case, the following will hold:
S judges that under $\langle B_2 \rangle$, $\langle \alpha_2 \rangle$ kauses $\langle \beta_2 \rangle$.

In short, like effekts under like circumstances have like kauses. Provided that the world cooperates, judging in accordance with the backward version of the principle of kausal transference will allow the subject to find means to a given end. Notice that when the principle of kausal transference is applied in the backward version, the action class surrounding the envisioning of the effekt ($\langle B_2, \beta_2 \rangle$) will consist of envisionings of events leading up to the effekt rather than of envisionings of subsequent transformations. They will be, in a sense, hypothetical kauses.

The second principle of kausal judgment that I will appeal to is the *principle of kausal combination:*

Suppose that S judges all of the following:
Under background $\langle B_1 \rangle$, $\langle \alpha_1 \rangle$ kauses $\langle \alpha_2, \psi_1 \rangle$.
Under background $\langle B_2 \rangle$, $\langle \alpha_3 \rangle$ kauses $\langle \alpha_4, \psi_2 \rangle$.
Under background $\langle C \rangle$, $\langle \beta_1 \rangle$ kauses $\langle \varphi_1, \alpha_7 \rangle$.
Under background $\langle D \rangle$, $\langle \beta_2 \rangle$ kauses $\langle \varphi_2, \alpha_8 \rangle$.
$\langle B, \alpha_1, \alpha_2, \psi \rangle$ is absolutely similar to $\langle B_1, \alpha_1, \alpha_2, \psi_1 \rangle$ relative to $\langle B \rangle$.
$\langle B, \alpha_3, \alpha_4, \psi \rangle$ is absolutely similar to $\langle B_2, \alpha_3, \alpha_4, \psi_2 \rangle$ relative to $\langle B \rangle$.
$\langle C, \beta, \varphi, \alpha_7 \rangle$ is absolutely similar to $\langle C, \beta_1, \varphi_1, \alpha_7 \rangle$ relative to $\langle C, \beta \rangle$.

$\langle D, \beta, \varphi, \alpha_8 \rangle$ is absolutely similar to $\langle D, \beta_2, \varphi_2, \alpha_8 \rangle$ relative to $\langle D, \beta \rangle$.
In that case, the following will hold:
S judges that under background $\langle B \rangle$, $\langle \beta \rangle$ kauses $\langle \varphi, \psi \rangle$.

(Notice the correlation between the B's and the ψ's and between the β's and the φ's.) What this says is basically that if a certain sort of action has two distinguishable aspects, one of which S judges to be the constant accompaniment of the background and the other of which S judges to be the constant accompaniment of a certain type of kause, then S will judge that that action will result from that kause in that background.

The third principle of kausal judgment is the *principle of kausal differentiation:*

Suppose that initially the following conditions hold:
S judges that under background $\langle B_1 \rangle$, $\langle \alpha_1 \rangle$ kauses $\langle \beta_1 \rangle$.
S judges that under background $\langle B_2 \rangle$, $\langle \alpha_2 \rangle$ kauses $\langle \beta_2 \rangle$.
S judges that $\langle B_2, \alpha_2 \rangle$ is absolutely similar to $\langle B_1, \alpha_1 \rangle$ relative to $\langle B_2 \rangle$.
S does *not* judge that $\langle B_2, \alpha_2, \beta_2 \rangle$ is absolutely similar to $\langle B_1, \alpha_1, \beta_1 \rangle$ relative to $\langle B_2, \alpha_2 \rangle$.
Under these conditions the action class around $\langle B_2 \rangle$ will *expand* so that subsequently:
S does *not* judge that $\langle B_2, \alpha_2 \rangle$ is absolutely similar to $\langle B_1, \alpha_1 \rangle$ relative to $\langle B_2 \rangle$.

In short, if initially the subject judges that like kauses have unlike effekts, then the subject will learn to differentiate between actions in such a way that the subject *no longer* judges that like kauses have unlike effekts.

The second of these three principles, the principle of kausal combination, has little special plausibility on its own and few applications outside of the context of language learning. The reason is that elsewhere the antecedent conditions are seldom satisfied. But this principle is perhaps plausible in light of the more general fact that our understanding of causal relations exhibits a great deal of productivity. That is, having learned a number of causal relations, we are able to form reasonable judgments concerning others that we have not observed. Having created a pond by building a dam, we may realize that we can drain a pond by digging a canal. Having discovered that we can catch antelope by driving them into a hole, we may realize that we can catch fish by driving them into a net. In a more complete theory I would hope that the principle of kausal combination would be a consequence of a more general account of this productivity of causal judgments.

Evidently, more "intelligent" versions of these principles could be formulated. That is, one could formulate principles less liable to err in uncooperative environments. For instance, the principle of kausal combination might be formulated to say that the subject will not form kausal expectations if he or she has already encountered counterexamples. Another enhancement to the principle of kausal combination would be a requirement that the variable factors (represented by the α's) actually be different from one another. But we should not expect to formulate principles that inevitably lead to true kausal predictions. And since here I am undertaking only an illustration of a strategy for explaining language, it does not seem useful at this stage to work very hard on refinements that might hide my basic conception behind a veil of complications.

Perhaps it will seem that in postulating these general principles of kausal reasoning I am ignoring my own critique of psychological laws in chapter 5. To resolve this apparent inconsistency, I must rely on a distinction between kinds of intentionality that I will not fully explain until chapter 14. There I will distinguish between three grades of intentionality: the *superfluous*, the *merely dispensable*, and the *indispensable*. Kausal judgments, similarity judgments, and reflections possess only the second grade of intentionality. They are merely dispensable. They are not indispensable, for the attribution of such states is not necessary for purposes of communication (that is, of actually participating in linguistic exchanges). However, their attribution is useful for purposes of getting a theoretical grip on something that we have been unable to understand in any more fundamental way, namely, how language is possible. The propositional thoughts that in chapter 5 I argued were lawless were not these but rather the sort that, as we will see, we must attribute for purposes of communication.

6. Finally, as promised, I return to the prospects for a theory of causality grounded in the idea that causal judgment is transformed kausal judgment. Roughly, the plan would be to define a causal relation as the relation that must obtain in order for a causal judgment to be true and then to define causal judgments in terms of the necessary transformations of kausal judgment. (Naturally, independent assumptions about causation might influence what sorts of transformations we take to be necessary.) Call this the *kausal judgment theory of causality*. Since I have not given a complete account of the necessary transformations of kausal judgment, I do not really have a kausal judgment theory of causality to offer. It is nonetheless possible to make a few brief remarks on behalf of this strategy.

The present theory might be compared to various theories of causality, but the one that most people will probably compare it to is the *constant conjunction* theory of causality, which is associated with Hume.[3] The present theory bears comparison to the constant conjunction theory because both take the form of theories of judgments of causality. The main difference between them is that the present kausal judgments theory grounds causal judgments in kausal judgments and similarity judgments, while the constant conjunction view grounds causal judgments in observations of regularities. Roughly, it says that we judge that x

---

[3] Two other important competitors are the counterfactual theory, represented by Lewis 1973a, and the theory of probabilistic causality, represented by Eells 1991.

causes y when x is an F and y is a G and F's are regularly followed by G's. A problem for any such theory is to explain how we are able, as we sometimes are, to recognize that this particular F is definitely not going to be followed by a G even if we have observed a very regular conjunction between F's and G's.

For instance, suppose I have a car that has almost always started right up whenever I have turned the key in the ignition and pressed my foot on the gas pedal. According to the the constant conjunction theory, I should judge that this time too my turning the key, and so on, will cause the car to start. But suppose I notice that the headlight switch is on and the headlights are off. In that case I may know full well that turning the key, and so on, will have no effect. How can I know this? It is not enough to say that in the present instance conditions are different, that this is not a pure instance of the type of event governed by the regularity. It is not enough to say this, because things are *always* different. One morning I may get into my car with my left shoelace untied. That may never have happened before. Yet it does not prevent me from expecting the car to start. What is the difference between my shoelace's being untied and the head-light switch's being on such that under the first condition I should expect the car to start and under the second condition I should not? An obvious difference is that I know that leaving the headlights on causes a change in the car such that causal relations that normally hold no longer hold, whereas my shoelace has no effect on the car whatsoever. But this sort of answer is not available to the proponent of the constant conjunction theory, since this sort of knowledge is knowledge of causal relations, which is precisely the sort of knowledge the origin of which the constant conjunction theory is supposed to explain.[4]

The kausal judgment theory avoids this sort of problem. Suppose that it has happened to me just once before that I have tried to start the car after noticing that the headlight switch was on and the headlights were off and that on that occasion the car failed to start. Since the present occasion may be more similar to that occasion than to any other occasion on which I have tried to start the car, I may judge, by the principle of kausal transference, that on the present occasion the car will not start. The fact that turning the key, and so on, has much more frequently kaused the car to start is irrelevant. But suppose that on some occasion my car fails to start when my left shoelace is untied. This does not

[4] This all by itself is not a criticism of Hume. Hume's account of our expectations of effects allows a role to reasoning by analogy (*Treatise*, 142) and to the principle that "like objects plac'd in like circumstances, will always produce like effects" (*Treatise*, 105, cf. 173), and consequently to the principle that if two like circumstances result in different effects, then the cause lies in that wherein the circumstances differ (*Treatise*, 174). Rather, my criticism of Hume would be twofold: First, it is hard to see how Hume's conception of the operations of the mind allows the possibility of the general rules that he thinks correct the influence of constant conjunction. Second, his idea that there is a role to be played by constant conjunction in determining a causal judgment is a consequence of a mistaken theory of the fixation of belief, namely, that repetition is necessary in order for an impression of the cause to produce an idea of the effect possessing the vivacity that, according to Hume, is characteristic of belief.

mean that the next time I get into my car with my left shoelace untied I will not expect the car to start, for on other occasions when I have tried to start the car with my shoelace undone, the car will have started. By the principle of kausal differentiation, I will infer that there is some relevant difference between these circumstances and then try to determine which one the present circumstance is most similar to.

Still, this is not a perfect solution to the problem. In fact we are much better at recognizing exceptions to the rule than this account allows. I may never have left the headlights on before or even have heard of a such a thing's ever happening. And yet on the basis of a little knowledge of how cars work I might foresee that the car is not going to start. Also, the solution rests on some fairly ad hoc assumptions about similarity judgments. If the last time I found that I had left the headlights on was at nighttime in the winter, and this time I find out during daylight in the summer, then it is not so clear that the present circumstances really are more similar to the last time I left the headlights on than to other occasions when I have tried and succeeded in starting the car. But I will not try to accommodate these facts here, since to do so I would have to take into account the kind of cognition, namely, knowledge of general truths, that arises only in the context of language, which I have not yet begun to explain.

Those with certain sorts of ontological scruples may consider it absurd to try to explicate causality in terms of causal judgments. Causality, they will say, is not a kind of judgment or any kind of mental entity at all, and so, as with anything else that is not itself a kind of mental entity, its nature ought to be explicable without any essential reference to mental entities. No one would expect to gain an understanding of the nature of gold or fermentation or earthquakes by studying the concepts *gold* or *fermentation* or *earthquakes*. Likewise we should not expect a study of the nature of causality to take the form of a study of the concept *causality*. But why should we believe that causality is like gold, fermentation, and earthquakes in this respect? Granting that causal relations hold between things not in the mind, why should we expect to be able to understand the nature of causality apart from an understanding of causal judgments and their origin?

Causality, I agree, is real. Likewise, color is real. Color might *exist* even in a universe where no one could *see* it. Still, one cannot fully explain the nature of color without citing the nature of human vision. Of course, one might explain that a certain thing is red because it reflects electromagnetic radiation of a certain kind, and that is an explanation that makes no mention of human vision. But even the kausal judgment theory may likewise acknowledge that x qualifies as the cause of y because certain objective relations hold between x and y having nothing to do with the human mind. But one cannot explain the *nature* of color without bringing in human vision. What the kausal judgment theory says is that likewise we should not expect to understand the nature of causality apart from human judgment.

But causality, it may be said, is more real than color, for causality is something that would have to be countenanced by any rational creature whatsoever, and color need be countenanced only by creatures who can see it. Well, I do not know whether causality would have to be countenanced by any rational creature whatsoever, but I will not try to deny it. Still, this would not show that an investigation into the nature of causality should not take the form of an investigation into causal judgments. At most it would show that there is something about the problem of knowing or controlling one's environment that necessitates a solution that makes use of the concept of causality. That might be a consequence, for instance, of one's being much larger than the basic components of matter on which the course of the universe depends, or of the fact that what happens within the field of observation depends on events outside of it, or of the fact that one must distinguish one's own perspective on the world from the objective order of things (Strawson 1966).

10

Command and Assertion

1. Language is an extremely complicated creature. In order to begin to understand the phenomenon of language, it is necessary to develop some conception of the basic function of language on which an understanding of the complications can be based. In part A of this book I criticized the Lockean conception of language, according to which the basic function of language is to express thoughts. In this chapter I will set out an alternative conception of the basic function of language. In this and the subsequent chapters, I will then try to use this conception to explain some of the important aspects of language that need to be explained.

My procedure will be to describe a series of models of languages, which I will call simply *languages*. The language at the start of the series may be thought of in two ways: First, it embodies in the simplest form my basic conception of the function of language. Second, it serves as a simplified and perhaps idealized model of a very early form of language in a speculative, very much simplified history of the early evolution of language. Accordingly, each next language in the series of models will be supposed to differ from its predecessor in two respects: First, it will be a better approximation to the languages we actually speak. Second, it will represent a later episode in my speculative, simplified history of the evolution of language.

Provided that certain conditions are met, such a series of models will, I believe, qualify as an explanation of language. The conditions that must be met are at least these: First, there must be definite mental mechanisms by which human beings could acquire a language like the first language in the sequence and then, having reached a given stage in the sequence, advance to the next stage. Second, in the limit the sequence must approximate in certain definite respects the languages that we actually speak. Any characteristics of human languages that we do not find in the limit will be characteristics unexplained. The characteristics of languages that I particularly aim to explain in this way are that languages facilitate cooperation, that languages are learned, that sentences possess logical structure, and that language can be a medium of thought.

What I expect to achieve is far less than what I seek. My earliest models are probably poor approximations to the earliest languages. At the very least, one can be sure that early languages were fluid and alive, whereas my models are rigid and mechanical. My explanation of learning will reach only the earliest stages in the sequence, and even here there will be some important gaps and some vagueness and a lot of oversimplification. Toward the end of the sequence, in chapter 13, I will be unable to preserve a clear sequence of definite models. So while the languages toward the end may be fairly good approximations to the languages we speak, it will not be clear that they are the inevitable culmination of the earlier sequence. So what I actually produce will be at most an illustration of the sort of explanation of language that one might hope to produce without relying on the Lockean conception of language. I do not claim that my alternative is any less problematic than the Lockean conception. The good things about it are that it is thoroughly non-Lockean and that it has not been refuted *yet*.

The ambition, if not the act, is to produce a speculative history of the evolution of language. There is a reciprocal dependency between such a history and a theory of language learning. In one direction, the speculative history depends on a theory of language learning, for it must be possible to explain how a population that had learned the language of a prior stage might learn the language of the next stage. In the other direction, we might expect that an account of how children learn sophisticated languages might make use of a theory of the evolution of language. The assumption is that when it comes to language, ontogeny recapitulates phylogeny to some extent. Features of the most primitive languages will be preserved in the more highly developed languages, and it is those features that children will somehow latch onto first. And in general, they will master earlier those features of their language that are found earlier in the evolution of language.

Philosophers of language influenced by Grice have sometimes conceived of language as originating in a kind of deliberation concerning the beliefs and intentions of other people. David Lewis (1969), for instance, thinks of it as the solution to what he calls a *coordination problem*. Coordination problems include such things as the problem two people face in trying to decide who should call back after they have been disconnected on the telephone or in trying to decide where to meet after losing one another in the shopping mall. Each thinks to himself or herself, roughly, as follows: "I want to go where he will go. He will go where he thinks I will go. So I want to go where he thinks I will go. So he will go where he thinks I think he thinks I will go . . ." This would result in an impasse except for the fact that there may be some other factor, however slight, aside from his or her consideration of what the other might do that might incline one party to one course of action rather than another. For instance, if one place in the mall rather than another stands out in the minds of both of them—because it is where they met once in the past or because it is where they think they must have lost one another—then it will be the only possibility that escapes the regress, and so it may emerge as the solution (1969, 35–36). For Lewis, the origin of language is like that, except that what has to be selected is not a place to meet but an entire language considered as an abstract set of rules pairing words with meanings.[1]

Jonathan Bennett (1976) offers a Gricean theory of language origin that is somewhat more realistic than Lewis's in acknowledging that languages are accretions and do not spring full-grown from the heads of Zeuses. For Bennett, the process is something more like the following (the example is mine, not Bennett's, but see pp. 138–41 of Bennett): One day Bob and Ted come across a snake. They watch it for a while, and Bob hisses at it playfully. Later that day, they are hiking through the tall grass when Ted sees that Bob is about to walk through a spot where Ted has just noticed a poisonous snake. In order to try to prevent Bob from stepping on the snake, Ted makes the same hissing noise that Bob had made earlier that day. Bob reasons, and Ted expects him to reason, that Ted would imitate that hissing noise only if he intended Bob to be reminded of snakes and that Ted would wish to remind Bob of snakes only if he, Bob, were now in immanent danger of stepping on one. In this manner, Bob's hissing noise takes the first steps toward becoming a sentence meaning *Watch out for snakes!*

These theories of language origin, I submit, make no contact whatsoever with the reality of human nature. Languages are not airplanes. They are not devices that we have contrived in order to do things that our physiology is not especially suited to do, such as fly. In many ways our physiology is suited for language. The human supralaryngeal vocal tract is no accident of evolution. It is clearly an adaptation serving the production of articulate sounds. Our brains, moreover, are in many ways adapted to the production and comprehension of speech. It does not seem likely that these brain adaptations are distinct functional or anatomical modules or layers embedded in an otherwise complete organ of human thought. They extend deep into the phylogenetically older regions of the brain and are inextricably bound up with circuitry subserving both the higher and the more primitive forms of intelligence (Lieberman 1991, ch. 3).

I do not claim that every Lockean account of language origin has to be as unrealistic as Lewis's and Bennett's. After all, my criticism of the Lockean conception of language in part A was not that it presupposed too much intelligence on the part of language learners. But it is useful to bear such theories in mind as examples of what an opponent of the Lockean conception, such as I, will want to avoid. What I seek is a conception of the basic function of language that lends itself to a theory of language learning and language origin that heeds

---

[1] My attribution to Lewis of this view of the origin of language is not based on any text that I can quote but on the fairly obvious implications of what he has written. He does not explicitly characterize the origin of language as the solution to a coordination problem, but he does characterize conventions in general as originating as solutions to coordination problems (1969, 36–42), and he includes the problem of choosing a language in a list of examples (7–8). And he does characterize the use of a language, considered as an abstract structure, as conventional (179).

the capacities of the language-learning infant and the language-inventing protohuman.

Nonetheless, I will pay scant attention to the vast literature on first language acquisition, for it offers little help with the task I have set. A lot of it is more or less explicitly committed to the Lockean conception of language, which I have rejected. This is certainly true of the literature on classification, including the writings of Rosch, Markman, and Keil (see chapter 4). These authors do not even explicitly think of themselves as dealing with language acquisition. They think of themselves as dealing with concept formation and assume that word learning is a matter of somehow mapping words to concepts. There is another large body of acquisition literature that deals explicitly with the functions of words (e.g., Halliday 1975). Much of it amounts to taxonomizing the functions of language and the stages of acquisition. Some of this may be useful and in some ways congenial to the theory of language I will be advancing, but most of what I have seen is so utterly vague as to be perfectly useless to me.

A large proportion of the literature on language acquisition focuses on the acquisition of syntax. The task is to explain how the child learns to distinguish between strings of words that are grammatical in its linguistic community and strings that are not. This is only a small part of what has to be explained. A person might in principle be able to distinguish perfectly well between grammatical and ungrammatical strings and yet have no idea what to do with them. The main thing that has to be explained is how they learn what to do with them. Of course, it is unlikely that children will learn their grammar without also learning how to use words. So one might expect that studies of acquisition of syntax might also contain some insights into the question of use. But in fact, all of the work on the acquisition of syntax with which I am acquainted makes quite unreasonable assumptions about the child's grasp of meanings. The work of Steven Pinker (1984; 1989, ch. 8) is a good example. Pinker's account of the acquisition of syntax is founded on what he calls the *semantic bootstrapping hypothesis*. According to this hypothesis, children are able to learn their grammars because when they hear a sentence, they are often able, prior to having learned the language, to determine what is being said. Specifically, they often know what object is being referred to by each noun in the sentence and whether that object is the agent or the patient in the action being described. How the child might come to know that is something about which Pinker has nothing to say.

Even if I am allowed to hold at arm's length all studies of language acquisition tainted by dubious presuppositions, I might be held accountable to the more or less purely descriptive histories of language acquisition (e.g., Brown 1973). Here, I confess, I am vulnerable, but I will not try to defend myself on this flank, because I am not competent to do so. I can offer only two additional excuses: First, it is fair for me to ask that my efforts be evaluated above all on the basis of whether the story I am going to tell is even possible in light of some very basic facts, such as that most concepts are not decomposable into innate conceptual atoms, for as I think I have shown through my critique of the Lockean conception, it is a challenge to achieve even that much. Second, even the most careful observer will exercise selective attention. The data he or she collects will either confirm or conflict with whatever theoretical conceptions occupy his or her mind. If the reported data appear to conflict with my theory, then since the observers will not have had my theory in mind, it might be worthwhile to look again. Those immersed in this literature will probably condemn my failure to come to grips with it, but those who, like me, have had some taste of it and found it unenlightening may appreciate a fresh approach.[2]

2. Here, without further ado, is the basic conception I aim to develop: The fundamental elements of a language are *commands* and *assertions*. A *command* is an utterance whose basic function is to initiate a response on the part of the addressee. For instance, by commanding, "Bring the rock!" the chief may cause the subordinate to bring a rock. An *assertion* is an utterance whose basic function is to create conditions under which commands may be efficacious. If there are many rocks in the vicinity, the subordinate may run from one rock to another, unable to select any particular rock to bring. But if the chief prefaces his command by asserting, "The rock is red," then when he commands, "Bring the rock!" the subordinate may be able to bring the uniquely most salient red rock in the vicinity.

An assertion can condition a command in various ways. In the example of the red rock, the assertion "The rock is red" enables the subordinate to determine which rock to bring. An assertion may also enable the addressee of a command to *find* the object toward which the commanded action is directed. For example:

Buffalo are by the lake. Hunt them down!

Also, the assertion may identify what needs to be done in order to complete the commanded action:

The bulb has burned out. Fix the lamp!

An assertion can condition a command other than by *directing* the commanded action. For instance, an assertion may give the hearer a motive to perform the commanded action:

We need to prop up this corner. Bring me another strut!

Or the assertion may simply establish that the speaker has the proper authority:

The captain sent me. Take this envelope to the major!

---

[2] The one body of literature on language learning in which I have found some inspiration is E. Sue Savage-Rumbaugh's writings on the linguistic abilities of chimpanzees (e.g., Savage-Rumbaugh, Rumbaugh, and Boysen 1978; and Savage-Rumbaugh 1981, 1986). See Gauker 1990a and Savage-Rumbaugh's insightful reply, 1990.

But I do not wish this last example to suggest that the practice of giving and taking commands requires that a command always issue from someone who has established authority. Cooperation often carries its own rewards.

The first thing I should say about this basic conception of language is that I do not propose to squeeze all of language into this particular mold. Clearly, the practice of making assertions has a life of its own that is largely independent of the practice of making commands. We often talk and talk and talk for long stretches without uttering a command. My proposal is to explain this fact by first characterizing a language in which assertions condition commands in a fairly immediate way and then characterizing more sophisticated languages as developments of this more primitive language. I will not be able to reach languages like the one I am now using, in which the practice of commanding is almost entirely internalized, but I will reach languages in which the practice of asserting begins to take on a life of its own.

Nonetheless, this account will place commands at center stage in a manner that is almost unheard of in philosophical writing on language. So I wish to point out that there are many more commands in ordinary discourse than philosophers are wont to recognize. One reason why commands in my sense do not stand out is that many utterances that I, for my purposes, would label as commands take the grammatical form, not of imperatives, but of requests, recommendations, questions, or even indicatives. For instance, "Would you please shut the door?" and "You had better shut the door" qualify as commands in my broad sense of the term. Another reason for the inconspicuousness of commands is that by the time we have become adults and have learned many of the routines of conversation, many of the commands that operate upon us can go without saying altogether. If I tell an adult, "That cheese will spoil if you leave it out," it will not be necessary for me to add, "And so you had better put it in the refrigerator." But if I tell that to a child, it may have no effect until I say, "So put it in the refrigerator!" Finally, among the commands on which language rests I count all those directives we give to ourselves, out loud or in inner speech. A person may say to himself, silently, but in English, "Don't forget to mail the letters!" In my sense, that will count as a command.

This conception of language as consisting of commands that initiate responses and of assertions that condition commands will serve as an alternative to the Lockean conception only if we can explain how commanding and asserting perform their functions without reinvoking the Lockean conception. How does the chief's saying "The rock is red" enable the subordinate to pick out the red rock? One tempting answer is that from this utterance the subordinate can infer that when the chief tells him to bring a rock, it is the red rock that the chief has *in mind*. But this leads straight back to the Lockean conception of language. Or one might be tempted to answer that there is a kind of word-world correspondence by virtue of which the subordinate can employ the chief's assertion as a kind of map leading to the rock the chief has told him to bring. But as we saw in chapter 6, an investigation into the nature of this correspondence relation is also liable to lead back to the Lockean conception. This doubt about my alternative, namely, whether it ultimately depends on the Lockean theory, will be answered in the course of my carrying out the subsequent steps of my project.

3. The next step will be to define a language that embodies in a very pure form the conception of language as consisting of commands and assertions that condition commands and then to explain how such a language might be learned. I will not appeal to any of the cognitive devices that belong exclusively to the Lockean tool box. So to begin, I wish to itemize the basic mental operations that I will appeal to in carrying out my task. These will be the cognitive entry points in my account of language learning.

Reflections. Here are some of the important points to remember about reflections from chapter 9: If a subject forms a kausal judgment or similarity judgment concerning x, y, and z, then there are discriminable mental states of the subject representing x, y, and z such that it is by virtue of there being some relation between those three states that the judgment is attributable to the subject. In the case where these judgments are not formulated in language, these representations are what I call *reflections*. The things that reflections represent are either agents in action or backgrounds, and the agents that reflections represent are individuated by the criterion of kinematic cohesion. Further, reflections may have various aspects, corresponding to various aspects of the things they represent. Reflections may be either impressions or envisionings. We may speak of an impression as an impression of some particular object, namely, that object that caused the impression, but the object of an envisioning is the *sort* of thing that, in the sense defined, corresponds to that type of reflection.

Similarity judgments. Recall from chapter 8 that the similarity judgments of interest here are *aspectual* similarity judgments. Their form is: *x's R is more similar than y's R to z's R*. Recall also that similarity judgments are potentially objective. Further, a similarity judgment, like a kausal judgment, is a mental relation between representations. In this chapter, the representations that similarity judgments will relate will be reflections. More precisely, since the kind of similarity at issue is a relation between aspects of things, such as shape or color or function or manner of motion, a similarity judgment will be a mental relation between *aspects* of reflections. However, in what follows I will in fact often ignore this relativization of similarity to aspect. In effect I will be assuming that all pertinent similarity judgments are judgments concerning the overall *appearance* of things. Relativizing to a variety of aspects rather than just this one might make possible an even more plausible account than I am about to give by supplying us with a more varied array of cognitive entry points—a richer collection of explanatory tools. But I do not now see how to exploit that greater wealth.

Recall also that, in terms of similarity judgments, I defined in chapter 9 what I called *absolute* similarity judgments. These depend on what I have called *action classes*. The action class around a reflection is determined by processes other than similarity judgments.

Kausal judgments. Here are some of the important points from chapter 9 to bear in mind about kausal judgments: First, they are not causal judgments. To judge that *x's F-ing* kauses *y's G-ing* given *B* is merely to judge that a certain sequence of events took place against an unchanging background *B*. Second, the relata of the kausal judgments that I will appeal to are represented by reflections, which are components of the judgment. Third, kausal judgments have value only in an environment that cooperates. Inasmuch as the account of language learning that I will offer rests on kausal judgments, therefore, it requires an environment that cooperates. Finally, kausal judgments are governed by three *principles* of kausal judgment: the principle of kausal transference (in both the forward and the backward versions), the principle of kausal combination, and the principle of kausal differentiation.

It is important to bear two things in mind about the terms I will use in ascribing similarity judgments and kausal judgments. First, they do not necessarily characterize the aspects of the relata that correspond to the aspects of the reflections that figure in the judgment. If I characterize the object of a similarity judgment or kausal judgment in English, then I am merely speaking approximately. In that case, my characterization undoubtedly is not determined by the character of the reflections that enter into the judgment. The bracket notation is a means of avoiding misleading characterizations in actual English without knowing what the characterization determined by the reflections might actually be. The second thing to bear in mind about the terms I will use in ascribing similarity judgments and kausal judgments is that in no case does the use of a term in ascribing such a judgment imply that the subject possesses the concept that the term expresses. Certainly, in ascribing to *S* the judgment that some red thing is more similar than something to something, I do not imply that *S* has the concept *red*. Moreover, in ascribing to *S* the judgment that $\langle \alpha_1, \alpha_2, \ldots, \rangle$ is more similar than something to something, I do not ascribe to *S* the concept α_1.

Now I want to introduce one more concept, namely, that of a *favorable outcome*. I will assume that subjects can distinguish between favorable and unfavorable envisioned events. I will also assume that when a subject envisions that an action of its own will kause a favorable event, then the subject performs that action. Favorable outcomes may be of many sorts. Praise or getting something to eat may be a favorable outcome, but so may be success in some cooperative enterprise, such as piling up wooden blocks. Further, there is no bar to altruism: a favorable outcome may very well be that someone *else* gets something to eat. In assuming that subjects choose favorable outcomes, I am not invoking the sort of psychological law that I questioned in chapter 5, for the behavior I am assuming here is fairly stupid behavior that subjects will improve upon in the context of more sophisticated languages.

In what follows I will assume, for simplicity, that agents always act in order to achieve some definite favorable outcome, but I want to acknowledge that in at least one way that is very wrong. On many occasions, compliance with a command may be motivated solely by the prospect of a favor in return, such as compliance to one's own commands. But moreover, compliance may bring the agent no special benefit beyond his or her helping in a small way to preserve the practice of giving and complying with commands, which is beneficial to humankind on the whole. It would be biologically naive to assume that agents always seek some definite benefit, whether for themselves or for others. On the contrary, there may be an innate disposition to comply with commands, and in consequence of this disposition an agent may normally refrain from complying with a command only when he or she has not learned how to comply or envisions some positively unfavorable outcome. However, to the extent that compliance is not directly rewarded, the agent, while learning the language, will have to rely on some recognizable sign from the issuer of a command (a smile, a nod) to determine whether his or her response is compliant. In that case, we can, for simplicity, regard this sign as a favorable outcome.

4. The next step, as I said, is to define a language that embodies in the purest form my conception of language as consisting of commands and assertions that condition commands. Let the language L_0 consist of a finite list of imperatives $C_1, C_2, \ldots, C_n$, which are used to make commands, and a finite list of indicatives $A_1, A_2, \ldots, A_m$, which are used to make assertions. Moreover, an utterance of an indicative of L_0 will be considered well-formed if and only if it is followed by an imperative of L_0. Such an utterance of an indicative followed by an utterance of an imperative is what I will call an *assertion-command pair*. When I say "followed by" here I do not mean *immediately* followed by, but I do mean that no other utterance of L_0 intervenes. So much for the syntax of L_0. In giving examples, I will use English sentences such as "Bring it!" and "Eat it!", in place of imperatives of L_0 and English sentences such as "There is a duck" and "There is a red one" in place of indicatives of L_0.

My definition of L_0 includes a definition of a *compliant response* to an assertion-command pair in L_0 and a definition of an *effective utterance* in L_0. For each imperative of L_0 there is some *corresponding* type of action. For each indicative of L_0, there is some *corresponding* type of object or object-in-a-location. A *response* to an assertion-command pair of L_0 is *compliant* if and only if it is an action of the type corresponding to the imperative used in making the command and that action is directed toward an object of the type corresponding to the indicative used in making the assertion. An *utterance* of an assertion-command pair in L_0 is *effective* if and only if that utterance does in fact cause someone to perform a compliant response. What sort of action constitutes a compliant response to an assertion-command pair will be clear enough from the English sentences that I use for the imperatives and indicatives of L_0. For instance, a compliant response to "There is a red one—Bring it!" is an action of bringing the speaker something red.

I recognize no sharp distinction in L_0 between uttering an imperative and making a command or between uttering an indicative and making an assertion. Even for a language like L_0 we might draw a distinction between sentences spoken in earnest, where the speaker envisions some response on the part of an audience actually present, and sentences muttered during daydreams. For present purposes, I think it will do no harm simply to ignore the latter. The more significant distinction that might be drawn is between saying something without an intention to bring about a certain effect on the thoughts of the hearer and saying something *with* that sort of intention. But L_0 is not a language for which such a distinction can sensibly be drawn. It can be drawn only in the context of languages much further along the sequence of languages that I am trying to describe.

A *fragment* of L_0 is any subset of the assertion-command pairs belonging to L_0. Notice that I have not defined a fragment as the set of assertion-command pairs generated by some subset of the imperatives of L_0 and some subset of the indicatives of L_0. So while the indicative A and the command C might both occur in the same fragment, the assertion-command pair consisting of A and C might not occur in that fragment.

I will say that a subject *comprehends* L_0 if and only if, when an assertion-command pair is directed to him or her and a compliant response would be possible, he or she reliably responds in compliance. Similarly, a subject comprehends a given *fragment* of L_0 if and only if, when possible, he or she reliably responds in compliance to any assertion-command pair from that fragment. I will not try to define in a general way when a compliant response is *possible*, but what I have in mind is that in the relevant sense a compliant response is possible for the subject whenever a compliant response is compatible with the subject's capacities for motion and the constitution of the subject's environment. (I recognize the somewhat question-begging features of this characterization.) For example, if the chief commands, "Capture buffalo!" when there are no buffalo anywhere to be found, then compliance is impossible. But unwillingness does not make compliance impossible in the relevant sense. Notice that I have not said that a subject comprehends who merely *tries* to comply. Here I will not try to distinguish between trying and doing.

I will say that a subject *employs* L_0 if and only if he or she reliably utters an assertion-command pair of L_0 only when such an utterance will be effective. Similarly, a subject employs a *fragment* of L_0 if and only if he or she reliably utters an assertion-command pair of that fragment only when such an utterance will be effective. I will say that a subject has *mastered* L_0 (or some fragment thereof) if and only if he or she both comprehends and employs L_0 (or the fragment). (I ignore the situation in which these conditions are satisfied vacuously just because the subject is not exposed to and does not make utterances of the language.)

Now I can define my task regarding L_0. It has two stages: First, I want to explain how a subject might acquire mastery of a fragment of L_0 on the basis of examples of each type of assertion-command pair in that fragment. Second, I want to explain how the subject, having mastered a fragment of L_0 through examples in this way, might acquire mastery of a larger fragment of L_0 without exposure to a complete set of examples. This will fulfill my goal of explaining in a simpleminded way how the basic functions of assertions and commands, as I have characterized them above, might be learned, and it will do so in such a way as to show that what is learned possesses at least a limited sort of productivity.

First, I need to explain some notation. I will use capital roman letters and hyphenated pairs of capital letters for types of event. "A" will denote a type of assertion, "C" will denote a type of command, and "A-C" will denote a type of event consisting of an assertion of type A and a command of type C. Capital letters in square brackets will be used to denote types of event that are *species* of the type denoted by the expression between the brackets, and subscripts will be used to distinguish between several species. For instance, "$[C]_1$" and "$[C]_2$" will stand for two species of the type that "C" stands for. For instance, "$[C]_1$" might stand for an utterance of C in a certain high-pitched voice, and "$[C]_2$" might stand for an utterance of C in a certain low-pitched voice. I will use "B" to stand for a type of background, and I will further identify a type of background by putting an expression for some particular thing between parentheses after the "B." For instance, "$B([A]_1)$" will stand for a background in which a species of assertion of type A has occurred.

First, I will explain how a subject S_1 might learn to comprehend a single assertion-command pair of L_0 on the basis of explicit examples. Suppose that the following conditions obtain:

S_2 utters $\langle[A\text{-}C]_1\rangle$.

S_3 executes response $\langle R_1\rangle$.

S_1 judges that under background $\langle B([A\text{-}C]_1)\rangle$, $\langle R_1\rangle$ kaused $\langle O_1\rangle$.

S_4 utters $\langle[A\text{-}C]_2\rangle$.

S_1 judges that $\langle B([A\text{-}C]_2), R_2\rangle$ is absolutely similar to $\langle B([A\text{-}C]_1), R_1\rangle$ relative to $\langle B([A\text{-}C]_2)\rangle$.

S_1 judges that $\langle B([A\text{-}C]_2), R_2, O_2\rangle$ is absolutely similar to $\langle B([A\text{-}C]_1), R_1, O_1\rangle$ relative to $\langle B([A\text{-}C]_2), R_2\rangle$.

Under these conditions, the following condition will also hold, by the principle of kausal transference (forward version):

S_1 judges that under background $\langle B([A\text{-}C]_2)\rangle$, $\langle R_2\rangle$ kauses $\langle O_2\rangle$.

Given the right sorts of action classes, similarity judgments, and responses, S_1's tendency to form kausal judgments in this way means that S_1 will have learned, in effect, that compliant responses to A-C kause a certain sort of outcome. So suppose, in addition:

$\langle R_2\rangle$ is an action *by* S_1 that S_1 envisions.
$\langle O_2\rangle$ is a favorable outcome for S_1.

According to my assumption about favorable outcomes, this means that under background $\langle B([A\text{-}C]_2)\rangle$, S_1 will perform an action of type $\langle R_2\rangle$. So, provided that compliant responses to A-C tend to have favorable outcomes, S_1 will tend to comply with assertion-command pairs of type A-C. Having acquired such a tendency, S_1 will have learned to *comprehend* A-C.

Now let us see how S_1 might learn to *employ* a given assertion-command pair of L_0. Suppose that the following conditions hold:

S_2 utters $\langle [A\text{-}C]_1\rangle$.
S_3 executes response $\langle R_1\rangle$.
S_1 judges that under background $\langle B_1\rangle$, $\langle [A\text{-}C]_1\rangle$ kauses $\langle R_1\rangle$.
S_1 judges that $\langle B_2, R_2\rangle$ is absolutely similar to $\langle B_1, R_1\rangle$ relative to $\langle B_2\rangle$.
S_1 judges that $\langle B_2, [A\text{-}C]_2, R_2\rangle$ is absolutely similar to $\langle B_1, [A\text{-}C]_1, R_1\rangle$ relative to $\langle B_2, R_2\rangle$.

Under these conditions, the following condition will also hold, by the principle of kausal transference (backward version):

S_1 judges that under background $\langle B_2\rangle$, $\langle [A\text{-}C]_2\rangle$ kauses $\langle R_2\rangle$.

Given the right sorts of action classes, similarity judgments, and responses, S_1's tendency to form kausal judgments in this way means that S_1 will have learned, in effect, that utterances of A-C kause a certain sort of response. So suppose, in addition:

$\langle [A\text{-}C]_2\rangle$ is an action by S_1 that S_1 envisions performing against the given background $\langle B_2\rangle$.
$\langle R_2\rangle$ is a favorable outcome for S_1.

Since $\langle R_2\rangle$ is a favorable outcome for S_1, S_1 will perform the action of uttering $\langle [A\text{-}C]_2\rangle$. So S_1 will have learned, in effect, to utter A-C in order to bring about R. Moreover, provided that compliant responses will be favorable outcomes for the hearer, S_1 will tend to utter an assertion-command pair of type A-C only when it will be effective. Having acquired such a tendency, S_1 will have learned to *employ* A-C.

So far, we have seen only how a subject S might learn to comprehend and employ assertion-command pairs that S first observes. Now I wish to explain how, having mastered some fragment of L_0 in this way, S might become master of some larger fragment of L_0, including assertion-command pairs that S has never before observed. The first thing to be explained is how S learns to make the requisite kausal judgments. That is, where A-C is a novel assertion-command pair and R is the corresponding response, how does S learn to judge that under backgrounds in which A has been asserted, command C will kause response R? The answer is that provided that S has mastered the use of A and the use of C in other assertion-command pairs, and provided that S forms the requisite action classes and makes the requisite similarity judgments, it will follow by the principle of kausal combination that S will judge as needed for mastery of A-C. Suppose that S on several occasions has judged that an utterance of "There is a red one" followed by some command kaused an action directed toward a red thing and on several occasions has judged that an utterance of "Stack it!" kaused an action of stacking. Then, according to the principle of kausal combination, assuming that S forms the right action classes and makes the right sorts of similarity judgments, S will judge that under the background of an assertion of "There is a red one," an utterance of "Stack it!" will kause a person to stack a red one. This may be so even if S has never before encountered an assertion of "There is a red one" followed by the command "Stack it!"

In order to explain how S's mastery of some fragment of L_0 may lead to S's mastery of novel assertion-command pairs of L_0, however, it is necessary to explain not only how S forms the requisite kausal judgments concerning the novel assertion-command pair but also why S might respond in compliance to the novel assertion-command pair and might sometimes effectively utter that pair himself or herself. As for compliance, the explanation is that the response that S envisions in response to the novel assertion-command pair may be his or her own response to that pair, and that response may be one that S envisions to kause an outcome that is favorable to himself or herself. As for employment, the explanation is that the response to the novel assertion-command pair may be one that is favorable to S himself or herself and in turn has outcomes that are favorable to the hearer.

One thing that my explanation of a subject's learning of L_0 has assumed is that compliant responses to assertion-command pairs will be mutually beneficial for both the speaker and the hearer. Of course, it is not really necessary that a compliant response *always* be favorable, either to the speaker or to the hearer. What is necessary is only that a compliant response be favorable often enough to make compliance worth the expense. What is often enough will depend on the size of the potential gains and losses. Where potential gains are large and potential losses small, what is often enough need not be very frequent. Still, is it reasonable to suppose that a compliant response will be mutually beneficial even often enough? This is actually two questions. First, is it reasonable to suppose that when a speaker addresses an assertion-command pair to the learner S, then often enough a compliant response on the part of S will be mutually beneficial? Yes, for we may suppose that the speaker is a master of L_0 and would not address an assertion-command pair to S unless he or she could count on a compliant response from S and thus often enough would not utter the assertion-command pair unless a compliant response would in fact be favorable to S. But second, is it reasonable to suppose that when S is the learner and judges that uttering a certain assertion-command pair will cause a certain response on the part of the hearer, then often enough that response would be mutually beneficial? Perhaps, but here we have to suppose that the action classes and the similarity judgments that S generates are such as to secure this result. That is something I think I may reasonably take for granted, although it is not obvious.

An important feature of these explanations, which might easily be over-looked, concerns the learners' judgments of absolute similarity between backgrounds. In my explanation of how S_1 learns to employ a fragment of L_0, for instance, I assumed that S_1 judges that $\langle B_2, [A\text{-}C]_2, R_2 \rangle$ is absolutely similar to $\langle B_1, [A\text{-}C]_1, R_1 \rangle$ relative to $\langle B_2, R_2 \rangle$. Such judgments have to be more than merely judgments to the effect that a given utterance-response pair is absolutely similar to a second utterance-response pair. What must be judged absolutely similar are the larger scenarios to which the two utterance-response pairs belong. Otherwise, the kausal judgments that result will usually be mistaken. For instance, suppose that S judges that an utterance of "There is a box in the next room—Bring it to me!" kauses someone to bring the speaker a box. This judgment must not lead S to judge on some later occasion that saying "There is a box in the next room—Bring it to me!" will result in someone's bringing a box if on that later occasion there is in fact no reason to think that any box may be found in the next room. If such mistaken judgments are to be avoided, then in judging that backgrounds are similar, S must, so to speak, pay attention to the broader context of the utterance, including those things that, from our perspective, indicate whether the judgment might be correct. In the present example, S must judge that the two backgrounds are similar not only with respect to the utterance of "There is a box in the next room" but also with respect to such things as whether, as we would put it, there is a box in the next room. Perhaps it would not be possible for someone with only a language as primitive as L_0 to recognize the similarity between situations in which a box is in the next room. In that case, "There is a box in the next room" is not a good example of the sort of assertion such a language might contain.

5. That completes my simpleminded account of how a productive mastery of the simple language L_0 might be achieved. Here are some of its virtues: First, the mental capacities it postulates are only such as we might expect to find throughout the animal world. Thus it allows that the rudiments of language may have arisen in the course of evolution prior to a high degree of intelligence. Second, it does not invoke any of those sorts of things that proved so intractable in my discussion of the Lockean conception of language. In particular, neither reference relations nor the mental grasp of reference relations is involved. Nor is any process of abstraction involved.

In two ways, it might appear that I have rested my conception of language on reference relations. First, I have explained similarity judgments and kausal judgments in terms of a relation of representation between reflections and things in the world. So it might appear that I have introduced a reference relation at that point. But I have already explained, in chapter 9, why the postulated representation relation is not reference. Second, I have now introduced a relation of correspondence between *words* and the world, for I defined the efficacy of assertion-command pairs in terms of a correspondence between assertions and types of object and between commands and types of action. The thing to notice about this second correspondence relation is that it played no role in my account of the mental processes by which L_0 might be learned. Learning was explained entirely in terms of kausal judgments and similarity judgments. I spoke of this correspondence between words and actions only in order to characterize mastery of L_0. But the language learner does not, according to my account, *achieve* mastery by *conceiving* of mastery in this way.

Moreover, my characterization of mastery in terms of a correspondence between words and actions does not commit me to conceiving of this correspondence relation as a real relation in need of analysis. Rather, I would give a metalinguistic account of it, as I proposed to do for reference in chapter 6. Roughly, to say that a certain assertion corresponds to the presence of a red object, for instance, is just to say that the translation of that assertion into English is, roughly, "There is a red object." If we happen to be dealing with an untranslatable language (I have acknowledged the possibility of such in chapter 4), then in fact it will not be possible to characterize mastery simply by stating the sorts of action or object that correspond to each sentence. The main point is that the characterization of mastery depends on interpretation in a broad sense.

It is tempting to reason as follows: To learn a language is to master it. So to learn a language, what one has to learn is what the conditions are under which one is a master of it. Therefore, if mastery is characterizable in terms of word-world correspondences, then what one has to learn is these correspondences. The fallacy occurs at the second step. Mastering a language is not a matter of learning the conditions under which one is master. From the point of view of someone who already knows a language and thus is in a position to interpret a second language in terms of one that he or she already knows, mastery may be characterized in terms of word-world correspondences. But those will not in general be correspondences that someone learning a first language can grasp; so mastering a first language cannot be a matter of grasping them.

As for abstraction, one might suppose that I had smuggled abstraction into my account somehow if the sorts of objects that are said to correspond to indicatives of L_0 had to be recognized as belonging to those sorts by anyone who had mastered L_0, but this is not so. There are aspects of things to which aspects of reflections correspond, but these need not coincide with the sorts to which indicatives correspond. Carelessly characterized, the principle of kausal combination might seem to presuppose a capacity to abstract. Abstraction will seem to be presupposed if the principle is supposed to be that the learner can isolate or abstract the aspect of things to which a given assertion corresponds. But that is simply not what it says. A speaker whose judgments accord with this principle need not in any way generalize concerning corresponding aspects.

Still, it might seem that I am presupposing an ability to generalize in supposing that the language learner can appropriately form the action classes in terms of which absolute similarity is defined. The problem of learning to generate action classes can be called a problem of *abstraction* (the word can be used in that way), but it is not the sort of problem that I complained about in the context of the Lockean conception of communication. In particular, it is not the sort of thing that might stand in the way of our learning to understand an extraterrestrial language in the way abstraction heuristics stood in the way in the context of the network theory of conceptual development.

The problem in chapter 4 was that in the context of the network theory, as in the Lockean theory, one conceives of both language learning and communication as involving interpretation. Consequently, from the perspective of the network theory it looked as though in order to learn to understand a language, one must solve the very same problems that must be solved in order to learn it as a first language. On the present approach, in contrast, learning a first language is not a kind of interpretation. So we may allow that it is possible to learn to understand a second language if one already understands a language, even if one would be in no position to learn that second language as a first language. So we may allow that one might exploit one's prior possession of a language in order to gain an understanding of another language, and then one might use one's understanding of that language to figure out how native speakers learn the language to begin with. As masters of a language, we may interpret the speakers of another language and then use that interpretation to work out the mechanisms by which they learn their language, such as the mechanisms that generate action classes.

If it is legitimate to appeal to similarity judgments as I have done in explaining language acquisition, why is it not likewise legitimate to explain concept formation in terms of similarity judgments? Why can we not treat concept formation as a kind of grouping by similarity and then explain word learning as matter of mapping words into concepts? I explained in chapter 1 why this will not work. One problem is that similarity cannot determine the boundaries of a category. The present theory escapes that problem inasmuch as no determination of the boundaries of a category is called for. Instead, we require only ad hoc judgments of what I call absolute similarity. The other problem was that in the case of categories that strike us as natural, like *dogs*, there often does not seem to be any antecedently recognizable respect in which every member is more similar to any other member than to any nonmember. The present account posits no such respects.

In chapter 1, I granted that if a large number of things were divided into groups, then judgments of similarity might suffice for deciding which of these groups to place further objects in. But then the basis for the given grouping would still be unexplained. In the context of the present theory, the question about the basis of classification does not arise in the same way, for we do not have to find any sufficient basis in the things themselves for their being grouped together. But a question arises in its place, namely, how the language originates and is sustained. The answer is basically that it is sustained inasmuch as it is mutually beneficial for hearer and speaker and learnable, as I have explained. As for the origin of a language as simple as L_0, the answer might be basically that a series of accidents produces something sustainable.

We may now explain away the child's apparent attempts to define the extension that a general term "applies" to. The adult points to a llama and says, "Llama!" The child repeats "llama" and later points to a llama and says, "Llama!" The child might mistakenly call a goat a "llama" or may fail to recognize a spotted llama as a "llama." It is very tempting to interpret these events as the child's attempt to form a general concept of the type to which "llama" applies. Quite apart from any theory of mine, one should recognize that this interpretation might easily be wrong inasmuch as it abstracts from the larger context of language learning. By now it should be clear that there are indeed other possibilities. In particular, the child might say "Llama!" in the presence of a llama because relative to the current situation, in view of the actions that are feasible in that situation, saying "Llama!" is absolutely similar in my sense to an earlier occasion in which saying "Llama!" had some favorable outcome such as approval.

6. L_0 is not much of a language. More interesting languages will be introduced in subsequent chapters. But L_0 is already a language suitable for *intrasubjective* use. Mastery of L_0 might enable a subject to do things that, other things being equal, he or she could not have done without that mastery. In acquiring his or her mastery of L_0, the subject learns a recipe for kausing others to do things: First, make an assertion, which prepares the hearer to act on a command. Then, when the moment is right, issue the command. This very same procedure may be a means by which the subject brings himself or herself to do certain things. Before acquiring his or her mastery of L_0, the subject might have had no means of preparing himself or herself to act in a certain way when the moment was right. But now, having mastered L_0, the subject may first declare, "Herds near lake," and then, when it is time to hunt, command himself or herself to "Find herds!"

The idea that commands might have a first-person, self-directed use has seemed to some philosophers absurd. For instance, C. L. Hamblin writes; "Talking to oneself can serve an important purpose, but its merits should not be sought by examining the actual words uttered. . . . As Wittgenstein said about private languages, there are no objective tests; what is right is whatever *seems* right" (1987, 36). In other words, there can be no important first-person use of commands, because it cannot matter what words one utters. Hamblin does not elaborate. So apparently he regards this as obvious. It is not obvious. In issuing a command to someone else, my choice of words matters very much. Why should it not matter equally in commanding myself?

Hamblin offers this further argument: "Imperatives are generally understood to create some sort of pressure, personal or rational, for the enjoinee to do what they say," but first-person, self-directed imperatives "create none at all" (37). This argument better reveals Hamblin's presuppositions. He is assuming that obeying a command is a matter of deliberately deciding to obey for some reason. Presumably, if one had a reason to do something sufficient to compel one's obedience to one's command to oneself, then that reason would be sufficient reason to act even without one's having commanded oneself, so the command plays no crucial role.

The problem with this argument is that it begs the question against someone who, like me, maintains that language is itself the medium of a certain kind of thought. Consider this deliberation that Hamblin supposes leads the recipient of a command to obey. What kind of process is that, and how is the ability to deliberate in this way acquired? No doubt, nonlinguistic and prelinguistic creatures are capable of some kind of deliberation. Call it *nonlinguistic deliberation*. To see clearly that Hamblin begs the question, consider the possibility that there is a different sort of deliberation, one that is possible only for creatures who have acquired a language and can thus, in a sense, talk to themselves. Call this *linguistic deliberation*. Now, which sort is it that, as in Hamblin's argument, makes first-person commands superfluous? Nonlinguistic deliberation may indeed determine whether a subject obeys a command from someone else. But nonlinguistic deliberation does not render first-person commanding superfluous. A first-person command may be precisely what creates the occasion for the nonlinguistic deliberation that leads to the action that amounts to obeying the command. Nor does linguistic deliberation render first-person commanding superfluous, because first-person commands may themselves be essential elements of linguistic deliberation.

We exercise control over ourselves in many ways. If I am irritated or anxious, I cannot by means of any mere act of the will calm myself, but I can perhaps "by an act of the will" bring about conditions under which I am likely to become calmer. For instance, I can pour myself some bourbon. If I am supposed to return a rented videocassette to the video store, I may set it by the door, where I am bound to see it on my way out. Perhaps if I am able to remember what I am supposed to do with the cassette when I see it, namely, return it, then I should be able to remember to return the cassette without setting it out where I will see it. Ideally, that might be true, but in fact people do not work that way. At least I do not. I can remember to return the video, but only by doing something now that will ensure that I take the right steps when the time comes.

That commanding oneself may be an important means of self-control is perhaps clearest where one has to execute a complicated series of instructions. In following a cooking recipe, one may memorize the instructions and then give them to oneself as one executes the plan. Here the commands come from the book, not from oneself, but in other cases the plan may come from oneself. Before I go out to do errands, I may tell myself, "OK, first pick up the dry cleaning, then go to the hardware store, and then go the grocery store," and then, as I complete each action, I may repeat to myself the next part of the plan. Perhaps I could do all these things without telling myself to do them, but I could not *make sure* that I did all these things, and did them in the right order, without telling myself to do them.

My hypothesis is that first-person commands, in a public language like L_0, may serve as an even more fundamental means of self-control. In my examples in the preceding paragraph, the problem I overcome in giving myself commands is remembering to do the things I planned to do, and in the right order. But moreover, even in cases where one acts as soon as the motive to act arises, a first-person command may be what makes the action possible. Granted, if opening the door would be favorable for me right now, and in order to open the door I need perform only one simple action, then my commanding myself to open the door may be a pointless flourish. But consider those cases in which the response that would bring about the favorable outcome whose envisioning occasions action depends on a state of affairs that is not perceptually evident at the moment of action. For instance, suppose it is time to hunt, but it is not obvious from the perceivable situation *where* to hunt. What determines where to hunt may in that case be that it has recently been asserted, by the agent himself or by someone else, "Herds by the lake." But how can it make a difference that these words have been spoken? Possibly only by engaging the agent's mastery of the language. In that case, the necessary complement to the assertion, without which it has no effect on where the agent hunts, may be the command, "Find the herds!"

To this it may be objected that when the occasion arises to hunt, what determines where the agent hunts is only the agent's memory of where the herds are. When this information has been obtained by the agent himself, and has not been communicated to him by others, the agent has no need to "engage his mastery of the language" in deciding where to hunt but only needs to remember where the herds are. Even if others are the source of the information, then in deciding where to hunt, he can use that information in the same way he would use it were he himself the source, and so again there is no need to "engage his mastery of the language" and issue himself a command. But how are these things possible? How, having once perceived the herds by the lake, does the agent remember this for later use? My answer is that one way he may do it is precisely by preparing the situation by means of an assertion, "Herds by the lake." In that case, "Find the herds" might be the necessary complement that initiates hunting.

Of course, language is not always a necessary means of remembering where things are. A lioness can remember the herds of wildebeest by the lake without having to tell herself anything. So I do not claim that a language as simple as L_0 is ever necessary for the sort of self-control that I have been discussing. My aim has only been to show that it can have an intrasubjective use, which it has if it is used for this kind of self-control even when the same effect could be had in some other way. Farther up the ladder of languages I am climbing, we may come upon some languages that facilitate a kind of self-control entirely lacking in creatures who lack such languages.

I distinguish between several kinds of talking to oneself. First, there is talking to oneself out loud. Second, there is talking to oneself silently. Call this second type *inner speech*. Inner speech, in turn, comes in two varieties. First, there is inner speech accompanied by auditory or visual mental imagery of words. As one talks to oneself, one may have the experience of an inner voice talking to oneself. This voice, like imagery in general, may be more or less vivid. But inner speech is by no means to be identified with this verbal imagery. Inner speech is no more to be identified with verbal imagery than the speech of another person is to be identified with the sensation of sound that it produces in the hearer. Rather, the verbal imagery of one's own inner speech is a medium for one's observation of one's own thoughts, just as auditory and visual sensations may be the medium for one's observation of the speech of others.[3] But inner speech is possible as well without verbal imagery. As I move about the kitchen making lunch, I do various things from which it might be inferred that I am moved by various acts of inner speech: "The mayonnaise is in the refrigerator. Get it now before you open the bread." But it need not be the case that I experience verbal imagery by means of which I can observe these thoughts. It is as though someone were getting me to do various things by saying things to me even though I am not aware of being spoken to. However, in this case the speaker and the audience are one.

If it seems that talking to oneself has got to be pointless, then perhaps that is because one is thinking of talking out loud. Sometimes talking to oneself out loud may serve to focus one's attention on one's task. Sometimes it may be somehow important actually to hear a sound. However, it may often be true that

---

[3] Various empirical issues arise in connection with the role of auditory imagery, and I would not wish this remark to be taken as prejudging any of those. For instance, one can ask and try to answer through controlled experiments whether one's acquaintance with one's own thought depends on something like listening to one's own inner speech. It is not obvious that that is so. See MacKay 1992.

talking to oneself out loud serves no purpose that would not equally be served by talking to oneself silently. Talking to oneself out loud may seem foolish because it is what people do who have not reached a certain level of normal development.

7. It is a commonplace that language differs from other causal processes, such as evaporation or photosynthesis, in being subject to a kind of normative evaluation to which the others are not. Evaporation or photosynthesis may be good or bad according to whether they serve our purposes or not. But talk, while it might be good or bad in that way too, is subject to normative evaluation in the further sense that it is shaped by the normative evaluations of those who already know how. A language may be a more or less effective medium of cooperation, and in that way it may serve our purposes well or not. But language is subject to normative evaluation in the further sense that the practice of speaking includes a kind of speaking that tends to prevent or to encourage a kind of speaking in turn.

It is a short step from L_0 to a language L_1 that exhibits this further normative dimension in a primitive form. Let L_1 be just like L_0 except that it contains a single sentence that functions as a *reply* to a command, namely, "No!" meaning, roughly, "No, I won't do it." One reason a person who comprehends the language may refuse to obey a command is because it is contrary to his or her own best interests. Another is that some apparent presupposition of the speaker does not obtain. For instance, if I tell you to bring the butter from the refrigerator, you may refuse on the grounds that there is no butter in the refrigerator. In L_1, however, there is no distinguishing between these various reasons for noncompliance.

The "No!" reply serves an instructive function by virtue of the principle of kausal differentiation. A subject who forms kausal judgments in accordance with this principle will learn to generate action classes large enough and varied enough that backgrounds in which a certain assertion-command pair is likely to cause a reply of "No!" will no longer be judged absolutely similar to those backgrounds in which that assertion-command pair will be effective. Thus the practice of uttering "No!" serves to ensure that assertion-command pairs are normally only uttered when they will kause a compliant response.

How might someone who has mastered L_0 go on to master L_1? Given mastery of L_0, comprehension of L_1 is just a product of kausal differentiation. So the only task is to explain employment. As usual, this will stem from the subject's observation of kausal relations. If the speaker fails to elicit a response from the hearer by uttering a certain assertion-command pair, then the speaker may try to elicit the same response or another one by means of a different assertion-command pair. The subject may observe that the "No!" reply kauses the speaker of the assertion-command pair to utter a different pair in response to that reply, which is in turn followed by a compliant response, which in turn may have various consequences. The speaker might, as we would put it, think of a better way to do things. Thus on a given occasion the subject may envision that his or her saying "No!" will initiate a chain of kauses and effekts that will have some favorable outcome for himself or herself.

In subsequent chapters, the sequence of languages will be extended much further. However, I have already said in this chapter all that I am going to say about language learning. I think each of the steps I take, at least in the next chapter, will be small enough that it should seem plausible that they may be taken by means of mental mechanisms not very different from those I have appealed to in this chapter. But how in fact they might be taken is presently beyond my power to speculate.

8. Various general considerations may seem to weigh against the basic conception of language I propose to put in place of the Lockean one. For instance, anyone who has listened to the jabbering of toddlers knows that they are often making no attempt whatever to affect the behavior of others or to create conditions under which behavior may be affected by commands. To this I have an easy answer: Much of children's verbal behavior may consist in rehearsing a verbal repertoire that they have relatively few occasions to exercise in a manner that gives it a point.

Apparently I am trying to derive the capacity for language from the sorts of functions that might produce a more general kind of intelligence. We might expect similarity judgments and kausal (or causal) judgments to be at work wherever intelligent behavior is exhibited. This in itself might seem to count against my approach, for it is clear that people whose mental powers are diminished or ruined in many respects may retain their mastery of their native language. I agree that this is a reasonable concern, but I do not consider it a sufficient reason to abandon my approach. One threat is that we will find that some people retain their ability to learn language while entirely losing the ability to make the sorts of judgments on which language learning, according to my account, rests, but I have not come across any evidence of this. What is familiar (from, e.g., Luria 1972) is cases of people who retain their mastery of language but lose their ability to remember recent events or to organize their thoughts.

Conversely, my account might seem to be threatened by cases of people who retain much of their general intelligence, including the ability to judge similarities and causes, but lose their ability to speak. But what exactly do they lose? I think I can acknowledge, without faulting my general approach, that comprehension and production of language, whether written or spoken, involves specialized mechanisms of perception and control that do not belong to general intelligence. Consider, for instance, the role of grammar. The languages that are truly usable (and not merely in principle understandable) by creatures with brains like ours might be limited to those that possess a certain sort of grammar. The capacity to produce effective sentences and to react in compliance with sentences possessing such grammars may not, as far as my theory goes, be bound up with the functions of general intelligence. So the loss of this capacity might destroy the capacity for fluid discourse, while leaving much of general intelligence intact. Of course, insofar as language is itself the medium for a certain kind of thought, we should find that the capacity for that kind of thought is at least hindered whenever the capacity for language is lost. Even that need not be entirely lost, however, if other kinds of thinking are able partially to compensate for whatever specific element of that capacity is lost.

11

Structure and Assertibility

1. One could not expect a committed Lockean to be impressed by the results of the previous chapter. The languages L_0 and L_1 are so primitive that it is hardly surprising that their function can be conceptualized without recourse to the devices of the Lockean theory of communication. Notice, in particular, that the sentences of L_0 and L_1 lack internal structure. The sentences of English that I have used as sentences of L_0 possess internal structure by virtue of their belonging to English but not by virtue of their belonging to L_0. The Lockean may well protest that it is only in connection with internal structure that the need for the Lockean conception becomes apparent.

From the Lockean viewpoint, the importance of internal structure is this: Only by virtue of the fact that sentences possess an internal structure is it possible for a language to express the indefinite variety of thoughts that we are capable of thinking and to display the interconnections between these thoughts. For given that the thoughts we express in words may be indefinitely various, it is only by virtue of such internal structure that hearers are able to infer the content of the speaker's thought from the speaker's choice of words. So I will not have a serious competitor to the Lockean conception of communication until I have presented an alternative conception of the function and possibility of internal structure.

One kind of internal structure is *logical structure*. For the Lockean it is not strictly true that *sentences* must possess an internal structure in order to bear logical relations to one another, for logical relations between sentences merely reflect the logical relations between the *thoughts* they express. Nonetheless, even the Lockean will acknowledge that an aspect of sentential structure is logical structure, that this is an aspect that is important in enabling hearers to understand what is being said, and that it is normally by virtue of logical structure that we detect logical relations. In some sense, the sentences "The rock is red" and "The flower is red" both logically imply "Something is red." What makes it possible for us to recognize such logical relations is, in part, that all three sentences contain the predicate "is red." The distinction between the predicate and the rest of the words in these sentences is a distinction pertaining to the logical structure of these sentences. It is such logical structure that I aim to explain in this and the following chapter.

My working assumption will be not merely that there is a *connection* between the logical structure of a sentence and the logical relations between that sentence and others but that there is no more to logical structure than what we must posit in order to exhibit logical relations. In this respect my conception of logical structure differs from that of those who believe in referential semantics, for whom logical structure must be exhibited not only to explain logical relations between sentences but also to explain the relations to the world on which truth and falsehood depend.[1]

Not all aspects of internal structure qualify as aspects of logical structure, however. For instance, the relative pronoun "who" enables us to say, "A man who called yesterday called again today," instead of, "A man called yesterday and that man called again today," but the difference between these two sentences is probably not a logical difference. The aspects of structure such as the one that distinguishes these two sentences probably concern the things that hearers depend on to grasp the larger structure of the speaker's discourse. They enable the speaker to condense his or her speech. They enable the hearer to grasp pronominal cross-references. They enable the speaker to emphasize new or significant information, and they enable the hearer to recognize what the speaker is emphasizing. Unfortunately, I do not have a theoretical understanding of the ways these aspects of structure function in communication, and so I will not say much more about them.

The only other thing I want to say about them is that I do not accept the usual assumption that for every normal speaker there is a definite grammar that characterizes that speaker's language.[2] That grammar, it will be said, may not be the grammar that is prescriptively normal—the grammar that his or her teachers might wish him or her to conform to—but it is nonetheless in some way *in* him or her and somehow governs his or her speech production. Historically, there is a clear connection between the development of the generative-transformational paradigm that underwrites this conviction and the Lockean theory of communication. A fundamental assumption within this tradition is that the deep structure, or "underlying phrase marker," for a sentence, which is the core component of the representation of the syntax of the sentence, provides the framework on which a semantic interpretation of the sentence is, so to speak, hung. The underlying phrase marker is supposed to provide the structure of the speaker's message on which the formation of the speaker's spoken sentence is based and into which hearers translate the sentences they

---

[1] This concern with logical structure beyond what is necessary for purposes of exhibiting logical relations is evident in most of the literature concerned with the logic of ascriptions of propositional attitudes, that is, sentences of the form "*S* believes that *p*." David Kaplan's "Quantifying In" (1968), an early prototype, is a good example. Kaplan's concerns are so far from being exclusively logical (in my sense) that he thinks a semantic analysis of "*S* believes that *p*" must even distinguish between sentences of that form that would interest the FBI and sentences of that form that would not interest the FBI. His example is "Ralph believes that someone is a spy." In the case where the FBI might be interested, Kaplan writes it this way: "Ralph believes *of* someone that *he* is spy."

[2] For some unpersuasive arguments in favor, see Lightfoot 1982, 17–18, and Gleitman 1986. For an argument against, see Rosenberg 1988.

hear.[3] If we can free ourselves from Lockean prejudices, then alternative conceptions of grammatical matters might again seem viable.

Since logical structure is the only kind of internal structure I will try to explain, I am entitled to confine my attention to languages in which the only kind of internal structure possessed by sentences is logical structure. Accordingly, I will confine my attention to model languages having the grammars of the languages of formal logic. The grammars of such languages are *transparent*. In such languages all grammatical structure is logical structure, and the logical structure is determined entirely by the sequence of symbols that make up the sentence. There is no need to rely on context of utterance (as one must in order to decide the structure of the logically ambiguous sentence "Every rhyme is not a poem"), and there is no need to rely on lexical meaning (as one must in order to distinguish between the structures of "John is *easy* to please" and "John is *eager* to please").

2. I turn now to the main task of this chapter, which is to explain the function of logical structure. My procedure, in outline, will be this: First, I will define a language that differs from L_1 in that it permits *lists* of assertions prior to a command, including simple negations. I will then distinguish between an *efficacious* assertion in such a language and an *assertible* assertion. I will then define the concept of a *primitive context*, which will be, in essence, a list of assertible sentences. This done, I will then be able to introduce a language that permits disjunction. At that point it will be possible to define an elementary kind of logical validity (differing from classical validity) and thereby to introduce a language that permits logical inference. It will then be possible to define a *context* (*simpliciter*) as a set of indicatives closed under logical implication of this elementary sort. In terms of that it will be possible to define the assertibility conditions for sentences containing modal operators, conditionals, and quantifiers.

In the following chapter, the various concepts introduced informally in this chapter will be used in stating a formally precise definition of validity for languages containing these various operators. The ultimate product will be a logical theory formulated wholly without appeal to reference relations. This theory, moreover, will corroborate the various observations in chapter 7 concerning particular forms of argument.

Let L_2 be a language like L_1 except for two differences: First, L_2 contains a

---

[3] See Katz 1966, 98–175. Even in a work as late as *Aspects of the Theory of Syntax* (1965) the Lockean theory is not particularly evident in Chomsky's own writings. But in *Cartesian Linguistics* (1966) Chomsky makes it quite clear that he feels a strong affinity for theories of language that qualify as Lockean in my sense. Strangely, Chomsky considers Descartes, not Locke, to be his predecessor. But as Aarsleff explains in his essay "The History of Linguistics and Professor Chomsky" (reprinted in Aarsleff 1981), there is good reason not to take Chomsky's historical remarks very seriously.

greater variety of indicatives than L_1. In addition to indicatives that, when asserted, prepare the hearer to perform an action toward a particular sort of object or object-at-a-location, there are indicatives in L_2 that, when asserted, prepare the hearer to act toward or in a certain distant place or at some later time. Second, L_2 differs from L_1 in that a whole series of assertions may precede a command. Thus, the chief might speak to his subordinates as follows:

> *It is buffalo. It is by the lake. Tomorrow is when. Hunt!*

The compliant response to this string of sentences of L_2 will be the subordinate's act of hunting buffalo near the lake tomorrow. Call such a string of assertions followed by a command an *assertion-command string*.

Let L_3 be a language like L_2 with just this difference: In L_3 the person to whom an assertion-command string is addressed can *reply* to an assertion-command string by making one or more assertions himself or herself. These replies may be thought of as amendments to the original assertion-command string. They might, for instance, further narrow the class of compliant responses by specifying a time or a place or some other feature of the response. Or they might contradict some assertion in the original assertion-command string (in the sense that the efficacy conditions of the two assertions relative to the remainder of the assertion-command string are incompatible). The first speaker, who issued the original assertion-command pair, can either reject the amendment by saying "No!" or say nothing. If the speaker says nothing in response, then the amendment is *instituted* in the sense that it determines what sort of response will qualify as complying with the assertion-command string. Let us call an assertion-command string modified by its instituted amendments (if any) a *ratified* assertion-command string.

In the previous chapter, compliance and efficacy conditions were defined for assertion-command pairs of sentences of L_0. The concept of efficacy for assertion-command strings may be extended to L_3 as follows. First, we define the efficacy conditions for indicatives of L_3 as follows:

> An assertion of an indicative p is *effective* relative to a ratified assertion-command string Σ if and only if the response to Σ has the aspect to which p corresponds.

For instance, "Tomorrow is when" will be effective in an assertion-command string if and only if the response to that string takes place the next day. We may now define the sense in which an assertion-command string of L_3 may itself be effective:

> An assertion-command string Σ is effective if and only if the response to Σ is an action of the type to which the command in Σ corresponds and every indicative in Σ is effective.

The sort of response to Σ that is necessary in order for Σ to qualify as effective is the sort that I will say is *in compliance with* Σ. In speaking of the aspects of responses to which indicatives correspond, I am not sneaking a reference relation into my theory of language. Nor am I presupposing an independent account of the speaker's grasp of generality. I explained these disclaimers in the previous chapter in connection with L_0, and so I will not elaborate here.

Since L_3 already contains the reply "No!" and allows other sorts of replies as well, it is a short step from L_3 to a language containing negation. Where p is a sentence, say that "Not p" is the *negation* of p. Let L_4 be a language in which every sentence is either a sentence of L_3 or the negation of a sentence of L_3. There are no multiple negations in L_4. Every negation in L_4 is a *simple* negation, that is, the negation of an atomic sentence. Having defined the efficacy conditions for simple indicatives of L_3, we may define the efficacy conditions for L_4 by adding the following:

An assertion of "Not p" is *effective* relative to a ratified assertion-command string Σ if and only if p is *not* effective relative to Σ.

Negations may serve at least two important functions. First, like the simple "No!" of L_1, the hearer's assertion of a negation may force a revision in the speaker's assertion-command string. For instance, suppose the subordinate asserts, "Not tomorrow is when." Then the chief, yielding to the subordinate's refusal to wait until tomorrow, might utter a revised assertion-command string thus:

It is buffalo. It is by the lake. Today is when. Hunt!

Second, a negation may play an important role as a member of an initial assertion-command string. Not everything about a hearer's response to an assertion-command string need always be determined by the assertions in the string. For instance, suppose the chief utters:

It is a rock. It is red. Bring it!

Then the subordinate may try to bring a red rock from the immediate vicinity without the chief's having specified that the red rock come from the immediate vicinity. Thus the assertion-command string may be ineffective if there is no red rock in the immediate vicinity. A response will have, so to speak, certain *default* features. A negation can be used to cancel such default features. Suppose the chief utters:

It is a rock. It is red. Not it is here. Bring it!

The effect of the additional negative assertion may be that the subordinate searches for and brings a red rock from outside the immediate vicinity.

I now wish to introduce the important concepts of assertibility, deniability, and irrelevance. But first I need to introduce the idea of a *cooperative effect*. At any given time there will be various things that speaker and hearer are conditionally motivated to do. That is, there are things they will be motivated to do if certain other things happen. (In speaking of conditional motivation in this way,

I acknowledge, I am speaking of one of those kinds of nonpropositional thinking the precise nature of which I am declining to try to specify.) In particular, there will be things that each party is motivated to do provided that the other does his or her part. For instance, it takes two to lift a large log, one to lift each end. It takes two to hunt a snipe, one to hold the bag and the other to drive the snipe into the bag. Furthermore, cooperation may be less direct. For instance, the typical member of the tribe may be willing to do as the chief commands, whether or not the chief helps out, provided that the chief adequately performs his or her role as coordinator of the tribe's several activities. Those things that a person would be willing to do provided that the others involved did their part are what I will call *cooperative effects in the broad sense*.

For any given conversational situation and given command, there will often be more than one cooperative effect in this *broad* sense. But there will be only one cooperative effect in the *narrow* sense. Suppose that there are buffalo both by the lake and over the hill. In that case, the cooperative effects in the broad sense that might result from a command to hunt will include both hunting by the lake and hunting over the hill. However, there are various dimensions along which effects may be evaluated, and it is unlikely that any two of them will both qualify as best overall. The relevant dimensions include such things as level of benefit, ease of execution, and salience. For purposes of explaining the possibility and function of language, we may safely assume that no two effects are ever exactly equal in value as measured along these several dimensions. Say that the *best* of the cooperative effects in the broad sense, given a situation and a command, is *the* cooperative effect in the narrow sense relative to the situation and command. (Obviously, I am presupposing some method of individuating effects. The basic principle will be that distinctions that can make no difference to what is asserted in L_4 do not count.) From now on, when I speak of cooperative effects, I will mean cooperative effects in this narrow sense.

Assertibility and deniability in L_4 are to be evaluated relative to cooperative effects in this sense. Suppose we are dealing with a certain conversational situation and a certain command. Suppose, moreover, that some variety of response in compliance with such a command would qualify as the cooperative effect in that conversational situation. In that case:

- An indicative of L_4 is *assertible* relative to the conversational situation and the given command if the only responses in compliance with such a command that would be likely (in fact) to bring about the cooperative effect are those that would be in compliance with an assertion-command string *containing* that indicative.
- An indicative of L_4 is *deniable* relative to the conversational situation and the given command if the only responses in compliance with such a command that would be likely to bring about the cooperative effect are those that would be in compliance with an assertion-command string *lacking* that indicative.
- Indicatives of L_4 that are neither assertible nor deniable are *irrelevant*.

Evidently, the cooperative function of the language that gives it value and makes it learnable will be enhanced insofar as speakers are able to confine themselves to *assertible* assertions.

For example, suppose the chief commands as follows:

Today is when. It is buffalo. It is by the lake. Hunt!

Suppose, moreover, that in order for this command to hunt to be at all effective, and thus in order for it to bring about the cooperative effect, the hearers must begin their hunting today. If they wait until tomorrow, then they will arrive at the lake too late. In other words, "Today is when" corresponds to a necessary feature of any response in compliance with the command to hunt that is likely to produce the cooperative effect. In that case, "Today is when" is *assertible*.

But suppose that instead the chief commands as follows:

Tomorrow is when. It is buffalo. It is by the lake. Hunt!

Suppose that by tomorrow the buffalo will no longer be near the lake. In that case, this assertion-command string will not bring about the cooperative effect, namely, killing buffalo, because it will not be effective. (I am assuming that hunting here means more than just running around with no prospect of catching.) Or suppose that the hearer cannot wait until tomorrow because tomorrow is his initiation day. Then again the assertion-command string will not bring about a cooperative effect, because the hearer will not wait until tomorrow. In either case, an assertion-command string lacking the assertion "Tomorrow is when" would be more likely to bring about the cooperative effect. Relative to this assertion-command string, then, "Tomorrow is when" is *deniable*.

Finally, consider the following:

Today is when. It is buffalo. It is by the lake. It has horns. Hunt!

The last of these assertions, namely, "It has horns," is peculiar. Its presence does nothing to undermine the efficacy of the assertion-command string or in any other way prevent the bringing about of the cooperative effect. But in view of what are evidently the aims of the tribe, namely, that the tribe kill some buffalo, "It has horns" contributes nothing. Relative to the aims of the tribe, which are to eat and collect pelts, it is not at all important whether the buffalo they hunt have horns. Since "It has horns" is not deniable but, on the other hand, contributes nothing, it is *irrelevant*.

Notice that it would not be possible to define assertibility and deniability wholly in terms of efficacy rather than in terms of cooperative effects. However we define these concepts, we will have to compare two different assertion-command strings, one containing p and the other lacking p. So if we were to seek a definition wholly in terms of efficacy, we would have to consider two different responses, namely, an effective response to the one and an effective response to the other. Relative to which, if either, would assertibility and deniability be judged? Alternatively, one might try to explain assertibility in terms of the speaker's intentions. For instance, one might say that an assertion is assertible if a response must possess the corresponding aspect in order to realize the speaker's intentions. But that answer is mistaken. The function that assertibility is supposed to promote is not the realization of the speaker's intentions. The pertinent function is cooperation, and neither the speaker alone nor the hearer alone gets to decide what qualifies as cooperation. The hearer may be uncooperative in failing to do what it would be in some sense good for him or her to do, but the speaker may be uncooperative in commanding what it is in some sense wrong for him or her to command.

I do not imagine that my characterization of the cooperative effect is precise enough to enable us in all situations to decide whether a given assertion is assertible, deniable, or irrelevant. But I think that in light of the conversational situation, it will often be fairly clear what the cooperative effect would be and what kinds of actions would tend to bring it about. For instance, in a case where the tribe is hunting for food and pelts, seeking game with horns is not a necessary part of the cooperative effect. But if the tribe practices some kind of game management that requires sparing the lives of the younger buffalo, then seeking exclusively game with horns might be a necessary feature of the cooperative effect. In the latter case, but not in the former, "It has horns" will be assertible.

Notice that it is not necessary that every assertible indicative actually be asserted at some point in time. Some things may simply *go without saying*. Suppose, for instance, that the speaker utters the following assertion-command string:

It is a rock. It is red. Bring it!

Here it may be unnecessary for the speaker to assert "It is near" because the hearer will bring the nearest red rock even if the speaker does not assert that. And yet "It is near" will be assertible if all compliant responses that qualify as the cooperative effect are bringings of red rocks that are nearby. In that case it *goes without saying* that the rock to be brought is near. Or in the buffalo-hunting example, it may be unnecessary for the speaker to add "Today is when" if the buffalo are near the lake today, since if he says nothing, the hearer will respond to the assertion-command string by hunting today. Still, "Today is when" may be assertible and so go without saying. The assertible indicatives that need actually be asserted will be those that do not in this sense go without saying.

3. I now define the concept of a *primitive context*. Bear in mind that assertibility as defined above is relative to a given conversational situation and a given command. Let us say that the *primitive context* relative to a given situation and command is the set of all indicatives of L_4 that are assertible in that situation relative to that command. Notice that it will never happen that both a sentence and its negation belong to the same primitive context. Notice also that it is possible for a primitive context to contain neither a given sentence nor its negation.

Again, assertibility is relative to the conversational situation. A primitive context comprises the indicatives of L_4 that are assertible. So assertibility *in a primitive context* may be understood as assertibility in the conversational situation in which the members of the primitive context are assertible. In other words, if Λ is a primitive context, then let us say that p is *assertible in* Λ if and only if $p \in \Lambda$. Likewise, let us say that p is *deniable in* Λ if and only if "Not p" $\in \Lambda$. If "Not p" $\in \Lambda$, then a compliant response to the given command is likely to bring about the cooperative effect only if it lacks the aspect to which p corresponds. So p is deniable relative to the conversational situation and given command. Conversely, if p is deniable, then "Not p" is assertible. In that case, since Λ comprises everything assertible, "Not p" $\in \Lambda$.

These conventions may be summed up in the following principles of assertibility and deniability:

(A0)   If $p \in \Gamma$, then p is assertible in Γ.
(ACl)   Nothing else is assertible in Γ.
(D0)   If "Not p" $\in \Gamma$, then p is deniable in Γ.
(DCl)   Nothing else is deniable in Γ.

These are the first of the *axioms of assertibility and deniability,* to which we will continually be adding in this chapter as we proceed up the hierarchy of languages. (I will use "Λ" as a variable over specifically *primitive* contexts. In stating the axioms I use "Γ" because these axioms will continue to hold even after I have introduced contexts of other sorts.)

We are now in a position to introduce a language L_5 permitting *disjunction* as well as *general negation*. Say that p is a sentence of L_5 if and only if either (i) p is a sentence of L_4, or (ii) $p =$ "Not q" and q is a sentence of L_5, or (iii) $p =$ "(q or r)" and both q and r are sentences of L_5. I say that L_5 permits *general* negation because it includes not only the simple negations already in L_4 but also negations of negations, negations of disjunctions, negations of disjunctions of negations, and so on. (Primitive contexts remain sets of indicatives of L_4 as defined above.)

The concept of assertibility may be extended to L_5 as follows. Between A0 and ACl in the above list of axioms, insert the following:

(A¬)   If p is deniable in Γ, then "Not p" is assertible in Γ.
(A∨)   If p is assertible in Γ or q is assertible in Γ, then "(p or q)" is assertible in Γ.

And between D0 and DCl in the above list, insert the following:

(D¬)   If p is assertible in Γ, then "Not p" is deniable in Γ.
(D∨)   If p is deniable in Γ and q is deniable in Γ, then "(p or q)" is deniable in Γ.

It is not necessary to state efficacy conditions for sentences of L_5, because for any sentence of L_5 that is not a sentence of L_4, we can decide whether it is assertible, deniable, or neither entirely on the basis of these axioms and the membership of the pertinent primitive context.

All by itself, however, this account of the assertibility conditions for disjunctions leaves the function of disjunctions mysterious. Notice that according to this account, "(p or q)" is assertible in a primitive context Λ only if either p is assertible in Λ or q is assertible in Λ. So why should a speaker ever assert "(p or q)" instead of just asserting p or just asserting q? In order to explain the value of disjunctions, I wish to distinguish between assertibility and deniability in the *primary sense* and assertibility and deniability in a *secondary sense*. Assertibility and deniability in the primary sense is just assertibility in a given primitive context as defined by the above axioms. Sentences that are assertible (or deniable) in the secondary sense, by contrast, are those that are assertible (or deniable) in the primary sense in every primitive context in a given *range* of primitive contexts. Thus, assertibility in the primary sense is relative to a given primitive context and assertibility in the secondary sense is relative to a given *set* of primitive contexts.

Disjunctions behave differently with respect to assertibility in the primary sense than they do with respect to assertibility in the secondary sense. As I pointed out, if a disjunction "(p or q)" is assertible in the primary sense in primitive context Λ, then either p is assertible in Λ or q is assertible in Λ. But "(p or q)" may be assertible in the secondary sense relative to a given range of primitive contexts even when neither p nor q is assertible in the secondary sense relative to that range of primitive contexts. For instance, that will be the case if the range is $\{\Lambda_1, \Lambda_2\}$ and p is assertible in the primary sense in Λ_1 but not in Λ_2 and q is assertible in the primary sense in Λ_2 but not in Λ_1.

Disjunctions acquire a useful function in the language inasmuch as assertibility in the secondary sense, and not assertibility in the primary sense, may on occasion be the pertinent dimension of evaluation for assertions. One way this may come about is that, as we would put it, neither the speaker nor the hearer is in a position to know which primitive context he or she is in (that is, which indicatives of L_4 are assertible relative to the conversational situation). For instance, one primitive context might be that in which both of the following are assertible in the primary sense.

It is buffalo. It is by the lake.

A different primitive context might be that in which both of the following are assertible in the primary sense.

It is buffalo. It is over the hill.

But circumstances may be such that the speaker cannot reasonably be held responsible for including every assertion that (*a*) does not go without saying and (*b*) is assertible in the primary sense. Still, it may be that the speaker can reasonably be held responsible for including every assertion that (*a*) does not go without saying and (*b*) is assertible in the primary sense in *both* of these primitive contexts, that is, in whichever of the two primitive contexts the speaker and hearer are in. For instance, the speaker might reasonably be expected to utter the following:

It is buffalo. It is by the lake or it is over the hill. Hunt!

Thus disjunctions assume a valuable function inasmuch as they allow the linguistic community to impose standards of comprehensiveness even where comprehensiveness in the making of assertions that are assertible in the primary sense is too high an ideal.

There is a second way in which assertibility in the secondary sense may become the pertinent dimension of evaluation and thus a second way in which disjunctions may serve a valuable function. It may happen that relative to the aims of the speaker, it does not *matter* which of a certain range of primitive contexts is the one the speaker and hearer are actually in. For instance, suppose that an inexperienced hunter is trying to instruct a novice in the art of hunting. Here what matters may not be whether there are tracks in the sand or whether there are buffalo nearby but only that either one will find no tracks or one will find buffalo nearby. Thus, the sentence "Either there are no tracks in the sand or there are buffalo nearby" may be assertible in the secondary sense even though neither disjunct is assertible in the secondary sense. Here the range of primitive contexts to which assertibility in the secondary sense is relative is not the range comprising those that, as far as the speaker can be expected to know, the speaker and hearer might actually be in. Rather, the range is a certain subset of the primitive contexts that the hearer might have been in or come to be in, namely those that are pertinent to the topic of the speaker's instruction.

L_1 was a language in which the recipient of a command could reject a command, and L_3 was a language in which a speaker could offer an amendment, but in a language containing disjunction as well as negation, it is possible, moreover, for one speaker to *decide* another speaker's disjunction. Suppose one speaker utters an assertion-command string containing "(*p* or *q*)" and another speaker utters the assertion "Not *p*." The assertion-command string containing "(*p* or *q*)" and the unrejected assertion "Not *p*" form a ratified assertion-command string having the efficacy conditions of a string containing *q* in place of "(*p* or *q*)." So we might say that the two speakers have jointly *decided* what to do.

In the case where one of the disjuncts is itself a negation, however, an alternative perspective on such collaborations is perhaps more natural. The disjunction "Not-*p* or *q*" is, in effect, the material conditional "*p* ⊃ *q*." Assertions, we have been supposing, can be thought of as creating conditions under which commands can be effective. The assertion of a material conditional

"$p \supset q$" can be thought of as creating conditions under which an assertion of p will create a condition under which the condition that q creates will be created, which may be a condition under which a command will be effective. For instance, the assertion "Tracks in sand $\supset$ buffalo nearby" may create a condition under which, if anyone else asserts "Tracks in sand," then everything will be just as if the original assertion had been "Buffalo nearby." So instead of thinking of the speaker of "$p \supset q$" and the speaker of p as together making a *decision*, it might be more natural to think of the speaker of "$p \supset q$" as providing *instruction*, which the hearer then *applies* on the occasion of his or her assertion of p.

Beyond deciding and instruction, there is *inference*. Inference involves more than deciding, as this has been described, for it requires actually drawing the conclusion. The first step toward explaining inference is to define a kind of logical validity, characterized in terms of assertibility. The requisite concept of validity—call it *0-validity*—may be defined as follows:

> Where A is a set of indicatives and p is an indicative, $A /\therefore p$ is a *0-valid* argument ($A \models_0 p$) if and only if the following holds for every primitive context Λ: if every member of A is assertible in Λ, then p is assertible in Λ as well.

For example, an argument of the form "(p or q), not p; therefore q" will be 0-valid. Here is the proof: Suppose that (i) "(p or q)" is assertible in primitive context Λ and (ii) "Not p" is assertible in Λ. By (i) and A$\lor$ and ACl, (iii) either p is assertible in Λ or q is assertible in Λ. But by (ii) and A$\neg$, p is deniable in Λ. But no sentence of L_5 is both assertible and deniable in Λ (this can be proved inductively). So p is not assertible in Λ. So, q is assertible in Λ.

0-validity differs from validity as it is understood in standard semantics (see chapter 7) in at least one important respect. According to standard semantics, certain sentences validly follow from any set of premises whatsoever (including the empty set). That is not so for 0-validity. For instance, in standard semantics, "$\varnothing /\therefore (p$ or not $p)$" qualifies as a valid argument. But it is not 0-valid, for "(p or not p)" will not be assertible in a primitive context in which neither p nor "Not p" is assertible. In most other respects, however, 0-validity is like classical validity.

0-validity characterizes the inferences that may be drawn. It remains for us to characterize the conditions under which inferences actually will be drawn. This may happen when several speakers get together and, so to speak, *pool* their assertions. On such occasions, one of the speakers may perceive an opportunity to simplify the pool of assertions. Where one speaker has said "(p or q)" and another has said "Not p," a speaker may simplify the total collection by uttering, "(p or q), Not p; therefore q." This process of simplifying the total pool of assertions, guided by 0-validity, might qualify as a primitive form of inference. Let L_6 be a language like L_5 except that it permits this kind of pooling of information, together with the simplifying operation of logical inference.

If we think of the series of languages I am describing as an idealized model of the history of language, then what I am suggesting is that logical inference originates in dialogue. This distinguishes my conception of the rudiments of logical inference from some other common conceptions of the rudiments of logical inference. Commonly, logical inference is conceived as originating in an association between sentences describing *things* that are associated. For instance, inasmuch as smoke is a sign of fire, the sentence "There is smoke" is thought to warrant the sentence "There is fire." This pattern can then become codified in a conditional sentence, "If there is smoke, then there is fire," which may be thought of as either *recording* the pattern among atomic sentences or *licensing* others to make the inference from one atomic sentence to the other (Sellars 1963c, Brandom 1985). This is a conception of the origins of logic that I reject. It takes its inspiration straight from the isomorphism theory of representation, which I criticized in chapter 6.[4]

4. At this point I wish to generalize somewhat from the concepts pertinent to L_6. I will generalize in two directions. First, I will consider a language in which assertions are less tightly bound to commands than they are in L_6, where every assertion is part of some definite assertion-command string. I will apply the concept of assertibility to this new language even though my explanation of assertibility in connection with earlier languages rested on the fact that every assertion is part of some definite assertion-command string. Second, I will broaden the concept of a context by defining a context *simpliciter* as a certain sort of set more inclusive than a primitive context. This broadening of the concept of a context will have the effect of tightening the concept of assertibility in a context.

Let L_7 be a language formally like L_6 except that indicatives in L_7 need not always occur in connection with some particular command. Despite this difference, I will speak of indicatives of L_7 as assertible and deniable. Sentences of L_7 will be assertible or deniable according to whether they enhance or undermine linguistically mediated cooperation. Where the meaning of this is questioned, I will appeal to the special case of assertibility and deniability in earlier languages as illustration.

L_7 will serve us primarily as a stepping-stone by which we may gain entry into languages containing additional logical structure. In order to introduce these further languages, I want to define the concept of a *context (simpliciter)*,

---

[4] It is very clear that Brandom 1985 aims to develop a conception of semantics that throws off the referential paradigm. Nonetheless, he persists in the conception of a conditional as the codification of a pattern: "The idea is to introduce conditionals, for instance, as an explicit way of *saying* that a certain inference is appropriate, where before that appropriateness was merely implicit in practices of undertaking and attributing assertional commitments" (1985, 38).

which will be a certain sort of set of sentences of L_7. Say that a set of sentences of L_7 is *0-consistent* if and only if for some primitive context Λ every member of the set is assertible in Λ. Say that a *base* B_Γ is a 0-consistent set of sentences of L_7. In other words, B_Γ is a set of sentences of L_7 such that, for some primitive context Λ of L_7 every member of B_Γ is assertible in Λ. Formally speaking, a context Γ is any set of sentences consisting of such a base, and everything that 0-validly follows from the base and nothing else. In short, $\Gamma = \{p \mid B_\Gamma \models_0 p\}$. Aside from the fact that a context is closed under a certain kind of implication, an important difference between contexts and primitive contexts is that a context may contain disjunctions. Moreover, a context may contain a disjunction without containing either disjunct. Since $(p\ or\ q) \not\models_0 p$ and $(p\ or\ q) \not\models_0 q$, "$(p$ or $q)$" may belong to a base B_Γ, and thus to Γ itself, although neither p nor q belongs to Γ.

It remains, however, to say something substantive about what determines, in any given conversational situation, what the membership of the pertinent context will be. Here I cannot simply repeat what I said about assertibility in a primitive context in L_4. My account of the membership in a primitive context depended on a prior account of the efficacy conditions of indicatives of L_4. In terms of efficacy conditions I defined assertibility relative to the conversational situation, and in terms of that I defined primitive contexts. Now, in L_7, we have sentences, such as disjunctions, for which no efficacy conditions are given. Nonetheless, the content of a context (*simpliciter*) can be explained in terms of primitive contexts. A context (*simpliciter*) consists of all those sentences that are assertible in every member of a given set of primitive contexts. For instance, suppose $B_\Gamma = \{(p\ or\ q)\}$, so that $\Gamma = \{s \mid (p\ or\ q) \models_0 s\}$. In that case, every member of Γ is assertible in every primitive context in which either p is assertible or q is assertible. In other words, a context consists of those sentences that are assertible in what I earlier called the secondary sense relative to a given range of primitive contexts. The pertinent range of primitive contexts, as I explained, might be the range within which the speaker could not reasonably be expected to isolate his or her own primitive context or the range in which the proffered instruction applies.

Notice that by the axioms of assertibility and deniability stated above, a sentence of L_7 is assertible in a context if and only if it belongs to the context. Not every sentence of L_7 assertible in a primitive context was a member of the primitive context. But now that we have shifted from primitive contexts to contexts *simpliciter*, which are closed under 0-implication, assertibility equals membership. This will not be so, however, when we come to more advanced languages. In more advanced languages we will have sentences that may be assertible with respect to a context without belonging to that context.

Recall that I pointed out in connection with assertibility in L_4 that not every assertible indicative need actually be asserted. Some assertible indicatives might in a sense go without saying. In L_4 the sense in which that was so could be explained in terms of how hearers were disposed to respond to assertion-command strings. Likewise some members of contexts in L_7 may, in an analogous sense, go without saying. In particular, everything that 0-validly follows from the base but is not in the base may go without saying. Moreover, even some members of the base may go without saying.

Membership in a context, like assertibility in a primitive context, transcends the minds of the speaker and the hearer. That is, a speaker may assert an indicative of L_7 that does not belong to the context. A speaker may be unwilling to assert an indicative of L_7 that does belong to the context and might even deny an indicative that does belong to the context. And the hearer may acquiesce in any such errors. These things are so despite the fact that standards for assertibility may be tailored to what can reasonably be expected from the speaker.

As observers of a conversation, we may employ our construal of the context as a reference in order to follow the course of the conversation. Participants in a conversation at the level of L_7 cannot yet explicitly employ the context to guide their participation. But as we will see in chapter 13, speakers of higher-level languages can actually speak of the context, as "what was meant," and their doing so may help determine their responses.

5. At this point I will let the sequence of model languages *branch*. I will describe three languages, one for conditionals, one for modal operators, and one for quantifiers. Any one of them might equally be conceived as the one that succeeds L_7 in a series that is to serve the explanatory role that I envision.

I begin with the language L_C, which differs from L_7 only in that it contains two conditional operators. An *indicative* conditional is an indicative of the form "If p then q," where p and q are other indicatives. A *subjunctive* conditional is a sentence of the form "If p were the case, then q would be the case." I will say that a subjunctive conditional is an indicative *sentence*, to contrast it with imperatives. So while every conditional is an indicative *sentence*, not every conditional is an indicative *conditional*.

In this presentation of the assertibility conditions for conditionals, we will see for the first time how the concept of context that I have been belaboring may be put to good use. Contexts will remain the sorts of sets of sentences of L_7 that I have defined. So they may contain negations and disjunctions, but they will not contain conditional operators. Rather, conditional sentences are to be assertible in contexts without being members of contexts. However, the assertibility of a conditional in a context will depend on nothing but the membership of the context. So it might be helpful to think of a conditional as a means of *indicating* something about the membership of a context.

The axioms of assertibility and deniability for conditionals may be stated *roughly* as follows:

(A>)   If $\Gamma \cup \{p\}$ implies q, then "If p then q" is assertible in Γ.

(D$>$)   If $\Gamma \cup \{p\}$ implies "Not q," then "If p then q" is deniable in Γ.

(A$\geqslant$)   If $\Gamma \cup \{p\}$ implies q and neither "Not p" nor q is assertible in Γ, then "If p were the case, then q would be the case" is assertible in Γ.

(D$\geqslant$)   If $\Gamma \cup \{p\}$ implies "Not q" and neither "Not p" nor "Not q" is assertible in Γ, then "If p were the case, then q would be the case" is deniable in Γ.

The reason these statements of the axioms of assertibility and deniability for conditionals are rough is that I have not yet defined the pertinent notion of implication. Where p and q are not themselves conditional sentences (which means, here, that they are sentences of L_7), the relevant concept of implication is simply the "$\models_0$"-relation defined above. I will postpone until the next chapter substitution of the fully general validity concept. I will also postpone until the next chapter an exploration of the logic this account of conditionals generates.

Suppose p and q are both sentences of L_7. Then it is evident from these assertibility conditions that an indicative conditional, "If p then q," is assertible in context Γ if "Not-p or q" belongs to Γ, for in that case p and Γ together will imply q. One way it can happen that "If p then q" is assertible, then, is that either "Not p" belongs to Γ or q belongs to Γ, for Γ is closed under 0-implication, and each of these 0-implies "Not-p or q." However, the subjunctive conditional, "If p were the case, then q would be the case," is assertible in Γ only if neither "Not p" nor q belongs to Γ. The idea is that since "Not p" implies "Not-p or q," and q implies "Not-p or q," the assertibility of "Not-p or q" would be had too cheaply if either "Not p" belonged to the context or q belonged to the context. That is, the assertibility of "Not-p or q" would in that case be had too cheaply for it to license the assertion of "If p were the case, then q would be the case."

The members of the prevailing context, as I explained above, are all those sentences of L_7 that are assertible in every member of a given range of primitive contexts. So "Not-p or q" will belong to Γ, while neither "Not p" nor q belongs to Γ if "Not-p or q" is assertible in every member of the given range of primitive contexts, but neither "Not p" nor q is. That might be the case, for instance, if, as we might put it, no one were in a position to know whether not-p or q. For instance, a young scout comes back to the camp and reports that he saw no buffalo. When the chief asks him whether he saw any tracks, the scout replies that he did not look for tracks. In that case, no one could be expected to assert, "There were no buffalo by the lake," even if there had been no buffalo by the lake, and no one could be expected to assert, "There were tracks," even if there had been tracks. The most one could be expected to assert, if it did not go without saying, would be something that would be assertible in either of those two cases, namely, "Either there were no buffalo or there were tracks." So that disjunction, but neither disjunct, might be assertible in the context relative to which assertibility is defined in this scenario. In that case, the subjunctive conditional, "If there had been buffalo by the lake, then there would have been tracks," would be assertible in the context.

In this example, the subjunctive conditional was assertible because, as we might put it, no one could be expected to know that there were no buffalo, even if there were none, and no one could be expected to know that there were tracks, even if there were some. But even if it is common knowledge between the scout and the chief that there were no buffalo, the chief might say, "If there had been buffalo by the lake, then there would have been tracks." This is something that it might be useful for the chief to assert in order to instruct the young scout in the art of finding buffalo. But given the common knowledge between the scout and the chief, how can this be assertible, when according to the assertibility conditions for subjunctive conditionals, the negation of the antecedent must not be assertible? The answer is that common knowledge does not guarantee assertibility. In this example, the negation of the antecedent may not be assertible, despite its being common knowledge, because the range of primitive contexts relative to which assertibility is evaluated in this case will include some in which "There were no buffalo" is not assertible.

As I explained in chapter 7, it is a mistake to think that in asserting a subjunctive conditional one must presuppose the negation of the antecedent. (The example was, "If there were a strike, then I would honor the picket line.") What is right, I said, is that we must presuppose neither the antecedent itself nor the negation of the antecedent. The present account of the assertibility conditions for subjunctive conditionals directly affirms that claim. The claim that a subjunctive conditional is assertible only if the negation of the antecedent is not assertible is an immediate consequence of A≫ (together with the closure clause ACl). Moreover, A≫ tells us that the consequent must not be assertible either. But the consequent would be assertible if the antecedent were assertible and the context together with the antecedent implied the consequent. So, since the context together with the antecedent must imply the consequent if the conditional is to be assertible, the antecedent must not be assertible either.

Now that I have given the concept of context some work to do, I can illustrate the mind transcendence of contexts. Consider the following exchange:

A: If we hadn't stopped for lunch, we would be there by now.
B: No, look how wet the road is. If we hadn't stopped, we would have driven through a thunderstorm. That would have slowed us down, and we still wouldn't be there.

A's assumption is that anyone driving nonstop under the conditions that obtain in their case and at the rate they travel when on the road covers the distance they are going within the time that has passed since they started out. What B does, in effect, is deny that this generalization belongs to the context. B does this by pointing out what the local conditions really are. In other words, A was wrong about the content of the context that governs his assertion. Presumably, he would not have made that assertion if he had known the content of the context that governs his assertion, and so he did not know. While *B* in this instance has a better grip on the content of the context, she too might have been oblivious to the prevailing conditions, in which case she might have agreed with *A* and made the same mistake as *A*.

From this example we can see what would be wrong with thinking of the context as the state of a speaker's mind. If the context were always some subset of the speaker's beliefs (the speaker's *presuppositions* in one sense of the term), then there could be no significant disagreement over conditionals. Whether a conditional were assertible in the context would be something the speaker could hardly be wrong about. Any mistake in asserting a conditional would be merely some kind of slip, like a fallacy, in which one merely failed to make proper use of what one had in mind. In denying another's asserted conditional, one would be merely indicating such a slip or perhaps accusing the speaker of some kind of deception—of pretending to speak under a certain context when in fact he or she took the context to be some other. But on the contrary, there must be the possibility of denying another speaker's conditional on nonpsychological grounds while holding the context constant. In other words, there must be the possibility of factually mistaken conditionals. Only then will conditionals be significant instruments of the dialectical give and take that leads to knowledge.

Recognizing the mind transcendence of contexts is important to an understanding of the difference between indicative conditionals and subjunctive conditionals. In asserting indicative conditionals we do not in any sense imply either that the negation of the antecedent is assertible or that the consequent is assertible, but we are asserting something that will be assertible even if it turns out that the negation of the antecedent is assertible or that the consequent is assertible. Suppose, for instance, that someone says, "If there is a strike, then Smith will honor the picket line" (an indicative conditional). This allows that it may turn out that the context contains, unbeknownst to the speaker, the fact that no strike will take place or the fact that Smith will honor the picket line. So where subjunctive conditionals are available, the indicative conditional is a way of avoiding commitments concerning the content of the context.

6. The next language I wish to consider is the language L_M, which differs from the language L_7 only in containing the modal operator "necessarily." In order to set out the assertibility conditions of modal sentences, it is necessary to add a wrinkle to the theory of contexts. What must be added is that contexts contain *cores* and belong to *shells*. Both cores and shells are sets of sentences satisfying the formal definition of a context. A *core* of a context is a subset of the context consisting of sentences that govern the conversation in some particularly crucial way. A core of a context may itself have a core, and this core of a core is itself a core of the context. A *shell* of a context, on the other hand, is a superset of the context. A shell contains every sentence in the context as well as additional sentences that govern the conversation in some more remote way than the sentences in the governing context do. While for any two cores, one must include the other, there may be several distinct, overlapping shells. The basic idea will be that the assertibility of a modal sentence in a context depends on what is in the cores and the shells of the context that governs the conversation. Like conditional sentences, modal sentences may be assertible *in* contexts but are never members of contexts.

The axioms of assertibility and deniability for modal statements may now be stated, thus:

(A□) If p is assertible in some core of Γ, then "Necessarily p" is assertible in Γ.

(D□) If p is deniable in some shell of Γ, then "Necessarily p" is deniable in Γ.

The idea behind D□ is to ensure that "Not necessarily not p," or, in other words, "Possibly p" is assertible in Γ if p is assertible in some shell of Γ. If p is assertible in some shell of Γ, then "Not p" is deniable in that shell, which means, by D□, that "Necessarily not p" is deniable in Γ, which means that "Not necessarily not p" is assertible in Γ. I will postpone until the next chapter an exploration of the logic that this account of modality generates.

The idea is that "Necessarily p" is assertible in a context just in case p belongs to the core of the context, that is, a set of indicatives in some way especially central to the context. One way a sentence can be central is by expressing something whose opposite one cannot imagine, or by expressing something that one is very certain of. Another way is by expressing a condition that it is very important to meet. Another way is by expressing something that qualifies as part of the framework of one's investigations of other things. The idea is also that "Possibly p" is assertible in a context just in case p belongs to the shell of the context, that is, a set of indicatives that governs the context in a remote way. One way a sentence can govern remotely is by expressing certain conditions that *will* govern the conversation if one makes a certain decision or if certain other things come to pass. Another way is by expressing something for which one has *some* evidence but not much.

Above I said that our construal of the context may serve as a reference enabling us to follow the course of a conversation. Here is an example of this: Shortly before the guests are due to arrive, John tells Mary that he *might have to* go out for more beer, that is, that it is possible that it is necessary that he will procure more beer. Consequently, Mary may conclude that it is possible that more people will come to their party than she had expected. Here is why: She assumes that John's assertion that he might have to go out for more beer was assertible in the context. In light of the circumstances, a context in which more people come to their party than expected may be the only sort of context in which the assertion that more beer is procured is central. So a context in which it is assertible that it is possible that more people are coming than she had expected may be the only sort of context in which John's assertion that he may have to go out for more beer is assertible. Having thus concluded that more people may come than she had expected, Mary may have a need to know how many more people might come and so ask John, "How many people are you expecting?" So we may explain why Mary asked this question by citing the context of John's assertion.

7. The quasi-English sentences that I have used in examples in this and the previous chapter contain distinct subject terms and predicates. In the languages described heretofore I have in no way exploited the distinction between subject and predicate. It is now time at long last to introduce a real distinction between them. In doing so, it is important to distinguish between the *grammatical* subject and the *logical* subject. In some cases, a single term may be both. For instance, in "Socrates is snub-nosed" the term "Socrates" is both. In the sentence "John loves Mary" both "John" and "Mary" are logical subjects, but only "John" is a grammatical subject. In the sentence "All dogs bark" the grammatical subject is "all dogs," and there is no logical subject at all. Similarly, we have to distinguish between grammatical predicates and logical predicates. The subject/predicate distinction that concerns me here is the logical distinction, not the grammatical one.

To begin, notice that in order for the assertion of a given indicative sentence to guide the course of the hearer's action, it must be evident to the hearer which command and which other assertions that assertion is to be associated with. In languages as advanced as L_2, it could be assumed that an assertion was in the pertinent way associated with the other sentences in the assertion-command string to which the assertion belonged. Languages allowing replies, such as L_6, also create no special difficulty in associating assertions with commands. But in a language such as L_7 it must be possible to reassemble assertion-command strings from assertions and commands spoken at various times. Demonstrative pronouns, proper names, and other sorts of noun phrases that may serve as subject terms are devices that enable the hearer to do just that.

Suppose, for example, that the chief speaks as follows to his subordinate:

It is red. It is yellow. It is in tree. It is on ground. Eat it! Stay away from it!

In a primitive language such a string might be ineffective. It might be impossible for the subordinate to decide whether the compliant response would consist in eating a red thing in the tree and staying away from a yellow thing on the ground or eating a yellow thing in the tree and staying away from a red thing on the ground. But suppose instead that the chief spoke as follows:

This is red. That is yellow. This is in tree. That is on ground. Eat this. Stay away from that.

By means of these different pronouns, "this" and "that," the several assertions and commands might be cross-indexed in such a way that the compliant responses were completely determinate. The compliant response to this string would consist in eating the red thing in the tree and staying away from the yellow thing on the ground.

Where the number of groups of interrelated assertions and commands may be greater than the number of distinct pronouns in the language, other solutions are called for, such as the device of proper names. Several different assertions may be cross-referenced in this way by setting the same name at the start of each, as in: "Gogan is chief. Gogan is angry." In languages with grammatical devices beyond those available in the languages of logic to which I am confining myself, another solution is the device of noun phrases. An assertion such as "This is red" might be converted into a noun phrase such as "This red," which might then serve as the index relating several distinct assertions, such as "This red is in tree" and "This red is edible."

I am now in a position to introduce the language L_Q, which will allow quantification. First I will define the language L_P, and then I will define the language L_Q in terms of L_P. L_P will contain an indefinitely extendable list of cross-indexing devices, which I will call *individual constants*, or just *constants* for short. These are to be understood as serving the cross-indexing function that I have just described. In addition, L_P will contain a finite number of predicates (in the logical sense), and atomic sentences of L_P will consist of a single predicate followed by a finite number of such constants. Compound sentences of L_P (indicatives) will be formed from atomic sentences of L_P by means of the operators "not" and "or," and no others. (I am ignoring the grammar of imperatives in L_P.)

L_Q will be a language just like L_P except for two differences. First, for purposes of forming quantifications, L_Q will contain an indefinitely extendable list of expressions called *variables*. Second, if ψ is an indicative of L_Q and $\psi v/c$ is the result of putting a variable v in place of constant c throughout ψ and $\varphi = \psi v/c$, then the *existential quantification*, "For some v, φ," will be a sentence of L_Q as well. I will also speak of the *universal quantification*, "For all v, φ," as if it belonged to L_Q, but officially this is to be understood as an abbreviation of "Not for some v not φ."

Adding conditional and modal operators to the language was a matter of stating conditions under which conditional and modal sentences were assertible in a context without belonging to the context. By contrast, adding quantifiers is just a matter of redefining contexts in such a way that quantified sentences may actually belong to contexts. This enhancement of the concept of context proceeds in three stages. First we enhance the concept of a primitive context. Second, we state the assertibility conditions for existential quantifications (which pertain to both primitive contexts and contexts *simpliciter*). Finally, we state the new definition of contexts. In addition, we make some stipulations concerning the relation of contexts to their cores and shells so that we may combine this account of L_Q with our prior account of L_M.

A primitive context will now be a set of literals (simple indicatives and their negations) in L_P. With each primitive context Λ in this sense we will associate a *domain* N_Λ. A *domain* N_Λ for Λ is a set of individual constants that includes at least every constant that occurs in any member of Λ and perhaps others in addition. I should emphasize that N_Λ is a set of *words*, not a domain of possibly nonlinguistic objects.

The axioms of assertibility and deniability for quantifications may now be formulated:

(A∃)   If for some constants $c_1, c_2, \ldots, c_n$, "$\varphi c_1/v$ or $\varphi c_2/v$ or $\ldots$ $\varphi c_n/v$" is assertible in Γ, then "For some v, φ" is assertible in Γ.

(D∃)   If for all constants $c \in N_\Gamma$, $\varphi c/v$ is deniable in Γ, then "For some v, φ" is deniable in Γ.

The idea behind D∃ is to ensure that "Not for some v, not φ," or in other words, "For all v, φ," is assertible in Λ if for all constants $c \in N_\Lambda$, $\varphi c/v$ is assertible in Λ. If for all constants $c \in N_\Lambda$, $\varphi c/v$ is assertible in Λ, then for all constants $c \in N_\Lambda$, "Not $\varphi c/v$" is deniable in Λ, which means, by D∃, that "For some v, not φ" is deniable in Λ, which means that "Not for some v, not φ" is assertible in Λ. It turns out to be unnecessary to mention the domain in A∃. I will postpone until the next chapter an exploration of the logic that this account of quantification generates.

"For all v, φ" should be assertible in Λ if every instantiation of φ by a constant in N_Λ is assertible in Λ, because N_Λ is the class of all cross-indexing devices at issue in the context. If a universal quantification is to fail to be assertible in a given context, then the domain must contain a counterexample, that is, a constant such that the result of dropping the words "for all v" and putting the constant in place of the variable is a sentence that is *not* assertible in the context. It will be best to I illustrate in English rather than in L_Q proper. Suppose that N_Λ = {"Al," "Bill"} and Λ is just {"Al wears glasses," "Bill wears glasses"}. Then "Everyone wears glasses" will be assertible in Λ. But if Λ is just {"Al wears glasses," "Bill wears glasses"} and N_Λ = {"Al," "Bill," "Cathy"}, then "Everyone wears glasses" will not be assertible in Λ.

We are now in a position to redefine contexts *simpliciter*. First, let a *base* B_Γ for a context be a 0-consistent set of indicative sentences of L_P (not L_Q). A *domain* is a set of constants N_Γ such that if constant c occurs in any member of any sentence in B_Γ, then $c \in N_\Gamma$. In short, N_Γ includes all of the constants in B_Γ but may include others as well. We now generalize on the concept of 0-validity by defining N-validity as follows:

Where A is a set of sentences of L_Q and φ is a sentence of L_Q, say that A /∴ φ is N-valid ($A \models_N \varphi$) if and only if the following condition holds for every primitive context Λ that has a domain $N_\Lambda = N$: if every member of A is assertible in Λ, then φ is also assertible in Λ.

(N_Γ-validity is the special case in which $N = N_\Gamma$.) Finally, we define a *context* as any set of sentences consisting of such a base B_Γ and everything that N_Γ-validly follows from the base and nothing else. In short, $\Gamma = \{p \mid B_\Gamma \models_{N\Gamma} p\}$. Notice that while N-validity and, hence, N_Γ-validity pertain to arbitrary arguments of L_Q, in defining contexts we are interested only in what N_Γ-validly follows from a set of sentences of L_P, namely, the base of B_Γ.

For purposes of combining the present account of quantification with the above account of modal sentences, it is necessary to place a restriction on the domains associated with contexts. Recall that for purposes of stating the assertibility conditions for sentences containing modal operators, we supposed that contexts possess cores and shells. These cores and shells are themselves formally contexts. We want to make sure that as we climb from a core to the context that governs the conversation and from the governing context to its shells, the possibilities do not decrease and thus the number of assertible universal quantifications does not decrease. To this end, we require that the domain associated with the core of the governing context *include* the domain of the governing context and that the domain of the governing context include the domains of all of its shells. Thus we can be sure that if "Necessarily for all v, φ" is assertible in Γ, then "For all v, φ" is assertible in Γ as well.

I said at the beginning of this chapter that my aim was to explain logical structure. So far I have introduced the basic concepts of assertibility and context that I will use to try to explain this and have illustrated their usefulness in understanding conversations. Moreover, I have defined some elementary kinds of logical validity that pertain to languages containing negation, disjunction, and quantification. But I still have not defined the concept of logical validity that will pertain to arguments containing conditionals and modal operators in addition. That is what I will do in the next chapter. Having done that, I will then be better able to defend the theory of assertibility that I have introduced here by showing that the arguments that prove to be valid on that account are those that really ought to qualify as valid.

12

Context Logic

1. The purpose of this chapter is to set out formally precise definitions of logical validity for languages containing conditionals, modal operators, and quantifiers. These definitions and the devices employed in them constitute what I will call *context logic*. This chapter should be thought of, not as advancing the sequence of languages I have been describing, but as detailing those arrived at in the previous chapter.

Recall that I argued in chapter 7 that referential semantics leads to a mistaken account of logical validity. Referential semantics does not, and in some cases arguably cannot, validate exactly those arguments that truly are valid. The context-logical conception of validity, as we will see, steers clear of all of those errors I pointed to in chapter 7. Thus this chapter will serve as confirmation of the superiority of the conception of language I have been developing in this book over any conception that, like the Lockean theory, leads to a referential semantics. At several points I will take for granted several general theorems that I will not stop to prove. (The proofs are not always simple.)

In principle I could define a single language containing all of the operators I wish to account for and proceed directly to a definition of logical validity for that language. This procedure would be hard to follow, however, since the reader would have to absorb a great many technical details before seeing any results. So instead I will first confine my attention to a language containing only logical operators for negation, disjunction, and necessitation. To that I will be able to add fairly directly two conditional operators. Then I will backtrack and redefine contexts in such a way as to allow quantifiers together with modal operators. I will not address combinations of quantifiers and conditionals.

2. Let S be a sentential language with the the logical constants "$\vee$," meaning *or*, and "$\neg$," meaning *not*. I will use capital roman letters "A," "B," and "C" for arbitrary atomic sentences of S, and I will use italicized lowercase letters "p," "q," "r," and "s" as schematic letters for arbitrary sentences of S. Say that p is a sentence of S if and only if either (i) p is an atomic sentence of S, or (ii) $p =$ "$\neg q$" and q is a sentence of S, or (iii) $p =$ "$(q \vee r)$" and q and r are sentences of S. I will use italicized uppercase letters, for example, "A," for *sets* of sentences of S. S is the formal analogue of L_7 discussed in the previous chapter.

The first step is to set out the initial *axioms of assertibility and deniability* for sentences of S. Assertibility and deniability are relative to context Γ. But since various concepts of context will be at issue, I will set out the initial axioms of assertibility and deniability for sentences of S before I define any sort of context:

(A0)   If $p \in \Gamma$, then p is assertible in Γ.
(A¬)   If p is deniable in Γ, then $\neg p$ is assertible in Γ.
(A∨)   If p is assertible in Γ or q is assertible in Γ, then $(p \vee q)$ is assertible in Γ.
(ACl)   Nothing else is assertible in Γ.
(D0)   If $\neg p \in \Gamma$, then p is deniable in Γ.
(D¬)   If p is assertible in Γ, then $\neg p$ is deniable in Γ.
(D∨)   If p is deniable in Γ and q is deniable in Γ, then $(p \vee q)$ is deniable in Γ.
(DCl)   Nothing else is deniable in Γ.

Define a *primitive context* Λ as any set of literals in the language S such that for no sentence p of S is it the case that both $p \in \Lambda$ and $\neg p \in \Lambda$. (A literal is any atomic sentence or negation of an atomic sentence.)

In terms of assertibility in a primitive context, it is possible to define *0-validity*: Where A is a set of sentences of S and p is a sentence of S, say that $A /\therefore p$ is *0-valid* $(A \models_0 p)$ if and only if for every primitive context Λ, if every sentence in A is assertible in Λ, then p is also assertible in Λ. Where A is a set of sentences of S, say that A is *0-consistent* if and only if for some primitive context Λ, every member of A is assertible in Λ.

Some noteworthy facts about 0-validity follow:

- For all p, $\varnothing \not\models_0 p$. (There are no 0-valid sentences.)
- $p \not\models_0 ((p \,\&\, q) \vee (p \,\&\, \neg q))$. (Assume that "&" is defined in the usual way.)
- $p, \neg p \models_0 q$. (A contradiction 0-implies anything.)
- $p \models_0 \neg\neg p$ and $\neg\neg p \models_0 p$. (Double-negation is 0-valid.)
- $p \models_0 (p \vee q)$, and $(p \vee q), \neg p \models_0 q$. (Addition and disjunctive syllogism are 0-valid.)
- $\neg p, \neg q \models_0 \neg(p \vee q)$, and $\neg(p \vee q) \models_0 \neg p$. (DeMorgan's laws are 0-valid.)

Say that Λ is a *maximal* primitive context if and only if for every atomic sentence p in S, either $p \in \Lambda$ or $\neg p \in \Lambda$. Say that a maximal primitive context Λ *corresponds* to a classical valuation Σ if and only if $\Lambda = \{s \mid r$ is atomic and either $s = r$ and $\Sigma(r) =$ Truth or $s = \neg r$ and $\Sigma(r) =$ Falsehood$\}$. If maximal primitive context Λ corresponds to classical valuation Σ, then p is assertible in Λ if and only if $\Sigma(p) =$ Truth, and p is deniable in Λ if and only if $\Sigma(p) =$ Falsehood. To every classical valuation there corresponds a maximal primitive context. Consequently, every 0-valid argument of S is classically valid (even though, as we have seen, not every classically valid argument is 0-valid). Moreover, if Λ and Π are primitive contexts and $\Pi \subseteq \Lambda$, then every sentence of S assertible in Π is assertible in Λ. So A is 0-consistent if *and only if A* is classically consistent.

My choice of the concept of 0-validity as a starting point is not a consequence of some odd distaste for tautologies. It is a choice more or less forced by later developments, especially in the theory of quantification. (See note 2 to R48 below.)

3. Define a *context* (*simpliciter*) Γ as any 0-consistent set of sentences of S such that for every sentence p of S, if $\Gamma \models_0 p$, then $p \in \Gamma$. In other words, a context is a 0-consistent set of sentences of S closed under 0-implication. (This definition will be modified when quantifiers are introduced.)

Define a *tree* Θ as any countable set of contexts such that (*a*) for some $\Gamma_0 \in \Theta$, for all $\Gamma_i \in \Theta$, $\Gamma_0 \subseteq \Gamma_i$ and (*b*) for all Γ_i, Γ_j, $\Gamma_k \in \Theta$, if $\Gamma_i \subseteq \Gamma_k$ and $\Gamma_j \subseteq \Gamma_k$, then either $\Gamma_i \subseteq \Gamma_j$ or $\Gamma_j \subseteq \Gamma_i$. For all trees Θ and all contexts Γ_i and Γ_j in Θ, define Γ_i to be a *core* of Γ_j if and only if either (*a*) $\Gamma_i \subset \Gamma_j$ or (*b*) $\Gamma_i = \Gamma_j$ and there is no context Γ_k in Θ such that $\Gamma_k \subset \Gamma_j$. (Here "$\subset$" will mean *properly includes*.) Define Γ_j to be a *shell* of Γ_i if and only if $\Gamma_i \subseteq \Gamma_j$. For all trees Θ, define Γ_i to be the *innermost* core of Θ if and only if $\Gamma_i \in \Theta$ and there is no context $\Gamma_j \in \Theta$ such that $\Gamma_j \subset \Gamma_i$.

Here are some consequences of these definitions: If Γ_k is a context in tree Θ and Γ_i and Γ_j are two distinct cores of Γ_k, then either $\Gamma_i \subset \Gamma_j$ or $\Gamma_j \subset \Gamma_i$. However a context Γ_i in Θ may have two shells, Γ_j and Γ_k, such that neither $\Gamma_j \subset \Gamma_k$ nor $\Gamma_k \subset \Gamma_j$. Further, a context is its own core if and only if it is the innermost core, but every context is a shell of itself.

Further, assume that in each tree there is a single context called the *governing* context. For every tree Θ, if Γ^* is the governing context in Θ, then $\Gamma^* \in \Theta$, and for every context $\Gamma \in \Theta$, either $\Gamma \subseteq \Gamma^*$ or $\Gamma^* \subseteq \Gamma$. In other words, no branches stem from any core of the governing context. In specifications of the membership of a tree, the governing context will always be marked with an asterisk, thus: Γ^*. (See fig. 12.1, where Γ^* is the governing context, Γ_1 is its only core and is the innermost core, and Γ_2, Γ_3, Γ_4, and Γ_5 are all shells of Γ^*.)

The several features of trees as so defined are fairly immediate consequences of the basic idea that shells represent possibilities and cores represent necessi-

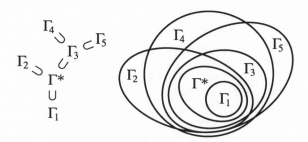

Figure 12.1. Two views of a tree.

ties. The idea behind selecting a single context to be the governing context and then forbidding any branches from stemming from below the governing context is this: What is possible only relative to what is necessary relative to the governing context may not be possible relative to all that belongs to the governing context. The idea behind requiring that of any two cores of a given context one must include the other is this: Since any two cores must be a subset of the governing context, their union must be consistent. So their union would itself be a set of necessities and thus a core, and there would be no point in distinguishing between them. The same cannot be said about shells, since the union of two shells need not be consistent.

Next, let M be a language just like S except that it contains the additional logical constant "□," meaning *necessarily*. That is, p is a sentence of M if and only if either (i) p is a sentence of S, or (ii) p = "$\neg q$" and q is a sentence of M, or (iii) p = "$(q \vee r)$" and q and r are sentences of M, or (iv) p = "$\Box q$" and q is a sentence of M. M is the formal analogue of L_M discussed in the previous chapter. Although sentences containing the constant "□" are never *members* of contexts, that will not prevent us from speaking of sentences containing "□"'s as assertible in Γ or deniable in Γ.

In the list of axioms of assertibility in the previous section, insert the following before ACl and DCl, respectively:

(A□)   If p is assertible in some core of Γ, then $\Box p$ is assertible in Γ.
(D□)   If p is deniable in some shell of Γ, then $\Box p$ is deniable in Γ.

I now define validity (*simpliciter*) in the context-logical sense: Where A is a set of sentences of M and p is a sentence of M, $A / \therefore p$ is *valid* ($A \models p$) if and only if for every tree Θ, if Γ^* is the governing context in Θ, then if every sentence in A is assertible in Γ^*, then p is assertible in Γ^*.

Finally I define consistency (*simpliciter*) in the context-logical sense: Where A is a set of sentences of M, say that the members of A are *co-assertible* if and only if there is a tree such that all the members of A are assertible in the governing context in the tree.

THEOREM 1: If p is a sentence of S, then (1) p is assertible in Γ if and only if $p \in \Gamma$, and (2) p is deniable in Γ if and only if $\neg p \in \Gamma$. (A sentence of M will be a sentence of S if it contains no "□"'s.)

THEOREM 2: For any sentence p of M, (1) $\neg p$ is assertible in Γ if and only if p is deniable in Γ, and (2) $\neg p$ is deniable in Γ if and only if p is assertible in Γ.

THEOREM 3: (1) If $(p \vee q)$ is a sentence of M and not of S (i.e., contains "□"'s), then $(p \vee q)$ is assertible in Γ if and only if p is assertible in Γ or q is assertible in Γ, and (2) in general, $(p \vee q)$ is deniable in Γ if and only if p is deniable in Γ and q is deniable in Γ. (But notice that if $(p \vee q)$ contains no "□"'s, then $(p \vee q)$ may be assertible in Γ even if neither p nor q is assertible in Γ, for $(p \vee q)$ may belong to Γ even though neither p nor q does.)

Define $(p \, \& \, q)$ to be an abbreviation of $\neg(\neg p \vee \neg q)$.

COROLLARY: (1) In general, $(p \ \& \ q)$ is assertible in Γ if and only if p is assertible in Γ and q is assertible in Γ, and (2) if $(p \ \& \ q)$ is a sentence of M and not of S (i.e., contains "□"'s), then $(p \ \& \ q)$ is deniable in Γ if and only if p is deniable in Γ or q is deniable in Γ.

THEOREM 4: (1) $\Box p$ is assertible in Γ if and only if p is assertible in Γ in some core of Γ, and (2) $\Box p$ is deniable in Γ if and only if p is deniable in some shell of Γ.

Define $\Diamond p$ to be an abbreviation of $\neg \Box \neg p$.

COROLLARY: (1) $\Diamond p$ is assertible in Γ if and only if p is assertible in some shell of Γ, and (2) $\Diamond p$ is deniable in Γ if and only if p is deniable in some core of Γ.

THEOREM 5: For all sentences p of M, for all trees Θ, if Γ^* is the governing context in Θ, $\Gamma \in \Theta$ and $\Gamma \subseteq \Gamma^*$, then (1) if p is assertible in some core of Γ, then p is assertible in Γ, and (2) if p is deniable in some core of Γ, then p is deniable in Γ.

Note: Not everything assertible in some core of Γ^* or in Γ^* itself is assertible in every shell of Γ^*. For instance, suppose $\Theta = \{\Gamma^*, \Gamma_1, \Gamma_2\}$, where $\Gamma^* = \varnothing$, $\Gamma_1 = \{s \mid A \ \models_0 s\}$, and $\Gamma_2 = \{s \mid \neg A \ \models_0 s\}$. Then $\Diamond A$ is assertible in Γ^*, but $\Diamond A$ is not assertible in Γ_2, which is a shell of Γ^*.

It is now easy to prove some of the more interesting results. In demonstrating the validity of a given form of argument, it is sometimes possible to prove the stronger claim that if the premises are all assertible in a given context, whether it could qualify as a governing context or not, then the conclusion is assertible in that context. I will prove this stronger claim whenever possible.

R1: $\Diamond p$ and $\Diamond \neg p$ may be co-assertible. Let $p = A$, and let $\Theta = \{\Gamma^*, \Gamma_1, \Gamma_2\}$, where $\Gamma^* = \varnothing$, $\Gamma_1 = \{s \mid A \ \models_0 s\}$, and $\Gamma_2 = \{s \mid \neg A \ \models_0 s\}$. Since $A \in \Gamma_1$ and $\neg A \in \Gamma_2$, A is assertible in Γ_1 and $\neg A$ is assertible in Γ_2. Since Γ_1 and Γ_2 are both shells of Γ^*, both $\Diamond A$ and $\Diamond \neg A$ are assertible in Γ^*.

Note: This result is a consequence of the fact that trees may "branch," that is, that a single context may have overlapping shells. The possibility of branching trees is also exploited in the proof of R17 below.

R2: If p is a sentence of S (i.e., contains no "□"'s), then p and $\Diamond \neg p$ are not co-assertible. Suppose p is nonmodal and both p and $\Diamond \neg p$ are assertible in Γ^*. Then $\neg p$ is assertible in some shell Δ of Γ^*. Since p is nonmodal, $\neg p \in \Delta$. But since p is nonmodal, $p \in \Gamma^*$, and every context is included in all of its shells. So $p \in \Delta$ too. But that is impossible, since all contexts are 0-consistent. This is the example I used in criticizing the principle of inconsistency in chapter 7. The failure of the principle of inconsistency is a consequence of this result together with R12 below.

R3: $\Diamond p$ and $\Diamond \Box \neg p$ (i.e., $\Diamond \neg \Diamond p$) may be co-assertible. Let $p = A$ and $\Theta = \{\Gamma^*, \Gamma_1, \Gamma_2, \Gamma_3\}$, where $\Gamma^* = \varnothing$, $\Gamma_1 = \{s \mid A \ \models_0 s\}$, $\Gamma_2 = \{s \mid \neg A \ \models_0 s\}$, and $\Gamma_3 = \{s \mid \{\neg A, B\} \ \models_0 s\}$. Since $A \in \Gamma_1$, A is assertible in Γ_1. Since Γ_1 is a shell of Γ^*, $\Diamond A$ is assertible in Γ^*. Since $\neg A \in \Gamma_2$, $\neg A$ is assertible in Γ_2. Since Γ_2

is a core of Γ_3, $\Box\neg A$ is assertible in Γ_3. Since Γ_3 is a shell of Γ^*, $\Diamond\Box\neg A$ is assertible in Γ^*.

R4: $\Box\Diamond p$ and $\Diamond\Box\neg p$ (i.e., $\neg\Box\Diamond p$) may be co-assertible. This is illustrated by the same tree as in the previous result. Since Γ^* is the innermost core, it is its own core. Since $\Diamond A$ is assertible in the core of Γ^*, $\Box\Diamond A$ is assertible in Γ^*.

Note 1: At first glance this may look like a perfectly absurd result, which undermines the whole of context logic. On the contrary, the result is defensible. First, the context in which both $\Box\Diamond p$ and $\Diamond\Box\neg p$ are assertible is not a context in which *every* sentence of M is assertible ($\Box\Diamond p$, $\Diamond\Box\neg p$ $\nvDash q$). And second, we can imagine circumstances in which, intuitively, both would be assertible. Suppose I *may have* to be *out* of Cincinnati on Friday (because something may possibly happen that will make it necessary for me to be in Chicago). This is not contradicted by the supposition that I *may* be *in* Cincinnati on Friday. But if it *is* possible that I will be in Cincinnati, then it *has* to be possible, because anything possible with respect to what *is* the case is possible with respect to what *has* to be the case (see R8 below).

Still, this result may seem hard to maintain when $\Diamond\Box\neg p$ is written as $\neg\Box\Diamond p$. I offer the following diagnosis of this apparent strangeness: The appearance of absurdity in accepting both $\Box\Diamond p$ and $\neg\Box\Diamond p$ stems from *referential thinking*. If we think of logical relations along the lines of standard semantics, then assertions having these two forms will seem to say of a certain proposition both that it corresponds to reality and that it does not correspond to reality, which is absurd. In the context of context logic, what we have to acknowledge is only that $\Box\Diamond p$ can be both assertible and deniable in a single context. It can be assertible by virtue of the fact that p belongs to one of the shells of the governing context, and it can be deniable by virtue of the fact that $\neg p$ belongs to the core of some other shell of the governing context.

Note 2: The principle of substitutivity fails for context logic. $(A \vee B)$, $\neg B \vDash A$, for atomic A and B, but $(A \vee \Box\Diamond B)$, $\neg\Box\Diamond B \nvDash A$.

R5: $\Box p \vDash p$. Suppose for arbitrary tree Θ, Γ^* is the governing context in Θ and $\Box p$ is assertible in Γ^*. Then p is assertible in some core of Γ^*. So by Theorem 5, p is assertible in Γ^*.

Note: This result is a consequence of the facts that in each tree a particular context is designated to be the governing context, that branches do not stem from beneath the governing context, and that validity is defined as preservation of assertibility in the governing context.

R6: $p \vDash \Diamond p$. Suppose for arbitrary tree Θ and arbitrary $\Gamma \in \Theta$, p is assertible in Γ. But Γ is its own shell. So $\Diamond p$ is assertible in Γ.

Note: This result is a consequence of the fact that every context is its own shell.

R7: $\Diamond\Diamond p \vDash \Diamond p$. Suppose for arbitrary tree Θ and arbitrary $\Gamma \in \Theta$, $\Diamond\Diamond p$ is assertible in $\Gamma \in \Theta$. Then p is assertible in some shell of some shell of Γ. But a shell of a shell of Γ is a shell of Γ. So p is assertible in some shell of Γ. So $\Diamond p$ is assertible in Γ.

R8: $\Diamond p \models \Box \Diamond p$. Suppose for arbitrary tree Θ and arbitrary $\Gamma \in \Theta$, $\Diamond p$ is assertible in Γ. Then p is assertible in some shell of Γ, which is also a shell of every core of Γ. So $\Diamond p$ is assertible in some (indeed every) core of Γ. So $\Box \Diamond p$ is assertible in Γ.

R9: $p \models \Box \Diamond p$. By R6 and R8.

R10: If $p, q, \ldots \models r$, then $\Box p, \Box q, \ldots \models \Box r$. Suppose the antecedent, and suppose that $\Box p, \Box q, \ldots$ are assertible in Γ^*. Then p is assertible in some core of Γ^*, q is assertible in some core of Γ^*, etc. One of these cores includes all of the others. So by Theorem 5, there is some one core of Γ^* in which $p, q, \ldots$ are all assertible. So since any core of a governing context might be designated as the governing context in an otherwise identical tree, r is assertible in that same core of Γ^*. So $\Box r$ is assertible in Γ^*.

Note: This result is a consequence of the fact that for any two cores of a context, one must include the other.

R11: $(\Box p \& \Box q) \models \Box (p \& q)$. If $(\Box p \& \Box q)$ is assertible in Γ^*, then $\Box p$ and $\Box q$ are both assertible in Γ^*. So the result holds by R10.

R12: $p \not\models \Box p$. To see this, consider a tree in which some sentence belongs to the governing context but does not belong to any core of that context.

R13: $\Diamond p \not\models p$. Consider a tree in which some sentence belongs to some shell of the governing context but does not belong to the governing context.

R14: $\Box p \not\models \Box \Box p$. Let $p = $ A, and let $\Theta = \{\Gamma_1, \Gamma_2, \Gamma^*\}$, where $\Gamma_1 = \varnothing$, $\Gamma_2 = \{s \mid A \models_0 s\}$ and, $\Gamma^* = \{s \mid \{A, B\} \models_0 s\}$. Since $A \in \Gamma_2$, A is assertible in Γ_2. Γ_2 is a core of Γ^*. So $\Box$A is assertible in Γ^*. But since $A \notin \Gamma_1$, A is not assertible in Γ_1. So $\Box$A is not assertible in Γ_1 or Γ_2. So $\Box \Box$A is not assertible in Γ^*.

By R6 and R7, we have it that $\Diamond p$ and $\Diamond \Diamond p$ are in a sense equivalent. As I pointed out in chapter 7, however, if that is so, then by the principle of equivalence, $\Box p$ and $\Box \Box p$ ought likewise to be equivalent. The problem, I pointed out, is that $\Box p$ does not seem to imply $\Box \Box p$. Now we see by R14 that context logic affirms that appearance. So context logic corroborates my argument in chapter 7 against the principle of equivalence. As I also pointed out in chapter 7, the possible-worlds theory of modal logic tells us that $\Diamond \Diamond p /\therefore \Diamond p$ and $\Box p /\therefore \Box \Box p$ must either both be valid or both be invalid. So R14 and R7 also corroborate my argument in chapter 7 against the possible-worlds theory of modal logic.

R15: $\Diamond \Box p \not\models p$. Let $p = $ A, and let $\Theta = \{\Gamma^*, \Gamma_1, \Gamma_2\}$, where $\Gamma^* = \varnothing$, $\Gamma_1 = \{s \mid A \models_0 s\}$, and $\Gamma_2 = \{s \mid \{A, B\} \models_0 s\}$. Since A is assertible in Γ_1, and Γ_1 is a core of Γ_2, $\Box$A is assertible in Γ_2. Since Γ_2 is a shell of Γ^*, $\Diamond \Box p$ is assertible in Γ^*. But A is not assertible in Γ^*.

As I pointed out in chapter 7, the possible-worlds theory of modal logic also tells us that $p /\therefore \Box \Diamond p$ and $\Diamond \Box p /\therefore p$ must either both be valid or both be invalid. R9 and R15 show that in context logic that is not so.

R16: $\Box(p \lor q) \not\models (\Box p \lor \Box q)$. Let $p =$ A, and let $q =$ B. Let $\Theta = \{\Gamma^*\}$, where $\Gamma^* = \{s \mid (A \lor B) \models_0 s\}$. Since $(A \lor B)$ is a member of Γ^*, and Γ^* is its own core, $\Box(A \lor B)$ is assertible in Γ^*. But neither A nor B is assertible in any core of Γ^*, since neither belongs to Γ^*. So neither $\Box$A nor $\Box$B is assertible in Γ^*. So by Theorem 3, $(\Box p \lor \Box q)$ is not assertible in Γ^* either.

Note: This result is a consequence of the fact that a context may contain a disjunction without containing either disjunct.

R17: $(\Diamond p \,\&\, \Diamond q) \not\models \Diamond(p \,\&\, q)$. Let $p =$ A, and let $q =$ B. Let $\Theta = \{\Gamma^*, \Gamma_1, \Gamma_2\}$, where $\Gamma^* = \varnothing$, $\Gamma_1 = \{s \mid A \models_0 s\}$, and $\Gamma_2 = \{s \mid B \models_0 s\}$. Since A is assertible in Γ_1, and Γ_1 is a shell of Γ^*, $\Diamond$A is assertible in Γ^*. Similarly, $\Diamond$B is assertible in Γ^*. But $(A \,\&\, B)$ is not assertible in Γ^*, Γ_1, or Γ_2. So $\Diamond(A \,\&\, B)$ is not assertible in Γ^*.

R18: $(p \lor q) \not\models (\Diamond p \lor \Diamond q)$. Let $p =$ A and $q =$ B, and let $\Theta = \{\Gamma^*\}$, where $\Gamma^* = \{s \mid (A \lor B) \models_0 s\}$. Then $(A \lor B)$ is assertible in Γ^*. But Γ^* is its own shell and is its only shell, and neither A nor B is assertible in it. So neither $\Diamond$A nor $\Diamond$B is assertible in Γ^*. So $(\Diamond A \lor \Diamond B)$ is not assertible in Γ^*, by Theorem 3.

R19: $\Diamond(p \lor q) \not\models (\Diamond p \lor \Diamond q)$. By R6 and R18.

Note: The failure of the inference from $(p \lor q)$ to $(\Diamond p \lor \Diamond q)$ is defensible if we think of possibilities as speculative extensions of the context that governs the conversation. From the fact that either a man or a woman will perform the surgery, it does not follow that it is either part of any speculative extension of the story that a man will do it or part of any speculative extension that a woman will do it. However, it would be easy to define an alternative to the present system in which the inference from $(p \lor q)$ to $(\Diamond p \lor \Diamond q)$ would be valid. Let us say that a disjunction $(p \lor q)$ is *decided* in a tree if and only if either p or q belongs to some context in that tree. If we required that every disjunction in any context in a tree were somewhere decided in this sense, then every context containing a disjunction would have a shell containing one of the disjuncts, and this inference would be valid.

4. I now take up the subject of conditionals. Let C be a language just like S except that it contains the additional logical constants ">" and "≫." The logical constant ">" is intended to represent the indicative conditional, and "≫" is intended to represent the subjunctive conditional. C is the formal analogue to L_C discussed in the previous chapter. Let MC be a language just like C except that it contains the logical constant "$\Box$." Insert the following two new axioms before ACl:

(A>) If p, $\Gamma \models q$, then $(p > q)$ is assertible in Γ.

(A≫) If (i) p, $\Gamma \models q$, (ii) $\neg p$ is not assertible in Γ, and (iii) q is not assertible in Γ, then $(p \gg q)$ is assertible in Γ.

And insert the following two new axioms before DCl:

(D$>$) If p, $\Gamma \models \neg q$, then $(p > q)$ is deniable in Γ.

(D$\gg$) If (i) p, $\Gamma \models \neg q$, (ii) $\neg p$ is not assertible in Γ, and (iii) $\neg q$ is not assertible in Γ, then $(p \gg q)$ is deniable in Γ.

Toward defining validity for MC, we first define *pure validity* thus: Let A be a set of sentences of MC, and let p be a sentence of MC. Let $Pure(p)$ be the result of substituting "$>$" for every occurrence of "$\gg$" throughout p, and let $Pure(A)$ be the result of substituting "$>$" for every occurrence of "$\gg$" throughout every sentence in A. Then A /$\therefore$ p is *purely valid* if and only if for every tree Θ, if Γ^* is the governing context in Θ, then if every sentence in $Pure(A)$ is assertible in Γ^*, then $Pure(p)$ is assertible in Γ^*. In short, pure validity is validity in the old sense with indicative conditionals in place of all subjunctive conditionals.

Now define validity (*simpliciter*) thus: Let A be a set of sentences of MC, and let p be a sentence of MC. Then A /$\therefore$ p is *valid* $(A \models p)$ if and only if (i) A /$\therefore$ p is purely valid, and (ii) for every tree Θ, if Γ^* is the governing context in Θ, then if every sentence in A is assertible in Γ^*, then p is assertible in Γ^*. Notice that there is no vicious circularity in this way of defining validity in terms of assertibility and defining the assertibility of conditionals in terms of validity.[1]

All of the theorems and results stated above for M continue to hold (with "MC" substituted for "M"). In addition we have:

THEOREM 6: (1) $(p > q)$ is assertible in Γ if and only if p, $\Gamma \models q$; and $(p > q)$ is deniable in Γ if and only if p, $\Gamma \models \neg q$, and (2) $(p \gg q)$ is assertible in Γ if and only if p, $\Gamma \models q$ and $\neg p$ is not assertible in Γ and q is not assertible in Γ; and $(p \gg q)$ is deniable in Γ if and only if p, $\Gamma \models \neg q$ and $\neg p$ is not assertible in Γ and $\neg q$ is not assertible in Γ.

THEOREM 7: If p and q are distinct literals of S, then (1) $(p > q)$ is assertible in Γ if and only if $(\neg p \lor q) \in \Gamma$, and (2) $(p > q)$ is deniable in Γ if and only if $(\neg p \lor \neg q) \in \Gamma$. (To see why the theorem is restricted to distinct literals, consider $(p > p)$ and $((p \& r) > (p \& q))$.)

THEOREM 8: If p is a sentence of C and p is assertible in Γ and $\Gamma \subseteq \Delta$, then p is assertible in Δ. (This does not necessarily hold for sentences of MC.)

R20: If A, p /$\therefore$ q is an argument in C, and A, $p \models q$, then $A \models (p > q)$. Suppose A, $p \models q$. Then (i) if every member of A is assertible in Δ and p is assertible in Δ, then q is assertible in Δ. By Theorem 8, (ii) if every member of A is assertible in Γ and every member of Γ is assertible in Δ, then every member of A is assertible in Δ. By (i) and (ii), if every member of A is assertible in Γ and p is assertible in Δ and every member of Γ is assertible in Δ, then q is assertible in Δ. So if every member of A is assertible in Γ, then p, $\Gamma \models q$. So $A \models (p > q)$.

R21: Modus ponens is valid for indicative conditionals: $(p > q)$, $p \models q$.

---

[1] The present account of conditionals is similar to my account in my 1987a. The primary difference is that the definition of context has undergone an improvement since that paper, where contexts were defined as closed under *classical* implication rather than under 0-validity.

Suppose (i) $(p > q)$ is assertible in Γ^* and (ii) p is assertible in Γ^*. By (i), p, $\Gamma^* \models q$. So for all trees Ω, if Δ^* is the governing context in Ω, then if p is assertible in Δ^* and every member of Γ^* is assertible in Δ^*, then q is assertible in Δ^*. So if p is assertible in Γ^* and every member of Γ^* is assertible in Γ^*, then q is assertible in Γ^*. But of course every member of Γ^* is assertible in Γ^*. So by (ii), q is assertible in Γ^*.

R22: Likewise modus ponens is valid for subjunctive conditionals: $(p \gg q)$, $p \models q$. This inference is purely valid since modus ponens is valid for indicative conditionals. Moreover, in every context in which both $(p \gg q)$ and p are assertible, q is assertible, because $(p \gg q)$ and p are never assertible in a single context.

Note: While it is desirable that modus ponens qualify as valid for subjunctive conditionals, we do not want every argument having $(p \gg q)$ and p as premises to qualify as valid. But $(p \gg q)$ and p are never assertible in a single context. So if every argument qualified as valid provided only that the conclusion was assertible in every governing context in which the premises were assertible, then every argument having these premises would qualify as valid. However, not every argument having $(p \gg q)$ and p as premises is *purely valid*, since $(p > q)$ and p may both be assertible in a single context. So not every argument having $(p \gg q)$ and p as premises is valid as defined. This is a consequence of the requirement that an argument be purely valid in order to qualify as valid.

R23: $\Box(p > q)$, $\Box p \models \Box q$. By R21 and R10 (extended to MC).

R24: $\Box(p > q) \not\models (\Box p > \Box q)$. Let $p = A$, $q = B$, and $\Theta = \{\Gamma^*\}$, where $\Gamma^* = \{s \mid (\neg A \lor B) \models_0 s\}$. Since Γ^* is its own core, $\Box(A > B)$ is assertible in Γ^*. Let $\Omega = \{\Delta_1, \Delta^*\}$, where $\Delta_1 = \{s \mid A \models_0 s\}$ and $\Delta^* = \{s \mid \{A, B\} \models_0 s\}$. In that case, A is assertible in Δ_1, which is the core of Δ^*, but B is not assertible in any core of Δ^*. Moreover, every member of Γ^* is assertible in Δ^*. So $\Box A$ is assertible in Δ^*, every member of Γ^* is assertible in Δ^*, but $\Box B$ is not assertible in Δ^*. So $\Box A$, $\Gamma^* \not\models \Box B$. So $(\Box A > \Box B)$ is not assertible in Γ^*.

Note: R23 and R24 together demonstrate that conditional proof is not in general valid in context logic.

R25: If p and q are distinct literals of S, then $(p > q)$, $\neg q \models \neg p$ (modus tollens). Suppose p and q are distinct literals of S and $(p > q)$ is assertible in Γ. By Theorem 7, $(\neg p \lor q) \in \Gamma$. So, since Γ is closed under 0-implication, if $\neg q$ is assertible in Γ, that is, if $\neg q \in \Gamma$, then $\neg p \in \Gamma$, that is, $\neg p$ is assertible in Γ.

R26: $(p > \Box \Diamond p)$, $\neg \Box \Diamond p \not\models \neg p$. By R9, $(A > \Box \Diamond A)$ is assertible in every context. But $\neg \Box \Diamond A \not\models \neg A$ (see R15).

R27: $(p > (q > r))$, $\neg(q > r) \not\models \neg p$. Let $p = A$, $q = B$, and $r = C$. Let $\Theta = \{\Gamma^*\}$, where $\Gamma^* = \{s \mid \neg B \models_0 s\}$. B, $\Gamma^* \models C$. So $(B > C)$ is assertible in Γ^*. By Theorem 8, $\Gamma^* \models (B > C)$. So A, $\Gamma^* \models (B > C)$. So $(A > (B > C))$ is assertible in Γ^*. Moreover, B, $\Gamma^* \models \neg C$. So $(B > C)$ is deniable in Γ^*. So $\neg(B > C)$ is assertible in Γ^*. But $\neg A$ is not assertible in Γ^*.

R25–R27 further illustrate the failure of the principle of substitutivity in context logic. R26 is the form of argument (B) in chapter 7, and R27 is the form of argument (C) in chapter 7.

R28: $\neg(p > q)$ $\not\models (p \,\&\, \neg q)$. Let $p = $ A and $q = $ B. Let $\Gamma^* = \{s \mid (\neg A \lor \neg B)\ \models_0 s\}$. $(A > B)$ is deniable in Γ^*. So $\neg(A > B)$ is assertible in Γ^*. But since A $\notin \Gamma^*$ and $\neg B \notin \Gamma^*$, $(A \,\&\, \neg B)$ is not assertible in Γ^*.

R28 distinguishes the context-logical conditional from the material conditional, since $\neg(p \supset q)$ /∴ $(p \,\&\, \neg q)$ is classically valid. Thus the context-logical conditional better represents the English indicative conditional, since the following argument is surely not valid: "It is not the case that if I am rich, then I drive a Chevrolet; therefore, I *am* rich and I do *not* drive a Chevrolet."

R29: $\neg(p > q)$ $\models (p > \neg q)$. By Theorem 2, $\neg(p > q)$ is assertible in Γ if and only if $(p > q)$ is deniable in Γ. But $(p > q)$ is deniable in Γ if and only if p, $\Gamma \models \neg q$, which is precisely the condition under which $(p > \neg q)$ is assertible in Γ.

R30: $(p > \neg q)$ $\models \neg(p > q)$. By the proof of R29 run backward.

R31: $\neg(p \gg q)$ $\models (p \gg \neg q)$. By R29 and the fact that for both $\neg(p \gg q)$ and $(p \gg \neg q)$, what the subjunctive requires over the indicative is that neither $\neg p$ nor $\neg q$ be assertible.

R32: $(p \gg \neg q)$ $\models \neg(p \gg q)$. Similarly, using R30.

R30 and R32 further distinguish the context-logical conditionals from the material conditional, since $(p \supset \neg q)$ /∴ $\neg(p \supset q)$ is *not* classically valid.

R33: $((p \,\&\, q) > r)$ $\not\models ((p > r) \lor (q > r))$. Let $p = $ A, $q = $ B, and $r = $ C. Let $\Gamma^* = \{s \mid (\neg(A \,\&\, B) \lor C))\ \models_0 s\}$. $((A \,\&\, B) > C)$ is assertible in Γ^*, but $(\neg A \lor C) \notin \Gamma^*$ and $(\neg B \lor C) \notin \Gamma^*$. So by Theorem 7, neither $(A > C)$ nor $(B > C)$ is assertible in Γ^*. So by Theorem 3 (with "MC" in place of "M"), $((A > C) \lor (B > C))$ is not assertible in Γ^*.

R33 is the form of argument discussed in chapter 7 in connection with the principle of equivalence (the example of the motor with two switches). The rest of the argument in chapter 7 against the principle of equivalence is that if p, q, and r are distinct literals of S, then (i) $(\neg p \lor q)$ $\models (p > q)$, (ii) $(p > q)$ $\models (\neg p \lor q)$, (iii) $((p \,\&\, r) > q)$ $\models (\neg(p \,\&\, r) \lor q)$, and (iv) $(\neg(p \,\&\, r) \lor q)$ $\models ((\neg p \lor q) \lor (\neg r \lor q))$. (i) and (ii) are consequences of Theorem 7, and (iii) and (iv) are plainly true as well. R33 further distinguishes the context-logical conditional from the material conditional, since $((p \,\&\, r) \supset q)$ /∴ $((p \supset q) \lor (r \supset q))$ is classically valid.

R34: If q is a sentence of C, then q $\models (p > q)$. Suppose q is a sentence of C and is assertible in Γ. By Theorem 8, p, $\Gamma \models q$. So $(p > q)$ is assertible in Γ.

R35: If p is a sentence of S, then $\neg p$ $\models (p > q)$. If p is a sentence of S and $\neg p$ is assertible in Γ, then p and $\neg p$ cannot both be assertible in any context. So trivially, p, $\Gamma \models q$.

R36: q $\not\models (p \gg q)$. If q is assertible in Γ^*, then one of the necessary conditions for the assertibility of $(p \gg q)$ in Γ^* is transgressed.

R37: $\neg p$ $\not\models (p \gg q)$. Similarly.

R38: Strengthening of the antecedent is valid for indicatives: $(p > r)$ $\models ((p$ & $q) > r)$. Suppose $(p > r)$ is assertible in Γ. Then p, Γ $\models r$. So $(p \& q)$, Γ $\models r$. So $((p \& q) > r)$ is assertible in Γ.

R39: Strengthening of the antecedent is not valid for subjunctives: $(p \gg r)$ $\not\models ((p \& q) \gg r)$. Even if $\neg p$ is not assertible in Γ, $\neg(p \& q)$ might be. (Recall the match example, argument (*D*), from chapter 7)

These last six results distinguish the subjunctive conditional from the indicative conditional. R36, R37, and R39 further distinguish the context-logical subjunctive conditional from the material conditional. R36, R37, and R39, moreover, agree with the Stalnaker-Lewis account of the subjunctive conditional. Some (e.g., Stalnaker 1975) would maintain that these forms of argument ought to be invalid even for the indicative conditional. But I disagree. Consider the following instance of the argument form q /∴ $(p > q)$: "I will call you tomorrow. Therefore, if I die tonight, I will call you tomorrow." Why should this count as valid when it rings so odd? The answer, I think, may be just that we do not take the conclusion at face value. We "hear" the conclusion either as the subjunctive conditional, "If I died tonight, I would call you tomorrow," or as the *even-if/still* conditional, "Even if I die tonight, I will call you tomorrow." If the conclusion were either of these, then the argument would indeed be invalid. (See R36 and the discussion of *even-if/still* conditionals below.)

I should point out that R30 and R35 imply that both $(p > q)$ and $\neg(p > q)$ will be assertible in Γ if $\neg p$ is a sentence of S and assertible in Γ. This is a further result that calls for explanations like those I gave in connection with R4. In addition, it might be helpful to point out that $(p \gg q)$ and $\neg(p \gg q)$ will both be assertible in Γ only if p is not assertible in any context.

R40: Hypothetical syllogism for indicatives is valid: $(p > q)$, $(q > r)$ $\models (p > r)$.

R41: Hypothetical syllogism for subjunctives is valid: $(p \gg q)$, $(q \gg r)$ $\models (p \gg r)$. This result distinguishes the context-logical theory of the subjunctive conditional from the Stalnaker-Lewis theory of the subjunctive conditional. (Recall the J. Edgar Hoover example, argument (*E*), in chapter 7).

Recall that Stalnaker and Lewis argue against the validity of hypothetical syllogism for subjunctive conditionals by arguing as follows that if hypothetical syllogism is valid then strengthening of the antecedent must be valid:

$(p \gg q)$	*Premise*
$((p \& r) \gg p)$	*Tautology*
$((p \& r) \gg q)$	*By hypothetical syllogism*

The problem with this argument, I said in chapter 7, is that in fact $((p \& r) \gg p)$ does not follow from $(p \gg q)$. That is, $(p \gg q)$ might be assertible in Γ even if $\neg r$ is assertible in Γ. But in that case $\neg(p \& r)$ will also be assertible in Γ, which means that $((p \& r) \gg p)$ will not be assertible in Γ.

R42: If p and q are distinct literals, then $(p > q) \models (\neg q > \neg p)$.

R43: If p and q are distinct literals, then $(p \gg q) \models (\neg q \gg \neg p)$.

R43, too, distinguishes the context-logical theory of the subjunctive conditional from the Stalnaker-Lewis theory of the subjunctive conditional. Recall Lewis's counterexample (argument (G) in chapter 7): "If Boris had gone to the party, Olga would still have gone. Therefore, if Olga had not gone, Boris would still not have gone." In chapter 7 I indicated that what might be wrong with this counterexample is that it is not truly an instance of $(p \gg q) / \therefore (\neg q \gg \neg p)$. It is disqualified because of the presence of the little word "still." Now I can explain a little more fully how the word "still" might make a difference.

For present purposes, I wish to introduce a further operator: "$+\gg$." The assertibility conditions for sentences formed from this operator are these: $(p +\gg q)$ is assertible in Γ if and only if (i) p, $\Gamma \models q$ and (ii) $\neg p$ is not assertible in Γ. In other words, the assertibility conditions for $(p +\gg q)$ are like the assertibility conditions for $(p \gg q)$ except that we do not require that the consequent not be assertible. We find that the rule of contraposition is invalid for this new conditional. That is, $(p +\gg q) \not\models (\neg q +\gg \neg p)$. Suppose q is assertible in Γ. Then $(p +\gg q)$ might still be assertible in Γ, but $(\neg q +\gg \neg p)$ cannot be, since the negation of its antecedent, namely, $\neg\neg q$, will be assertible in Γ.

My claim is that the logic of "$+\gg$"-conditionals, as here defined, is the logic of *even-if/still* conditionals of the form "*Even if p* were the case, q would be the case," or "If p were the case, then q would *still* be the case." Contraposition fails in the story of Olga and Boris because the conditionals in that story are even-if/still conditionals. This treatment of even-if/still conditionals confirms my claim above that the following argument is invalid: "I will call you tomorrow. Therefore, even if I die tonight, I will call you tomorrow." For $q \not\models (p +\gg q)$. To see this, consider a context in which both $\neg p$ and q are assertible. Notice that $\neg p \not\models (p +\gg q)$ as well.

R44: $(p > \neg q) \not\models \neg(p > \Diamond q)$. Let $p = A$ and $q = B$. Let $\Theta = \{\Gamma^*\}$, where $\Gamma^* = \{s \mid (\neg A \vee \neg B) \models_0 s\}$. Clearly, $(A > \neg B)$ is assertible in Γ^*. Let $\Omega = \{\Delta_1, \Delta^*\}$, where $\Delta_1 = \varnothing$ and $\Delta^* = \{s \mid \{A, \neg B\} \models_0 s\}$. A is assertible in Δ^*, and every member of Γ^* is assertible in Δ^*, but since $\neg B$ does not belong to Δ_1, the core of Δ^*, $\neg \Diamond B$ is not assertible in Δ^*. So A, $\Gamma^* \not\models \neg \Diamond B$. So $(A > \Diamond B)$ is not deniable in Γ^*. So $\neg(A > \Diamond B)$ is not assertible in Γ^*.

By R44, it follows that $(p \gg \neg q) \not\models \neg(p \gg \Diamond q)$. I suggest that "$(p \gg \Diamond q)$" is a reasonable translation of "If it were the case that p, then it *might* be the case that q." Thus, context logic explains the apparent *in*validity of an inference such as the following. "If I were rich, then I would not drive a Chevrolet. Therefore, it is not the case that if I were rich, then I might drive a Chevrolet." The context-logical theory of conditionals is in this respect superior to Lewis's theory, according to which this inference is valid (1973b, 21).

A good objection to the present context-logical theory of the subjunctive conditional is that it entails that the following argument is invalid: $((p \vee q) \gg r)$ $/ \therefore ((p \gg r) \& (q \gg r))$. That seems to be an inexcusable result. The problem is that even if $\neg(p \vee q)$ is not assertible in Γ, one or the other of $\neg p$ and $\neg q$ might be assertible in Γ, in which case either $(p \gg r)$ or $(q \gg r)$ will not be assertible in Γ. Moreover, according to the present account, $(p \gg (q \,\&\, r))$ /∴ $((p \gg q) \,\&\, (p \gg r))$ is not valid either. This is also inexcusable. The situation can be repaired as follows:

Let us say that p and q are *equivalent* just in case $p \models q$ and $q \models p$. Say that d is a *disjunct in an equivalence to* p if and only if for some sentence q, p is equivalent to $(q \vee d)$. Say that c is a *conjunct in an equivalence to* p if and only if for some sentence q, p is equivalent to $(q \,\&\, c)$. For instance, $(A \vee B)$ is a conjunct in an equivalence to $(A \,\&\, B)$ because $(A \,\&\, B)$ is equivalent to $(((\neg A \vee B) \,\&\, (A \vee \neg B)) \,\&\, (A \vee B))$. Further, say that s is *trivial* if and only if s is assertible in every context. Say that s is *absurd* if and only if s is deniable in every context.

Next, alter the assertibility and deniability conditions for subjunctive conditionals as follows:

(A≫*)   If (i) p, $\Gamma \models q$, (ii) if d is a nonabsurd disjunct in an equivalence to p, then d is not deniable in Γ, and (iii) if c is a nontrivial conjunct in an equivalence to q, then c is not assertible in Γ, then $(p \gg q)$ is assertible in Γ.

(D≫*)   If (i) p, $\Gamma \models \neg q$, (ii) if d is a nonabsurd disjunct in an equivalence to p, then d is not deniable in Γ, and (iii) if c is a nontrivial conjunct in an equivalence to $\neg q$, then c is not assertible in Γ, then $(p \gg q)$ is deniable in Γ.

Notice that in both axioms condition (ii) may sometimes be satisfied even though an absurd sentence is always a disjunct in an equivalence to p. Similarly, condition (iii) may sometimes be satisfied even though a trivial sentence is always a conjunct in an equivalence to q.

Two simple ideas lie behind these refinements. Think of a disjunct as one of the ways in which the disjunction might be assertible, and think of a disjunctive antecedent as giving alternative ways in which the consequent might become assertible. Then the first simple idea is that if one of the ways in which the consequent of a conditional might become assertible is already deniable, then it is pointless to mention it as one of the ways in which the consequent might become assertible. Next, think of a conjunct as part of the information content of a conjunction, and think of a conjunctive consequent as spelling out the information we would have if the antecedent became assertible. Then the second simple idea is that if part of this information is already assertible, then it is pointless to mention it as information we would have if the antecedent became assertible.

With this refinement in place, we may assert:

R45: $((p \vee q) \gg r) \models ((p \gg r) \,\&\, (q \gg r))$.
R46: $(p \gg (q \,\&\, r)) \models ((p \gg q) \,\&\, (p \gg r))$.

As I pointed out in chapter 7, R45 is not valid according to the Stalnaker-

Lewis account of the subjunctive conditional (argument (*H*)). I also drew attention to Ellis's (1979) argument for the invalidity of this argument. Ellis's point is that if this inference were valid, then we could argue for strengthening of the antecedent as follows:

$(p \geqslant r)$ *Premise*

_____

$(((p \ \& \ q) \vee (p \ \& \ \neg q)) \geqslant p)$ *Tautology*
$((p \ \& \ q) \vee (p \ \& \ \neg q)) \geqslant r)$ *Hypothetical syllogism from the above*
$((p \ \& \ q) \geqslant r)$ *By R45*

My answer to this is that $(((p \ \& \ q) \vee (p \ \& \ \neg q)) \geqslant p)$ does not in fact follow from $(p \geqslant r)$, for $(p \ \& \ q)$ may be deniable even if p is not.

5. Finally I wish to develop a context-logical account of quantification. This will require backtracking. I will have to redefine primitive contexts, and then in terms of this redefined concept of primitive contexts I will redefine contexts *simpliciter*.

Let P be a language containing countably many *n*-ary predicates, denumerably many individual constants, and the logical constants "$\vee$" and "$\neg$." φ is an *atomic* sentence of P if and only if for some *n*-ary predicate F of P and some n constants $c_1, c_2, \ldots c_n$ of P, $\varphi = Fc_1c_2 \ldots c_n$. φ is a sentence of P if and only if either (i) p is an atomic sentence of P, or (ii) $\varphi =$ "$\neg\psi$" and ψ is a sentence of P, or (iii) $\varphi =$ "$(\psi \vee \sigma)$" and ψ and σ are sentences of P. (P is thus quantifier-free.)

Let Q be a language containing all of the vocabulary of P but containing denumerably many individual variables and the quantifier "$\exists$" as well. That is, φ is a sentence of Q if and only if either (i) φ is a sentence of P, or (ii) $\varphi =$ "$\neg\psi$" and ψ is a sentence of Q, or (iii) $\varphi =$ "$(\psi \vee \sigma)$" and ψ and σ are sentences of Q or (iv) where ψ is a sentence of Q and $\psi v/c$ is the result of substituting an occurrence of the variable v for zero or more occurrences of the constant c, $\varphi = \exists v \psi v/c$. (Vacuous and overlapping quantifiers are thus permitted.) $\exists$-sentences are our symbolic equivalents of existential generalizations, and the symbol "$\exists$" followed by a variable is said to be an *existential quantifier*. Let $\forall v \varphi$ be an abbreviation for $\neg \exists v \neg \varphi$.

Let QM be a language containing all of the vocabulary of Q plus the logical constant "$\square$." QM is the formal analogue of the combination of L_M and L_Q, which I discussed in the previous chapter. I will distinguish between *formulae* and *sentences* of Q and QM. The difference is that formulae may contain free variables (or not), but sentences are always closed. (A free variable is a variable v not in the scope of the quantifier $\exists v$.) Assertibility and deniability pertain only to sentences.

Let $\varphi c/v$ stand for the sentence that results from substituting the constant c for the variable v wherever v occurs free in the formula φ.

$$\textit{Define } \bigvee_{i=1}^{n} \varphi c_i / v = \begin{cases} \varphi c_i/v \text{ if } n = 1 \\ (\bigvee_{i=1}^{n-1} \varphi c_i/v \vee \varphi c_n/v) \text{ if } n > 1. \end{cases}$$

Let the axioms of assertibility and deniability include all of those we have encountered so far. In addition, the following two axioms are to be inserted before ACl and DCl, respectively:

(A∃) If for some constants $c_1, c_2, \ldots, c_n$, $\bigvee_{i=1}^{n} \varphi c_i/v$ is assertible in Γ, then $\exists v \varphi$ is assertible in Γ.

(D∃) If for all constants $c \in N_\Gamma$, $\varphi c/v$ is deniable in Γ, then $\exists v \varphi$ is deniable in Γ.

N_Γ is understood to be a nonempty set of individual constants called the *domain* of the context Γ. Notice that D∃ does, and A∃ does not, mention the domain.

Before defining contexts proper, we first define a *primitive context* as follows:

A *primitive context* (in the new sense) is a pair $\langle \Lambda, N_\Lambda \rangle$ such that
(i) Λ is set of literals in the language P such that not both $\varphi \in \Lambda$ and $\neg\varphi \in \Lambda$.
(ii) N_Λ is a nonempty set of individual constants that includes every individual constant that occurs in any member of Λ (and possibly other constants as well).

N_Λ is the *domain* of the primitive context. Although a primitive context is officially a pair of the sort just defined, in practice I will employ a somewhat different terminology. In practice, instead of using the term "primitive context" to refer to the pair $\langle \Lambda, N_\Lambda \rangle$, I will use the term "primitive context" to refer to just the first member of that pair, that is, the set Λ. However, I will assume that each primitive context Λ in this sense is *associated* with a unique domain N_Λ. Accordingly, I will speak of primitive contexts Λ and Π as distinct primitive contexts when their associated domains are distinct, as well as when their memberships are different.

Primitive contexts do not form trees. Consequently, assertibility in primitive contexts is defined only for sentences of Q, not for sentences of QM.

Say that a primitive context Λ *realizes* a set of sentences A if and only if every member of A is assertible in Λ. Say that A is *realizable* if and only if there is some primitive context that realizes A.

We now define a second kind of validity, or rather a family of validity relations, namely, N-validity. This is not yet validity proper but will be used in defining contexts *simpliciter*. Where N is a set of individual constants of the language Q, A is a set of sentences of Q, and φ is a sentence of Q, say that $A /\therefore \varphi$ is *N-valid* ($A \vDash_N \varphi$) if and only if for every primitive context Λ such that $N_\Lambda =$ N, if Λ realizes A, then φ is assertible in Λ.

We may now proceed to the definition of a *context*:

A *context* (in the new sense) is a triple $\langle \Gamma, B_\Gamma, N_\Gamma \rangle$ such that

  (i) B_Γ is a realizable set of sentences of P (not necessarily literals),

  (ii) N_Γ is a nonempty set of individual constants that includes every individual constant that occurs in any member of B_Γ (and possibly other constants as well), and

  (iii) Γ is a set of sentences of Q (not QM) such that $\Gamma = \{\varphi \mid B_\Gamma \models_{N\Gamma} \varphi\}$.

B_Γ will be the *base* of the context. N_Γ will be the *domain* of the context. The restriction of Γ to the language P is a context in the old sense (except that the language is P, not S). Although a context is officially a triple of the sort just defined, in practice I will use the term "context" to refer to just the first member of that triple, that is, the set Γ. However, I will assume that each context Γ in this sense is associated with a unique base B_Γ and a unique domain N_Γ, in terms of which Γ is defined. Accordingly, I will speak of contexts Γ and Δ as distinct contexts when their associated bases or domains are distinct, as well as when their memberships are different. I recognize that this notation is somewhat unusual, but it is more economical in the long run than referring to each context in terms of its domain and base.

The next step is to define a tree. The definition will be similar to that given in section 3 above, except that here we have to take into account the fact that there are two ways for one context to include another: either by having a more inclusive base or by having a *less* inclusive domain. To ensure that contexts grow larger as we climb the branches of a tree, we will require that if the base of one context is *strictly included in* the base of another context in a tree, then the domain of the first will *include* the domain of the second. In other words, the domain of a context will include the domains of all of its shells. The idea will be that a domain amounts to a set of *potential counterexamples* to *denials* of existentially quantified statements. Or equivalently, it is a set of potential counterexamples to universally quantified statements. The motivation for requiring the domain of a context to include the domains of its shells is that as we ascend the branches of a tree to ever more contentful contexts, the number of potential counterexamples ought to decrease.

Define a *tree* Θ as any countable set of contexts $\{\Gamma_0, \Gamma_1, \ldots\}$ such that (a) for some $\Gamma_0 \in \Theta$, for all $\Gamma_i \in \Theta$, $B_{\Gamma 0} \subseteq B_{\Gamma i}$ and $N_{\Gamma i} \subseteq N_{\Gamma 0}$, and (b) for all $\Gamma_i, \Gamma_j, \Gamma_k \in \Theta$, if $B_{\Gamma i} \subseteq B_{\Gamma k}$ and $B_{\Gamma j} \subseteq B_{\Gamma k}$, then either $B_{\Gamma i} \subseteq B_{\Gamma j}$ or $B_{\Gamma j} \subseteq B_{\Gamma i}$, and (c) for all $\Gamma_i, \Gamma_j \in \Theta$, if $B_{\Gamma i} \subset B_{\Gamma j}$, then $N_{\Gamma j} \subseteq N_{\Gamma i}$. For all trees Θ and all contexts Γ_i and Γ_j in Θ, define Γ_i to be a *core* of Γ_j if and only if either (a) $B_{\Gamma i} \subset B_{\Gamma j}$, or (b) $N_{\Gamma j} \subset N_{\Gamma i}$, or (c) $\langle B_{\Gamma i}, N_{\Gamma i} \rangle = \langle B_{\Gamma j}, N_{\Gamma j} \rangle$ and there is no context Γ_k in Θ such that $B_{\Gamma k} \subset B_{\Gamma j}$ or $N_{\Gamma j} \subset N_{\Gamma k}$. Define Γ_j to be a *shell* of Γ_i if and only if $B_{\Gamma i} \subseteq B_{\Gamma j}$ and $N_{\Gamma j} \subseteq N_{\Gamma i}$. In each tree, we designate one member context as the *governing* context in that tree, subject to the following condition: If Γ^* is the governing context in Θ, then for all $\Gamma \in \Theta$, either $B_\Gamma \subseteq B_{\Gamma *}$ and $N_{\Gamma *} \subseteq N_\Gamma$ or $B_{\Gamma *} \subseteq B_\Gamma$ and $N_\Gamma \subseteq N_{\Gamma *}$.

For example, let Θ be a tree with the following properties:

$\Theta = \{\Gamma_0, \Gamma_1, \Gamma_2\}$, where
$B_{\Gamma 0} = \{Fa\}$, and $N_{\Gamma 0} = \{a, b, c, d\}$,
$B_{\Gamma 1} = \{Fa, Fb, \neg Gb\}$, and $N_{\Gamma 1} = \{a, b\}$,
$B_{\Gamma 2} = \{Fa, (Ha \lor Gc)\}$, and $N_{\Gamma 2} = \{a, c\}$.

Γ_1 and Γ_2 are both shells of Γ_0, but neither is a shell of the other. $N_{\Gamma 2}$, the domain of Γ_2, must contain at least "a" and "c," since these occur in the base $B_{\Gamma 2}$; $N_{\Gamma 1}$, the domain of Γ_1, must contain at least "a" and "b," since these occur in the base $B_{\Gamma 1}$; and $N_{\Gamma 0}$ must contain at least "a," since "a" occurs in $B_{\Gamma 0}$, but also "b" and "c," because the domains of the shells of Γ_0, namely, $N_{\Gamma 1}$ and $N_{\Gamma 2}$, must be included in the domain of Γ_0. Here are some illustrative facts about Θ:

- $\forall x Fx \in \Gamma_1$, since both Fa and Fb are assertible in any primitive context that realizes $B_{\Gamma 1}$, which means that both $\neg Fa$ and $\neg Fb$ are deniable in any primitive context that realizes $B_{\Gamma 1}$, which means that $\exists x \neg Fx$ is deniable in any primitive context Λ ($N_\Lambda = N_{\Gamma 1}$) that realizes $B_{\Gamma 1}$, which means that $\neg \exists x \neg Fx$ is assertible in any primitive context Λ ($N_\Lambda = N_{\Gamma 1}$) that realizes $B_{\Gamma 1}$, which means that $B_{\Gamma 1} \models_{N\Gamma 1} \neg \exists x \neg Fx$.
- Nonetheless, Fc $\notin \Gamma_1$, since there is a primitive context Λ ($N_\Lambda = N_{\Gamma 1}$) that realizes $B_{\Gamma 1}$ but in which Fc is not assertible, which means that $B_{\Gamma 1} \not\models_{N\Gamma 1}$ Fc. For instance, let $\Lambda = \{Fa, Fb, \neg Gb\}$ and domain $N_\Lambda = N_{\Gamma 1} = \{a, b\}$.
- $\forall x Fx \notin \Gamma_0$, since b, c, d $\in N_{\Gamma 0}$ but Fb, Fc, and Fd are not assertible in all primitive contexts Λ ($N_\Lambda = N_{\Gamma 0}$) that realize $B_{\Gamma 0}$, which means that $\neg Fb$, $\neg Fc$, and $\neg Fd$ are not all deniable in all primitive contexts Λ ($N_\Lambda = N_{\Gamma 0}$) that realize $B_{\Gamma 0}$, which means that $\exists x \neg Fx$ is not deniable in all primitive contexts Λ ($N_\Lambda = N_{\Gamma 0}$) that realize $B_{\Gamma 0}$, which means that $\neg \exists x \neg Fx$ is not assertible in all primitive contexts Λ ($N_\Lambda = N_{\Gamma 0}$) that realize $B_{\Gamma 0}$, which means that $B_{\Gamma 0} \not\models_{N\Gamma 0} \neg \exists x \neg Fx$. For instance, let $\Lambda = \{Fa\}$ and $N_\Lambda = N_{\Gamma 0} = \{a, b, c, d\}$.
- $\exists x Fx$ will be a member of all three contexts, since Fa is assertible in any primitive context that realizes any of the three bases. For instance, Fa is assertible in any primitive context that realizes $B_{\Gamma 0}$, which means that $\exists x Fx$ is assertible in any primitive context that realizes $B_{\Gamma 0}$, which means that $B_{\Gamma 0} \models_{N\Gamma 0} \exists x Fx$, which means that $\exists x Fx \in \Gamma_0$.
- $(\exists x Hx \lor \exists x Gx) \in \Gamma_2$, since for any primitive context that realizes $B_{\Gamma 2}$, either Ha or Gc will be assertible in it, which means that either $\exists x Hx$ or $\exists x Gx$ will be assertible in any primitive context that realizes $B_{\Gamma 2}$, which means that $(\exists x Hx \lor \exists x Gx)$ will be assertible in any primitive context that realizes $B_{\Gamma 2}$, which means that $B_{\Gamma 2} \models_{N\Gamma 2} (\exists x Hx \lor \exists x Gx)$.

To motivate the definition of validity in QM that I am about to set forth, I want to point out that my way of defining the assertibility conditions of quantifications in terms of a countable domain of constants creates a certain problem. Suppose that a, b, c, . . . exhausts the constants of QM. And consider the argument Fa, Fb, Fc, . . . /∴ ∀xFx. This is known as the *omega rule*. Clearly we do not want the omega rule to qualify as valid. But in any context in which Fa, Fb, Fc, . . . are all assertible, ∀xFx will be assertible as well (since there can be no counterexamples). More generally, if for all but a finite number n of constants c of QM, every premise Fc is assertible in Γ, then an assertion to the effect that no more than n things are not F will be assertible in Γ. The way to avoid validating such arguments is to define validity in such a way that an argument is valid only if every argument that has a certain structural similarity is valid too.

Here is how: Say that a one-to-one function from the constants of QM *into* the constants of QM is a *rewrite* function, and say that the argument φ_1', φ_2', . . . /∴φ' is a *rewrite* of φ_1, φ_2, . . . /∴ φ if and only if there is a rewrite function π such that the argument φ_1', φ_2', . . . /∴ φ' results from simultaneously substituting, for all c, $\pi(c)$ for c wherever c occurs in φ_1, φ_2, . . . /∴ φ.

Next, we define the concept of *near validity*. Assume that A is a set of sentences of QM and φ is a sentence of QM. Then A /∴ φ is *nearly valid* if and only if for every tree Θ, if Γ^* is the governing context in Θ, then if the members of A are all assertible in Γ^*, then φ is assertible in Γ^* as well. (Notice that the right-hand side of this definition is identical to the definition of validity given earlier for language M.) In terms of near validity we can define validity proper: A /∴ φ is *valid* ($A \models \varphi$) if and only if every *rewrite* of that argument is *nearly* valid.

On this account, the omega rule and its kin will be invalid. Fa, Fb, Fc, . . . /∴ ∀xFx is not valid because it has a rewrite that is not nearly valid. For every nth constant in some enumeration of the constants, substitute the $2n$th constant. If the constants are enumerated in alphabetical order, then the result is Fa, Fc, Fe, . . . /∴ ∀xFx. This is not nearly valid, because there is a context in which Fa, Fc, Fe, . . . are all assertible but ∀xFx is not. Suppose Fa, Fc, Fe, . . . $\in \Gamma$ and Fb $\notin \Gamma$, but b $\in N_\Gamma$. (I learned this technique for defining validity in terms of rewrites from Leblanc 1976.)

All of the theorems stated above for M hold as well for QM. In addition, we have the following:

THEOREM 9: (1) ∃$v\varphi$ is assertible in Γ if and only if for some constants c_1, c_2, . . . , c_n, $\bigvee_{i=1}^{n}\varphi c_i/v$ is assertible in Γ. (2) ∃$v\varphi$ is deniable in Γ if and only if for all $c \in N_\Gamma$, $\varphi c/v$ is deniable in Γ.

COROLLARY: (1) ∀$v\varphi$ is assertible in Γ if and only if for all $c \in N_\Gamma$, $\varphi c/v$ is assertible in Γ. (2) ∀$v\varphi$ is deniable in Γ if and only if for some c_1, c_2, . . . , c_n, $\&_{i=1}^{n}\varphi c_i/v$ is deniable in Γ.

THEOREM 10: Suppose c does not occur in φ_1, φ_2, . . . , or ψ. If $\varphi_1 c/v$, $\varphi_2 c/v$, . . . $\models \psi c/v$, then for all constants d, $\varphi_1 d/v$, $\varphi_2 d/v$, . . . $\models \psi d/v$.

COROLLARY: Suppose c does not occur in φ_1, φ_2, . . . , or ψ. If φ_1, φ_2, . . . $\models \psi c/v$, then for all d, φ_1, φ_2, . . . $\models \psi d/v$ too.

COROLLARY: Suppose c does not occur in φ, σ_1, σ_2, . . . , or ψ. If $\varphi c/v$, σ_1, σ_2, . . . $\models \psi$, then for all d, $\varphi d/v$, σ_1, σ_2, . . . $\models \psi$ too.

Let us consider how close we can come to the usual inference rules for existential and universal quantifications. In proving that a certain form of argument is valid it will suffice to show that it is nearly valid, for in all cases to be considered, we may assume that every rewrite is nearly valid as well.

R47: For all c_1, c_2, . . . c_n, $\bigvee_{i=1}^{n}\varphi c_i/v \models \exists v\varphi$. This is an immediate consequence of Theorem 9.

R48: For all c_1, c_2, . . . , c_n, $(\bigvee_{i=1}^{n}\varphi c_i/v \vee \psi) \models (\exists v\varphi \vee \psi)$. Suppose $(\bigvee_{i=1}^{n}\varphi c_i/v \vee \psi)$ is assertible in Γ. *Case 1:* $(\bigvee_{i=1}^{n}\varphi c_i/v \vee \psi) \in \Gamma$. For every primitive context Λ ($N_\Lambda = N_\Gamma$) that realizes B_Γ, either $\bigvee_{i=1}^{n}\varphi c_i/v$ is assertible or ψ is assertible in Λ. So for every primitive context Λ ($N_\Lambda = N_\Gamma$) that realizes B_Γ either $\exists v\varphi$ or ψ is assertible in Λ. So $(\exists v\varphi \vee \psi)$ is assertible in Λ. So $(\exists v\varphi \vee \psi) \in \Gamma$ too. *Case 2:* $(\bigvee_{i=1}^{n}\varphi c_i/v \vee \psi)$ is not in Γ but is assertible in Γ. In that case, the sentence contains "$\square$"'s. So either $\bigvee_{i=1}^{n}\varphi c_i/v$ or ψ is assertible in Γ. In either case, $(\exists v\varphi \vee \psi)$ is assertible in Γ. This and the previous result constitute the context-logical version of the usual rule of existential generalization.

Note 1: Case 1 of R48 depends on the fact that contexts may contain sentences containing quantifiers. (Compare R18.)

Note 2: R48 also depends on the fact that contexts are defined in terms of N-validity and not in such a way as to ensure that the restriction of a context to the language P is closed under classical implication. If the restriction of a context to P were closed under classical implication, then every classical tautology, such as (Fa $\vee$ $\neg$Fa), would belong to every context. But ($\exists$xFx $\vee$ $\neg$Fa) would still not be assertible in every context. Let $B_\Gamma = \varnothing$ and $N_\Gamma = \{a\}$. In that case, there will be a literal context Λ realizing B_Γ ($N_\Lambda = N_\Gamma$) such that neither $\exists$xFx nor $\neg$Fa is assertible in Λ.

R49: Suppose c does not occur in φ_1, φ_2, . . . , or ψ. If φ_1, φ_2, . . . $\models \psi c/v$, then φ_1, φ_2, . . . $\models \forall v\psi$. Suppose φ_1, φ_2, . . . $\models \psi c/v$. By the first corollary to Theorem 10, φ_1, φ_2, . . . $\models \psi d/v$ for all d. So suppose φ_1, φ_2, . . . are all assertible in Γ. Then for all d, $\psi d/v$ is assertible in Γ. So, a fortiori, for any $d \in N_\Gamma$, $\psi d/v$ is assertible in Γ. So by the corollary to Theorem 9, $\forall v\psi$ is assertible in Γ. So φ_1, φ_2, . . . $\models \forall v\psi$. This is the context-logical version of the rule of universal generalization.

R50: Suppose c_1, c_2, . . . , c_n do not occur in φ, σ_1, σ_2, . . . , or ψ. If $\bigvee_{i=1}^{n}\varphi c_i/v$, σ_1, σ_2, . . . $\models \psi$, then $\exists v\varphi$, σ_1, σ_2, . . . $\models \psi$. Suppose $\exists v\varphi$, σ_1, σ_2, . . . are assertible in Γ. Then, by Theorem 9, for some d_1, d_2, . . . , d_n, $\bigvee_{i=1}^{n}\varphi d_i/v$ is assertible in Γ. But if $\bigvee_{i=1}^{n}\varphi c_i/v$, σ_1, σ_2, . . . $\models \psi$ when c_1, c_2, . . . , c_n do not occur in φ, σ_1, σ_2, . . . , or ψ, then by the second corollary to Theorem 10, $\bigvee_{i=1}^{n}\varphi d_i/v$, σ_1, σ_2, . . . $\models \psi$. So in that case, ψ is assertible in Γ. This is the context-logical version of existential instantiation.

R51: $\forall v\varphi \not\models \varphi c/v$. $\forall v\varphi$ may be assertible in Γ^*, and yet $\varphi c/v$ may fail to be assertible in Γ^* if c is not a member of N_{Γ^*}. So the context-logical theory of quantification does not allow anything like the usual rule of universal instantiation. As we saw in chapter 7, this is a desirable result. We are partially compensated for the failure of universal instantiation by the following three results:

R52: Suppose c does not occur in φ_1, φ_2, . . . , or ψ. If $\varphi_1 c/v$, $\varphi_2 c/v$, . . . $\models$ $\psi c/v$, then $\forall v\varphi_1$, $\forall v\varphi_2$, . . . $\models \forall v\psi$. Suppose $\forall v\varphi_1$, $\forall v\varphi_2$, . . . are assertible in Γ. Then, for all $e \in N_\Gamma$, $\varphi_1 e/v$, $\varphi_2 e/v$, . . . are assertible in Γ. So if $\varphi_1 c/v$, $\varphi_2 c/v$, . . . $\models \psi c/v$, then by Theorem 10, for all $e \in N_\Gamma$, $\varphi_1 e/v$, $\varphi_2 e/v$, . . . $\models$ $\psi e/v$. So, for all $e \in N_\Gamma$, $\psi e/v$ is assertible in Γ too. In that case, $\forall v\psi$ is assertible in Γ.

R53: $\forall v\varphi \models \exists v\varphi$. Suppose $\forall v\varphi$ is assertible in Γ. Then for all $c \in N_\Gamma$, $\varphi c/v$ is assertible in Γ. Thus for *some* c, $\varphi c/v$ is assertible in Γ. (N_Γ is by definition nonempty.) So, $\exists v\varphi$ is assertible in Γ.

R54: Say that a set of sentences S is *c-forcing* if and only if whenever all members of S are assertible in Γ, $c \in N_\Gamma$. We find that if S is c-forcing, then $\forall v\varphi, S \models \varphi c/v$. If every member of S is assertible in Γ and S is c-forcing, then $c \in N_\Gamma$. So if $\forall v\varphi$ is also assertible in Γ, which means that for all $d \in N_\Gamma$, $\varphi d/v$ is assertible in Γ, then $\varphi c/v$ is assertible in Γ. (For instance, $\forall xFx, Ga \models Fa$. But $\forall xFx, (Ga \lor Hb) \not\models Fa$.)

R55: $\Box\forall v\varphi \models \forall v\Box\varphi$. Suppose $\Box\forall v\varphi$ is assertible in Γ_j. In that case, $\forall v\varphi$ must be assertible in some core Γ_i of Γ_j. So for all $c \in N_{\Gamma i}$, $\varphi c/v$ must be assertible in Γ_i. So for all $c \in N_{\Gamma i}$, $\Box\varphi c/v$ must be assertible in Γ_j. Since $N_{\Gamma j} \subseteq N_{\Gamma i}$, this means that for all $c \in N_{\Gamma j}$, $\Box\varphi c/v$ is assertible in Γ_j. So $\forall v\Box\varphi$ is assertible in Γ_j.

The apparent problem with R55 is that if φ says that v exists, then the premise, which says that necessarily everything exists, implies that everything necessarily exists. This will look wrong if "Everything necessarily exists" is understood as meaning that everything that exists in the actual world also exists in every possible world. But in the context of the context logical conception of modality, it does not mean that. What it means is that everything that exists according to the current context also exists according to the core of the current context. That will not ordinarily be the case, but it will be if in the core of the current context it is already assertible that everything exists. In context logic the sentence "Everything exists" is not the trivial assertion that it is in other systems, for the domain associated with a context may contain names for nonexistent objects.

R56: $\exists v \Diamond \varphi \models \Diamond \exists v\varphi$. Suppose $\exists v \Diamond \varphi$ is assertible in Γ. Then by Theorem 9, there are c_1, c_2, . . . , c_n such that $\bigvee_{i=1}^{n} \Diamond \varphi c_i/v$ is assertible in Γ. By Theorem 3, for some c, $\Diamond \varphi c/v$ is assertible in Γ. So by the corollary to Theorem 4, $\varphi c/v$ is assertible in some shell of Γ. So $\exists v\varphi$ is assertible in that shell of Γ. So $\Diamond \exists v\varphi$ is assertible in Γ.

In a familiar way, "$\exists$" corresponds to "$\lor$," and "$\forall$" corresponds to "&." When we consider the arguments of QM that in this way correspond to the arguments of M examined above, we find that *in*validity in M is preserved in the corresponding arguments of QM. For example, just as we found that $\Diamond (p \vee q)$ $\not\models (\Diamond p \vee \Diamond q)$ (R19), we get the following result:

R57: $\Diamond \exists v \varphi \not\models \exists v \Diamond \varphi$. Let $\Theta = \{\Gamma^*\}$, where $N_{\Gamma^*} = \{a, b\}$ and $B_{\Gamma^*} = \{(Fa \vee Fb)\}$. $\Diamond \exists xFx$ is assertible in Γ^* because Γ^* has a shell, namely itself, where for some c_1, c_2, namely, "a" and "b," $\bigvee_{i=1}^{2} Fc_i = (Fa \vee Fb)$ is assertible. But $\exists x \Diamond Fx$ is not assertible in Γ^*, because there is no series of constants $c_1, \ldots , c_n$ such that $\bigvee_{i=1}^{n} \Diamond Fc_i$ is assertible in Γ^*. For instance, $(\Diamond Fa \vee \Diamond Fb)$ is not assertible in Γ^*, since neither Fa nor Fb belongs to any shell of Γ^*.

However, *validity* in M is not always preserved in the corresponding arguments of QM. For example, although we found that $(\Box p \& \Box q) \models \Box (p \& q)$ (R11), we get the following result:

R58: $\forall v \Box \varphi \not\models \Box \forall v \varphi$. Let $\Theta = \{\Gamma_1, \Gamma^*\}$, where $N_{\Gamma_1} = \{a, b\}$, $N_{\Gamma^*} = \{a\}$, $B_{\Gamma_1} = \{Fa\}$, and $B_{\Gamma^*} = \{Fa\}$. Fa is assertible in Γ_1, which is the core of Γ^*, and so $\Box Fa$ is assertible in Γ^*. But "a" is the only constant in N_{Γ^*}. So $\forall x \Box Fx$ is assertible in Γ^*. But $\forall xFx$ is not assertible in Γ_1, since $b \in N_{\Gamma_1}$ but Fb is not assertible in Γ_1. So $\Box \forall xFx$ is not assertible in Γ^*. This result illustrates the importance of associating each context with its own domain rather than defining a single domain for the whole tree.

R57 and R58 are important results because it is widely believed that these inferences are subject to easy intuitive counterexamples. (They correspond to what is known as the *Barcan formula*.) Expositions of the usual counterexamples are often inextricably bound up with the possible-worlds account of necessity and possibility (see chapter 7). For instance, it might be said that the inference from $\forall v \Box \varphi$ to $\Box \forall v \varphi$ is invalid because even if everyone who exists in the actual world must necessarily pay homage to Xerxes, since Xerxes is stronger than anyone, it is not necessary that everyone pay homage to Xerxes, because there is a possible world in which some nonactual merely possible person is stronger than Xerxes (Bonevac 1987, 350). But I think that counterexamples can be made persuasive even without this commitment to possible worlds semantics. Suppose we are talking about the group of people gathered together in a certain room. Suppose we may say of each person in the room that it is necessary that that person have a ticket, because there is no one present who would have been let in without a ticket. But that does not mean that it is necessary that everyone have a ticket. For instance, if Madonna showed up, we would let *her* in without a ticket.

The theory of quantification developed here is a species of what is known as the *substitutional* theory of quantification, because the logic of quantifications is explained in terms of the results of *substituting* names for variables rather than in terms of assignments of objects to variables. Through my definition of validity in terms of rewrites, I have obviated the only really "logical" objection to substitutional theories, namely, that concerning the omega rule. Still, one might suspect that the relativization of assertibility to a countable domain of constants will inevitably have intuitively undesirable consequences. For instance, it seems to entail that the assertibility of a universal quantification might be had too cheaply. If the domain contains exclusively names of integers, and the context contains, for each of these names c, the sentence "c is an integer," then "Everything is an integer" will be be assertible in that context. Consequently, the false sentence "Every real number is an integer" will be assertible in that context too. But this is not a serious objection. There are also contexts in which "Every real number is an integer" is *not* assertible, and even in standard semantics that sentence may come out true if the domain of discourse is limited to integers.

It is no objection to the present system that the universe may contain uncountably many individuals or that there may be individuals that have no name in the language. The present system does not in any way posit a universe of discourse consisting of the individuals discoursed of, and so no such positing provides an opportunity to overlook any individuals. Still, it seems that unnamed individuals might *pertain* to a given context, and so it might seem that in some contexts the individual constants in the associated domain may underrepresent the individuals that pertain to the context. This might happen in either of two ways. First, we might want to say that *something* is F even when there is nothing we can name that is F. Second, we might want to *withhold assent* from the proposition that *everything* is F on the grounds that for some unnamed something it is not assertible that it is F.

Both of these intuitions can be accommodated in terms of context logic. But to see this, it is important not to think of the constants of context logic as terms to which individual objects are related by some one-to-one relation of reference. A constant in context logic may be a mere "this" or "that." Thus it may be assertible that something is F provided only that there is something of which one can, in context, say, "This is F." Obviously, a thing referred to as "this" need not be something directly perceivable. The intuition that unnamed objects may be counterexamples to universal quantifications may likewise be accommodated. The domain associated with a context may contain constants that do not occur in the base of the context. We may think of these extra constants as representing unmentionable counterexamples to universal quantifications. The counterexamples may be unmentionable in the sense that nothing assertible can be said of them, perhaps because nothing is known of them. This conception of the extra constants might make no sense if every constant were in some sense assigned an object from some domain of objects, since unmentionable objects might not be assignable. But the present system in no way involves such assignments of objects to constants.

13

Interpretation

1. According to the Lockean, ascriptions of belief and meaning are what first make communication possible. Since beliefs, for the Lockean, are states of mind that one ought to be able to cite in a theoretical explanation of linguistic communication, belief states must be ontologically, even if not developmentally, independent of language. And meanings must somehow derive from these ontologically independent states of mind. Accordingly, a theory of interpretation has to take the form of a methodology for discovering these independent mental states in a person. In part A we saw how hard it is to explain the nature of belief and interpretation along these lines.

From the perspective of my non-Lockean alternative, the concepts of belief and meaning play only a tertiary role. From this perspective, it is not necessary to explain belief and meaning in such a way that we can then explain communication in terms of them, for communication on at least at a primitive level is possible apart from ascriptions of meaning and belief. On the contrary, we may take linguistic communication as a given and then explain how attributions of belief and meaning enhance the process of linguistic exchange. In explaining this, as we will see, it is not necessary to conceive of the process as one in which the interpreter seeks to discover some independently constituted state. On the contrary, an account of what belief and meaning are can take the form of an account of their attribution. These are the theses that I will try to develop in this and the next chapter.

A consequence of my adopting this strategy is that I will have to draw a distinction between the case of attributing beliefs and meanings to speakers of one's own linguistic community and the case of attributing beliefs and meanings to members of other linguistic communities. From the point of view of the Lockean, this is not an important distinction, for as we saw in chapter 5, the Lockean will hold that interpreting a speaker of one's own language is essentially the same kind of thing as interpreting a speaker of a different language. The majority of this chapter will concern the nature of interpretation in the *intra*linguistic case. I will postpone discussion of the *inter*linguistic case to the final section.

In explaining the concepts of belief and meaning, I am going to employ the concept of *appropriateness*. I explain this in two ways. First, I define it: An act of speech is *appropriate* if it is of the sort that facilitates cooperation in the way that gives language value and makes it learnable. I define it this way, in terms of *sorts*, in order to allow the possibility of an appropriate act that does not facilitate cooperation. This definition is extremely vague, and that, I am sorry to say, is how I must leave it. But I can explain appropriateness in a second way, by comparing it to assertibility, which I treated at length in chapters 11 and 12: As it pertains to assertion, appropriateness is the larger space of constraints on assertion of which assertibility is but one dimension.

2. One might wonder whether there really is any such thing as belief per se. After all, there are so many belieflike attitudes that one can take toward a proposition: One can hold that p is subject to no serious doubt. One can be willing to bet one's life on the proposition that p. One can sincerely assert that p. One can ascribe a probability of .92 to p. One can accept that p for the sake of argument. One can act under the assumption that p. One can hold that p is the best supported of the plausible hypotheses. One can take for granted that p without really realizing it. One can have an intuition that p. One can concede for the sake of argument that one has no reason to doubt whether p. One can favor p over any other well-developed hypothesis. One can have noticed, in a way, that p but not have fully registered that p, so that one acts just as if one did not know that p but still recognize one's error in so acting as soon as it is pointed out.[1] And so on. Which of these attitudes is belief per se? It would be easy to get the impression that belief-talk is just loose talk and that wherever we have reason to be precise, we will speak of these other, more definite attitudes rather than of belief. Or we might suppose that some of these more specific attitudes are the paradigm cases of belief and that the others in various contexts are similar enough along context-relative dimensions of similarity to justify our speaking of belief.

Here is a different proposal: The *primary* role of an ascription of a belief to S is to *make an assertion on behalf of S*. (Various secondary roles will be introduced later.) If A and B are talking and A asserts that p, then various continuations of the dialogue become appropriate that would not have been appropriate if something else had been said, and various continuations cease to be appropriate that might have been appropriate if something else had been said. And if A and B are talking and B asserts, "So, you believe that p," and A replies, "Yes," then what is appropriate is almost the same as what would have been appropriate had A volunteered that p. For example, it becomes appropriate at this point for B to make assertions amounting to challenges to p and for A to make further assertions that qualify as supporting p. Of course, making an assertion on behalf of someone else must not be misunderstood as a way of asserting the same thing oneself.

In putting forward this theory, I am not drawing a sharp distinction between

---

[1] See Dennett's example of the lemonade seller in his essay "Making Sense of Ourselves," reprinted in Dennett 1987, 84–86.

saying and believing. "Says" might be the appropriate term where the assertion one makes on behalf of another is an assertion that one supposes the other has also made. "Believes" might be the appropriate term in other cases. In treating advanced linguistic communities, we will have to distinguish as well between terms like "believes," "suspects," "anticipates," "remembers," and so on, but I will not attempt to draw such distinctions here.

Let us consider some further ways in which assertions on behalf of another might play a role in communication that assertions *simpliciter* could not so easily play. One case is that in which the speaker does not have proper authority and so needs to cite the authority of someone else. For instance, Gogan meets the scout, who says to Gogan, "Buffalo near the lake!" Gogan cannot simply go to the tribe and report, "Buffalo near the lake!" because Gogan has not been gone long enough to actually have been to the lake himself. So Gogan's assertion, "Buffalo near the lake!" would not be effective in causing the hunters to head toward the lake. Instead Gogan says, "Scout says buffalo near the lake," or, "Scout believes buffalo near the lake."

Another case is that in which a speaker is willing to serve as a conduit for someone else's assertion but is not willing to make that assertion himself or herself. Misleading one's hearers, we may suppose, carries certain undesirable consequences. So one would not wish to assert "Buffalo near the lake!" if the result would be that the hunters would go to the lake and come back empty-handed. At the very least one might in this way lose credibility. That is, one might lose the capacity to affect other people's behavior through speech. Suppose that the scout has been unreliable recently. His recent assertions have been misleading. In that case, Gogan may not be willing simply to assert "Buffalo near the lake" even if that is what the scout asserted and Gogan himself possesses the proper authority. Gogan would prefer to make this assertion on the scout's behalf by saying, "Scout says buffalo near the lake!" In this way he absolves himself from most of the responsibility in case the scout's assertion proves misleading. (I say he absolves himself of *most* of the responsibility because speakers may also be expected to make assertions only on behalf of reliable speakers.)

Yet another sort of case might be that in which one makes an assertion on someone else's behalf that that person is unwilling to make himself or herself. Gogan may have observed that Boffo was present when the tribal chief stole the grain from the tribal storage house. Thus if the question arises at a meeting of dissidents, Gogan may assert, "Boffo believes the chief is a thief," even though Boffo would never himself dare to assert "The chief is a thief."

We saw in chapter 11 how the context (in my sense) that governs a conversation may contain elements that "*go without saying.*" Thus a further function of assertions on behalf of another may be to check up on the content of the context from the speaker's point of view. Suppose that the chief says, "There is a red one—bring it!" In this case, what goes without saying is that the red one is somewhere in the immediate vicinity. But this may not go perfectly without saying from the hearer's point of view, and so the hearer may choose to check up on the content of the context from the speaker's point of view by saying to the chief, "Chief believes it is nearby." (In this simple example, I concede, this function might be served as well by a simple question, "Is it nearby?")

One of the functions of making assertions on behalf of another may be to provide an opportunity for another to deny or disavow something. In an appropriate conversation, certain things may be permitted if not forbidden, and so the conversation may in certain respects proceed as if one of the speakers had asserted that p unless that speaker explicitly disavows belief that p either by denying that p or by rejecting someone's ascription to him or her of the belief that p. In addition, assertions on behalf of another may serve simply to raise the question whether p, which can have a value even where it is not an issue whether the other will avow that p. Further, making an assertion on behalf of another can serve as a way of setting the stage for further inquiry and of making salient what is most relevant.

Self-ascriptions of belief, according to this account, are simply assertions on behalf of oneself. Self-ascription makes sense precisely because assertions of p on someone's behalf have functions beyond those possessed by assertions of p. Making an assertion on behalf of oneself can serve as a way of raising the question whether p while acknowledging one's own commitment to p. Or in making an assertion on behalf of oneself, as opposed to simply asserting, one may make clear that it is the stage-setting sort of enterprise that one is engaged in. Moreover, assertions on behalf of one's *past* self can have many of the same functions possessed by assertions on behalf of others.

Notice that this account of ascriptions of belief does not rest on a prior account of the nature of belief. Thus we are free to explain the nature of belief in terms of a theory of the attribution of belief. The legitimacy of this kind of explication will be the subject of the next chapter. Assuming that this kind of explication is legitimate, we may conclude that a belief that p is none of the so-called belieflike relations, such as being willing to bet one's life that p, accepting that p for the sake of argument, and so on. Belief is none of these because none of these is a relation in which a speaker always stands to the proposition that p whenever one may assert on his or her behalf that p. Moreover, there need be no such specific disposition toward a proposition that one is in whenever one believes that p, for the conditions for appropriate ascription of belief are not to be understood in terms of any such disposition.

I should emphasize that I am not saying that a belief is a disposition to assert. If a belief were a disposition to assert, then an account of the conditions under which beliefs are correctly attributable to a person would take the form of an account of the conditions under which a subject will be disposed to assert something. But that is not what my account of the conditions under which a belief is attributable looks like. Very roughly, an ascription to S of a belief that p

is correctly made just in case it is appropriate for an interlocutor to make an assertion of p on S's behalf. But for any number of reasons—sleepiness, stubbornness, silliness—a person may not be disposed to assert what may appropriately be asserted on his or her behalf. So a belief, according to my account, is not a disposition to assert.

To see clearly how far I am from treating an ascription of belief as a description of a state ontologically independent of language, imagine a society in which the division of epistemic labor is structured somewhat differently than it is in our society. Imagine that there is a person who is a kind of combination priest/debate-coach. In this society the priest/debate-coach has the right to "assign" assertions to people by making assertions on their behalf that they might not make of their own accord. For instance, the priest/debate-coach might say, "Gogan believes that the enemy will attack today" and "Boffo believes the enemy will not attack today." Having had opposing assertions assigned to them, these two people bear the responsibility of defending the assertions assigned to them. They may then be allowed to go out in search of experiences that might put them in a position to do so. Finally, the opposing parties argue it out, and the tribe adopts the assertion of the winner. This is the tribe's way of settling empirical questions.

Someone might think that what I have imagined is a society in which people may be required to defend propositions that they do not believe, but I reject this characterization. There is no fact of the matter about what a person believes apart from the assertions that may appropriately be made on his or her behalf. One thing that makes this conclusion so surprising, I think, is that we tend to think of the members of the tribe I have described as if they were members of our own linguistic community. If we follow the practices of Gogan's own linguistic community, then we will interpret him as believing that the enemy will attack tomorrow, whereas if we interpret him in accordance with our own practices, we may find it most natural to interpret him as believing that the enemy will *not* attack tomorrow. Which interpretation is correct? I will answer this in terms of a distinction that I will spell out in the next chapter. The answer is that the only *indispensable* kind of intentionality is that which we must attribute for the sake of linguistic communication. So the linguistic practices of Gogan's own community are the proper standard by which to interpret him.

Incidentally, the present account of the attribution of belief should by no means be construed as a semantic analysis of sentences of the form "S believes that p." In particular, I am certainly not saying that sentences, or assertions, are the "objects of the attitudes." (So my theory should not be assimilated to Davidson's in his 1968.) In my view, we should expect to find only as much logical structure as it is necessary to identify for purposes of articulating logical relations. That will inevitably be less than what most of those presently engaged in semantic analysis expect to find (see n. 1 in chapter 11). In my view, what has to be done is to define logical validity for languages containing sentences that function as sentences of the form "*S* believes that *p*" function in our language. I will not try to do that here.

Ascriptions of desire may be understood along similar lines as ascriptions of belief. Desires stand to commands as beliefs stand to assertions. To ascribe to *S* the desire that *p* is to issue on *S*'s behalf the command that *p* be the case. Of course, a command issued by *A* on behalf of *B* is not to be understood as a command from *A*, not even as a command from *A* originating in *B*. This account of ascriptions of desire may be even harder to accept than my account of ascriptions of belief. One reason is that we think of commands as directed to someone in particular, whereas a desire may not be a desire for anyone in particular to do anything. But many desires that cannot be construed as commands to anyone other than the desirer can in fact be construed as commands to the desirer. So in evaluating my account, it is important to bear in mind the intrasubjective use of language that I am taking for granted.

In putting forward this theory of ascriptions of desire, I am construing the term "desire" rather broadly to include intentions as well as mere hopes and wishes. An intention is not necessarily directed toward the immediate present, for one may intend to do something next year. An intention is, roughly, a command to oneself to do something rather specific. But usage is not very tightly controlled. Thus one might say, "I intend to be happy," which is not very specific. Moreover, this characterization of intentions is not much help when it comes to explaining the nature of doing something *intentionally*. At the other end of the spectrum are mere hopes and wishes, which may not be directed toward oneself or toward anyone at all. For instance, I hope that my house will not be swept up in a tornado. If we insist on treating these as commands, as I do, then we have to allow the possibility of commands that do not seriously call on anyone to do anything. Such commands may be thought of as by-products of the linguistic function of commanding, which do not perform the function that keeps the practice of commanding alive.

3. Certainly there are uses for attributions of belief and desire beyond those I have set forth. In particular, we sometimes explain or even predict people's behavior by citing their beliefs and desires. To understand how this is possible, it necessary to bear two things in mind. First, the languages I have introduced function *intra*subjectively, and not only as a means of cooperation between different people. One may command oneself as well as others and prepare oneself for commands to oneself by making assertions. Further, one may argue with oneself. Something occurs to me, and I write it down. But I want my assertions to withstand objections, and so I take the part of an opponent and raise those objections myself. In the end I may persuade myself that my initial assertion was mistaken. Or I may concede something and modify my initial position in some way to withstand such objections. A series of assertions and counterassertions takes place and culminates in a final position, namely, a set of assertions on which the execution of subsequent commands will be based.

From the perspective of the Lockean theory of language, this conception of thought as like an inner debate will seem to put the cart before the horse. From the Lockean perspective, a debate between people is the *product* of thought. People decide what to assert and decide how to answer objections by thinking. So even if thinking sometimes seems like an inner debate, really it is not that. Rather, thinking is that more fundamental process that drives debates between two people. In one way, the Lockean is perfectly right about this. There is indeed some mental process underlying speech, and that mental process deserves to be called a kind of thinking. The mistake is to suppose that that kind of thinking consists of *thoughts*, which words *express*, to suppose that that kind of thinking is the locus of propositional attitudes, to suppose that that kind of thinking can move an agent without language in all the same ways that it moves the agent by means of language.

The second thing to bear in mind is that it is often possible to follow the course of a conversation without witnessing every utterance. The characters in a movie whisper in the dark. I do not catch every word. Yet I know what they have decided to do and can guess at some of what I missed. One desperado told the other desperado to get back to the ranch. So they must have figured out that the federal marshals were on their way. There may be a limited variety of paths from one utterance to a later utterance such that each of these paths would preserve appropriateness at every step. These paths may differ in many ways, so that something that happens much later surprises me because I had incorrectly guessed the intervening steps. But as a speaker of the language, I have some sense, even if not explicit knowledge, of what some of those paths might be.

In attributing a belief, I have said, one makes an assertion on behalf of another. In attributing a desire, one makes a command on behalf of another. Where our objective is to confront a person with his or her beliefs or desires, it is not necessary to think of these assertions and commands made on behalf of another as having been made also by the subject of our attributions. But in other cases we can think of them in that way, as having been made at some point in a conversation. This, I suggest, is how we ought to conceive of beliefs and desires when we cite them in explanations of behavior. We can even think of them in that way without thinking of them as having been made overtly so that they might be observed by others. So my claim is that in citing a person's beliefs and desires in explaining his or her behavior, we are making assertions and commands on his or her behalf that we take to have been made in some actual conversation that may or may not have been observable to others.

In other words, an explanation of behavior in terms of beliefs and desires is a recounting or reconstruction of a conversation. It may be the case that each of the beliefs and desires we attribute is exhibited in the conversation by an overt assertion or command. Or our attributions of belief and desire may belong to a reconstruction of parts of the conversation that did not occur overtly. The covert parts may be parts of a conversation in which two people speak just as if one of them had said something that in fact went unspoken. Or the entire conversation may be carried on covertly within a single person.

These attributions serve as explanations because we may expect that the subjects to whom we make these attributions, as speakers of the language, will react appropriately to the assertions and commands they are supposed to have made. These appropriate responses may be either verbal or nonverbal deeds. Sometimes there may be just one appropriate response, and we may be able to reconstruct the course of the covert conversation prior to observing the overt response. In that case, we may be able to *predict* the response. Alternatively, there may be many possible appropriate responses, or we may be unable to reconstruct the course of the covert conversation prior to the response. In either case we will be unable to predict the response, but we may nonetheless be able to *explain* the response after the fact.

In supposing that certain conversations occur covertly, it is not necessary to suppose that mental images of words, either visual or auditory, pass before some kind of inner sense in the mind of the speaker. There are many senses in which a person may be *aware* of something, and there may be some sense in which a person must be aware of the covert assertions and commands that can correctly be attributed to him or her. But I see no reason to suppose that the person must be aware of some particular sensory quality, such as a tone of voice or a style of handwriting, or even be aware of something that *has* such a quality (whether or not the person is aware of its having that quality). It is not even necessary to suppose that for each covert utterance that we postulate there is some discrete physical event with which that utterance might be identified. An inner utterance might have to have such a physical identity if we were to carry the analogy between covert and overt utterances very far, since each overt utterance is in fact some physical event, but I know no reason to carry the analogy that far (see Gauker 1988).

In light of this conception of belief-desire explanation, one can better comprehend the possibility that there are no psychological laws of the sort I discussed in chapter 5. A conversation can make sense, have a direction, and achieve something even though none of its component utterances is a necessary consequence of the components that preceded it. To see this, consider your own role as a participant in a conversation. It may be that a question is being discussed and an answer occurs to you. That means that you *say* what you think might be an answer. If you are asked, you might be able to cite something you know, that the others may not know, that presumably made it possible for you to think of this answer. But you probably cannot *derive* this answer from the question being discussed or the conversation that preceded your statement of your proposal. Your answer may *make sense* as an answer to the question at hand but may not ultimately be an acceptable answer. Someone else might think of some objection that you and everyone else agree is a good objection. Again, no general principles imply that under the circumstances such an objection would come forward. But the objection, like your answer, makes sense and moves the conversation forward toward a given end.

In short, conversations can make sense and achieve something even if there are no general principles determining the course a conversation will take. So likewise, if the thinking we cite in explanation of a person's behavior is like a conversation, that thinking can lead in the direction of the result we wish to explain without there being any general psychological laws. Notice that I can say this without begging the question against those who hold that each component utterance is a consequence of general principles pertaining to the psychology of that particular speaker, for what makes sense without general principles, I am claiming, is the conversation, involving several speakers. I am not here presupposing that there are no general principles governing the speech of the several participants.

4. Any account of ascriptions of belief must come to grips with ascriptions of meaning as well, for there is a well-known trade-off between ascriptions of belief and ascriptions of meaning (Davidson 1974). If a pop star declares, "The only true love is love at first sight," shall we interpret her as having what strikes us as a very strange belief, namely, that the only true love is love at first sight, or shall we interpret her word "love" as meaning, not *love*, but something more like *instant infatuation* or *animal lust*? An answer to this can come from either a theory of belief or a theory of meaning, and the answers from these two sources must not conflict. So a theory of belief puts constraints on a theory of meaning, and conversely.

Moreover, various *theories* of meaning have tended to conflict with otherwise defensible ascriptions of belief. Holistic theories of meaning hold that the meaning of a word is a matter of its overall function in the language to which it belongs. So if two people use a word in fundamentally different ways, then it has different meanings for the two of them. Suppose that Isaac Newton meets Albert Einstein. Newton says, "Mass is conserved." Einstein says, "Mass is not conserved." This difference between the things they say reflects the difference between their fundamentally distinct conceptions of physical reality. So the holistic theory of meaning tells us that the meaning of "mass" for Newton is different from the meaning of "mass" for Einstein.

This conclusion conflicts with something it seems right to say about their beliefs, namely, that Einstein believes the opposite of what Newton believes. That is not to say that Newton could not be persuaded but only that at the start, before they talk things over, Einstein believes *precisely the negation of that which* Newton believes. So the words that Einstein speaks express a belief that is precisely the negation of the belief expressed by the words Newton speaks. So there is some one proposition such that Newton's words express that proposition, and Einstein's words express the negation of that *very same* proposition. So, Einstein's word "mass" must mean exactly the same thing as Newton's word "mass." But this contradicts the conclusion we drew from the holistic theory of meaning. So it is evident that belief and meaning have to be treated together.

It should be noted that the concept of meaning has played no role whatsoever in the account of communication and logic I have been developing in these chapters. On the contrary, in chapter 3, I offered a *reductio ad absurdum* on the very idea that we might put the notion of *content*—the mentalistic cousin of *meaning*—to any serious theoretical use. Since I assign no theoretical role to meaning, I am free to give the same sort of deflationary account of it that I have offered for belief. Just as I explain belief in terms of ascriptions of belief, I will explain meaning in terms of ascriptions of meaning. To do this, I need to identify the distinctive dialectical role played by assertions about meaning.

I want to distinguish between four kinds of talk about meaning. The first is a kind that treats meaning as a property of a person's words. To say that a certain form of words has a certain meaning in this way is not necessarily to say that anyone else attaches the same meaning to those words. However, it does imply that at least that one person does engage in a certain practice in his or her use of those words. The meaning we speak of in this case is not entirely unique to a particular occasion. The second kind of talk about meaning, which I will discuss in the next section, concerns the sorts of phenomena discussed in the literature under the heading "speaker's meaning" or "speaker's occasion meaning" (I am drawing no sharp distinction between these two). Here the meaning we speak of is something potentially unique to a particular occasion. The third kind of talk about meaning is a kind that occurs in connection with literally translating between two languages.

A fourth kind of talk of meaning is exhibited when someone makes some obscure remark and the rest of us ask, "What did he mean by that?" This is just a request for more information of one sort or another. We want to know what motivated him or her to say that, or we want to know about the events surrounding the incident that he or she was referring to, or we want to know how what he or she said was relevant to what he or she had said just prior to that. This fourth kind of talk of meaning has no special interest to us here. Only the first three kinds encourage philosophers to develop *theories* of meaning.

The first kind of meaning, which we speak of as pertaining to words and expressions, becomes an issue in connection with what I will call, in neutral terms, *conflicts in assertion*. The conflict in my example of Newton and Einstein is an illustration of this, or at least a caricature. So is the example of the pop star's claims about "love," since the problem only arises inasmuch as we imagine ourselves wishing to *deny* what she says. A conflict in assertion, in its simplest form, is a situation in which one person makes an assertion using a certain form of words and another person makes another assertion using a form of words that qualifies as the negation of the form of words used by the first.

Some conflicts in assertion are resolvable by what I will call the *standard method*. The standard method of resolving conflicts in assertion is to bring together those whose assertions conflict and let them state their hypotheses and present their evidence and, where necessary, run experiments and collect more evidence. In short, it is the scientific method. I will not try to explain the standard method in any more detail than this. I acknowledge the possibility that in saying no more I may be begging some of the questions I am trying to answer. The important points about the standard method are just these: In resolving conflicts in assertion through the standard method, the language itself does not come under scrutiny. The upshot, if all goes well, should be harmony in assertions. This may take a few minutes or it may take millennia.

Meaning becomes an issue when conflicts in assertion cannot be resolved by the standard method. The standard method may fail for a variety of reasons. Pride and prejudice, stubbornness and stupidity are some common causes. When the standard method seems not to work, we may dismiss the conflict as due to such character traits. Alternatively, we may try out the hypothesis that the parties in conflict *mean different things by their words*. The putting forward of such a hypothesis, when the time is right, should have the effect of making language itself the object of discussion. It occasions the defining of terms, the description of paradigm cases, and a variety of other devices.

The diagnosis of conflict as due to a difference in meanings is liable to be overused and abused. Too often it may serve simply as a bad excuse for not continuing the debate, for not trying to come up with better arguments, for not going out and collecting more evidence, or for not giving in when one has failed to make a strong case. It ought not to be that. A diagnosis of a difference in meaning ought to be an occasion for seeking harmony in a different way, a way that makes the language itself the object of discussion, as the standard method had not.

I say we *can try out the hypothesis* of a difference in meaning, because we may find that that diagnosis gets us nowhere, that the conflict in assertions remains as forceful as ever even after the examination of language occasioned by the diagnosis. In this case, two further diagnoses are possible: One possibility is that the question is subjective (see chapter 8), but subjectivity carries its own characteristic marks. Where these are lacking, we may have to conclude that one or the other of the interlocutors is not fully rational. That is the other possibility.

Here then is my theory of the first kind of meaning: First, this kind of meaning becomes an issue only where there is some prospect of a *difference* in meaning (which is not to say that we may not conclude that meanings are the same). Second, to ascribe a difference in meaning is to initiate a shift in the pattern of discourse amounting to an examination of the language in which the discourse has been carried on up to that point. Finally, the function of this examination of language is to resolve conflicts in assertion.

On my theory, meaning is not something fundamental the real nature of which we have to understand in order to understand the nature of language. Yet, my theory gives answers to the sorts of questions about belief and meaning that I spoke of in introducing the topic of meaning. In particular, the conflict between Newton and Einstein is not a difference in meaning, because it is not a case in which the diagnosis of a difference in meaning is appropriate. Rather, their conflict is just a case in which the standard method requires a great deal of expensive work and a great deal of creative hypothesizing. The temptation to say that "mass" means something different for Newton from what it means for Einstein has several sources. One of these is probably just the confusion of the first kind of meaning with the fourth kind of meaning, which we may speak of in calling for elaboration. Another, more important source is the theoretical presumption that there is something—the meaning—that each word has and by virtue of which the word can function as it does in the language. Since Newton's word and Einstein's word seem to have nothing in common but a *reference*, one may be tempted to conclude that their *meanings* must differ. But according to my account, there is no theoretical use for this conception of meaning.

The pop star's theory of love, on the other hand, might be a good example of a genuine difference in meaning. It will not be one if her utterance is not a genuine assertion at all and she is merely being ironic or provocative or is only trying to create a certain impression of herself or to carry on the conversation when she cannot think of anything else to say. But if she will argue with us, by describing her experiences of love at first sight, by citing classic examples of love at first sight, and so on, and yet does not persuade us, then we may have to conclude that there is a real difference in meaning between her word "love" and ours. Sometimes recognizing a difference in meaning may have no other result than a realignment of terminology. What makes the case of the pop star more interesting and more difficult is that our diagnosis of a difference in meaning may reveal a deep difference between her and us over questions of value. Our pop star may know perfectly well what sort of thing we call "love" but believe that that sort of thing does not have the value we attach to it and that what truly has that value is the sort of thing that *she* calls "love." For this reason she may deliberately choose to speak a different language from ours. Thus if the diagnosis succeeds in creating harmony in assertions, it will only be by showing us a way of talking suited to a way of life that we may be disposed to join.

This theory of meaning, moreover, makes direct contact with the history of the subject. Recall from chapter 1 Locke's example of the meeting of physicians where the question arose "whether any Liquor passed through the Filaments of the Nerves" (III.ix.16). I argued that Locke's own version of the Lockean theory of communication was an attempt to prescribe a remedy for such disputes, which are merely verbal. What I am now proposing, in effect, is to explicate meaning by taking us back to that starting point. As Locke clearly saw, certain sorts of disputes are indeed to be resolved by distinguishing meanings. The mistake is to take this concept of meaning, which plays a regulatory function within a language, and treat it as the fundamental theoretical entity in terms of which the functioning of language is to be explained.

5. Next I want to address some phenomena related to *speaker's meaning*, which is the second kind of meaning I listed above. Recall that I suggested in chapter 2 that the specification of a conversational parameter, such as the domain of discourse or a presupposition, could be understood as a principle of conversational potential. In other words, by identifying a conversational parameter, we in some way specify which sorts of continuations of the conversation would be appropriate. I can now explain better what I meant. In our more advanced languages, recall, conversations are governed by what I have called *contexts* (see chapter 11). What is assertible and what is deniable depends on this context. So my claim is that to specify a conversational parameter is to do something on the order of specifying some aspect of the context that governs the conversation. I say "something on the order of" in order to acknowledge that the full account of conversational dynamics must go beyond the simple picture I have drawn.

Consider, for instance, the following case: I told Alice I would meet her at noon in front of the department store. It is now noon, and she is not here. I assumed she knew I meant the Matsuzakaya Department Store, since that is where we met last time. But maybe she thought I meant the Mitsukoshi Department Store, since that is the one we like better. So now I *predict* that I will find her in front of Mitsukoshi, because I conjecture that she believes that that is where we planned to meet. The reason she believes this, I say, is that she *misunderstood* what I *meant*. In saying this, what I am saying, in effect, is that the context governing my utterance was one thing and that, as evidenced by her response, she took the context to be something else. I *meant* that we should meet in front of Matsuzakaya. In other words, the context included, "The department store is Matsuzakaya." But she thought I *meant* that we should meet in front of Mitsukoshi. In other words, she *took* the context to include, rather, "The department store is Mitsukoshi." When at noon I fail to find her in front of Matsuzakaya, I suddenly become sensitive to the possibility of taking the context in her way and realize that when it came time for her to meet me, she was led, by the way she took the context, to assert to herself, "We will meet in front of Mitsukoshi." I conjecture, in other words, that she believes we will meet at Mitsukoshi.

Generalizing from this example, I propose to construe a misunderstanding of a speaker's meaning as a mismatch between the context that the speaker takes to govern the conversation and the context that the hearer takes to govern the conversation. Notice that it is not necessary to suppose that the context that governs the conversation really is what either of the participants takes it to be. We may distinguish between what appears to the participants to be appropriate and what really is appropriate, all things considered. What appears to a participant to be appropriate depends on what he or she takes the context to be, as exhibited in his or her speech. What really is appropriate depends on what the context really is.

Incidentally, when we say that someone thought that so-and-so meant that p, it is not necessary to suppose that that person attributed the *belief* that p to so-and-so. Alice thought that I meant we should meet at Mitsukoshi, but she need not have actually made on my behalf the assertion that we should meet at Mitsukoshi. To suppose that she had done that would be to suppose that she had reflected on our conversation in a way that in fact she did not. She misunderstood my meaning, because she misunderstood the context, not because she made the wrong assertion on my behalf. To suppose that every misunderstanding involves a mistaken attribution of belief is to yield to the temptations of the Lockean conception of communication. *Mis*understanding a speaker need be no more a kind of interpretation of the speaker than understanding need be.

This account makes sense of our characterization of the pertinent sort of misunderstanding as a misunderstanding of what the speaker *meant*. We say that what I *meant* was that we would meet in front of Matsuzakaya, but Alice misunderstood what I *meant*. Thus this second kind of meaning, like the first kind, serves to characterize a disagreement. Again it is a disagreement that cannot be resolved by what I called the standard method. The disagreement would be resolved, if it were noticed, by an examination of language. If Alice had felt uncertain about where we were going to meet, the way for her to resolve her uncertainty would not have been to consult a directory of Tokyo department stores or to try to recall where she and I have tended to meet in the past, but to ask me, "Which department store are you talking about?" and in this way focus our attention on my speech.

Next let us review the cases discussed in chapter 2. The first case was that in which a burglary victim declares, "Everything is gone!" and we say that the domain of discourse was the class of transportable objects of non-negligible value that had been in the apartment earlier. It should now be obvious what I will say about this: the domain of discourse so specified is a feature of the context, namely, the domain as I defined it in chapter 11. The second case was that in which A says, "Her husband is kind to her" and in so doing presupposes that Mrs. Green's companion is her husband. Here my claim is that to say that she presupposes this is to say that "Mrs. Green's companion is her husband" belongs to the governing context. In anticipation of a misunderstanding of meaning, we may in both cases consider our specification of the context as a specification of what the speaker *meant*.

Finally, consider again the case from Grice in which a teacher writes a letter that describes a student as punctual, and so on, meaning thereby that the student is not very talented. Here we wish to say that in a sense the teacher *meant* that the student was not very talented, although that is not what he *said*. Again I want to take this as a specification of the governing context. What has to be shown is that in such a case, the context would include the proposition that the student is not very talented. One way to show this is to explain why it would be reasonable for a reader of the letter to treat that as part of the context governing the teacher's writing of the letter. Here is why: Given that the letter is a letter of recommendation, the reader may assume that the context contains everything most pertinent to the student's qualifications. Thus the context must include either that the student is talented or that he is not. So if the letter writer does not explicitly address this question, the reader may presume that what the context includes is that the student is not very talented. The reader's presuming this may mean either that the reader actually infers it or merely that it comes to be included in what the reader takes to be the context governing the reader's own actions in response. (In either case, this result might depend on the hearer's employing assumptions about the psychology of the letter writer.)

So in order for the teacher to have *meant* that the student was not very talented, it was not necessary for the teacher to have foreseen the reader's response or to have acted with the intention to bring about such a response. However, it is also possible for the teacher to have written the letter with such an intention. In that case, the teacher will have commanded himself, as it were, to bring about a certain response in the reader and will have chosen his words by envisioning the sorts of inner conversation that various formulations would elicit in the reader and then choosing those that would result in the intended effect.

Thus, I do acknowledge the possibility of making an assertion with certain intentions and, in particular, of making an assertion in order to fulfill a desire to get someone to believe something. However, asserting in order to instill a belief is not the normal case of assertion. In choosing his words in order to fulfill an intention, the teacher's choice of words depended on a prior sense of how words work. This prior sense of how words work does not amount to knowledge of what people intend to do with words. It is an understanding of what sorts of responses are appropriate that enables him correctly to envision people's responses. Quite apart from my treatment of this example, it should be clear that according to my account of how language works, asserting in order to fulfill a desire to instill belief cannot be the normal case of assertion. There are things that are achieved by making assertions, such as preparing the hearer for commands, and where such things could not be achieved by making assertions, there would be no practice of asserting. But that does not mean that assertions are made in order to fulfill the desire to achieve such things. According to my account, to attribute a desire to S is to make a command on S's behalf. So asserting in order to fulfill a desire is asserting in response to a command. But asserting and commanding belong to the same level of thought. So asserting in response to a command cannot be the normal case of assertion. So asserting in order to fulfill a desire cannot be the normal case of assertion.

How, on my approach, is it possible to lie? This might see to be a problem for my conception of language inasmuch as lying might seem to depend on the speaker's having certain sorts of intentions regarding the hearer's beliefs. I have acknowledged the possibility of such intentions in other-than-normal cases, but that does not seem to be enough of a concession to account for the possibility of lying, for lying seems to be possible even for creatures who have not reached the level of linguistic capacity at which these other-than-normal cases are found. Even nonhuman animals are capable of some simple sorts of deception (Cheney and Seyfarth 1991). The answer is simply that there can be a kind of linguistically mediated deception even at the lower levels of linguistic capacity. On the present approach, language is a means of social cooperation (a means that may acquire an intrasubjective role as well). As in any institution that serves the good of the community as a whole, there will be free riders who learn how to use it in a way that, while favorable to themselves, tends to undermine the institution. In the case of language, the cognitive capacities necessary to discover how to exploit the institution in this way may be none other than the very same abilities to judge similarities and causal relations that make language learning possible in the first place.

But how is it possible to assert something one does not believe? If an ascription of belief to S is an assertion on S's behalf and S asserts that p, then may we not ascribe to S the belief that p? On the contrary, S may be lying in asserting that p. The mistake here is to suppose that it is in every way correct to assert on S's behalf everything that S would assert. There may indeed be certain contexts in which it would be in a sense appropriate to assert on S's behalf anything S would assert. But by the same token, there is a sense in which a lie expresses a belief. It expresses a belief on the part of someone who S is pretending to be. In any case, there is definitely a way in which an assertion on S's behalf might fail to be appropriate even if S would make that assertion. For our assertions on others' behalf are appropriate in one way only insofar as they facilitate explanation. If we are taken in by a lie and thus assert on S's behalf anything that S would assert, we will be unable to provide an entirely coherent account of S's life as a whole. For instance, if the liar says he is going straight home, and we are taken in by this, then we may be unable to explain why he goes to the bar instead.

6. By *interpretation* I mean a certain kind of talk. Interpretive talk is talk about people's beliefs, desires, and other propositional thoughts and about meanings. Since talking out loud is in my view a kind of propositional thinking, talk about what another person has *said* will also count as interpretation in my sense. My topic up to this point in this chapter has been interpretation in the *intra*linguistic case, the case in which the interpreter and the person under interpretation speak the same language. This is the case in which we can understand interpretation as primarily a further function of the language, a function that in various ways enhances the process of cooperative interaction.

I now turn to interpretation in the *inter*linguistic case. This is the case in which the interpreter's home language is different from the home language of the person under interpretation. Broadly speaking, interlinguistic interpretation amounts to learning to understand the other person's language well enough that one can even attribute meanings and propositional thoughts using the language of the other person. There is more than one way to do this. The first way is just to learn the language as a child might. On my theory, this will amount to a process of making similarity judgments and kausal judgments. In its earliest stages it will not be an exercise in conceptual thought, although a capacity for conceptual thought will be the result. A second way involves taking advantage of the fact that one already speaks a language. This second way is to translate the foreign language into one's own home language.

I do not mean to imply that the individuation of languages is clear-cut. Much of what I say about translation between languages will pertain as well to the interpretation of subpopulations of speakers of what is in some broad sense one's own language. It will be evident that my account of translation does not rest on any very sharp cognitive distinction between understanding one's own home language and understanding a foreign language. Translation will be something that can be carried on in a very thorough going way or resorted to infrequently as need arises.

Radical translation, as I conceive of it, is just a special case of translation. It is the case in which one has to discover a translation without relying on help from anyone who is already a master of both languages or who already knows how to translate from one language to the other. This conception of radical translation is a little different from the usual conception, which treats translation as a special case of interpretation and radical translation as merely one aspect of something called radical *interpretation*. But this way of looking at things makes no sense for me, since on my approach, the capacity to *interpret* in the foreign language will be just a necessary consequence of a capacity to translate the foreign language.

How is radical translation to be performed? It is tempting to answer that translation is a process of comparing the functions of words and sentences (Sellars 1974). The idea is that each word or phrase or sentence in a language has a distinctive function in that language and that translation from L to L' is a matter of finding for each sentence s of L the sentence s' of L' such that the function of s in L is more similar to the function of s' in L' than to the function of any other sentence of L'. This is not the approach I will take, however. My objection to this conception of translation is just that there is no good reason to believe that there are functions of the requisite sort. If a word or a sentence has a function of the requisite sort, then it ought to be possible to say in a definitive way what that function is. If the Lockean theory were correct, then perhaps we could explain the distinctive function of each expression in terms of the sorts of thoughts it may be used to express. If there were reference relations such as I discussed in chapter 6, then perhaps we could identify the distinctive function of each nonlogical word by identifying its reference. But apart from these mistaken doctrines, I see no way to assign to each word or expression a definite, distinctive function.

Certainly the account of language I have been developing in these chapters generates no such assignment. An act of speech, according to my account, is indeed the product of a kind of thinking. At least in the simplest case, it is the product of similarity judgments and kausal (or causal) judgments. But each speaker views the world from a distinct perspective, and so there is no reason to expect that the judgments that explain one speaker's utterance of a given sentence will be the same as those that explain another speaker's utterance of that same sentence. Such explanations do not generalize. We cannot abstract a distinctive function for each sentence from such explanations.

Could the functionalist approach to translation be preserved by focusing on individual speakers? Perhaps we could get a translation of the speech of a single speaker by matching the functions of words for that speaker to the functions of words for us. The problem is that this presupposes that an individual's linguistic dispositions at a given time are entirely a matter of what is *in* the individual at that time and in that individual's nonlinguistic environment. Only in that case will there be something we can call *the* function of a word for that speaker (at a time) that is independent of other speakers' uses of that word. But in fact each speaker is ready to modify his or her manner of using words in light of others' manner of using words, as my account of language learning makes plain. Even someone who invents a language for his or her own private use will be responsible to his or her past usage. So even narrowing the scope of our inquiry to individual speakers would not enable us to avoid the impossible task of abstracting a general function.

In one respect, my account of language learning may have been somewhat misleading in this regard. I characterized mastery of some of the more primitive languages in terms of efficacy, and I characterized the efficacy of assertions and commands in terms of corresponding *aspects* of responses. But as I explained in chapter 10, this is a characterization that rests on a prior interpretation of the language. We discover the aspect corresponding to a given sentence only by translating that sentence into our own language. So the characterization of mastery is not a characterization of function on which we can rest a theory of interpretation.

Here is my conception of translation: Translation is a matter of finding a way to exploit one's prior mastery of a language in order to be able to cooperate with a foreign community by means of their language. In other words, what one seeks is a way of using sentences of one's home language in place of sentences of the foreign language, and conversely, such that appropriate responses, verbal and nonverbal, on one's own part to translations of sentences spoken in the foreign language, together with appropriate responses on the part of the foreign speakers to translations of appropriate sentences in one's own language, amount collectively to linguistically mediated cooperative interaction with speakers of the foreign language. This is not to say that one cannot also employ translation in order to understand the goings-on within a community without participating in that community, but in that case, one understands by imagining oneself participating.

So conceived, translation will conform, by and large, to two important guidelines inter alia (see Gauker 1986). The first is this:

> *The Principle of Uniformity:* If two people belong to the same linguistic community, translate their words *uniformly*.

Uniformity in translation means translating both speakers according to a single procedure, that is, one that distinguishes between two individuals only on general grounds. That translation should conform to such a principle is an immediate consequence of my account of the objective of translation together with my non-Lockean account of communication. Suppose I do not translate A and B uniformly. In that case, I will have to interpret A and B as understanding one another by means of translating one another. But by my non-Lockean account of language, this cannot be the normal case for two speakers who belong to a single linguistic community. To the extent that I cannot interpret the members of a linguistic community uniformly, therefore, I will fail to understand how they communicate with one another.

The second guideline for interpretation is my version of the principle of charity:

> *The Principle of Appropriateness:* Translate a person as saying what is *appropriate* under the circumstances.

To understand the rationale for the principle of appropriateness, one must bear in mind that the method of translation is one of exploiting one's mastery of one's own language in order to find a way to cooperate with speakers of the foreign language. Being master of one's own language means knowing what it is appropriate to say in one's own language and knowing how to respond appropriately to utterances in one's own language. Mastery equals knowledge of appropriateness. One will not be able to exploit one's mastery of one's own language to find a way of cooperating with speakers of the foreign language unless one's translation shows those speakers to be saying appropriate things and responding to speech appropriately. For to the extent that one's translation fails to translate speakers as speaking appropriately, one's sense of appropriateness in one's own language will not enable one to respond to what they say in ways they know how to respond to, or to anticipate what they will say or do in response to what is said to them, or to anticipate what they will say in response to their circumstances. If I translate Gogan as saying something that translates as "The buffalo are near the lake or over the hill," and if I have just come from the lake, where I saw no buffalo, then I may appropriately reply by saying what I translate as "There are no buffalo near the lake." And if my translation preserves appropriateness, then I may expect that Gogan will draw a conclusion that translates as "The buffalo are over the hill." But if I translate Gogan as saying "The clouds are words that no one can read," then, since I know of no appropriate response to such an assertion, our conversation comes to an end. To the extent that I have failed to explain exactly what appropriateness is, I concede, the content of this principle remains undecided.

Offhand, it might seem that we could translate the speakers of the foreign language as saying things that struck us as inappropriate and even quite bizarre but that after a while we might begin to discover a pattern in their discourse, as represented in our translation of it, and that we could explain what they say and do by citing these patterns. The problem is that novelty is pervasive. In almost every situation in which we have to explain or predict what someone will say or do, the situation that that person faces is in some possibly relevant respect different from any other that he or she or anyone else has ever faced. So the patterns we uncover must tell us also what the person will say and do in the face of novel situations. The way to ensure translatability even in the face of novelty is to translate the foreign speakers as speaking appropriately. Indeed, ensuring intelligibility even in the face of novelty is what gives translation a point. Otherwise we might try to understand wholly in terms of patterns discoverable in their actual speech and dispense with translation altogether. I do not wish to deny that this could in fact be done. In some sense it is what the child learning the foreign language as a first language does. But that, as I said at the start of this section, is a different style of language learning and not what we are concerned with in discussing translation.

Correctness in translation is not defined by these two principles. Correctness in translation is, rather, a matter of whether the translation really does enable one to exploit one's mastery of one's own language to cooperate by means of the foreign language. Still, these two principles might be deliberately adhered to in the course of a self-conscious and deliberate attempt to discover a system for translating a language. So it should be pointed out that these "principles" are not strict rules. One cannot expect that everything a person says will be appropriate or that the utterances of the several members of a linguistic community will always be uniformly translatable. On the contrary, these two principles may easily come into conflict. We may find that in order to translate uniformly, we must interpret a person as saying something inappropriate. Thus we may have to translate a person's assertion as "I am a parrot" if in the vast majority of cases we maximize appropriateness by translating a certain word as "parrot." Conversely, we may find that in order to translate a person as saying something appropriate, we have to interpret him or her as speaking a distinctive idiolect.

The fact that the principles of translation may yield to one another does not make them vacuous. Somehow it is possible to be guided by a guideline without strictly conforming to it. I do not know how this is possible, but clearly it is. It may serve a purpose for me to tell my students, "Don't use too many quotations," even if I do not tell them exactly how many is too many. Part of the answer in the present case may be that we have an independent measure of whether we have interpreted well, namely, whether our translation facilitates cooperation. Another part of the answer is that we may allow only those exceptions that seem explicable in one way or another. We will readily recognize a malapropism where one word is used in place of another that sounds a lot like it. We will readily allow inappropriateness if the error belongs to a common type.

It must be emphasized that translation is not necessarily possible at all. It is not necessarily possible even where there is a genuine language that facilitates cooperation in the characteristic way. As I argued in chapter 4, every language should be *understandable* to us (provided its speakers are not intellectually superior to us in the sense explained), but not every language need be *translatable* into our own current languages. This distinction between translatable and merely understandable languages raises the question, What accounts for the difference? What do intertranslatable languages have in common? I doubt whether any very clear answer to this is possible. Translation may be successful in degrees and more successful along some dimensions than along others. It is fair to say, however, that creatures who can translate one another's languages will have to be significantly alike in certain ways. Some of the relevant dimensions of likeness will be the sort of environment to which the language to be translated is suited, the sorts of sense organs possessed by speakers of that language, and the aspects of things by which they spontaneously choose to judge similarities.

Let me emphasize the ways in which the present account of radical translation depends on the conception of language that I have been developing in these chapters. One pertinent feature of my conception is that language learning does not amount to a kind of interpretation. The Lockean, by contrast, will wish to explain the learning of a first language along basically the same lines as his or her explanation of radical translation (or interpretation). Only because my conception differs from the Lockean's in this way can I maintain that radical translation rests on a prior mastery of some language. Another important feature of my conception of communication is that it does not take the form of a theory of meaning. If language had been explained by explaining meaning, then translation could be defined simply as a meaning-preserving mapping. But here we have no account of meaning that can be applied interlinguistically independently of a prior translation. So it was necessary to define the objective of radical translation in some other way, which is what I have attempted to do here.

Nonetheless, in the context of the conception of translation that I have described, we may find a further use for the concept of meaning. Imagine two people trying to work together who speak different languages. Each speaks his or her own language, and neither responds appropriately to the other. This too is a conflict in assertions in a broad sense. It is not the first sort of case of a difference in meaning, as I characterized it above, in which one person asserts one thing, the other asserts the negation of that same thing, and their conflict cannot be resolved by means of the standard method. But it is similar, for it is a case in which discourse fails to facilitate cooperation and cooperation cannot be brought about by means of the standard method. Translation is a process that may bring about cooperation in this case. Inasmuch as translation resolves this kind of conflict, translation can be considered an investigation into meaning. Moreover, as translation proceeds and the translators test their understanding in real-life discourse employing the foreign language, differences in meaning of the first sort are bound to arise quite frequently. So translation will be a process intimately concerned with meanings even in the first sense.

14

Interpretationism

1. In the previous chapter I explained that to attribute a belief to another person is to make an assertion on that person's behalf. But to say that much about the attribution of belief is not yet to say what beliefs *are*. Assuming that we understand something about the function of an assertion in general, I have explained something about the function of a particular kind of assertion, namely, one that is, as we say, *about* someone's belief. But from the point of view of someone making assertions about the beliefs of another, something more might seem to be necessary. In order to understand what one is doing in the course of attributing beliefs, one might want an account of what beliefs *are*. So the question appears to remain, What *are* beliefs?

On the contrary, I think I have already answered this, albeit very sketchily, in setting out my account of attribution of belief. It is one thing to specify the function of attributions of belief and, one might have thought, something else again to say what beliefs are. But in this chapter I intend to argue that, no, an account of what beliefs are need not be anything over and above an account of their attribution. I will call this doctrine *interpretationism*. The official formulation is this: An account of what beliefs *are* may take the form of an account of the attribution of beliefs. More generally: An account of what propositional thoughts *are* may take the form of an account of the attribution of such thoughts.

Talking, I suggest, may be viewed as a kind of thinking. But that does not mean that my interpretationism is an alternative to the theory of talking that I have been advancing in these chapters. It is not a thesis about the act of speech as such. Rather, it is a thesis about the kinds of thing we attribute when we interpret a person in the ways I discussed in the previous chapter. Thus, it is a thesis about the act's *being the thought that p*, as well as a thesis about other propositional thoughts that may not be embodied in overt or covert acts of speech. Moreover, I have acknowledged that there are kinds of thinking in addition to propositional thought, and interpretationism is not a thesis about any of those.

In this chapter I will take up a variety of general, metaphysical objections against the interpretationist thesis that an account of what thoughts are can take the form of an account of their attribution. In addition, I will explain the distinction, promised in an earlier chapter, between several grades of intentionality.

2. First of all, interpretationism might seem to be a clear case of confusing epistemology and ontology. Many illustrations can be adduced of the difference between an account of what a thing *is* and an account of how we *know* of such things. Consider, for instance, the case of electrons. An account of what electrons are would tell us that electrons are negatively charged components of atoms, that they may possess various levels of excitation, that they are shared by atoms bound together in molecules, that they are leptons, which are distinct from quarks and gauge bosons, and so on. An account of our *knowledge* of electrons would be quite different. It would tell us about the various experiments with electricity that led people to accept the electron theory.

But I think that, quite apart from the question of the nature of thought, it is necessary to recognize some interdependencies between matters of epistemology and matters of ontology. An account of what a certain sort of thing *is*, we have to recognize, may include an important epistemological component. This is true in more than one way. Our account of a kind of thing may involve an epistemological component because things of that kind belong together only by virtue of their presenting themselves to us through the same sort of sign. Alternatively, and this is the case of real interest here, it may happen that an explanation of the nature of a thing will instill understanding only if it addresses the problem of *recognizing* certain sorts of thing.

A case of the first sort might be the *quasar*. A quasar, or *quasi-stellar object*, is just any of a variety of deep-space sources of intense radio waves that have extremely red-shifted spectra. As it stands, what they are known to have in common is only this sort of detection profile. But they might turn out to be very different from one another in physical structure. If it turns out that most of them are the same sort of thing structurally, then the term "quasar" might come to stand for just that sort, and the rest might be dismissed as "pseudo-quasars." But until that happens, *quasar* will be an essentially epistemological sort. But epistemological sorting such as we find in the case of quasars is not the epistemological dependency of sorting that I wish to draw attention to. It does not serve my purpose, because it is clearly only an expedient. It is a kind of classification that we may use before we understand very well the things that belong to the sort.

The epistemological dependency of sorting that I wish to emphasize is different. An account of the nature of a thing can be more or less elaborate. The depths to which we have to reach in order to explain what a certain sort of thing is will depend on what our audience understands to begin with. To someone suitably prepared, it may be possible to give a wholly *ontological* account of a thing, that is, to explain what a certain sort of thing is without having to say anything about how anything may be recognized as being of that sort. But on the other hand, a person may be so naive that in order to prepare him or her for the wholly ontological account, one has to train the person to recognize certain sorts of thing—not necessarily the sort at issue. This is the dependency of ontology on epistemology that I want to emphasize and that I want to say is particularly direct in the case of thoughts.

For example, consider again the case of electrons. Students who learn just the textbook theory of electrons and not the method of their discovery can indeed be said to understand what electrons are. But that is because they already have a practical understanding of many of the concepts presupposed in stating the textbook theory. They can *tell* when one thing is a component of another. In certain cases they can *tell* whether or not an electrical current is flowing. They can understand the force of attraction between electrons and protons because they can tell when a magnet is the cause of the motion of a nail or because they can solve various problems employing the sort of elementary mathematics by which Coulomb's law is defined. Moreover, we will not credit them with much understanding unless they are able to put forth reasonable conjectures about electrons and are able to recognize confirmations of the electron hypothesis when confronted with such. To anyone not so prepared for the wholly ontological account of a thing, the account will have to address epistemological matters directly.

In the case of electrons, much may be said without addressing epistemological matters. In the case of other sorts of things, however, there may be little to say without addressing the epistemological questions. What interpretationism says is that in the case of thoughts, the epistemological entanglements are fairly immediate. It is not easy, in other words, to sustain in this case the illusion of explaining without addressing the problem of recognition. In the case of thought, unlike in the case of electrons, there is not a large body of other terms by means of which we can proceed to explain while postponing epistemological issues until we come to the problem of explaining those other terms.

Why should thoughts differ from electrons in this regard? Why are the epistemological entanglements more immediate in the case of thought? Perhaps the answer is that talk of what people think and want is so fundamental to talking and thinking in languages such as ours that we will not find a person who can understand our explanations of things and yet has simply never heard of thinking and has never spoken of thoughts himself or herself and simply needs to be informed. So if one asks, What are thoughts? this is a sign of a philosophical problem about a concept with which one is already well acquainted. So the reason why epistemological entanglements are so immediate in the case of thoughts is that these philosophical problems tend to be entangled with epistemology.

The case is different with electrons. Even if humanity someday reached a stage where everyone did in fact learn about electrons at an early age, and even if it came to pass that everyone were actually in the business of studying the structure of matter, it would remain true that one could speak the language with great facility and understand what others were saying about other things perfectly well without employing one's understanding of electrons. So electron talk is largely independent of the rest of talk. Consequently, even in such a society, as well as in ours, people might frequently reach a stage in their linguistic development where mere theory, unaccompanied by instruction in problems of recognition, could explain to them the nature of electrons.

One thing I am assuming here, which is not quite obvious, is that an explanation of the nature of a thing is whatever it has to be in order to instill understanding. This does not mean that everything we call an *explanation* will in fact instill understanding. A string of words that fails to instill understanding may still qualify as an explanation by virtue of what it was supposed to do. Even a good explanation may fail to instill understanding through some fault of the hearer. A very different perspective on explanations of the nature of a thing is possible, according to which an explanation of the nature of a thing amounts to spelling out the laws of nature to which things of that sort must conform. But even if this is a viable conception of explanation in certain domains (which I doubt), it is certainly not one that we can adopt in the domain of propositional thoughts. As I argued in chapter 5, we have no reason to believe that there are also laws of the requisite sort governing propositional thoughts.

Still, it might seem that an interpretationist account of thought must inevitably beg the question. The charge of begging the question comes in a couple of forms. First, it may be said that an account of interpretation cannot *be* an account of what thoughts are because it will inevitably *presuppose* an account of what thoughts are. If we had an independent account of what thoughts are, then we could attribute thoughts by locating the things so characterized. Without an account of what thoughts are, on the other hand, it might seem that we could not attribute thoughts at all, because we would not know what we were looking for. To this I reply simply that in the previous chapter I set out an account of interpretation that does not in the manner stated presuppose an independent account of the nature of thought.

There is a second way the interpretationist theory of thought might be charged with begging the question. An explanation of a given sort of thing, whether purely theoretical or epistemologically entangled, must not presuppose a prior understanding of that very sort of thing. So if an account of the attribution of thought is to qualify as an account of the nature of thought, the account must not refer to thoughts as such except in directing us to attribute certain thoughts. But an account of the attribution of thoughts, it seems, is bound to transgress this constraint in directing the interpreter to draw certain *conclusions*, make certain *observations*, formulate certain *hypotheses*, and try certain *predictions*, for conclusions, observations, hypotheses, and predictions are all various types of propositional thought.

My answer to this second charge of begging the question is that the account of attribution may refer to observations, hypotheses, and the rest without begging the question, because it may refer to them without referring to them as thoughts. While the account might set out certain instructions, these instructions may be conceived as instructions for making certain assertions in a particular language, such as English. Where we may presuppose the categories of thought, we may characterize these assertions as observations, hypotheses, and so on. But in the context of our account of attribution, where an understanding of the categories of thought cannot be presupposed, these types may be understood instead in terms of functional and syntactic characteristics of assertions in the interpreter's native language. For instance, an observation report is roughly an assertion that (*a*) takes the form of a present-tense, subject-predicate sentence and (*b*) does not originate as a response to another assertion. Hypotheses are, roughly, assertions containing the operator "maybe." Predictions are, roughly, assertions in the future tense. No doubt these reductions fail to capture what is common between the observations, hypotheses, and so on, of different languages. No doubt they are distortions of even the language-specific categories that we can grasp after we understand what thought is. Nonetheless, they might suffice for an understanding of the method of interpretation that the interpretationist puts forward as an account of what thoughts are.

If an account of attribution constitutes an account of what thoughts are, then apparently the thoughts that exist according to that account are those whose attribution is sanctioned by the given account of attribution. They need not be attributable on the basis of the evidence we actually have, but may be attributable only on the basis of events and states of affairs now out of reach. Still, this idea may not seem very promising. Surely there are thoughts that do not manifest themselves in what we say and do. The most striking case of apparently hidden thoughts is the case of those occurrent thoughts associated with soundless verbal imagery. By "soundless verbal imagery" I mean those auditory (or visual) images of words that come to mind as, for example, we sit quietly looking out the window. As I explained in chapter 10, inner acts of speech are by no means to be identified with episodes of such verbal imagery. Verbal imagery is only the medium of one's own observation of one's acts of inner speech and is not at all a necessary accompaniment of that speech.

What I want to say about these occurrent thoughts accompanied by soundless verbal imagery is that they are not in any relevant sense hidden at all. Certainly they are not hidden from the person who has them. But that means that they are also not in any relevant sense hidden from others. What counts as evidence for an interpretation need not be confined to observations that each interpreter could make for himself or herself. The evidence for an interpreter's interpretation may include observations that only others could make and, in particular, may include the subject's observations of his or her own inner speech. That evidence is *available* to other interpreters in the sense that the subject could report those observations to them. This conception of the evidence for interpretation extends a general lesson in epistemology to the special case of thought attributions. This more general lesson is that science is best conceived as a cooperative endeavor and not as a matter of each mind's inferring reality for itself on the basis of data immediately present to it.

Thus an interpretationist may countenance certain apparently hidden thoughts by taking a liberal, egalitarian stand on the nature of the evidence. Further, the interpretationist's account of the evidence may also be broad enough to include neurological facts. I, for one, am doubtful about the possibility of literally identifying individual occurrent thoughts with individual events in the brain or identifying mental states such as belief with states of the brain (Gauker 1988; see also Horgan and Tye 1985), and the interpretationist account of propositional thoughts is one that does not depend on there being such identities. But even without identities, there might nonetheless be neurological *symptoms* of thinking from which thoughts might be inferred. For instance, even if propositional thoughts are not physical, mental imagery may be. Mental images may be physical in whatever way auditory and visual sensations are physical. If mental images are physically identifiable apart from attributions of thought, certain thoughts may be attributable on the grounds that their occurrence explains the subject's mental imagery. Another possibility is that we could in principle determine on neurological grounds what the subject would do in various counterfactual situations and attribute thoughts that explain why the subject would act that way. Of course, in reasoning counterfactually in this way, we would have to be sure to distinguish between counterfactual situations that reveal what the subject actually thinks and those that change the subject's mind.

These methods of discovering hidden thoughts in principle on neurological grounds give the interpretationist a way of making sense of the speculation that paralyzed and brain-damaged subjects have thoughts that do not occur out loud in overt speech and that do not manifest themselves in nonverbal action. Perhaps we could read their thoughts from their mental imagery, especially from the auditory images of words. Or perhaps we could tell what they would say and do if they were able. Of course, one problem would be to decide what portion of their neurology to hold constant while imagining them able to express themselves in words and deeds.

I still have not replied to what many will regard as the most decisive argument against interpretationism, namely, that it obscures the distinction between what is true and what we have reason to believe. Teachers of philosophy are accustomed to teaching their students to distinguish between truth and belief. One may have the best of reasons to believe something that is in fact false. Further, the truth may be something believed by no one. Most important, the fact that one believes something is no defense against doubts about its truth. These are lessons we must persistently drill into our students lest they settle for myths and fantasies because they are "true for me." We rightly reject any doctrine that denies these important lessons. The interpretationist theory of thought might seem to be guilty of transgressions because it makes a method for forming beliefs (about thoughts) constitutive of the object of belief (namely, thoughts).

On the contrary, acknowledging a dependency of ontology on epistemology in the way I have done does not at all threaten our useful pedagogical distinction between truth and belief. The practical implication of that distinction is that we must always be prepared to revise our beliefs and that we have a responsibility to address all reasonable doubts. But clearly this practical implication is not threatened by what I have said. No application of the method of interpretation I have described yields unrevisable certainty. Even the methods themselves are subject to revision. But the distinction between truth and belief is more than this practical implication. It is also part of an explanation of the permanent prospect of revision. Of course, if any explanation of this prospect depends on a correspondence theory of truth, then I will deny that explanation. But the explanation can do without the correspondence theory, for the explanation might be simply that omniscience is an impossible ideal. The distinction between truth and belief enters into the explanation inasmuch as we may express this impossibility as follows: There is always more that is *true* than anyone individually or intelligent life collectively will ever *believe*.

3. One philosopher who has longed advocated an interpretationist conception of propositional thoughts is Daniel Dennett (1981, 1982). I myself have been greatly influenced by Dennett, but my view is nonetheless quite different from his. A comparison will afford me the opportunity to defend my view against a number of objections and to draw the distinction I have promised (in chapter 9) between several grades of intentionality.

One way in which I differ from Dennett is in my account of interpretation. Basically, Dennett's view is that interpretation is a matter of attributing beliefs and desires that rationalize the subject's behavior. As Dennett understands the point, this entails that the propositional, or "notional," contents of the beliefs ascribable to an organism describe a world in which the organism would function optimally (1982). In explaining interpretation, Dennett helps himself to a conception of ideal rationality that he makes little effort to explain. This is a problem, from my point of view, because it is not clear to me that the requisite kind of rationality can be understood apart from a theory of language. Further, Dennett has been unable to recognize the importance of Burge's argument, which I discussed in chapter 3 (see his remarks on Burge in chapter 8 of Dennett 1987). What Dennett calls notional content is supposed to be a species of narrow content, the existence of which I disputed by means of my adaptation of Burge's argument.

A problem for Dennett's interpretationism is that it seems to imply that beliefs and desires are properly attributable to anything whatsoever (Haugeland 1982). For any object at all we can think of some beliefs and desires such that if the object had those beliefs and desires, then it would have a rationale to behave precisely as it does. In Dennett's own illustration of the point, the lectern from which he is lecturing in Oxford believes it is at the center of the civilized world and desires above all to stay there, and so it stays put (1981, 62). So it appears that on Dennett's conception of interpretation, we may interpret anything whatsoever as having intentional states. Call this the *everything-thinks objection*.

One answer to the everything-thinks objection might be that beliefs and desires are properly attributable to an object only when we have no better way of understanding the object's behavior than to explain it in terms of belief and desire. The trouble with this answer is that is seems to relativize an object's possession of beliefs and desires to the capacities of the interpreter. To illustrate the problem, Dennett asks us to imagine vastly superior intelligences who can tell what we are going to do on wholly physiological or microphysical grounds (1981, 64). If Dennett's interpretationism says that for a given interpreter only those things think that the interpreter can understand only in terms thought, then from the perspective of the superior intelligences, even we ourselves do not really think. Call this the *eye-of-the-beholder objection*.

The everything-thinks objection and the eye-of-the-beholder objection constitute a dilemma. If we reply to the everything-thinks objection by saying that the lectern does not really think because we have no need to attribute thoughts to the lectern in order to explain its behavior, then we get the eye-of-the-beholder objection. An obvious answer to the eye-of-the-beholder objection is that the superior intelligences *can* attribute thoughts to us even if they have no *need* to do so. But likewise we *can* attribute thoughts to the lectern. So that reply is subject to the everything-thinks objection.

Dennett's reply to the everything-thinks objection is that in the case of such things as lecterns, explanation in terms of propositional thought does not "recommend itself . . . for we get no predictive power from it that we did not antecedently have" (1981, 62). But this, as we have seen, leads to the eye-of-the-beholder objection. His reply to that objection is that there are certain objective behavioral patterns that are describable in terms of propositional thought (or in terms of intentional states more generally) and in no other way (1981, 64; see also Dennett 1991). So if the superior intelligences do not attribute thoughts to us, then they are missing something that is objectively there for all to discover. But if this reply is effective against the eye-of-the-beholder objection, then it ought to be effective as well against the everything-thinks objection. The reason that not everything thinks is that not everything exhibits the pattern of behavior describable only in terms of propositional thought. So we may take this as his reply to both objections.

Now consider these objective patterns of behavior describable only in terms of propositional thought. Dennett himself emphasizes that they are describable only in terms of propositional thought. To allow that they might equivalently be described in nonintentional terms would be to return to the logical behaviorism he renounced long ago (Dennett 1969). But since they are describable only in terms of propositional thought, we can pose the same dilemma all over again, this time as a problem about the presence of those patterns. Everything thinks, including the lectern, because everything exhibits a pattern of behavior describable only in terms of propositional thought (for example, going or staying, as one chooses). And if that is wrong, because in some cases there is no need to describe a pattern describable only in terms of propositional thought, then propositional thought is in the eye of the beholder.

Dennett is stuck with this dilemma because he recognizes no sharp distinction between interpretation of lecterns and thermostats, at one end of the spectrum, and interpretation of language-using human beings at the other. What distinguishes things at one end from things at the other end is that things at one end might function optimally in a very wide range of environments, whereas things at the other, human end would function optimally only in a narrower range of environments. The further we advance toward the human end of the spectrum, the more our interpretations are constrained by the internal structure of the object of interpretation. A line can be drawn, but there is nothing intrinsically right about one way of drawing it as opposed to some other. For Dennett, it is right not to draw any sharp distinction. The reason is that he is impressed by cases that appear to lie in the middle, for instance, chess-playing computers. He thinks that in such cases explanation in terms of propositional thought has a definite utility in view of our ignorance of the program that runs the computer. I, on the other hand, propose to escape the dilemma by drawing some sharp distinctions. I can do that because I am not so impressed by the interpretability of chess-playing computers.

I will distinguish between three grades of intentionality, or, more precisely, three kinds of attributions of propositional thought. The lowest grade is what I call *superfluous* intentionality. In this class I place our commonplace attributions of propositional thoughts to lecterns, thermostats, frogs, dogs, newborn babies, and chess-playing computers. Some of these, such as dogs, newborn babies, and maybe even chess-playing computers, may literally think, but as I have emphasized at several points, we must recognize all kinds of thinking in addition to propositional thinking. My position is that our commonplace attributions of propositional thoughts to such things—attributions of the form "*S* thinks that *p*"—are, in a sense to be defined, superfluous. I wish to stress that it is only our *commonplace* attributions of propositional thought to such things that I am classifying as superfluous, for I have a different category for attributions of propositional thought that might be made by an ethologist or a brain scientist in the course of attempting to model a complex system.

I will assume that when we attribute propositional thoughts to a thing, there are behaviors of the thing that form the *basis* for our attributions. For instance, if we interpret the thermostat as believing that the room temperature is less than 65°F and as desiring to keep the temperature at 65°F, then that is because we have observed that whenever the temperature falls below 65°F the thermostat turns the furnace on. Further, I assume that there is something we intend to explain by citing the propositional thoughts we attribute. For instance, in the case of the thermostat, we intend to explain why the thermostat turns the furnace on. Call the things we intend to explain the *explananda*.

I can now define what I mean by *superfluous*. Attributions of propositional thought are *superfluous* in the sense I mean if and only if the explananda can be equally well explained merely by generalizing from the basis as by postulating propositional thoughts. For instance, from the past behavior of thermostats in general or this thermostat in particular, we may generalize and say that the thermostat always turns the furnace on when the temperature falls below 65°. But the fact that the thermostat always turns the furnace on when the temperature falls below 65° is *already* an explanation of the fact that on some particular occasion when the temperature fell below 65°, the thermostat turned the furnace on. Adding that the thermostat believes that the room temperature is below 65° and desires to keep the temperature at 65° does not improve the explanation one bit.

Dennett (e.g., 1971) and others have so often extolled the virtues of explanation in terms of propositional thought, even in connection with such things as thermostats, dogs, and chess-playing computers, that I expect that many will balk at my suggestion that the virtues are simply illusory. Dennett's idea is that explanation in terms of propositional thought is useful in such cases if for no other reason than that, due to ignorance, we may be unable to explain behaviors in terms of physical structure or overall structural design. We may not know how the thermostat works or what the chess-playing computer's program says. And even if we did know these things, it might be difficult for us to work out the consequences in the case of something like the computer or the dog. Thus we might explain why a dog is sitting on the front porch by saying, "He expects his master to be home soon," or we might explain a chess-playing computer's action by saying, "It wants to get its queen out early." But in contrasting explanation in terms of propositional thought only with such other possibilities as these, Dennett is overlooking an important alternative, namely, explanation by generalization from past behavior.

Ethologists may have special insights into the behavior of dogs, and computer programmers may have special insights into chess-playing computers, but the rest of us, who may be inclined to make the sorts of attributions of propositional thoughts to dogs and computers that Dennett has in mind, know little about what dogs and computers will do that we could not deduce by generalization from their past behavior. We predict that the dog will stand watch near the door around 5:30 p.m., not because we know that he *expects* his master to come home, but because that is what he always does. I predict that the computer will take my rook, not because I know that it *desires* to win the game and *thinks* that taking my rook will help it win the game, but because I have observed or otherwise been informed that the computer regularly makes moves that increase its probability of its winning, and in the present circumstance taking my rook will clearly do so. We may sometimes make predictions of dogs and chess-playing computers that we cannot support except in terms of propositional thought, but then it is hardly more than coincidence if the things we predict actually do take place.

This is not to deny that there may be various good reasons for us to speak of propositional thoughts in explaining what the dog or the computer does. Saying that the dog expects his master to come home is a simple way of conveying to another what we know about the dog. The truth might not be simply that the dog always waits on the porch at 5:30 p.m. For instance, when the dog's master is working in the backyard on weekends at that time, the dog may not wait on the porch. We can avoid having to list the various qualifications by explaining the dog's behavior in terms of expectations that we speak of the dog as having. But the reason we do not expect the dog to wait when his master is home is not that we know that he *knows* that the master is at home but because we know that when the dog has recently seen (that is, laid eyes on) his master, he does not wait for him.

Bear in mind that I am not now trying to show that languageless creatures do not have propositional thoughts. I am simply arguing, against Dennett, that our attribution of propositional thoughts to languageless creatures is not justified by the explanatory power we derive from such attributions. So it would be irrelevant at this point to answer me by saying that in ascribing propositional thoughts to a creature, we explain the creature's behavior by describing a mechanism by which the creature's observable behavior is produced. That is an account of the explanation according to which the attributions of propositional thought are justified, not by the prospect of explanation, but by the internal structure of the organism.

Still, someone might object that I am assuming that the prospect of explanation will justify our attributions of propositional thoughts to animals only if these explanations yield predictions. On the contrary, someone might say, our attributions may enable us to *explain* even if they do not enable us to *predict*. For instance, we might explain why the dog is barking up a tree by saying that he *thinks* there is a squirrel in the tree even if we could not have predicted that this barking would take place or could have predicted it only in some other way. To this I reply that something has to make this attribution explanatory other than just that the dog would behave as he behaves if he did think the squirrel was up a tree. Otherwise we will have to attribute propositional thoughts to the lectern as well on the grounds that it would behave as it does if it had them. So if it is not a corresponding capacity to predict and it is not the description of a mechanism, then it must be something else. I do not know what that something else might be.

At this point I might be accused of exercising a double standard. I do not deny that we may rightly attribute propositional thoughts to people. Yet (as will become even clearer) I countenance only a limited capacity to predict what even people will do on the basis of attributions of propositional thoughts. But I am not exercising a double standard. There is a different sort of benefit, other than explanation or prediction, that we derive from our attributions of propositional attitudes to people: we enhance our communication with them. Obviously that cannot be a reason to attribute propositional thoughts to languageless animals, since we do not communicate with them (in the way I mean).

It is especially tempting to make superfluous attributions of intentionality when the generalizations to which we might otherwise appeal must be cast in terms of states of affairs that are not readily perceptible. For instance, suppose we find that female vervet monkeys behave as follows: If two of them are grooming one another and a third, higher-ranking female approaches them, then the lowest-ranking of the three will be replaced by the highest-ranking one. Here the generalization concerns a state of affairs involving social rank, and social rank is something not immediately perceivable. So it is very tempting to interpret the monkeys as "recognizing" or believing that a given monkey ranks higher than another (see Cheney and Seyfarth 1992). Since the generalization is cast in terms of imperceptible states, no doubt such a generalization will be true only insofar as the monkeys do perform some kind of thinking. But the attribution of *propositional* thoughts to them in order to explain such a generalization is entirely superfluous.

Someone might object that according to my account of superfluousness, the postulation of electrons is superfluous as well, for it may be said that the phenomena that we could have predicted on the basis of purported facts about electrons could just as well have been predicted directly on the basis of whatever phenomena led us to draw conclusions about electrons. But I deny this premise. It is not true that we could make the same predictions without postulating electrons that we make by postulating electrons. The main point to be made in defending this claim would be that we cannot effectively generalize exclusively in terms of observable kinds (see Sellars 1977). If we found that the postulation of propositional thoughts in languageless animals improved our capacity to construct projectible generalizations, then likewise that would be reason to believe that they really do have propositional thoughts. A careful study of learning in languageless animals might in this way give us reason to attribute propositional thoughts to them. These would be propositional thoughts having at least the next higher grade of intentionality. But our commonplace attributions of thought to them are not in fact justified in this way.

Notice that in defining superfluous intentionality I have not appealed directly to the account of belief attribution set out in the previous chapter. If that were available to me here, I might have said that a dog cannot really believe that p because one cannot make an assertion on behalf of a dog. Normally, one cannot, in the relevant sense, make an assertion on behalf of a thing that cannot make an assertion itself. But I did not offer that as a reason here, because doing so would be begging the question. The viability of that account of interpretation depends on whether I can sustain a viable interpretationism. I need to show that certain attributions of propositional thought are superfluous precisely in order to do that.

The second grade of intentionality is *merely dispensable* intentionality. Attributions of intentionality are *merely dispensable* in the sense I mean if and only if they are not superfluous but there is nothing we can explain in terms of them that we could not *in principle* explain just as well without them. They are not superfluous, because *in fact* we cannot explain the same things by generalizing from past behavior.

The proper place for merely dispensable attributions of propositional thought, as I conceive of them, is in constructing hypothetical models of complex systems. (This statement constitutes a departure from what I said in Gauker 1988.) Suppose, for instance, that we are trying to explain and predict what some sophisticated robot does. Here it might prove helpful to try to write out procedural rules that take assertions as input and generate commands as output, where the input assertions are assertions about the system's environment and the output commands are directions for moving body parts, or to apply this strategy to several hypothetical subcomponents of the robot. We might, that is, try to get some grip on the structural design of the thing by construing it as thinking in accordance with certain definite rules or by construing it as a team of thinkers talking to one another and thinking in accordance with certain definite rules. We might, in other words, pursue a homuncularization strategy such as Dennett (1975) and others (Haugeland 1978; Lycan 1987) have described. As these authors have emphasized, it is a strategy that might work as well with human beings. The propositional thoughts we attribute in the course of executing this strategy will be merely dispensable. It is a strategy that demonstrates the dispensability of such attributions of propositional thought, because the upshot, if we succeed, should be an account of the internal structure of the thing that we can cite in explanation instead of propositional thoughts.

In this book I have made extensive use of the merely dispensable grade of intentionality. The similarity judgments and kausal judgments that I cited in explaining language learning were examples of merely dispensable intentionality. One thing that distinguishes them from indispensable intentional states, which I will discuss shortly, is that they are bound by a stricter form of rule (such as the principles of kausal judgment) than indispensable intentional states are. In the future physiological psychology that I envision, the role that these judgments are said to play in language learning will be taken over by networks of neurons, whose behavior can be characterized in specifically neurological vocabulary.

Merely dispensable attributions of propositional thought, I should emphasize, are rare. Such attribution is practiced almost exclusively by cognitive psychologists, artificial intelligencers, and philosophers, and even they tend only to envision making merely dispensable attributions, and not actually to make any to any actual objects. Merely dispensable attribution of propositional thought is not what we are engaged in when in the course of everyday life we speak of people, or even animals or infants, as thinking. On such occasions we clearly do not have any reductive theoretical strategy in mind, however schematic, and our explanations and predictions cast in terms of propositional thought do not depend on any such theoretical strategy.

Finally I come to what I call *indispensable intentionality*. As I explained in the previous chapter, communication in advanced languages may involve the attribution of propositional thoughts. Attributions of propositional thoughts that may be appropriate in the course of conversation as part of the process of communication are what I call indispensable attributions. The paradigm case of an indispensable attribution is the attribution of a propositional thought to a language-using human being on the basis of his or her having said something that, as we say, expresses that thought. For example, if someone asserts, in English, "There's a ferret in the closet," and in consequence of that assertion I report, "He thinks there's a ferret in the closet," then that is a paradigmatic case of an indispensable attribution of propositional thought. Other examples include the attributions of belief that we make by way of reconstructing the inner conversation that we may cite in explanation of a language user's participation in a language-mediated exchange.

Indispensable intentionality is indispensable because communication depends on it. This is especially clear in the case of communication in sophisticated languages like our own. If I suddenly lost the ability to reconstruct the unspoken parts of a conversation in a language like ours, I would lose thereby the ability to carry on a normal conversation. I would be unable to do as I was told. I could not take a hint. I would not know when it was my turn to speak. I could not offer relevant suggestions or criticize bad ones. I would not be able to follow the course of a speaker's speech. I would not understand how what he or she was saying was relevant to what he or she had been saying before. I would be unable to learn anything from teachers. I could get nothing out of books. All of these things depend on my being able, by spelling out the speaker's (or writer's) presuppositions, implications, and ellipses, to make connections that are not made explicitly. But attributions of propositional thought can be indispensable even in more primitive languages. I offered a number of examples in the previous chapter.

It is possible to explain the behavior of a speaker of a language by citing what he or she says and what is said to him or her. And as I acknowledged in the previous chapter, a certain sort of explanation and prediction is possible through our reconstruction of an agent's covert conversation with himself or herself. So attributions of propositional thought may be indispensable to a certain sort of explanation of behavior as well. But that is not what I wish to emphasize in characterizing the indispensability of certain sorts of attributions of propositional thought. There is a possibility of explaining a person's behavior in this way only to the extent that he or she is engaged in a continuing conversation, in some broad sense, in the language of the covert conversation attributed. (The language of the covert conversation attributed may not be the language in which the attributions are made.)

Only creatures who possess and use a language may possess indispensable intentionality. For only attributions of propositional thoughts to speakers of a language will be "part of the process of communication" in the relevant sense. This does not mean, however, that every time one makes an attribution of indispensable intentionality, it must be an attribution to someone to whom one is speaking at that very moment. On the contrary, we may make attributions of indispensable intentionality to, for instance, long-dead philosophers. But these are to be understood as part of the continuing process of making sense of their recorded conversation, a process that is itself part of the process of communication. That only those who speak a language are subject to attributions of indispensable intentionality also does not mean that one must belong to a linguistic community in order to be a proper object of such attributions. Not at all, for nothing I have said denies that a loner could invent a language for purely intrasubjective use.[1]

My terminology is somewhat misleading, for I do not wish to claim that every attribution of indispensable intentionality is indispensable. Rather, indispensable attributions are attributions of a *sort* that is indispensable. No particular indispensable attribution need ever be indispensable. Above I defined indispensable attributions of propositional thoughts as "attributions of propositional thoughts that may be appropriately attributed in the course of conversation as part of the process of communication." Thus an attribution may belong to the indispensable sort if attributing it would be appropriate, and yet that attribution of propositional thought need not be in any sense necessary.

Further, in drawing a sharp distinction between superfluous attributions of propositional thought and indispensable attributions of propositional thought, I do not mean to imply that every attribution of the indispensable kind is unequivocally true or false (and of course I do not mean that we can always know which). Consider, for instance, our attributions to young children. We can make attributions of the superfluous sort to children, to adults, to anything whatsoever, even lecterns. But young children are subject also to *unclear cases* of attributions of the indispensable *sort*. The unclarity is due to their being potential and emerging members of the linguistic community who have not yet achieved a mastery of the language. Or consider the pop star from the previous chapter who says, "The only true love is love at first sight."

---

[1] Bar-On (1992) argues that a Robinson Crusoe could not invent a language if he did not already possess a language employed by a community, but her argument depends on the assumption that a Gricean account of the origin of language is correct, which I deny.

More generally, interpretation is subject to a certain kind of indeterminacy even when it is indispensable. By *indeterminacy* I mean the availability of alternatives between which we can choose at best on grounds of historical priority and not on grounds of intrinsic superiority (as evaluated by the methods of radical interpretation such as I presented in chapter 13). The possibility of indeterminacy that I envision is not the kind that Quine argues for (1960). For Quine, even the translation of a language into itself is every bit as indeterminate as the translation of one language into another. (That this is the distinctive feature of Quine's thesis is persuasively argued by Robert Kirk [1986].) I do not deny that the translation of a language into itself might be indeterminate. (Think of a language comprising two distinct vocabularies in which each word in one vocabulary has an exact synonym in the other.) But indeterminacy is not, as Quine imagines, inevitable. There might be a language such that only the identity mapping, which takes each sentence of the language into itself, preserves practical utility. The kinds of alternative translations that Quine envisions will typically not preserve practical utility. A sentence like "There are five simultaneous temporal rabbit stages in the garden" will certainly not have the same effect on a native speaker of English as "There are five rabbits in the garden."

The kind of indeterminacy I envision is that which may arise due to dissimilarities between two speakers or two linguistic communities. What I would like to say is that to the extent that the speakers of two languages *think differently*, translation is bound to be indeterminate. But since the only way to compare their thinking is through translation, this may seem to presuppose determinacy in translation only in order to deny it. So I will put the point this way: Suppose we can find no translation that conforms very well to the methodological constraints on interpretation such as I laid down in the previous chapter. This situation can be characterized as one in which no translation interprets the speakers of the language as thinking very like us. In that case, there will be no good reason to prefer one of the optimal translations over any of the others. (However, the possibility of a better, as yet undiscovered translation will remain.)

To wrap up this discussion, my answer to the everything-thinks objection is that *not* everything thinks, for in some cases our interpretations are superfluous. My answer to the eye-of-the-beholder objection is that attributions of propositional thought to language users may be indispensable to anyone who wishes to participate in the use of that language.

4. Attributions of belief and desire are types of assertion that play a distinctive role in conversation. The nature of belief and desire is to be understood in terms of this role. That, in short, is what I have been saying in this and the previous chapter. I do not deny that by attributing beliefs and desires, we may also sometimes explain a person's behavior. But it is a mistake to try to understand those attributions as descriptions of independently constituted mental processes. Having correctly made such attributions, we may certainly think of them as describing an inner process in the mind of the thinker. But it is a mistake to try to understand the correctness of these attributions as a matter of their aiming at description of the inner processes that they do, I acknowledge, describe.

The conception of beliefs and desires developed in these chapters contrasts with the conception of them as theoretical entities, such as electrons or force fields, postulated for the sake of explaining and predicting what will happen. My criticism in chapter 5 of the conception of beliefs and desires as described by psychological laws was already a criticism of this conception. In closing, I would like to take a further stab at the idea that attributions of belief and desire serve explanation and prediction quite apart from their role in conversation. Having explained my alternative conception, I am now in a position to *diagnose the temptation* to think of beliefs and desires as theoretical entities.

One point that must be stressed is that our predictions of people's behavior often are not based on attributions of beliefs and desires. We know that people will seldom try to walk across a freeway full of fast-moving traffic. We know that people who have been perspiring will drink potable liquids. We know that most people will return a friendly greeting. We know that most people will adopt the religion of their parents. In all these cases we can invent explanations in terms of beliefs and desires, and sometimes these explanations may even be correct. But our confidence in these predictions is actually independent of our explanations in terms of beliefs and desires. Our confidence rests on our knowledge of what people in general tend to do, or what people of the type in question tend to do, or what the particular person in question tends to do.

Still, it is tempting to suppose that we may sometimes predict a person's behavior based on attributions of belief and desire quite apart from any conversation we may be engaged in with him or her or others socially engaged with him or her. Imagine a Robinson Crusoe stranded on an otherwise uninhabited island. It is tempting to suppose that if we could observe him from afar, we might infer a rich mental life from his nonverbal behavior and on that basis make predictions that we could otherwise not make. But I doubt that this is really possible. No doubt we could make many good predictions. We could predict that when he first arrives, he will attempt to build himself some kind of shelter, that he will go around the island looking for sources of food, and so on. But these predictions do not depend essentially on a characterization of his mental life. We predict that Crusoe will seek shelter and food because we have learned that in general people take the steps most necessary to their survival. We may be even more specific in our predictions, of course. If there is a lot of good wood and Crusoe has an ax, then we may predict that eventually he will build himself a *wooden* shelter. But again, this prediction can be based on generalizations about what people in general tend to do or on what Robinson Crusoe in particular tends to do.

Suppose Robinson Crusoe is setting out to go fishing. We know that that is what he is doing because he is heading toward the lagoon, and he only goes to the lagoon when he is going to fish. But he has not brought along the jagged piece of metal that he uses as a hook. In this case, we may *predict* that before he gets to the lagoon, he will *remember* the hook and go back to get it. We may predict that he will go back, but what reason may we give for thinking he *remembers* the hook? We know from past experience that when Crusoe himself or people like him perform some activity that they are accustomed to performing, they bring along their usual tools. But that fact is itself sufficient basis for our prediction, without our having to postulate Crusoe's remembering anything.

Consider a more complicated case. Crusoe has built himself a cistern of wood and clay, but termites have been eating away the wood, and if he does not do something about it, they will eat a hole through the wall of the cistern. Further, Crusoe has been keeping the ants out of his pantry with a sticky resin that he can easily collect in large quantities. Thus, we may predict that Crusoe will *realize* that the termites are ruining his cistern, will *observe* that these are crawling, not flying, termites, and thus will *hypothesize* that the sticky resin would prevent the termites from climbing up the walls of the cistern. So we may predict that Crusoe will apply the resin around the base of the cistern. Really? Why should we expect Crusoe to be so clever? We might have reason to expect such cleverness. From past experience with Crusoe or others like him, we may know that whenever Crusoe faces a practical problem like this and the obvious solution is similar to solutions that Crusoe has achieved to similar problems in the past, then he generally executes the obvious solution. So the basis for our prediction is really something other than our attributions of propositional thoughts. The attributions of propositional thought only rationalize behavior that we predict independently.

What I am saying about Robinson Crusoe is much like what I said about the chess-playing computer in explaining superfluous intentionality. In terms of propositional thoughts we can tell a story that rationalizes the behavior of the chess-playing computer or the actions of Crusoe, but our predictions are not *based* on our attributions of propositional thoughts, because the basis for our attributions of propositional thoughts is equally a basis for our predictions without the attribution of propositional thoughts. In the case of the chess-playing computer I concluded that our attributions of intentionality are superfluous. However, I will not draw that conclusion in the case of Robinson Crusoe. If Robinson Crusoe speaks a language, then that is a crucial difference between him and the chess-playing computer.

If Robinson Crusoe is master of a language, then our attributions of thought, though we make them only in order to rationalize behavior that we predict independently, might turn out to be true. And in that way they might qualify as a good explanation, for if Robinson Crusoe speaks a language, then he is a legitimate subject for the indispensable sort of attributions of propositional thought. Our attributions might turn out to be true if at some later time we have occasion to engage him in conversation about the things he did on the island. For instance, if we ask him how he saved his cistern from the termites, the answer he gives may be that he had the thoughts we attributed to him in our rationalizing story. Or our attributions might turn out to be true if we discover a diary containing a written record that we can better understand by means of these same attributions. Moreover, our attributions may really be true even if we never discover that they are, for it may always be the case that they *would have been* necessary for our understanding our conversation with him even if we never happen to converse with him or in any way interact with him.

So the fact that Crusoe would accede to our account might be an important part of our grounds for accepting it as true. The reason why it is important is not that the rules of the language game of attributing propositional thought say that the subject of such attributions is always permitted to decide whether they are true or false. The reason is not that in acceding to our account Crusoe somehow compares our account with a memory trace of his own former thoughts somehow stored in his brain and detects a correspondence. And the reason is not that Crusoe's genuine possession of propositional thoughts somehow depends on our thinking of him as a member of our own linguistic community or on his potential for becoming one. The reason is, rather, that his agreement is overt verbal behavior that we may best understand by means of our attributions. (By *understanding* here I mean the kind of understanding on which linguistic communication depends.) Of course, Crusoe's agreement is important for other reasons as well. Crusoe may have access to details of his experience to which we have none. These may include memories of his own internal imagery.

Now I am in a position to diagnose the temptation to think of belief and desire as theoretical entities. In a case like that I have described, we are presented with someone whose behavior we can rationalize by means of attributions of propositional thoughts. Moreover, those attributions may be literally true and thus genuinely explanatory. We may even be able to predict the subject's behavior. Thus, the case may seem to be one in which the propositional thoughts we attribute are theoretical entities postulated for the sake of explanation and prediction. In addition, there may seem to be no alternative construal of our attributions of propositional thought, since they may not, at the time they are made or at any other time, facilitate conversation with the subject to whom they are made. So it is very tempting to conclude from such a case that propositional thoughts are theoretical entities postulated for the sake of explanation and prediction. The mistake is twofold. First, it is a mistake to suppose that the true and explanatory attributions also facilitate or might have facilitated prediction.

Our predictions are based on other things. Second, it is a mistake to suppose that because these particular attributions do not facilitate conversation, the facilitation of conversation is not what makes them true. Our attributions in this case may be appropriate expressions of a practice that has the function of facilitating conversation even if that function is not realized in this particular case.

In theorizing about the nature of belief and desire, it is a mistake to take the point of view of someone standing outside the linguistic community who theorizes about the members of the community in the way one might theorize about the structure of matter on the basis of vapor trails in a bubble chamber. A Lockean might take this "theoretical" attitude toward thoughts, because the Lockean must conceive of thoughts as having a nature independent of the attributions of propositional thought that we make for the sake of communication. Only inasmuch as propositional thoughts are independently constituted may the Lockean cite them in explanation of the very possibility of communication. The theoretical attitude toward thoughts is a way of trying to grasp that independent nature. But from a non-Lockean perspective, one can see that this attitude inverts the proper explanatory order of things. What is independently constituted is linguistic communication. Its function is to facilitate cooperative interaction, and it is the product of mental processes that are characterizable in terms of propositional thought in only a dispensable way. Indispensable attributions of propositional thought are among the linguistic devices by which languages of a certain advanced sort facilitate cooperative interaction.

References

Aarsleff, Hans. 1981. *From Locke to Saussure: Essays on the Study of Language and Intellectual History*. University of Minnesota Press.

Abelson, R. 1981. Psychological status of the script concept. *American Psychologist* 36:715–29.

Adams, E. 1965. The logic of conditionals. *Inquiry* 8:166–97.

Alston, William P. 1964. *The Philosophy of Language*. Prentice-Hall.

Armstrong, D. M. 1973. *Belief, Truth, and Knowledge*. Cambridge University Press.

Armstrong, S., L. Gleitman, and H. Gleitman. 1983. What some concepts might not be. *Cognition* 13:263–308.

Aune, Bruce. 1967. *Knowledge, Mind, and Nature*. Random House.

Avramides, Anita. 1989. *Meaning and Mind*. MIT Press.

Bach, Kent. 1987. *Thought and Reference*. Oxford University Press.

———. 1988. Burge's new thought experiment: Back to the drawing room. *Journal of Philosophy* 85:88–97.

Baker, Lynne Rudder. 1989. On a causal theory of content. In *Philosophical Perspectives*. vol. 3, *Philosophy of Mind and Action Theory*, ed. James Tomberlin, 165–86. Ridgeview.

Bar-On, Dorit. 1992. On the possibility of a solitary language. *Noûs* 26:27–45.

Bennett, Jonathan. 1976. *Linguistic Behavior*. Cambridge University Press.

Berkeley, George. [1710] 1957. *A Treatise concerning the Principles of Human Knowledge*. Ed. Colin Turbayne. Bobbs-Merrill.

Biro, John. 1979. Intentionalism in the theory of meaning. *The Monist* 62:238–57.

Blackburn, Simon. 1984. *Spreading the Word*. Oxford University Press.

Block, Ned. 1986. Advertisement for a semantics for psychology. In *Midwest Studies in Philosophy*, vol. 10, *Studies in the Philosophy of Mind*, ed. Peter A. French, Theodore E. Uehling, Jr., and Howard K. Wettstein, 615–78. University of Minnesota Press.

Bonevac, Daniel. 1987. *Deduction*. Mayfield.

Brandom, Robert. 1984. Reference explained away. *Journal of Philosophy* 81:469–92.

———. 1985. Varieties of understanding. In *Reason and Rationality in Natural Science*, ed. Nicholas Rescher, 27–51. University Press of America.

Brown, Roger. 1973. *A First Language: The Early Stages*. Harvard University Press.

Bullock, M., R. Gelman, and R. Baillargeon. 1982. The development of causal reasoning. In *The Developmental Psychology of Time*, ed. William. J. Friedman, 209–54. Academic Press.

Burge, Tyler. 1979. Individualism and the mental. In *Midwest Studies in Philosophy*, vol. 4, *Studies in Metaphysics*, ed. Peter A. French, Theodore E. Uehling, Jr., and Howard K. Wettstein, 73–121. University of Minnesota Press.

Carey, Susan. 1982. Semantic development: The state of the art. In *Language Acquisition: The State of the Art*, ed. E. Wanner and L. Gleitman, 347–89. Cambridge University Press.

———. 1988. Cognitive development in childhood. In *Cognition and Representation*, ed. Stephen Schiffer and Susan Steele, 131–59. Westview Press.

Cheney, Dorothy, and Robert M. Seyfarth. 1991. Truth and deception in animal communication. In *Cognitive Ethology: The Minds of Other Animals*, ed. Carolyn Ristau, 127–51. Lawrence Erlbaum.

———. 1992. The representation of social relations by monkeys. In *Animal Cognition*, ed. C. R. Gallistel, 167–96. MIT Press.

Chomsky, Noam. 1965. *Aspects of the Theory of Syntax*. MIT Press.

———. 1966. *Cartesian Linguistics*. Harper and Row.

Clark, E. 1973. What's in a word? On the child's acquisition of semantics in his first language. In *Cognitive Development and the Acquisition of Language*, ed. T. Moore, 65–110. Academic Press.

———. 1977. Strategies and the mapping problem in first language acquisition. In *Language Learning and Thought*, ed. J. Macnamara, 147–68. Academic Press.

Clark, Herbert H. 1992. *Arenas of Language Use*. University of Chicago Press.

Cummins, Robert. 1989. *Meaning and Mental Representation*. MIT Press.

Davidson, Donald. 1967. Truth and meaning. *Synthese* 17:304–23. Reprinted in Davidson 1984b.

———. 1968. On saying that. In *Words and Objections: Essays on the Work of W. V. Quine*, ed. Donald Davidson and Jaakko Hintikka, 158–74. D. Reidel. Reprinted in Davidson 1984b.

———. 1970. Mental events. In *Experience and Theory,* ed. L. Foster and J. W. Swanson, 79–101. University of Massachusetts Press. Reprinted in Davidson 1980.

———. 1973. Radical interpretation. *Dialectica* 27:313–28. Reprinted in Davidson 1984b.

———. 1974. Belief and the basis of meaning. *Synthese* 27:309–23. Reprinted in Davidson 1984b.

———. 1975. Thought and talk. In *Mind and Language*, ed. Samuel D. Guttenplan, 7–23. Oxford University Press. Reprinted in Davidson 1984b.

———. 1977. Reality without reference. *Dialectica* 31:247–53. Reprinted in Davidson 1984b.

———. 1980. *Essays on Actions and Events*. Oxford University Press.

———. 1984a. Communication and convention. In Davidson 1984b, 265–80.

———. 1984b. *Inquiries into Truth and Interpretation*. Oxford University Press.

———. 1986a. Judging interpersonal interests. In *Foundations of Social Choice Theory*, ed. Jon Elster and Aanund Hylland, 195–211. Cambridge University Press.

———. 1986b. A nice derangement of epitaphs. In *Truth and Interpretation: Perspectives on the Philosophy of Donald Davidson*, ed. Ernest Lepore, 433–46. Basil Blackwell.

———. 1990. The structure and content of truth. *Journal of Philosophy* 87:279–328.

Dennett, Daniel. 1969. *Content and Consciousness*. Humanities Press.

———. 1971. Intentional systems. *Journal of Philosophy* 68:87–106. Reprinted in Dennett 1978.

———. 1975. Why the law of effect will not go away. *Journal of the Theory of Social Behavior* 5:169–87. Reprinted in Dennett 1978 and Lycan 1990.

———. 1978. *Brainstorms*. MIT Press.

———. 1981. True believers: The intentional strategy and why it works. In *Scientific*

Explanation, ed. A. F. Heath, 53–75. Oxford University Press. Reprinted in Dennett 1987.

———. 1982. Beyond belief. In *Thought and Object: Essays on Intentionality*, ed. Andrew Woodfield, 1–95. Oxford University Press. Reprinted in Dennett 1987.

———. 1987. *The Intentional Stance*. MIT Press.

———. 1991. Real patterns. *Journal of Philosophy* 88:27–51.

Devitt, Michael. 1981. *Designation*. Columbia University Press.

———. 1984. *Realism and Truth*. Princeton University Press.

———. 1990. A narrow representational theory of the mind. In Lycan 1990, 371–98.

Devitt, Michael, and Kim Sterelny. 1987. *Language and Reality: An Introduction to the Philosophy of Language*. MIT Press.

Donnellan, Keith. 1966. Reference and definite descriptions. *Philosophical Review* 75:281–304.

Dretske, Fred. 1986. Misrepresentation. In *Belief: Form, Content, and Function*, ed. Radu J. Bogdan, 17–36. Oxford University Press. Reprinted in Lycan 1990.

———. 1988. *Explaining Behavior*. MIT Press.

Eells, Ellery. 1991. *Probabilistic Causality*. Cambridge University Press.

Ellis, Brian. 1979. *Rational Belief Systems*. Rowman and Littlefield.

Ellsberg, Daniel. [1961] 1988. Risk, ambiguity and the Savage axioms. In *Decision, Probability, and Utility*, ed. P. Gärdenfors and N. Sahlin, 245–69. Cambridge University Press.

Enderton, Herbert. 1972. *A Mathematical Introduction to Logic*. Academic Press.

Etchemendy, John. 1990. *The Concept of Logical Consequence*. Harvard University Press.

Field, Hartry. 1972. Tarski's theory of truth. *Journal of Philosophy* 69:347–75.

Finke, Ronald A. 1989. *Principles of Mental Imagery*. MIT Press.

Fivush, R. 1987. Scripts and categories: Interrelationships in development. In *Concepts and Conceptual Development*, ed. Ulric Neisser, 234–54. Cambridge University Press.

Fodor, Jerry A. 1975. *The Language of Thought*. Harvard University Press.

———. 1982. Cognitive science and the twin earth problem. *Notre Dame Journal of Formal Logic* 23:98–118.

———. 1987. *Psychosemantics*. MIT Press.

———. 1990. A theory of content II: The theory. In *A Theory of Content and Other Essays*, 89–136. MIT Press.

Fodor, Jerry A., M. Garrett, E. Walker, and C. Parkes, 1980. Against definitions. *Cognition* 8: 1–105.

Fodor, Jerry A., and Ernest Lepore. 1992. *Holism: A Shopper's Guide*. Basil Blackwell.

Frege, Gottlob. [1892] 1952. On sense and reference. In *Translations from the Philosophical Writings*, trans. Max Black and P. T. Geach, 56–78. Basil Blackwell.

Gallistel, C. R. 1992. Representations in animal cognition: An introduction. In *Animal Cognition*, ed. C. R. Gallistel, 1–22. MIT Press.

Garson, James. 1983. Quantification in modal logic. In *Handbook of Philosophical Logic*, ed. D. Gabbay and F. Guenther, vol. 2, 249–309. D. Reidel.

Gauker, Christopher. 1986. The principle of charity. *Synthese* 69:1–25.

———. 1987a. Conditionals in context. *Erkenntnis* 27:293–321.

————. 1987b. Language as tool. *American Philosophical Quarterly* 24:47–58.

————. 1987c. Mind and chance. *Canadian Journal of Philosophy* 17:533–52.

————. 1988. Objective interpretationism. *Pacific Philosophical Quarterly* 69:136–51.

————. 1990a. How to learn a language like a chimpanzee. *Philosophical Psychology* 3:31–53.

————. 1990b. Semantics without reference. *Notre Dame Journal of Formal Logic* 31:437–61.

————. 1991a. If children thought like adults: A critical review of Markman's *Categorization and Naming in Children* and Keil's *Concepts, Kinds and Cognitive Development. Philosophical Psychology* 4:139–46.

————. 1991b. Mental content and the division of epistemic labor. *Australasian Journal of Philosophy* 69:302–18.

————. 1992. The Lockean theory of communication. *Noûs* 26:303–24.

————. 1993. An extraterrestrial perspective on conceptual development. *Mind and Language* 8:105–30.

————. 1994. Review of *Animal Cognition*, ed. C. R. Gallistel. *Philosophical Psychology*. Forthcoming.

Gleitman, Lila R. 1986. Biological dispositions to learn language. In *Language Learning and Concept Acquisition*, ed. W. Demoupolous and A. Marras, 3–28. Ablex.

Godfrey-Smith, Peter. 1989. Misinformation. *Canadian Journal of Philosophy* 19:533–50.

Goldman, Alvin. 1989. Interpretation psychologized. *Mind and Language* 4:161–85.

Goodman, Nelson. [1955] 1983. *Fact, Fiction, and Forecast*. 4th ed. Harvard University Press.

Grandy, Richard. 1987. In defense of semantic fields. In *New Directions in Semantics*, ed. Ernest Lepore, 259–80. Academic Press.

Green, Georgia M. 1989. *Pragmatics and Natural Language Understanding*. Lawrence Erlbaum.

Grice, H. P. 1957. Meaning. *Philosophical Review* 66:377–88. Reprinted in Grice 1989c.

————. 1968. Utterer's meaning, sentence-meaning, and word-meaning. *Foundations of Language* 4:225–42. Reprinted in Grice 1989c.

————. 1989a. Logic and conversation. In Grice 1989c, 22–40.

————. 1989b. Meaning revisited. In Grice 1989c, 283–303.

————. 1989c. *Studies in the Way of Words*. Harvard University Press.

Grover, Dorothy, Joseph Camp, Jr., and Nuel Belnap. 1975. A prosentential theory of truth. *Philosophical Studies* 27:73–125.

Hacking, Ian. 1975. *Why Does Language Matter to Philosophy?* Cambridge University Press.

Halliday, Michael. 1975. *Learning How to Mean*. Edward Arnold.

Hamblin, C. L. 1987. *Imperatives*. Basil Blackwell.

Haugeland, John C. 1978. The nature and plausibility of cognitivism. *Behavioral and Brain Sciences* 1:215–26.

————. 1982. The mother of intention. *Noûs* 16:613–19.

————. 1985. *Artificial Intelligence: The Very Idea*. MIT Press.

Herrnstein, R. J. 1992. Levels of stimulus control: A functional approach. In *Animal Cognition*, ed. C. R. Gallistel, 133–66. MIT Press.

Hill, Christopher. 1987. Rudiments of a theory of reference. *Notre Dame Journal of Formal Logic* 28:200–19.

Horgan, Terence, and Michael Tye. 1985. Against the token identity theory. In *Actions and Events: Perspectives on the Philosophy of Donald Davidson*, ed. Ernest Lepore and B. P. McLaughlin, 426–43. Basil Blackwell.

Horgan, Terence, and James Woodward. 1985. Folk psychology is here to stay. *Philosophical Review* 94:197–226.

Horwich, Paul. 1990. *Truth*. Basil Blackwell.

Hume, David. [1739–40] 1978. *A Treatise of Human Nature*. Ed. by L. A. Selby-Bigge. Rev. by P. H. Nidditch. Oxford University Press.

Jackendoff, Ray. 1983. *Semantics and Cognition*. MIT Press.

———. 1989. What is a concept, that a person may grasp it? *Mind and Language* 4:68–102.

Jackson, Frank, ed. 1991. *Conditionals*. Oxford University Press.

Jeffrey, Richard. 1983. *The Logic of Decision*. 2d ed. University of Chicago Press.

Johnson-Laird, Philip. 1983. *Mental Models*. Harvard University Press.

Kant, Immanuel. [1783] 1950. *Prolegomena to Any Future Metaphysics*. Ed. by Lewis White Beck. Macmillan.

Kaplan, David. 1968. Quantifying in. *Synthese* 19:178–214.

———. 1989. Demonstratives. In *Themes from Kaplan*, ed. Joseph Almog, John Perry, and Howard K. Wettstein, 481–563. Oxford University Press.

Katz, Jerrold J. 1966. *The Philosophy of Language*. Harper and Row.

Keil, Frank. 1981. Constraints on knowledge and cognitive development. *Psychological Review* 88:197–227.

———. 1989. *Concepts, Kinds, and Cognitive Development*. MIT Press.

———. 1990. Constraints on constraints: Surveying the epigenetic landscape. *Cognitive Science* 14:135–68.

Kirk, Robert. 1986. *Translation Determined*. Oxford University Press.

Kobes, Bernard. 1989. Semantics and psychological prototypes. *Pacific Philosophical Quarterly* 70:1–18.

Kripke, Saul. 1972. Naming and necessity. In *Semantics of Natural Language*, ed. Donald Davidson and Gilbert Harman, 253–355. D. Reidel.

———. 1982. *Wittgenstein on Rules and Private Language*. Harvard University Press.

Leblanc, Hugues. 1976. *Truth-Value Semantics*. North-Holland.

Lewis, David. 1969. *Convention*. Harvard University Press.

———. 1970. How to define theoretical terms. *Journal of Philosophy* 67:427–46.

———. 1973a. Causation. *Journal of Philosophy* 70:556–67.

———. 1973b. *Counterfactuals*. Harvard University Press.

———. 1975. Languages and language. In *Language, Mind, and Knowledge*, ed. Keith Gunderson, 3–35. University of Minnesota Press.

———. 1979. Scorekeeping in a language game. *Journal of Philosophical Logic* 8:339–59.

———. 1984. Putnam's paradox. *Australasian Journal of Philosophy* 62:221–36.

Lieberman, Philip. 1991. *Uniquely Human: The Evolution of Speech, Thought, and Selfless Behavior*. Harvard University Press.

Lightfoot, David. 1982. *The Language Lottery*. MIT Press.

Loar, Brian. 1981. *Mind and Meaning*. Cambridge University Press.

———. 1985. Social content and psychological content. In *Contents of Thoughts*, ed. R. Grimm and D. Merrill, 99–110. University of Arizona Press.

Locke, John. [1690] 1975. *An Essay concerning Human Understanding*. Ed. by P. H. Nidditch. Oxford University Press.

———. [1693] 1989. *Some Thoughts concerning Education*. Ed. by John W. Yolton and Jean S. Yolton. Oxford University Press.

Luria, A. R. 1972. *The Man with a Shattered World: The History of a Brain Wound*. Harvard University Press.

Lycan, William. 1987. *Consciousness*. MIT Press.

———, ed. 1990. *Mind and Cognition: A Reader*. Basil Blackwell.

MacKay, Donald G. 1992. Constraints on theories of inner speech. In *Auditory Imagery*, ed. D. Reisberg, 121–49. Lawrence Erlbaum.

Maloney, J. Christopher. 1990. Mental misrepresentation. *Philosophy of Science* 57:445–58.

Markman, E. 1987. How children constrain the possible meanings of words. In *Concepts and Conceptual Development*, ed. Ulric Neisser, 255–87. Cambridge University Press.

———. 1989. *Categorization and Naming in Children: Problems of Induction*. MIT Press.

Markman, E., and G. Wachtel. 1988. Children's use of mutual exclusivity to constrain the meanings of words. *Cognitive Psychology* 20:121–57.

McGee, Vann. 1985. A counterexample to modus ponens. *Journal of Philosophy* 82:462–71.

Mead, George Herbert. 1934. *Mind, Self, and Society*. University of Chicago Press.

Medin, D. 1983. Structural principles in categorization. In *Perception, Cognition and Development*, ed. T. Tighe and B. Shepp, 203–30. Lawrence Erlbaum.

Medin, D., and E. Shoben. 1988. Context and structure in conceptual combination. *Cognitive Psychology* 20:158–90.

Medin, D., W. Wattenmaker, and S. Hampson. 1987. Family resemblance, conceptual cohesiveness, and category construction. *Cognitive Psychology* 19:242–79.

Mervis, Carolyn. 1987. Child-basic object categories and early lexical development. In *Concepts and Conceptual Development*, ed. Ulric Neisser, 201–33. Cambridge University Press.

Millikan, Ruth Garrett. 1984. *Language, Thought, and Other Biological Categories*. MIT Press.

———. 1986. Thought without laws: Cognitive science without content. *Philosophical Review* 95:47–80.

———. 1989. Biosemantics. *Journal of Philosophy* 86:281–97.

Murphy, G. 1982. Cue validity and basic levels in categorization. *Psychological Bulletin* 91:174–77.

Murphy, G., and D. Medin. 1985. The role of theories in conceptual change. *Psychological Review* 92:289–316.

Nelson, K. 1974. Concept, word, and sentence: Interrelations in acquisition and development. *Psychological Review* 81:267–85.

Newell, Allen. 1990. *Unified Theories of Cognition*. Harvard University Press.

Nisbett, Richard E., and Lee Ross. 1980. *Human Inference: Strategies and Shortcomings in Social Judgment*. Prentice-Hall.

Nisbett, Richard E., and Timothy D. Wilson. 1977. Telling more than we can know: Verbal reports on mental processes. *Psychological Review* 84:231–59.

Owens, Joseph. 1987. In defense of a different doppelganger. *Philosophical Review* 96:521–54.

Palmer, Stephen E. 1978. Fundamental aspects of cognitive representation. In *Cognition and Categorization*, ed. E. Rosch and B. Lloyd, 259–303. Lawrence Erlbaum.

Peacocke, Christopher. 1983. *Sense and Content*. Oxford University Press.

Peirce, Charles S. [1878] 1934. How to make our ideas clear. In *Collected Papers of Charles Sanders Peirce*, ed. C. Hartshorne and P. Weiss, vol. 5, 248–71. Harvard University Press.

Perner, Josef. 1991. *Understanding the Representational Mind*. MIT Press.

Pettit, Philip. 1991. Decision theory and folk psychology. In *Foundations of Decision Theory: Issues and Advances*, ed. Michael Bacharach and Susan Hurley, 147–75. Basil Blackwell.

Pinker, Steven. 1984. *Language Learnability and Language Development*. Harvard University Press.

———. 1989. *Learnability and Cognition: The Acquisition of Argument Structure*. MIT Press.

Putnam, Hilary. 1980. Models and reality. *Journal of Symbolic Logic* 45:464–82.

———. 1989. Model theory and the "factuality" of semantics. In *Reflections on Chomsky*, ed. Alexander George, 213–64. Basil Blackwell.

Pylyshyn, Zenon W. 1984. *Computation and Cognition: Toward a Foundation for Cognitive Science*. MIT Press.

Quine, W. V. 1960. *Word and Object*. MIT Press.

———. 1969. Natural kinds. In *Ontological Relativity and Other Essays*, 114–38. Columbia University Press.

———. 1975. Mind and verbal dispositions. In *Mind and Language*, ed. Samuel D. Guttenplan, 83–95. Oxford University Press.

Ramsey, F. P. [1927] 1965. Facts and propositions. In *The Foundations of Mathematics*, ed. R. B. Braithwaite, 138–55. Little, Adams.

Resnik, Michael D. 1987. *Choices: An Introduction to Decision Theory*. University of Minnesota Press.

Rey, Georges. 1983. Concepts and stereotypes. *Cognition* 15:237–62.

———. 1985. Concepts and stereotypes: A reply to Smith, Medin, and Rips. *Cognition* 19:297–303.

Rosch, Eleanor. 1977. Human categorization. In *Studies in Cross-Cultural Psychology*, ed. N. Warren, vol. 1, 1–49. Academic Press.

———. 1978. Principles of categorization. In *Cognition and Categorization*, ed. E. Rosch and B. Lloyd, 27–48. Lawrence Erlbaum.

Rosch, Eleanor, and Carolyn Mervis. 1975. Family resemblances: Studies in the internal structure of categories. *Cognitive Psychology* 7: 573–605.

Rosch, Eleanor, Carolyn Mervis, Wayne Gray, David Johnson, and Penny Boyes-Braem. 1976. Basic objects in natural categories. *Cognitive Psychology* 8:382–439.

Rosenberg, Jay F. 1974. *Linguistic Representation*. D. Reidel.

————. 1988. About competence and performance. *Philosophical Papers* 17:33–49.

Russell, Bertrand. [1912] 1959. *The Problems of Philosophy*. Oxford University Press.

Savage-Rumbaugh, E. S. 1981. Can apes use symbols to represent their world? In *The Clever Hans Phenomenon: Communication with Horses, Whales, Apes, and People*, ed. T. A. Sebeok and R. Rosenthal, 35–59. Annals of the New York Academy of Sciences, 364. New York Academy of Sciences.

————. 1986. *Ape Language: From Conditioned Response to Symbol*. Columbia University Press.

————. 1990. Language as a cause-effect communication system. *Philosophical Psychology* 3:55–76.

Savage-Rumbaugh, E. S., D. M. Rumbaugh, and S. Boysen. 1978. Linguistically mediated tool use and exchange by chimpanzees (*Pan troglodytes*). *Behavioral and Brain Sciences* 4:539–54.

Schiffer, Stephen. 1972. *Meaning*. Oxford University Press.

————. 1991. Ceteris paribus laws. *Mind* 100:1–17.

Seager, William. 1993. Fodor's theory of content: Problems and objections. *Philosophy of Science* 60:262–77.

Searle, John R. 1958. Proper names. *Mind* 67:166–73.

Sellars, Wilfrid. 1963a. Empiricism and the philosophy of mind. In Sellars 1963b, 127–96.

————. 1963b. *Science, Perception, and Reality*. Humanities Press.

————. 1963c. Some reflections on language games. In Sellars 1963b, 321–58.

————. 1963d. Truth and "correspondence." In Sellars 1963b, 197–224.

————. 1969. Language as thought and as communication. *Philosophy and Phenomenological Research* 29:506–27.

————. 1974. Meaning as functional classification. *Synthese* 27:417–37.

————. 1977. Is scientific realism tenable? In *PSA 1976*, ed. Frederick Suppe and Peter D. Asquith, vol. 2, 307–34. Philosophy of Science Association.

————. 1979. *Naturalism and Ontology*. Ridgeview.

Shultz, Thomas R. 1992. Choosing a unifying theory for cognitive development. *Behavioral and Brain Sciences* 15:456–57.

Smith, E. 1978. Theories of semantic memory. In *Handbook of Learning and Cognitive Processes*, ed. W. Estes, vol. 6, 1–56. Lawrence Erlbaum.

Solomon, Miriam. 1989. Quine's point of view. *Journal of Philosophy* 86:113–36.

Spelke, Elizabeth. 1985. Preferential looking methods as a tool for the study of cognition in infancy. In *Measurement of Audition and Vision in the First Year of Postnatal Life: A Methodological Overview*, ed. G. Gottlieb and N. Krasnegor, 323–63. Ablex.

————. 1988. Where perceiving ends and thinking begins: The apprehension of objects in infancy. In *Perceptual Development in Infancy: The Minnesota Symposia on Child Psychology*, vol. 20, ed. Albert Yonas, 197–234. Lawrence Erlbaum.

————. 1990. Principles of object perception. *Cognitive Science* 14:29–56.

Sperber, Dan, and Deirdre Wilson. 1986. *Relevance: Communication and Cognition*. Harvard University Press.

Stalnaker, Robert. 1968. A theory of conditionals. In *Studies in Logical Theory*, American Philosophical Quarterly Monograph Series, no. 2, ed. N. Rescher, 98–112. Basil Blackwell. Reprinted in Jackson 1991.

————. 1975. Indicative conditionals. *Philosophia* 5:269–86. Reprinted in Jackson 1991.

Stampe, Dennis. 1979. Towards a causal theory of linguistic representation. In *Contemporary Perspectives in the Philosophy of Language*, ed. Peter A. French, Theodore E. Uehling, Jr., and Howard K. Wettstein, 81–102. University of Minnesota Press.

Stich, Stephen P. 1983. *From Folk Psychology to Cognitive Science*. MIT Press.

Strawson, P. F. 1966. *The Bounds of Sense*. Methuen.

Thagard, Paul. 1990a. Concepts and conceptual change. *Synthese* 82:255–74.

————. 1990b. The conceptual structure of the chemical revolution. *Philosophy of Science* 57:183–209.

Tversky, Amos. 1977. Features of similarity. *Psychological Review* 84:328–52.

von Neumann, John, and Oskar Morgenstern. 1944. *Theory of Games and Economic Behavior*. Princeton University Press.

Wellman, Henry M. 1991. From desires to beliefs: Acquisition of a theory of mind. In *Natural Theories of Mind*, ed. Andrew Whiten, 19–38. Basil Blackwell.

White, Stephen L. 1982. Partial character and the language of thought. *Pacific Philosophical Quarterly* 63:347–65.

Wittgenstein, Ludwig. [1921] 1963. *Tractatus Logico-Philosophicus*. Trans. by D. F. Pears and B. F. McGuinness. Routledge and Kegan Paul.

————. 1953. *Philosophical Investigations*. Trans. by G.E.M. Anscombe. Macmillan.

Index